MEASUREMENT IN PEDIATRIC EXERCISE SCIENCE

Published for the
Canadian Society for Exercise Physiology

David Docherty, PhD
University of Victoria
British Columbia, Canada

Human Kinetics

Library of Congress Cataloging-in-Publication Data

Measurement in pediatric exercise science / David Docherty, editor.
   p.   cm.
   "Published for the Canadian Society for Exercise Physiology."
   Includes bibliographical references and index.
   ISBN 0-87322-960-6 (case)
   1. Physical fitness for children--Testing.   2. Children--Growth--
Testing.   3. Exercise tests.   I. Docherty, David, 1942- .
II. Canadian Society for Exercise Physiology.
   RJ133.M43   1996
   613.7'042'0287--dc20   96-23786
                                                                  CIP

ISBN: 0-87322-960-6

Permission notices for material reprinted in this book from other sources can be found
on pages xi-xv.

Developmental Editor: Julia Anderson; **Assistant Editor:** Jacqueline Eaton Blakley;
Editorial Assistant: Alecia Mapes Walk; **Copyeditor:** June Waldman; **Proofreader:**
Dena Popara; **Indexer:** Diana Witt; **Typesetting and Layout:** Angela K. Snyder and
Julie Overholt; **Text Designer:** Judy Henderson; **Cover Designer:** Jack Davis; **Illustra-
tors:** Craig Ronto, Jennifer Delmotte, and Dianna Porter; **Printer:** Braun-Brumfield, Inc.

Printed in the United States of America

10   9   8   7   6   5   4   3   2   1

Human Kinetics
P.O. Box 5076, Champaign, IL 61825-5076
1-800-747-4457
Canada: Human Kinetics, Box 24040, Windsor, ON N8Y 4Y9
1-800-465-7301 (in Canada only)
Europe: Human Kinetics, P.O. Box IW14, Leeds LS16 6TR, United Kingdom
(44) 1132 781708
Australia: Human Kinetics, 2 Ingrid Street, Clapham 5062, South Australia
(08) 371 3755
New Zealand: Human Kinetics, P.O. Box 105-231, Auckland 1
(09) 523 3462

Contents

Preface

The considerable interest in the exercise testing of pediatric populations has resulted in a proliferation of testing protocols. Thomas Rowland's *Pediatric Laboratory Exercise Testing: Clinical Guidelines* (1993) indicated that there is little uniformity in the way that exercise tests are conducted on children. Consequently, it is difficult to compare results from different laboratories and develop a comprehensive understanding of the pediatric response to exercise and physical activity. Rowland has provided a valuable resource for professionals in sports medicine, exercise science, and clinical evaluation of pediatric populations.

Recommendations for fitness assessment protocols appropriate for use with youth and children have been identified as a high priority by the National Fitness Appraisal Certification and Accreditation (FACA) Program of the Canadian Society for Exercise Physiology (CSEP). CSEP, in partnership with the Fitness Program, Health Canada, organized and funded an expert Youth and Children Steering Committee to oversee the development of two manuals: *Critical Analysis of Available Laboratory Tests Used in Evaluating the Fitness of Children and Youth* and the *Critical Analysis of Available Field Tests Used in Evaluating the Fitness of Children and Youth*. This work provided the initial impetus for the development of *Measurement in Pediatric Exercise Science*. This book provides a more comprehensive coverage of the evaluation of pediatric populations in relation to growth, maturation, and physical activity. The measurement areas presented in each chapter are considered critical to the understanding of the impact of growth and maturation on physical activity and performance and the impact of physical activity on growth and maturation. The interaction of these variables is clearly described in the first chapter and provides a framework in which the measurement areas should be considered.

The purpose of this text is to describe standardized techniques for the measurement and evaluation of physical and physiological attributes of children and youth. Where possible, specific protocols are recommended to enable the gathering of data that will allow for comparisons in the literature and a more comprehensive understanding of the acute and chronic responses of children to exercise. At present no text has combined the recommended measurement techniques for both physical (anthropometric) and physiological attributes of children and youth. This volume allows readers to turn to one source where measurement techniques are conveniently presented and critically evaluated.

In addition to describing measurement techniques for the laboratory assessment of pediatric populations, the text provides a comprehensive review of field tests that are currently used in the fitness assessment of children and youth. The validity and reliability of specific tests and test batteries are critically evaluated. The text includes a discussion of the current trends and controversy that surround the use of fitness testing in schools and recommends approaches for the collection and interpretation of test results.

Because of its scope (the inclusion of physical and physiological measurements *and* a section on field testing), the text will be of interest to researchers, clinicians, and educators involved in the area of pediatric exercise science. It can serve as a reference text for researchers and clinicians directly involved with the exercise testing of children and youth. Given the structure of each chapter, the text is appropriate for undergraduate courses in growth and development and measurement and evaluation that focus on testing children. The section on laboratory assessment provides a clear description of the criterion measures, and the section on field testing allows the reader to assess the validity and reliability of the test items and test batteries traditionally used to assess the fitness of children and youth, especially in schools. *Measurement in Pediatric Exercise Science* is also appropriate for a graduate course dealing specifically with the issues and problems associated with the collection and interpretation of physical and physiological data on pediatric groups. Practical guidelines, based upon the experience of the authors, are provided for the testing of children in laboratory settings and should prove valuable for graduate students planning research in this area.

The chapter authors are knowledgeable and prominent leaders in the field of pediatric exercise science with particular expertise and practical experience in the measurement area they present. Readers will find the information theoretically sound and practically useful in the testing of young children. The chapter authors' expertise and practical experience with pediatric populations is a particular strength of this text and makes it unique in the area of physical and physiological assessment of exercise and physical activity. *Measurement in Pediatric Exercise Science* provides a reference text for children and youth equivalent to that provided in *Physiological Testing of the High-Performance Athlete* for adults, with the addition of a section on field testing. The text is divided into three parts that consider different aspects of evaluation in the pediatric population. Part I provides detailed information on the assessment of the physical status of children including anthropometry, body composition, and maturation. Part II focuses on the laboratory measurement of physical performance with particular reference to the assessment of anaerobic, aerobic, and strength abilities. In addition Part II includes a chapter on the current techniques for measuring physical activity levels in the pediatric population. Each chapter in these two sections of the book introduces a measurement area, explains the significance of collecting such data on pediatric subjects, and presents an overview of the developmental characteristics of the measurement variable in the chapter. A comprehensive review of the tests and protocols frequently used by researchers is included, along with guidelines and recommendations on the tests and protocols that should be used as the standardized technique for specific pediatric populations. Where appropriate and possible, each chapter concludes with normative standards developed from a broad source of data.

Part III addresses the area of field tests used in the assessment of fitness of children and youth. Rather than list the tests that are frequently presented in tests-and-measurements books in physical education and exercise, the section provides a critical analysis of the tests and the numerous test batteries that have been used to assess the fitness levels of children. The section reviews the history of fitness testing in children and identifies the current trends and recommended approaches in the collection and interpretation of such data. The inclusion of such a section will be of interest to educators as well as researchers who are interested in psychometrics and the development of fitness tests.

It is hoped that, as a result of this text, there will be progress toward a standardized approach to the measurement of physical and physiological attributes of children and youth. Such an approach will permit both the construction of developmental profiles and a clearer understanding of the interactive effects of growth, maturation, and physical activity. It is also hoped that identification of the problems and issues related to the field testing of children's fitness will lead to more discerning use of such tests and better utilization of the results to encourage active lifestyles.

Credits

Figures

Introduction

Figure 1: From "Physical Growth and Maturation" by J. Teeple. In *Motor Development: Issues and Applications* by M.V. Ridenour (Ed.), 1978, Pennington, NJ: Princeton Book Company Publishers. Copyright 1978 by Princeton Book Company Publishers. Adapted with permission.

Chapter 3

Figure 3.1: From "Monitoring Growth in Young Skaters," by W.D. Ross, S.R. Brown, R.A. Faulkner, A.S. Vajda, and M.V. Savage, 1976, *Canadian Journal of Applied Sport Sciences*, **1**, p. 165. Copyright 1976 by Canadian Association of Sports Sciences. Reprinted with permission.

Figure 3.2: From "Biological Maturation: Concept and Assessment," by R.M. Malina and C. Bouchard. In *Growth, Maturation, and Physical Activity* (p. 233), by R.M. Malina and C. Bouchard (Eds.), 1991, Champaign, IL: Human Kinetics. Copyright 1991 by Robert M. Malina and Claude Bouchard. Reprinted with permission.

Figure 3.3: From *Radiographic Atlas of Skeletal Development of the Hand and Wrist* (*second edition*, pp. 170-171), by W.W. Greulich and S.I. Pyle, 1959, Stanford, CA: Stanford University Press. Copyright 1950 and 1959 by the Board of Trustees of the Leland Stanford Junior University. Reprinted with permission.

Figure 3.4: From "Bone Growth and Maturation," by A.F. Roche. In *Human Growth: A Comprehensive Treatise* (Vol. 2, p. 37) by F. Falkner and J.M. Tanner (Eds.), 1986, New York: Plenum. Reprinted with permission.

Figure 3.5: From *Assessment of Skeletal Maturity and Prediction of Adult Height (TW2 Method)* (p. 85), by J.M. Tanner, R.H. Whitehouse, W.A. Marshall, M.J.R.

Healy, and H. Goldstein, 1975, London: Academic Press. Copyright 1975 by Academic Press. Reprinted with permission.

Figures 3.6-3.9: From *Growth at Adolescence* (*second edition*, pp. 32 and 37), by J.M. Tanner, 1962, Oxford: Blackwell Scientific. Copyright 1962 by Blackwell Scientific Publications. Reprinted with permission.

Figures 3.10-3.13: From "Validation of a Self-Administered Instrument to Assess Stage of Adolescent Development," by N.M. Morris and J.R. Udry, 1980, *Journal of Youth and Adolescence*, **9**, pp. 271-280. Copyright 1980 by Plenum Publishing Corporation. Reprinted with permission.

Chapter 4

Figures 4.3 and 4.4: Adapted from "Body Composition and Maximal Exercise Performance in Children," *Human Biology*, **44**, pp. 195-214, by C.T.M. Davies, C. Barnes, and S. Godfrey by permission of the Wayne State University Press. Copyright 1972 by Wayne State University Press. Adapted with permission.

Chapter 5

Figures 5.1, 5.2, and 5.3: From "Evolution de la Puissance Maximal Aérobie de L'enfance à L'âge Adulte: Influence de L'activité Physique et Sportive," by G. Falgairette, 1989, *Revue des Sciences et Techniques en Activités Physiques et Sportives*, **10**, pp. 43-58. Copyright 1989 by Association Francophone por la Recharche en Activité Physique et Sportive. Adapted with permission.

Figures 5.4 and 5.8: From *Maximal Aerobic Power—A Longitudinal Analysis* by R.L. Mirwald and D.A. Bailey, 1986, London, Canada: Sports Dynamics. Copyright 1986 by Sports Dynamics. Reprinted with permission.

Figure 5.5a: From "Maximal Aerobic Capacity of Canadian Schoolchildren: Prediction Based on Age-Related Cost of Running," by J.D. MacDougall, P.D. Roche, O. Bar-Or, and J.R. Moroz, 1983, *International Journal of Sports Medicine*, **4**, pp. 194-198. Adapted with permission.

Figure 5.5b: From "Energy Cost of Running, Cycling, and Stepping During Growth," by L. Léger, J. Cloutier, and D. Masciotte. In *Kinanthropometry III* (pp. 138-145) by T. Reilly, J. Watkins, and J. Borms (Eds.), 1986, London: E & FN Spon. Adapted with permission.

Figure 5.6: From "Capacité Aérobie des Québécois de 6 à 17 ans—Test Navette de 20 Mètres avec Paliers de 1 Minute," by L. Léger, J. Lambert, A. Goulet, C. Rowan, and Y. Dinelle, 1984, *Canadian Journal of Applied Sport Science*, **9**, pp. 64-69. Copyright 1984 by Canadian Association of Sports Sciences. Reprinted with permission.

Figure 5.7: From "The Relationship Between Changing Body Height and Growth Related to Changes in Maximal Aerobic Power," by J. Rutenfranz, M. Macek, K. Lange Andersen, R.D. Bell, J. Vavra, Radvansky, F. Klimmer, and H. Kylian, 1990,

European Journal of Applied Physiology, **60**, pp. 282-287. Reprinted with permission.

Figure 5.9: From "The Relationship Between Body Mass and Oxygen Uptake During Running in Humans," by V. Bergh, B. Sjodin, A. Forsberg, and J. Svedenhag, 1991, *Medicine and Science in Sports and Exercise,* **23**, pp. 205-211. Reprinted with permission.

Figure 5.10: From "Physiologic Responses to Treadmill Running in Adult Prepubertal Males," by T.W. Rowland, J.A. Auchinachie, T.J. Keenan, and G.M. Green, 1987, *International Journal of Sports Medicine,* **8**, p. 295. Copyright 1987 by Thieme Medical Publishers. Reprinted with permission.

Chapter 6

Figures 6.1 and 6.5: From Cameron J.R. Blimkie, Ph.D., "Age- and Sex-Associated Variation in Strength During Childhood: Anthropologic, Morphologic, Neurologic, Biomechanical, Endocrinologic, Genetic, and Physical Activity Correlates" in David R. Lamb and Carl V. Gisolfi, *Perspectives in Exercise Science and Sports Medicine, Vol. 2: Youth, Exercise and Sport.* Copyright 1989, Benchmark Press, Inc. Reprinted by permission of Times Mirror Higher Educaiton Group, Inc., Dubuque, Iowa. All rights reserved.

Figure 6.2: From "Testing Strength and Power," by D.G. Sale. In *Physiological Testing of the High-Performance Athlete* (*second edition*, p. 50) (Eds.) by J.D. MacDougall, H.A. Wenger, and H.J. Green (Eds.), 1991, Champaign, IL: Human Kinetics. Copyright 1991 by Canadian Association of Sport Sciences. Reprinted with permission.

Chapter 7

Figures 7.4 and 7.5: From "Daily Energy Expenditure in Free-Living Children: Comparison of Heart-Rate Monitoring With the Doubly Labelled Water ($^2H_2$ ^{18}O) Method," by M.B.E. Livingstone, W.A. Coward, A.M. Prentice, P.S.W. Davies, J.J. Strain, P.G. McKenna, C.A. Mahoney, J.A. White, C.M. Steward, and M.J. Kerr, 1992, *American Journal of Clinical Nutrition,* **56**, pp. 343-352. Copyright 1992 by Am. J. Clin. Nutr. American Society of Clinical Nutrition.

Figures 7.6 and 7.7: From *Active Living for Canadian Children: A Statistical Profile* (pp. 38 and 44), by S.J. Russell, C. Hynford, and A. Beaulieu, 1992, Ottawa, ON: Canadian Fitness and Lifestyle and Research Institute. Reprinted with permission.

Chapter 8

Figure 8.1: From *Measuring Body Fat Using Skinfolds* (Videotape) by T.G. Lohman, 1987, Champaign, IL: Human Kinetics. Copyright 1987 by Human Kinetics. Reprinted with permission.

Tables

Chapter 1

Table 1.1: From "Kinanthropometry," by W.D. Ross and M.J. Marfell-Jones. In *Physiological Testing of the High-Performance Athlete* (p. 286) by J.D. MacDougall, H.A. Wenger, & H.J. Green (Eds.), 1991, Champaign, IL: Human Kinetics. Copyright 1991 by Human Kinetics Publishers, Inc. Adapted with permission.

Tables on pp. 56, 79-83: From "Anthropometric Characteristics of Canadian Children, Birth to 19 Years. Based on Data Collected During the Nutrition Canada National Survey, 1970-1972" by M. Jetté, 1982, Ottawa, ON: University of Ottawa. Copyright 1982 by Maurice Jetté. Reprinted with permission.

Tables on pp. 57-59, 63, 67: From *Manual of Physical Status and Performance in Childhood* (p. 998), by A.F. Roche and R.M. Malina, 1983, New York: Plenum. Copyright 1983 by Plenum Publishing Corporation. Adapted with permission.

Tables on pp. 60, 64-65, 68, 74: From "Anthropometry of Infants, Children, and Youths to Age 18 for Product Safety Design" (p. 263), by R.G. Snyder, L.W. Schneider, C.L. Owings, H.M. Reynolds, D.H. Golomb, and M.A. Schork, 1977, Warrendale, PA: Society of Automotive Engineers. Copyright 1979 by Society of Automotive Engineers. Reprinted with permission.

Tables on pp. 61-62, 76-78: From "Anthropometric Prototypes: Ages Six to Eighteen Years," by W.D. Ross, D.T. Drinkwater, N.O. Whittingham, and R.A. Faulkner. In *Children and Exercise IX* (pp. 3-12) by K. Berg and B.O. Erikkson (Eds.), 1980, Baltimore: University Park Press. Adapted with permission of William D. Ross.

Tables on pp. 66, 69-73: From "Fitness and Lifestyle in Canada" by Canada Fitness Survey, 1981, Ottawa: Health and Welfare Canada. Distributed by the Canadian Fitness and Lifestyle Research Institute. Reprinted with permission of the Canadian Fitness and Lifestyle Research Institute.

Chapter 2

Table 2.1: From "The Assessment of the Body Fat Percentage by Skinfold Thickness in Childhood and Young Adolescence," by P. Deurenberg, J.J.L. Pieters, and J.G. Hautvast, 1990, *British Journal of Nutrition*, **63**, pp. 293-303. Copyright 1990 by The Nutrition Society of Cambridge University Press. Adapted with permission.

Chapter 3

Table 3.1: From *Assessment of Skeletal Maturity and Prediction of Adult Height (TW2 Method)* (p. 10), by J.M. Tanner, R.H. Whitehouse, W.A. Marshall, M.J.R. Healy, and H. Goldstein, 1975, London: Academic Press. Copyright 1975 by Academic Press. Reprinted with permission.

Chapter 5

Tables 5.2 and 5.3: From "Important Differences Between Children and Adults for Exercise Testing and Exercise Prescription," by O. Bar-Or. In *Exercise Testing and Exercise Prescription for Special Cases* (pp. 57-74) by J.S. Skinner (Ed.), 1993, Philadelphia: Lea & Febiger. Reprinted with permission.

Chapter 7

Table 7.1: From "Observational Measures of Children's Physical Activity," by T.L. McKenzie, 1991, *Journal of School Health*, **61**(5), p. 31. Copyright 1991 by American School Health Association, Kent, OH. Reprinted with permission.

Table 7.2: From "Self-Report Measures of Children's Physical Activity," by J.F. Sallis, 1991, *Journal of School Health*, **61**(5), pp. 216-217. Copyright 1991 by American School Health Association. Reprinted with permission.

Table 7.3: From "Electronic Motion Sensors and Heart Rate as Measures of Physical Activity in Children," by P.S. Freedson, 1991, *Journal of School Health*, **61**(5), p. 221. Copyright 1991 by American School Health Association. Reprinted with permission.

Introduction

The relationship between growth, maturation, and physical activity is very complex and requires a multidisciplinary approach to develop a comprehensive understanding. There have been many articles published that deal with the separate aspects of growth, maturation, and physical activity. Recently, Malina and Bouchard (1991) made a significant contribution to the literature by compiling information related to the areas of growth, maturation, and physical activity. However, they did not provide a theoretical model, as suggested by Teeple (1978), to help interrelate the various components and, in particular, identify how they are inextricably related to each other.

A Model for Growth, Maturation, and Physical Activity (Figure 1) has been adapted from Teeple (1978) and attempts to identify the many factors that need to be considered in trying to understand the complex relationship between growth, maturation, and physical activity. As in Teeple's original model there are status factors and change factors. *Status factors* of the child reflect a level of development that is the product of the two *change factors*. The measurement of the status factors forms the basis of this text. In addition, the text includes the measurement or quantification of physical activity in organized and spontaneous contexts. The impact of physical activity, growth (or both), and maturation can be identified by measuring the differences in the status factors over time. It is obviously important to identify changes attributable to growth and maturation and changes attributable to physical activity.

The model also attempts to recognize the interactive relationship between the different factors. For example, physical activity usually has a positive effect on growth and maturation that may enhance the optimal performance and development of the child. However, growth and maturation are also influenced by genetic inheritance, as well as by environmental factors, such as adequate nutrition. The combined effects of growth, maturation, and physical activity will enhance the child's ability to undertake more demanding and complex physical tasks that in themselves have a positive effect on growth and current status.

1

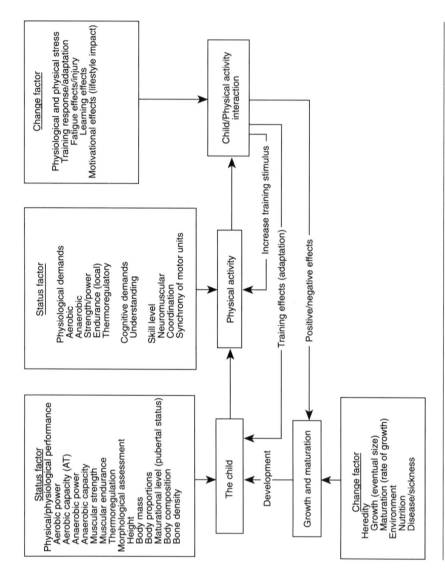

Figure 1 Factors affecting the physical/physiological performance of children. Adapted from Teeple (1978).

In extreme circumstances, it is possible that the demands of the physical activity, as well as the negative effects of inadequate nutrition and poor health, may have a detrimental effect on growth and development. Such possible negative outcomes should be of concern to young high-performance athletes who are exposed to high-volume and intense training regimens and the problems of retaining optimal body size and weight. Although beyond the scope of this text, it is important to recognize the psychological and social outcomes of the interaction between the child and physical activity. The experiences of young children in physical activity, including competitive sports, determine either negative or positive attitudes toward an active lifestyle.

PURPOSES OF PEDIATRIC EXERCISE TESTING

This text is primarily designed to suggest accurate techniques for the measurement of physical and physiological parameters in children and youth. Data collected from the various measurement areas provide a greater understanding of growth, maturation, and physical activity. The various measurements help to profile changes from childhood to adolescence and measure the acute and chronic effects of physical activity and training programs on children. More specifically, pediatric exercise testing can be used to serve the following purposes.

Develop Profiles That Describe Normal Patterns of Growth, Maturation, and Physical Performance

Measures related to growth, maturation, and physical performance can be charted as single variables to provide valuable information for the researcher, clinician, or teacher. There are many growth charts that provide normative information on the status of healthy children, usually based on chronological age. There have also been several cross-sectional and longitudinal studies that provide a developmental profile of various measures of motor performance. There are fewer normative data for physical-performance measures based on laboratory techniques (such as aerobic and anaerobic performance) because of the relatively recent advent of testing pediatric populations, the cost and time involved in collecting such data, and variations in the testing protocols reported in the literature.

Understand Individual Variation Within Normal Patterns of Growth, Maturation, and Physical Performance

There is considerable "normal variation" within any biological characteristic, especially during childhood. It is important to know the extent of this variation as it relates to growth, maturation, and physical activity. The charting of the kinanthropometrical measures should provide researchers, clinicians, and teachers with data to assess the status of an individual or group relative to their peers and identify when they fail to comply with the norms.

Assess Impact of Environmental Factors on Growth, Maturation, and Physical Performance

An individual's size, shape, proportion, and physical performance are largely determined by genetic inheritance, which produces considerable variation in these characteristics by adulthood. However, the processes are quite plastic, and can be influenced by a variety of environmental factors (Malina & Bouchard, 1991). In particular, nutrition, injury, disease, and physical activity (lifestyle) can have significant effects on growth, maturation, and physical performance. The assessment of various kinathropometrical measures provides an understanding of how these factors impact each other. For example, according to the World Health Organization, the assessment of growth is a strong indicator of health and nutritional status (Malina & Bouchard).

Assess Effects of Regular Physical Activity on Growth, Maturation, and Health

It has been proposed that physical activity is critical to optimal growth and maturation. Physical activity has also been linked to cardiovascular health and body composition. More active children generally have higher levels of cardiovascular fitness (Mirwald & Bailey, 1986), increased lean body mass, and decreased levels of body fat when they are compared to less active children. There are some indications that body composition, particularly body fat, may extend from childhood to adulthood as a potential coronary heart disease (CHD) risk factor (Wood, Williams, & Haskell, 1984). However, there is less indication that the cardiovascular fitness level of children affects the risks of CHD in adulthood. More recently, it has been proposed that the integrity of the skeletal mass in adulthood may depend on the level of physical activity during childhood (Bailey & McCulloch, 1992). Considerable research needs to be conducted to establish the link between physical activity during childhood and health status in adulthood.

Examine Trainability of Children During Circumpubertal Years

There has been considerable controversy about the trainability of young boys and girls during the circumpubertal years. Viewpoints range from the suggestion that prepubertal children do not respond to training programs to the belief that training during the pubertal years can actually enhance adult potential. Interest in the trainability of children continues, and despite recent insights many questions remain.

Monitor Potential Injury From Participation in High-Performance Sport During Circumpubertal Years

Many children participate in high-performance sports at very young ages. The physical demands of many activities (such as gymnastics and marathon running) and the volume and intensity of training required to perform at the elite level can have harmful effects on the immature body. There are surprisingly few studies that monitor the acute, chronic, and (especially) long term effects of high-performance sport competion and training. Regular monitoring of growth and performance measures throughout the circumpubertal years of children participating at the elite level would provide some answers to the many questions related to this topic.

Understand Acute Response of Children to Exercise at Varying Intensities

There is some evidence that children differ from adults in metabolic capabilities and energy kinetics. It has been reported that boys from 10 to 13 years of age have low levels of phosphofructokinase (PFK), the rate-limiting enzyme in glycolysis. This PFK level is believed to reduce the ability of children to perform short-duration, high-intensity work (Erikson, 1973). The oxygen kinetics of children differ from that of adults in that children achieve aerobic-steady-state within 1 min at a specific power output. Such rapid adjustment has been attributed to a shorter oxygen (O_2) uptake transient time (Godfrey, 1974). However, such findings and hypotheses need further testing and delineation. For example, the ability of children to generate force at different velocities of contraction offers a fertile area for inquiry.

Monitor Secular Trends

It is often suggested that the fitness level of children has declined over the past 20 to 30 years. Unfortunately, there are few data that permit comparison among children over long periods of time. Comprehensive monitoring of growth, maturation, and physical performance would provide a basis for determining secular trends. Several test batteries have been developed essentially for this purpose (NCYFS, 1985; Eurofit, 1988; The Australian Council, 1985). However, there is a need to collect more precise physiological data so the trends can be more accurately monitored.

ISSUES RELATED TO PEDIATRIC EXERCISE TESTING

It is generally agreed that children are not miniature adults. Therefore, exercise testing of children requires special considerations in the administration of the tests, the collection of the data, and the representation of the results. Researchers, clinicians, and educators not familiar with the testing of children need to consider the following issues.

Partitioning Out Differences in Performance Due to Size

It is generally agreed that *scaling*, or partitioning out differences in physiological performance due to size, is a necessary adjustment when testing children (Rowland, 1991; Winter, 1992). Traditionally, scaling has involved a simple ratio standard in which a physiological variable is divided by a measure of size, such as body weight. For example, relative $\dot{V}O_2$max (or $\dot{V}O_2$max scaled to size) is usually expressed in $ml \cdot kg^{-1} \cdot min^{-1}$. Winter provides a compelling argument that partitioning out differences by dividing a performance value by an anthropometric attribute is theoretically incorrect and misleading. The use of ratio standards tends to advantage small people and penalize large people. Winter also suggests the use of such a scaling technique explains the results of cross-sectional and longitudinal studies that have reported $\dot{V}O_2$ remains stable or decreases during maturation. Analysis of covariance (ANCOVA) is recommended as one alternative, provided that linearity of data exists. Alternatively, Winter suggests the use of *allometry* (adjustment for differences in body size), especially for assessment of individuals, intergroup comparisons, and identification of the relationship between physiological attributes and performance.

Rowland (1990) provides a comprehensive explanation of and rationale for the use of allometry based on dimensionality theory or principles. In essence dimensionality principles provide a technique for comparing the physiological functions of animals (including humans) that differ in size. Based on Euclidean geometry, areas of objects of different sizes can be related to each other by the square of their linear dimensions, and volumes can be compared by the cube of the linear dimensions (Rowland). Such relationships are based on the assumption that the animals being compared have similar body proportions. Consequently, a measure such as $\dot{V}O_2$max can be scaled by using the square of a linear measure such as height. Time (per minute) is expressed as a linear function of length, whereas $\dot{V}O_2$max (a volume) is expressed as a cube function (L^3/L or L^2). However, the recommended value based on experimental work is $L^{2.25}$ to $L^{2.46}$ (Bailey, Ross, Mirwald, & Weese, 1978; McMahon, 1973; Mirwald & Bailey, 1986).

Winter (1992) refers to this scaling technique as a *power function ratio*. It is more acceptable than a standard function ratio because it is based on a logarithmic transformation that allows the use of t tests or analysis of variance. It is tempting to recommend that correcting, or normalizing, physical and physiological measures by body weight be discontinued. However, this is the current convention and will need to be retained for some time to permit comparisons with existing data and permit a transition to statistically more appropriate procedures. It is recommended that at least one of the scaling techniques suggested by Winter, such as the power function ratio, be included in all future data analyses. In order to provide some standard procedure for comparison, it is suggested that $ht^{2.25}$ be used. This is slightly greater than the squared value that would result from dimensionality theory, but it has been found to work in practice and probably accounts for factors other than geometrical size that affect performance. Height is the recommended anthropometric measure because it is less subject to environmental factors and variance in body composition, and therefore a more accurate representation of size.

Impact of Growth, Maturation, and Development on Performance

It is important to distinguish among the terms growth, maturation, and development. *Growth* refers to an increase in the size of the body and occurs as the result of hyperplasia (an increase in the number of cells), hypertrophy (increase in the size of cells), or accretion (an increase in intercellular substances). There is a positive relationship between size and most physiological attributes that must often be considered in the study of physical activity during childhood (Docherty & Gaul, 1991). *Maturation* is described as the process of attaining the mature state, or maturity (Malina & Bouchard, 1991). The different biological systems will achieve a mature state at different times; for example, sexual maturity usually occurs prior to skeletal maturity.

However, maturation also refers to the tempo or rate of progress toward the mature state and will vary considerably among individuals within a specific biological system. Maturational rate does not necessarily parallel chronological age and is largely determined by biological inheritance (Malina & Bouchard, 1991). In general there is a positive correlation between level of maturity and physical performance, especially in adolescent boys. Early maturing males are usually more successful in competitive sports, especially those sports that require power and strength. Late maturity seems more advantageous to females, especially when they engage in activities that require agility and high levels of relative strength and power (gymnastics and skating). However, the relationship between maturity status and physical performance is compounded by the associated relationships with chronological age and changes in body size, proportions, physique, and composition. There are also the compounding effects of sociological and psychological pressures that accompany the period of adolescence, especially for young females. Nevertheless, it is important to consider the maturational status of the individual when analyzing physical performance, predicting ultimate performance capability, assessing the efficacy of training programs at different developmental stages, and investigating the relationship between physical activity and CHD risk factors.

Development is intimately related to growth and maturation, but has a biological and behavioral context (Malina & Bouchard, 1991). *Biological development* involves the differentiation of cells that enables them to perform specialized functions or to refine functions that already exist. It may or may not involve growth of tissue and usually occurs during the prenatal period. *Behavioral development* relates to the evolution of intellectual, psychological, and sociological attributes. *Motor development* has been defined as a progressive change in motor performance (Teeple, 1978), resulting from growth, maturation, and biological and behavioral development.

Ethical Considerations

It is generally agreed that children should not be subjected to invasive techniques in order to obtain physiological data. Muscle biopsies, catheterization, and any form of testing that places the child at physical or psychological risk are unjustified on ethical, legal, and humanitarian grounds (Rowland, 1990). There are times when blood sampling can be justified, especially in the analysis of hormonal responses to exercise or the monitoring of serum lipids. However, samples should be taken by a technician experienced in pediatric sampling techniques; the presence of a professional will reduce risk and psychological trauma. The researcher must be confident that any data collected while subjecting children to discomfort and anxiety is valid and reliable. Such data should contribute significantly to the understanding of physical activity in the pediatric population. Therefore, collecting of blood samples for analysis of serum lactates seems unjustified, given the questionable validity of this information in contributing to an understanding of physiological responses to exercise (Washington, 1993).

Many of the laboratory and field exercise testing techniques require maximal effort or exertion. In some instances this means the child exercises to exhaustion, which can be a painful and uncomfortable experience. Once again, the researcher needs to feel confident that the data gathered from such testing can be justified. Even simple anthropometric testing can be threatening to the child and should be conducted in a sensitive and caring manner with respect for the child's privacy. Some children even become anxious with the placement of electrodes for skin temperature or electrocardiogram (ECG) recording.

Creating a Nonthreatening Laboratory Environment

Researchers and technicians need to be sensitive to the physiological and psychological stresses experienced by children who are tested in the exercise laboratory setting. It is imperative to recognize the stress of the situation and try to create a nonthreatening laboratory environment. There are several ways in which this can be accomplished:

1. Always have a greeter outside the laboratory to meet the parent and the child. Have a comfortable area to sit and complete the necessary protocols. Greeters should introduce themselves to children, parents, guardians, and other guests and, after some brief informal discussion, explain the procedures. Forms and the letter of consent should be completed.
2. The greeter should escort the child and parent into the laboratory and introduce them to the technician who will conduct the first test.
3. It is often helpful to allow the parent, guardian, or sibling into the laboratory, but once the testing procedures begin the guest should be seated in an observation area away from the actual testing. The child and guardian should be encouraged to ask questions at any time.
4. The laboratory testing equipment (e.g., treadmill) can be psychologically threatening and noisy. Some time should be allowed for children to become familiar with the situation.
5. Music, posters, and pictures (especially of elite athletes who have been tested in the laboratory) are a good means of distraction and can help to introduce specific tests.

6. The technician should establish a friendly rapport and trust with the child. This is an essential part of making the testing procedure as pleasant as possible and assuring the accuracy and validity of the test results.

7. Following the test the child should continue to receive care and attention. A designated helper should escort the child to the waiting area, praise the child's effort and performance, and offer a choice of refreshments (drinks, muffins, cookies).

CONDUCTING THE EXERCISE TEST

Many of the exercise tests used for children are similar to those used with adults. However, children differ from adults in their physical, cognitive, social, and psychological status and cannot be regarded or treated as miniature adults (Tomassoni, 1993). Such differences have important implications for the way in which exercise testing is conducted.

Modify the Testing Equipment

Much of the equipment in an exercise-testing laboratory has been designed for adults. It may be necessary to modify the equipment to the size of the child. For young children, the cycle ergometer will need adjustments of the pedal crank shaft length, seat and handle bar height, and the magnitude of the power output increments (Bar-Or, 1983). The handrails on the treadmill and the configuration for supporting gas-analysis equipment will also need to be modified. In order to evaluate strength, the dynamometer apparatus will need special adjustments to accommodate a child's body size and proportions.

Children will often need to be taught to use the testing equipment. Walking on a treadmill is not an easy skill and must be explained and demonstrated. Even cycling may need some guidance since children often apply pressure to the pedal with the arch rather than ball of the foot. It is important to ensure that mechanical inefficiency or lack of skill does not confound the test data. Testing on the Cybex dynamometer may require some modification of protocol to obtain maximal performance (Docherty & Gaul, 1991). Studies have generally indicated that training helps mechanical efficiency in children and facilitates more accurate determination of metabolic responses to exercise (Daniels, Oldridge, Nagle, & White, 1978; Rowland, 1991). It has been suggested that some of the differences in performance between children and adults result from biomechanical rather than physiological factors (Rowland, 1990; Rowland, Auchinachie, Keenan, & Green, 1987).

Obtain Maximal Effort in Children

Few children will have ever performed to maximal exertion or experienced the effort required for many of the metabolic laboratory tests. They will generally not have a true sense of their physiological capabilities or limits and will often wish to terminate the test as soon as they experience some discomfort or anxiety. It is important to reassure children that they can safely perform at high levels of physical exertion and distract them from the subjective feelings of localized fatigue or discomfort. As Tomassoni (1993, p. 13) advises, the "tester must encourage or gently prod the child to perform maximal exercise by verbal encouragement and distraction from fatigue." It is important to carefully monitor for physiological signs of stress using an ECG and metabolic data and be alert to the more subjective symptoms, such as skin pallor, dizziness, syncope, dyspnea, and beaded sweating. The test should be terminated if there are any physiological or subjective signs of problem or risk. Tomassoni (1993) provides guidelines for conducting and terminating the pediatric exercise test in the clinical setting so as to obtain safe and valid data. Coaxing children to reach maximal exertion requires skill and motivational strategies on the part of the tester. The use of posters, heart rate monitoring equipment, setting goals, and rewards help to distract children from the effort of the test and to attain valid test results. Tests, such as $\dot{V}O_2$max, do require considerable exertion and, in some children, are likely to induce short-term discomfort and fatigue.

Consequently, it is important to rationalize the need and significance of the data or study. Although children may experience some discomfort from maximal testing, they rapidly recover and quickly forget any unpleasantness associated with the test (Tomassoni, 1993). This is particularly true when children are praised for their efforts and given some external form of reinforcement, such as a ribbon, badge, or T-shirt.

Obtain Informed Consent

As in most testing situations, it is important, and usually required by institutions, to obtain informed consent from the legal parent or guardian for the child to participate in the testing. Institutions usually have a standardized request form for projects or research that require the use of human subjects (see Figure 2). It is important that the rights of the subjects or patients are protected, particularly their right to confidentiality of the results and their right to withdraw. The right of the subject to withdraw from the study at any time should be clearly stated. Informed consent requires that the participants fully understand the nature of the study, the testing procedures (including level of exertion), and the potential risks.

Communicate During the Test

It is important to devise a system of communication for use during the test, especially for tests in which verbal communication is not possible due to the mouthpiece for collecting expired air. This can be accomplished by the use of hand signals that indicate "fine," "not fine," and "not sure." It is also important to realize that children generally do not communicate very effectively during exercise testing. The tester must monitor the child's response to the exercise intensity and keep seeking

---

Informed Consent

I, _____, the parent/guardian of _____, give my permission for his/her participation in the "Strength and Power Characteristics in Children" study proposed by Dr. Docherty, Dr. Gaul, and Adele Thompson. All testing will be done by Certified Fitness Appraisers at the University of Victoria Sport and Fitness Centre, and the subjects will be treated in a supportive, caring manner. I understand that all data will be kept confidential and that subjects will receive only their own results. I also understand that participation is completely voluntary and that subjects are free to withdraw at any time.

_____   _____
Signature   Date

Figure 2   Informed consent form.

some indication or reassurance that there is no major difficulty or problem. This is particularly necessary when the intensity or workload is changed.

Posttest Considerations

As in all testing that requires maximal or near maximal exertion, it is important to monitor the subject after the test until physiological indicators have returned to normal or resting state. Recovery is usually enhanced by continuing to exercise at submaximal levels for 2 to 5 min or until heart rate is $\leq 120b \cdot min^{-1}$. Subjects should be assisted from the treadmill or cycle ergometer in case localized muscular fatigue causes some loss of stability. They should then sit quietly for a short period (approximately 5 min) to ensure that there are no adverse residual effects. Juice or water should be available to help replenish the fluids lost during the testing procedures, as well as cookies or muffins.

SUMMARY

Exercise testing does not impose any risk to the normal, healthy child. However, there are considerations and procedures that are unique to pediatric-exercise testing. It is important to consider the impact of growth, maturational level, and development on physical performance. These factors need to be considered in evaluating, analyzing, and interpreting performance data. In order to assess the effect of physical activity or training programs on performance in children, it is necessary to partial out changes due to growth, maturation, and development. It should be recognized that the testing environment, especially laboratory settings, can be threatening to children. Efforts need to be made to reduce the anxiety level and familiarize the child with the testing protocols and equipment. Few children will have ever performed at maximal levels of effort. They frequently require coaxing to produce maximal physiological exertion, which may result in subjective feelings of discomfort. However, with appropriate strategies and techniques, it is possible to provide a challenging and satisfying experience that facilitates the willing retesting of the child. There are still many questions relating to physical activity, growth, and maturation in children. They can only be resolved by the careful design of studies, including the collection of valid and accurate data.

REFERENCES

The Australian Council for Health, Physical Education, and Recreation Inc. (1985). *Australian health fitness survey* Parkside, South Australia: Author.

Bailey, D.A., & McCulloch, R.G. (1992, October). Osteoporosis: Are there childhood antecedents for an adult health problem. *Canadian Journal of Pediatrics*, 130-134.

Bailey, D.A., Ross, W.D., Mirwald, R.L. & Weese, D. (1978). Size dissociation of maximal aerobic power during growth in boys. *Medicine and Sport*, **11**, 140-151.

Bar-Or, O. (1983). *Pediatric sports medicine for the practitioner*. New York: Springer-Verlag.

Daniels, J., Oldridge, N., Nagle, F., & White, B. (1978). Changes in oxygen consumption of young boys during growth and running training. *Medicine and Science in Sports*, **3**, 161-165.

Docherty, D., & Gaul, C.A. (1991). Relationship of body size, physique, and composition to physical performance in young boys and girls. *International Journal of Sports Medicine*, **12**, 525-532.

Erikson, B.O. (1973). Physical training, oxygen supply, and muscle metabolism in 11-13 year old boys. *Acta Physiologica Scandinavica* (Suppl. 384), 1-48.

Eurofit (1988). *European test of physical fitness*. Council of Europe, Committee for the Development of Sport. Rome: Edigrat Editionale Grafica.

Godfrey, S. (1974). *Exercise testing in children*. Philadelphia: Saunders.

Malina, P.M., & Bouchard, C. (1991). *Growth, maturation, and physical activity*. Champaign, IL: Human Kinetics.

McMahon, T. (1973). Size and shape in biology. *Science*, **199**, 1202-1204.

Mirwald, R.L., & Bailey, D.A. (1986). *Maximal aerobic power*. London, ON: Sports Dynamics.

NCYFS (1985). Summary of findings from national children and youth fitness study. *Journal of Physical Education, Recreation and Dance*, **56**, 43-90.

Rowland, T.W. (1990). *Exercise and children's health*. Champaign, IL: Human Kinetics.

Rowland, T.W. (1991). "Normalizing" maximum oxygen uptake, or the search for the Holy Grail (per kg). *Pediatric Exercise Science*, **3**, 95-102.

Rowland, T.W., Auchinachie, J.A., Keenan, T.J., & Green, G.M. (1987). Physiologic responses to treadmill running in adult and prepubertal males. *International Journal of Sports Medicine*, **8**, 292-297.

Teeple, J. (1978). Physical growth and maturation. In M.V. Ridenour (Ed.), *Motor development: Issues and applications* (pp. 3-30). Pennington, NJ: Princeton Books.

Tomassoni, T.L. (1993). Conducting the pediatric exercise test. In T.W. Rowland (Ed.), *Pediatric laboratory exercise testing* (pp. 1-18). Champaign, IL: Human Kinetics.

Washington, R.L. (1993). Anaerobic threshold. In T.W. Rowland (Ed.), *Pediatric laboratory exercise testing* (pp. 115-130). Champaign, IL: Human Kinetics.

Winter, E.M. (1992). Scaling: Partitioning out differences in size. *Pediatric Exercise Science*, **4**, 296-301.

Wood, P.D., Williams, P.T., & Haskell, W.L. (1984). Physical activity and high density lipoproteins. In N.E. Miller & G.J. Miller (Eds.), *Clinical and metabolic aspects of high density lipoproteins* (pp. 133-165). New York: Elsevier Science.

I

PHYSICAL ASSESSMENT

There is a need to monitor physical size during childhood and youth. Size can reflect the nutritional and health status of children and provide important information for health agencies. It is also important to consider the proportionality changes that occur during childhood and the possible impact they may have on motor performance and mechanical efficiency. The limbs generally grow faster than the trunk, affecting the location of the center of gravity. A higher center of gravity might affect balance and coordination in some activities. Changes in limb length can affect the ability to apply force, especially when there is a potential lag in muscular development behind the growth in bone length. The lag between muscle and bone growth can contribute to injury, such as Osgood-Schlatter's Syndrome and apophysitis, and loss of coordination (adolescent awkwardness). Eventually, changes in size can lead to improved mechanical efficiency that will affect the measurement of physiological performance. Size also has an effect on motor performance and needs to be considered in assessing the motor and physiological performance of children. Given the impact of body size and proportionality changes on performance, especially during childhood, it is important to be able to accurately monitor various components of physical growth. Sue Crawford's chapter on anthropometry (chapter 1) presents the standardized techniques for the measurement of body size, including mass, stature, lengths, girths, and breadths.

Body composition includes the fractionation of the mass into its constituent tissues. In particular, estimates of body fat, muscularity, and skeletal size are made to reflect the percentage of the various tissues that contribute to body mass. The contribution of each tissue mass to total body mass changes over time and is particularly variable during the transition from childhood to adolescence. The relative mass of the tissue can have a significant effect on health and physiological/motor performance. The relative amount and distribution of body fat have been related to health problems and poor motor performance. In contrast, an increase in the relative amount of muscle mass is associated with enhanced performance, especially in activities requiring strength and power. Increased skeletal mass during the growing years is considered to be an investment against osteoporosis in adulthood. Consequently, it would seem important to be able to describe children with regard to the tissue components that comprise body mass so they can be profiled or considered when analyzing motor and physiological performance. Alan Martin and Richard Ward's chapter on body composition (chapter 2) provides techniques to estimate body fat, muscularity, and skeletal size.

The Introduction noted the importance of maturation to performance and the normal variation in maturity level for children of the same chronological age. Variability is particularly noticeable during the pubertal years when the differential start of the growth spurt maximizes differences within and between sexes. Skeletal age assessment, in which the hand and wrist are X-rayed to determine the degree of closure in epiphyseal plates, is the criterion measure for maturation. Because of concern about repeated X-ray exposure, the use of skeletal age assessment is discouraged. However, there are other techniques used to assess the maturational level of children. Robert Faulkner's chapter on maturation (chapter 3) provides alternative techniques for assessing maturational level, including self-assessment. It is certainly recommended that any study on children include some indication of their maturational status in addition to chronological age. In longitudinal studies data are frequently realigned on some measure of maturational status, such as peak-height velocity.

1

Susan M. Crawford

Anthropometry

Anthropometry can serve many functions in the study of pediatric exercise science. Perhaps foremost, it provides the data used in the indirect appraisal of body composition. Girths and skinfolds can be entered into a number of established regression equations to estimate body density and, therefore, total body fat (Lohman, 1987). Skinfolds can be summed and, if desired, corrected for stature (Ross & Marfell-Jones, 1991) to assess relative body fatness. When corrected for overlying subcutaneous fat, trunk and limb girths provide estimates of relative muscle mass. These and other body composition techniques are addressed in more detail in chapter 2 by Martin and Ward.

Another critical application of anthropometry is the assessment and monitoring of growth. Growth in stature and weight are frequently used as markers of health and nutritional status, as well as adjuncts to the evaluation of developmental progress (refer to chapter 3). In that both absolute and proportional changes in specific body measures may influence strength (Birrer & Levine, 1987; Haywood, 1986), movement mechanics (Jensen, 1981; Jensen, 1987), and physiological parameters (Haywood; Houlsby, 1986; Hughson et al., 1986; Rutenfranz et al., 1982), anthropometric tracking of such measures will provide information regarding the effects of training or detraining of children beyond those changes normally anticipated with growth.

Morphological factors are known to directly influence human performance (Carter, 1978; Carter, 1985). Among adult elite athletes, sport-specific differences in physiques have been well documented (Carter, 1984; Hebbelinck, Ross, Carter, & Borms, 1980). The anthropometric techniques of proportionality assessment (Ross &

Ward, 1986; Ross & Wilson, 1974) and somatotyping (Carter, 1980) can be applied to the identification of common physical characteristics of elite young athletes within any given sport. With the collection of sufficient data, anthropometric prototypes for a sport can be created. Such prototypes assist in talent identification, training protocol development, and equipment design.

Anthropometric measurement has the advantage of being noninvasive and relatively easy to carry out; with a modest amount of training, it is possible to become skilled at acquiring reliable measures. Most techniques require the use of inexpensive equipment that is generally portable.

GROWTH CHARACTERISTICS
RELATED TO ANTHROPOMETRY

"In the absence of basic facts about human growth patterns, much that is said about children and sport is illusory."

J. Borms, 1986

Growth is a major, though highly variable, aspect of infancy, childhood, and adolescence. Growth and maturation are the characteristics that so obviously set children apart from adults, yet these characteristics are frequently overlooked when establishing physiological standards, interpreting test results, and selecting sports groupings. An understanding of the growth status of a young athlete is crucial for equitable assessment of performance both in absolute terms and in comparison with other athletes of the same age.

Somatic growth is more than the regular accretion of tissue mass in that it includes dramatic alterations in both size and proportion. The physique changes that accompany growth may affect the skill, exercise tolerance, and injury potential of an individual child over time. These changes can have a profound influence on the mechanics of movement and the physiological capacities of the growing organism. They are rarely linear and must be considered in terms of departure from geometric expectations (Ross, Drinkwater, Bailey, Marshall, & Leahy, 1980). The cumulative effects of growth on the physical capacities of children are, however, frequently of the direction and magnitude of changes anticipated with training so that it is difficult to separate the two (Bailey, Malina, & Mirwald, 1986). Accordingly, children within a given chronological age may be so heterogeneous in both size and proportion that one must consider their individual potentials rather than carry expectations for the group as a whole.

Measuring Growth

The U.S. National Center for Health Statistics (NCHS), the Fels Research Institute, and the Center for Disease Control (CDC) have collaborated to produce two sets of reference curves for evaluating physical growth through height (or length) and weight of children from birth to 36 months and from age 2 to 18 years (Hamill, Drizid, Johnson, Reed, & Roche, 1977; Neumann, 1979). These reference curves are based on a sample of approximately 20,000 children studied during the Health Examination Surveys from 1963 to 1975. While these standards may appear to be dated, it is apparent that secular trends for increasing height have ceased in the United States, and presumably in Canada (Roche & Himes, 1980). An important feature is that these data represent "all contemporary United States children" (Hamill, Drizid, Johnson, Reed, & Roche, 1979) rather than only upper middle-class children of north European ancestry, which was typical of growth norms used prior to the publication of the NCHS standards (Neumann, 1979).

Heights and weights are available on gender-specific tables of normative height-for-age (HA), weight-for-age (WA), and weight-for-height (WH) (Hamill et al., 1977). More frequently used in field examination of individual subjects are the smoothed percentile curves for HA, WA and WH (Appendix 1.1). In addition to percentile rankings, heights and weights can also be expressed as Z scores, or percentages of the median of the NCHS data using the microcomputer program ANTHRO (available from the Division of Nutrition, Center for Chronic Disease Prevention and Health Promotion, Centers for Disease Control, 1600 Clifton Rd., MSA08, Atlanta, GA 30333). This software will handle height and weight data for individuals up to 18 years of age, in batch or single mode.

Height-for-age and weight-for-age are generally used as indicators of nutritional status, though they may be useful in pediatric exercise science as bases for simple between-athlete comparisons and for longitudinal monitoring of height and weight status. Weight-for-height is in some ways a more useful parameter in that it describes whether the weight of a child is appropriate (according to the norms used) for height, irrespective of age. It is therefore less discriminatory of racial differences in stature, weight, or both at specific ages and is more suggestive of the proportionality of the child.

As with many other measures of children, WA, HA, and WH estimates lose their specificity in the circumpubertal years. When using WA and HA to interpret percentile rankings, maturational status must be taken into consideration. Further, it is recommended that the use of WH be limited to males through 138 months of age and smaller than 145 cm, and to females through 120 months of age and smaller than 137 cm (Sullivan & Gorstein, 1990; Waterlow et al., 1977). This usually avoids specious comparisons of pubertal children against the generally prepubertal normative database.

It is important that these norms not be confused with ratios or indexes such as the Quetelet or Body Mass Index (Weight/Height^2) that are addressed in chapter 2.

One criticism of the NCHS curves is that they are based on cross-sectional data (Tanner, 1986; Tanner & Davies, 1985). This presents a problem throughout the circumpubertal period when height and weight velocities vary more than at any other time of development. Cross-sectional data create a curve that is not the correct shape and does not represent the trajectory followed by any individual child (Tanner & Davies, 1985). Tanner and Davies have reconstructed the NCHS height-percentile curves using information on phase differences in the timing of growth spurts from smaller longitudinal studies to create growth charts which depict average, early, and late maturing norms.

Growth is a process rather than a state. As such, a true assessment of growth requires serial measurement rather than any single set of measures. Finding that the stature or weight of a child lies on the 25th percentile for age cannot determine whether that child is genetically small, developmentally slower than the norm, or is in some way growth-impaired. Serial measures must be taken under identical measuring conditions and using the same techniques. In addition, the time interval between measures must be sufficiently great to permit growth beyond that which would be expected as measurement error. This will differ according to the state of development of the child.

Growth and Proportional Change

Among the derivatives of the comparatively recent large-scale longitudinal growth studies have been descriptions of the differences in rates of growth of various dimensions of the body other than height and weight, including the timing of the growth spurt and the relative maturities of each. Although by no means universal (Cameron, Tanner, & Whitehouse, 1982; Jensen, 1987), a fairly generalized sequence of growth in segments of the axial and appendicular skeleton is apparent (Hauspie, 1979; Tanner, 1977), which results in recognizable differences of form throughout growth. The sequences are cephalo–caudal and distal–proximal, respectively.

Proportionality can be defined as the dimensions of various body parts in relation to each other. Assessment of proportionality can describe the static shape of an individual or homogenous sample, or can be used to depict the changes in physique that accrue with growth, maturation, and physical training (Attalah, 1980; Bookstein, 1978; Cameron et al., 1982; Healy & Tanner, 1981; Jensen, 1987).

Anthropometric proportionality is frequently described in bivariate or allometric terms such as ratios or percentages (e.g., the ratio of leg length to stature). This considerably restricts description of the body as a whole, and there are limits to the number of pairs which are meaningful in exercise science. Adjusting anthropometric data to a standard scale (such as Z scores) and comparing them graphically with normative or baseline values permits the use of all measures for which such values are available.

The choice of a norm will depend on the objectives of the measurer. Age- and gender-specific norms may be the most frequent choice, particularly if the physiques of athletes within a specific sport are to be compared with those of athletes in another sport, or with nonathletic children. However, differences in proportions between child and adolescent athletes within the same sport may need to be examined, in which case the use of the child's proportions as the object of comparison would be appropriate. Similarly, proportional differences can be examined among male and female athletes participating in the same sport. In this case either gender could be used as the standard.

If sufficient numbers are available, norms could also be constructed on a sport-specific basis. This is more appropriate in the observation of adult athletes where the objective is to gather data on the best athletes within the sport of interest and use these as the model against which other participants might be compared. However, as Hughson and colleagues (1986) have clearly stated,

> Selecting children for specific sports at young ages is a questionable procedure. Children can be given advice about potential success in specific sports based on body-build characteristics, but there is little relationship between body size and/or shape and success in sports during childhood.

The construction of standards for each comparative purpose is cumbersome. A solution is the use of an arbitrary gender- and sport-neutral physique as the prototype, plotting the anthropometric characteristics of individuals or groups of interest in terms of this device. An example of this is a procedure known as *proportionality deviation analysis* (Ross & Wilson, 1974). This method size-dissociates anthropometric data by geometrically scaling it to stature, then expresses it as standard scores of a metaphorical, or "phantom," model. The technique has been used to describe proportionality differences among athletes (DeRose, Crawford, Kerr, Ward, & Ross, 1989; Ross & Ward, 1984) as well as longitudinal anthropometric proportionality changes in growing children (Ross & Wilson).

PRACTICAL ASPECTS
OF MEASURING CHILDREN

The standard rules of anthropometric etiquette, such as measuring from the side rather than the front or back of a subject, gently assisting a subject into a preferred measurement position, measurer confidence, warm hands, and scrupulous personal hygiene, all hold for measuring children. Similarly, pediatric anthropometry requires a high degree of preparation and organization, informed consent of subjects, efficiency of movement, and precision of technique. Children will present additional challenges in that they may possibly be more curious, more cautious, less patient, and less capable of holding required positions than adult subjects.

Minimizing Chaos

It is important to ensure the presence of a number of attentive adults to assist in the organization and control of subjects while they are waiting to be measured or moving through testing stations. Need will depend on the number and age of the children to be measured. Enthusiastic cooperation from enlisted teachers, coaches, and parents may not always be forthcoming, in which case it may be prudent to offer a minor incentive or reward; for example, a free T-shirt bearing the logo of the child's team or the measurement project (Ross, June 21, 1990, personal communication).

If children have to wait more than a few minutes to be measured, arrange to have some form of entertainment available to them. This can be as simple as a few comic books or showing videos. Try not to have any distraction from which it would be difficult to separate a child when his or her turn arises. Finally, keep equipment, data, and recording instruments (pens, forms, microcomputers) in an area where they will not likely be tampered with by the curious and the bored.

Clothing

The children should be instructed to wear or bring with them appropriate clothing in which to be measured. The optimal attire is a racing-style swimsuit for males, and a two-piece swimsuit for females. An acceptable alternative for both is a baggy T-shirt with baggy shorts, ideally with an elasticized waistband. The emphasis is on loose fit because styles vary, and the simple instruction to wear shorts can produce anything from snug wool cycling gear to tailored fashion shorts. As some children will undoubtedly forget their attire, it is prudent to have a few spare pairs of large shorts and T-shirts on hand. Masking tape provides useful belting to secure large shorts onto the smallest subjects. It is not recommended that athletes such as gymnasts, skaters, and female swimmers be measured wearing the one-piece stretch body-suits in which they train. These may have minimal weight or bulk; however, they preclude the marking of landmarks and are too slippery for equipment such as skinfold calipers to grip adequately.

Arrange for subjects to have a private place in which to change their clothing. It is often incorrectly assumed that children do not mind disrobing in front of others. Very young children may require assistance with their clothes and shoes. Measuring large groups of early school-age (or younger) children often necessitates additional personnel to help with clothing.

Measuring Children

Ergonomic concerns are foremost when measuring children. Measurement error is much more likely when the anthropometrist is working in cramped or crouched positions. Arrange for a stable platform or wooden box on which to measure a standing child. The optimal height of this platform depends on the height of the subjects being measured. Common ergonomic practice is to keep work close to eye level and no more than a few feet below.

Children are curious and frequently want to see what the measurer is doing. This can distort posture, leading to misjudgment of landmarks and misapplication of instruments. If time allows, show each piece of equipment to the subject (or group of subjects) and demonstrate how each is applied. This is most important for skinfolds that can be a surprising and potentially upsetting pinch.

Once cooperation is ensured, there may be a tendency for the subject to overaccommodate the measurer (for example, lifting an arm high and out of the way of a trunk skinfold measure). As is the problem with the curious subject, measurement errors can be made by way of misidentified landmarks. One means by which this can be avoided is to gently maneuver the child's head, trunk, and limbs into the exact positions required before proceeding with the measurement.

Minimizing Assessment Error

In the technological milieu of exercise science, anthropometry appears to be simple. The equipment is generally mechanical and its application is self-evident. Similarly, the human body is familiar territory having obvious dimensions of length, breadth, and thickness. As a result, many investigators wrongly procede with anthropometric assessment having little of the knowledge or skill necessary to acquire accurate and reliable data. The result is a range of measurement error rarely experienced in the more instrument-intensive procedures of exercise physiology.

In general, the term *error* refers to the difference between the observed measures and the actual, or true, measures of an anthropometric dimension. Error is often classified as one of two types. Bias, or systematic error, is that for which a constant differential exists between the true and the observed measure. These include errors of equipment calibration or differences of individual measurement technique. Bias will reduce the accuracy of a measurement by affecting its median and mean value.

Random errors are by definition nonsystematic. Their degree fluctuates according to the conditions creating them (e.g., casual technique, mistakes in recording measurements) (Mueller & Martorell, 1988). These tend to produce the same mean and median value, but increase the variability about that mean (Gibson, 1990). Random error is more likely to be experienced in the measurement of younger children because of their inability to stand in the desired position for the length of time it may take to carry out reproducible measures.

It is important to recognize all potential sources of error and control these whenever possible. Foremost are the knowledge, skill, and attitude of the measurer. Training and practice will decrease the likelihood that techniques will vary beyond the written specifications of a standard anthropometric protocol (Cameron, 1986; Carter, 1980; Ross & Marfell-Jones, 1991; Weiner & Lourie, 1981). Cameron suggests that the anthropometrist should be obsessed with acquiring and maintaining measurement accuracy, while at the same time, relaxed and confident with both the human and technical elements of measurement. Measurement can be facilitated by the services of an assistant whose responsibilities include recording the measures read by the anthropometrist and monitoring the measurement process, thereby ensuring the correct identification of landmarks and application of instruments This individual will also alert the anthropometrist when repeated measures fall outside the acceptable range of error tolerance as outlined in Table 1.1. Additional sources of error can be controlled by the choice of appropriate equipment, which has been properly assembled and calibrated; a quiet, ergonomically optimal measurement environment; sufficient time to set up equipment and complete all measurements; and willing subjects in suitable clothing.

Reliability.   Formal recognition of measurement reliability and accuracy must be made during anthropometric assessment. It is critical to know that each anthropometrist is able to consistently acquire the same values on any given subject with repeated measurements. Equally important is the assurance that collected data can be compared to those found in available standards or norms.

Table 1.1 Anthropometric Tolerances

Weight	0.5 kg
Stature	3.0 mm
Lengths	2.0 mm
Breadths	
Trunk	1-2 mm
Bone	1.0 mm
Wrist	1-2 mm
Skinfolds	5%
Girths	
Lower limb	1.0 mm
Upper limb	2.0 mm
Chest	1-2%
Waist	2-3%
Abdominal	1.0 mm
Gluteal	1.0 mm

Adapted from Ross and Marfell-Jones (1991).

The extent to which repeated measurements of the same variable yield the same value (Mueller & Martorell, 1988) or the within-subject variance is often described by the terms *precision, consistency, reproducibility,* and *reliability* (Bailey, 1991; Gibson, 1990; Habicht, Yarbrough, & Martorell, 1979). It is most commonly expressed as the technical error of measurement (TEM) (s) (Cameron, 1986; Malina, Hamill, & Lemeshow, 1973; Meuller & Martorell, 1988; Ross, De Rose, & Ward, 1988) that is the standard deviation of the difference (*d*) between repeated measures by the same observer (×1) and (×2) over (*n*) subjects:

$$s = ([\text{sum } d^2/2n]^{0.5})$$

The TEM provides more information than the coefficients of reliability, stability, objectivity, and reproducibility, which are all simply Pearson's product–moment correlation coefficients of test–retest pairs. In anthropometry these numbers will always be close to 1.0, so they cannot provide sufficient discrimination of technical measurement error (Cameron, 1984; Ross, et al., 1988).

When a number of measurers will be employed in a single project, it is advisable to ensure a high degree of interobserver reliability as well. This can be accomplished by having each anthropometrist take repeated measurements on each of a number of subjects (Cameron, 1984). Analysis of variance (ANOVA) procedures permit the examination of intra- and interobserver variances across subjects (Mueller & Martorell, 1988). Detailed descriptions of these concepts and their algorithms can be found in Cameron (1984), Mueller and Martorell, and Marks, Habicht & Mueller (1989).

Accuracy. Accuracy denotes the degree to which the measured value reflects the true dimensions of the variable. This true measure can best be determined through repeated measures by an expert or *criterion anthropometrist*. To assess the extent of a measurer's accuracy, a paired *t* test between the original values and those of the criterion anthropometrist can be carried out.

Validity.   Finally, the term *validity* refers to the extent to which the anthropometric measure used reflects the parameter of interest. For example, body stature may be a measure carrying with it a high degree of reliability and accuracy, but may not be a valid representation of leg length, which is only one element of stature.

These concepts of error are important for quality control in anthropometry. Measurement drift, faulty calibration, and invalid assumptions about techniques can result in specious conclusions. Absence of quality control wastes a great deal of research time and resources and results in misleading inferences. Measurement error can lead to inaccurate assessment of body composition, incorrect interpretation of physiological test results, and misjudgment of growth status. Ultimately error can cause undue anxiety and confusion for the child being measured, along with the parents and coaches of that child.

ANTHROPOMETRIC TECHNIQUES

Ideally, the measurer should work from the side of the subject. A child standing in this position is able to see and anticipate most of the measurer's movements. Measurements which necessitate movement in sensitive areas should be carried out by approaching the landmark indirectly. For example, thigh girth measurement requires application of the tape around the thigh, 1 cm below the gluteal fold. Rather than attempting to wrap the tape around the thigh at this level, the anthropometrist can form the tape loop lower down on the leg and move it upwards, tightening it at the appropriate location.

Currently there is no worldwide convention regarding the side of the body on which measurements should be taken. Most of the large contemporary national surveys conducted in the United States and Canada have measured on the right side; the European convention is to use the left side (Martorell, Mendoza, Mueller, & Pawson, 1988; Weiner & Lourie, 1981). While evidence exists suggesting that handedness has an influence on the bilateral dimensions of at least the arm, the degree of difference between left- and right-side measures is usually less than measurement error (Martorell et al.).

With the exception of skinfolds, there is little difference in ease of measurement on one side as opposed to the other. When measuring skinfolds from the left side of a subject, the application of the caliper to anterior sites awkwardly forces a right-handed measurer to stand directly in front of the subject rather than to the side.

To an inexperienced measurer, the manipulation of anthropometric instruments while simultaneously checking for subject landmarks can be challenging. A general technique is to hold and guide the instrument in use with only the thumbs and forefingers. The remaining fingers can be used to palpate landmarks and for balance.

Unless otherwise noted the techniques outlined are those on which there is agreement in the descriptions by the International Biological Programme (Weiner & Lourie, 1981; Cameron, 1986; Ross & Marfell-Jones, 1991; and Lohman, Roche, & Martorell, 1988). For the majority of measurements, these are also the techniques used for the collection of the reference data listed in appendix 1.2. Differences are noted in the accompanying text.

In order to minimize error and ensure reliability, it is advisable to repeat the measurement protocol in triplicate. Observer error is sufficiently probable that single measures are usually inadequate for collection of accurate data. Duplicate measurement presents the difficulty of reconciling two different numbers, neither of which may be accurate. The calculated mean of two measures will be influenced by gross measurement errors, whereas recording the median value of triplicate measures is the protocol most likely to produce accurate values (Ross & Marfell-Jones, 1991).

Before any anthropometric measurements can be taken, the subject's body must be marked for specific skeletal and soft tissue landmarks. For identification of these landmarks, and for a majority of anthropometric procedures, the subject should be positioned on a flat surface in the anatomical position. This denotes standing erect with the head in the Frankfort Horizontal Plane, feet together with weight evenly distributed, and arms straight with hands by the side. In the Frankfort Horizontal Plane, the lower border of the orbit of the eye is in the same horizontal plane as the tragion. The line of vision is thus perfectly horizontal; the subject appears to be looking straight ahead.

Marks should be made with water-soluble ink, ensuring that the skin covering a landmark is not pulled out of its natural alignment by restrictive clothing, subject posture, or the marking process itself. At young ages, some of the bony landmarks may not be completely ossified, and may be more difficult to locate than is the case in adults. Each landmark should be double-checked before proceeding to the next one (see Figure 1.1).

MEASURING BODY MASS

Body weight should be obtained on an calibrated scale and recorded to the nearest 100 grams when using a beam-balance, and to 1/2 kg when using a spring scale. The subject should preferably be weighed nude although this is rarely feasible in any but clinical settings. Light clothing, such as shorts and a T-shirt, can be worn, and it is advisable to have young subjects check to see that any pockets are empty. Shoes must be removed. To obtain highly accurate values for body mass, subjects should be weighed in a fasting state and after voiding, generally first thing in the morning.

MEASURING STATURE

The recommended method for measuring stature is to position the subject barefoot on a level measuring platform directly in front of the vertical anthropometer, or

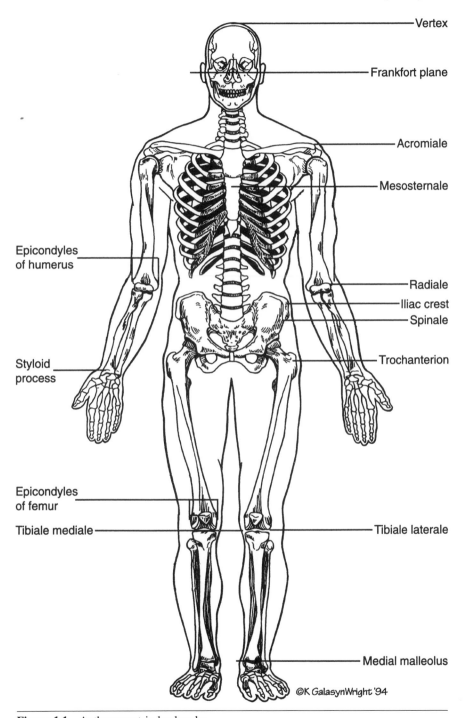

Figure 1.1   Anthropometric landmarks.
© K. Galasyn-Wright, Champaign, IL, 1994.

against a vertical wall (without a baseboard) or door on which a strip of paper has been taped. The subject stands erect with heels and toes together and arms hanging by the sides (see Figure 1.2).

The measurement is taken as the maximum distance from the floor to the vertex of the head, which is the highest point on the skull when the head is held in the Frankfort Plane. Using both hands, the measurer cups the subject's head along the mastoid processes to correctly position it in the Frankfort Plane. To measure stretch stature, gentle upward traction is applied from this position. This specific technique corrects for diurnal variations in stature (Cameron, 1986).

For measurement against a wall, a triangular headboard is brought firmly down and into contact with the vertex, crushing the hair. (Hair clips and ribbons worn by girls must be removed before stature is measured). A pencil mark is made on the paper, level with the underside of the headboard. The subject then steps away from the wall, the headboard is removed, and the vertical distance from the floor to the pencil mark is measured with the retractable measuring tape. The measurement is read to the nearest tenth of a centimeter.

It can be challenging to correctly position children for stature measurement. The usual directions given to a subject being measured—to stand tall, take a deep breath, and relax—are difficult for a child to execute. The tendency among younger subjects

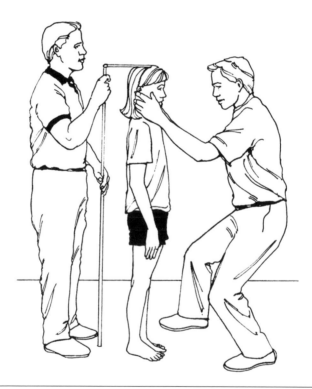

Figure 1.2   Measurement technique for stature.

Figure 1.3   Measurement technique for sitting height.

is to stiffen their bodies, shrug their shoulders, look upwards, and/or raise their heels, particularly if stretch stature is being measured. For these reasons, it is advisable to have two anthropometrists involved in this measurement: one to position the child and one to take the reading.

MEASURING SITTING HEIGHT

This is the distance from the vertex to surface on which the erect subject is seated. There is no concensus as to whether the feet should hang freely or be supported (Cameron, 1986; Martin, Carter, Hendy, & Malina, 1988); however, in either instance, the thighs should rest in a horizontal position with the knees flexed over the edge of, but not in contact with, the sittting surface. The subject's head is positioned in the Frankfort Plane, and gentle traction is applied to the mandibular processes while the subject is directed to sit up straight. The anthropometer is positioned flat on the sitting surface behind the subject, and the branch is lowered to make firm contact with the vertex (see Figure 1.3). As with stature, care must be taken to ensure that the subject does not reposition or push upwards with the hands or legs.

Subischial height is the length of the combined lower extremities, derived by subtracting sitting height from stature.

TECHNIQUES FOR MEASURING LIMB LENGTHS

Lengths of limb segments can be measured either directly between two skeletal landmarks or as vertical distances between a constant flat surface (such as the floor or anthropometric box) and a skeletal landmark. The latter are referred to as projected lengths which, through subtraction, yield a number of derived segment lengths. For example, trochanterion height minus tibiale height gives an estimate of the length of the femur or thigh. This method of measuring limb segments is not generally recommended for use with children because it is heavily reliant on the subject's ability to maintain the same, correct position throughout a series of measures. Detailed description of projected length techniques can be found in Ross and Marfell-Jones (1991), Cameron (1986), and Martin et al. (1988).

Two types of anthropometers are commonly used for the measurement of lengths (and breadths). The more conventional is the Martin-type Siber–Hegner (#101 GPM). This instrument consists of four 52-cm sections that join to become a single rod, a moveable branch casing, and two straight branches. A foot plate is a recommended addition. The rod to which the fixed branch is attached can be used alone as a sliding beam caliper and instead of a wide-spreading caliper for anterior–posterior chest depth, when two curved branches with olive tips are attached. It is critical that these adaptations be assembled properly. The sliding branch should be on the right-hand side of the measurer. When this sliding beam caliper is closed, its indicator should read 0.7 mm or the actual distance between branches. The Siber–Hegner anthropometer is accurate to 0.5 cm.

The Harpenden anthropometer differs in that its moveable parts run on ball-bearings and a digital counter may be used (Cameron, 1986). Consequently, its accuracy is on the order of 0.1 cm.

Upper Arm Length

The distance between the the most superior lateral point of the acromion process (or acromiale landmark) and the upper and lateral border of the head of the radius (or radiale landmark) consitutes the upper arm length. The arm hangs relaxed at the side of the subject, and the anthropometer branches are held perpendicular to the long axis of the arm (see Figure 1.4). Another version of the upper arm measurement is the shoulder–elbow length (Martin et al., 1988). This involves positioning the subject with the arm flexed to 90° so that the ulnar surface of the forearm and hand are horizontal, and the palms are facing medially with the fingers extended. The anthropometer branches are placed perpendicular to the vertical axis of the body, lying across the acromiale landmark and the posterior surface of the olecranon process of the ulna (Martin et al.).

Forearm Length

This is the distance from the head of the radius (radiale landmark) to the most distal point of the styloid process of the radius (or stylion). As with upper arm length,

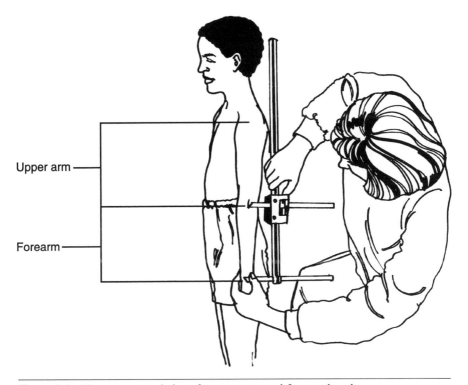

Figure 1.4   Measurement technique for upper arm and forearm lengths.

the arm is hanging relaxed at the side of the subject, and the anthropometer branches are held perpendicular to the long axis of the arm. Using the same positioning as when measuring the shoulder–elbow length, the lower arm can be measured for elbow–wrist length (Martin et al., 1988). The tips of the anthropometer branches are placed on the olecranon and the most distal palpable point of the styloid process of the radius (see Figure 1.4).

Hand Length

With the hand extended, palm upward in the direction of the longitudinal axis of the forearm, one anthropometer branch is placed across the styloid process at the base of the thumb while the other is retracted to touch the tip of the middle finger. Care must be taken that the hand is not overextended. This can be prevented by resting only the hand supine on a table surface.

Arm Span

This is the distance between the tips of the longest fingers of each hand when the arms are maximally outstretched to the sides, at the level of the shoulder. The subject is positioned against a vertical wall, facing outwards, with the middle finger on one of the outstretched arms touching an object fixed to the wall. This could be a door molding or a partially embedded nail. One measurer holds the anthropometric tape to the tip of this middle finger, while the other extends the tape along the wall behind the subject and takes a reading at the tip of the other hand. The tape must be horizontal and the subject must be reminded to fully extend the arms and keep them at shoulder height throughout the measurement.

Thigh Length

This measure is not specifically described in many of the standard anthropometric methodologies, possibly due to the lack of agreement on a universal proximal landmark, which in turn may be due to the difficulty in locating appropriate bony surfaces in this region. In most children, however, the head of the trochanter is relatively easy to palpate and can be used as the proximal landmark with the proximal–lateral border of the tibia serving as the distal site. Another technique is to derive the length of the thigh by subtracting the distance from the head of the tibia to the floor from the subischial height.

Tibial Length

This is the distance along the tibia from the proximal–medial border to the most distal border of the medial maleolus. The subject is seated with the ankle of the leg to be measured resting on the opposite knee so that the medial aspect of the tibia faces upwards. The branches of the anthropometer are placed perpendicular to the long axis of the tibia with the tips touching the two landmarks (see Figure 1.5). The projected length measurement of tibiale height encompasses the distance between the most superior aspect of the lateral tibial head and the floor when the subject is standing.

Foot Length

This is the distance between the most posterior part of the heel and the most anterior part of the longest toe when the foot is placed on a flat surface. Whether the foot should be weight-bearing remains equivocal (Cameron, 1986).

TECHNIQUES FOR MEASURING GIRTHS

The tape casing should always be held in the right hand with the tape stub secured in the left hand. An ample length of tape should be pulled from the casing before any measurement. This length is looped around the part to be measured and held so that the printed notches on the scale are next to each other (with some tapes,

Figure 1.5   Measurement technique for tibial length.

this means the stub end is pulled superior to the casing end, in others this is reversed). The objective is to avoid having to read across a blank space on the tape.

Each end of the tape is held in a thumb and forefinger while the remaining fingers palpate the measurement site and move the tape loop for correct measurement positioning. At the same time, the loop is tightened by allowing the excess length to reel back into the casing.

The tension applied to the tape will vary. Skin surfaces should not be compressed, nor should there be any observable space between the skin and the tape. Constant tension of the tape is not appropriate because of the range of inter- and intra-subject compressibility. For this reason tapes with spring casings are not recommended. Tape tension is an important concern when measuring children because their skin and underlying tissues are much more compressible than those of adults.

With the exception of head and neck girths, the tape loop should lie perpendicular to the long axis of a bone or body segment being measured. Under ideal conditions an assistant should be on hand to help monitor both tension and positioning. Measurements should be recorded to the nearest 0.1 cm.

Head Girth

This is the maximum circumference of the head when the tape is located immediately superior to the eyebrows and positioned at the back of the head, so that the maximum perimeter is measured. Care must be taken to keep the tape in the same plane on both sides of the head and the hair compressed to the extent that the measure is the best estimate of the cranial perimeter (Callaway et al., 1988).

Neck Girth

This is the perimeter of the neck taken slightly superior to the larynx. The subject is usually seated with the head oriented in the Frankfort Plane. The tape is located perpendicular to the long axis of the neck.

Midarm Girth

This is also known as arm circumference (Callaway et al., 1988), upper arm circumference (Cameron, 1986), biceps circumference (Cameron, 1986), and relaxed arm girth (Ross & Marfell-Jones, 1991). It is the circumference of the upper arm parallel to the long axis of the humerus when the subject is standing erect and the relaxed arm is hanging by the side. The tape is applied at the landmark midway between the acromiale and the head of the radius (see Figure 1.6).

Forearm Girth

This measurement is the maximal girth of the forearm when the arm is held relaxed downward but slightly posterior to the trunk, with the palm of the hand up. The tape is again placed perpendicular to the long axis of the forearm and moved up and down to position it at the maximal circumference (see Figure 1.7).

Wrist Girth

The perimeter of the wrist taken distal to the styloid process of the radius and ulna, perpendicular to the long axis of the forearm (see Figure 1.7).

Chest Girth

This is the circumference of the chest at the level of the mesosternale landmark. The chest should be bare, although adolescent girls may wear a strapless top. The subject stands in a natural, erect posture and abducts the arms to permit the passage of the tape around the chest. The tape is adjusted so that it is horizontal at the level of landmark (see Figure 1.8). The arms are returned to resting position, and the reading is obtained at the end of a normal expiration. This can be difficult to obtain in younger subjects as there is a tendency to breath-hold during the measurement. A recommended strategy is to ask the subject an open-ended question once the tape

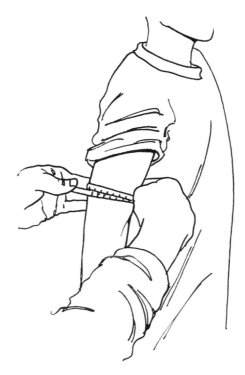

Figure 1.6   Measurement technique for midarm girth.

is in position. This will usually elicit sufficient verbal response to obtain the desired end-tidal reading.

Waist Girth

Waist girth is measured at the narrowest part of the torso when viewed from the anterior aspect. The subject should be standing comfortably erect, with the hands by the side, and neither intentionally contracting the abdominal muscles nor breath-holding. The tape is placed horizontally around the torso so that it is snug, but not compressing the skin and underlying tissue (see Figure 1.8). Clothing should be minimal as it can obstruct both identification of the measurement site and the measurement process. If an obvious narrowing is not evident, the measurement should be taken approximately halfway between the ribs and the iliac crest. Another measure sometimes confused with waist girth is abdominal circumference (Callaway et al., 1988; Weiner & Lourie, 1981), which is the perimeter distance around the torso at the level of the umbilicus.

Gluteal Girth

Also known as the buttocks or hip circumference, this is the perimeter at the level of the greatest posterior protuberance of the gluteals. The subject stands erect in

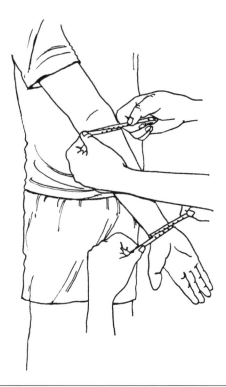

Figure 1.7   Measurement technique for forearm and wrist girths.

minimal clothing, with the feet together and no intentional contraction of the gluteal muscles. The tape is placed horizontally around the site, compressing any overlying clothing but not the soft tissues (see Figure 1.9).

Thigh Girth

This is the circumference of the thigh, which is measured when the subject stands erect with legs slightly parted and weight distributed equally on both feet. The tape is looped around the lower leg and raised to various levels.

- *For proximal or upper thigh*: until it is approximately 1 cm below the gluteal fold and horizontal to the long axis of the femur (Callaway et al., 1988; Cameron, 1986; Ross & Marfell-Jones, 1991; Weiner & Lourie, 1981).
- *For midthigh*: until it is middistance between the inguinal crease and the proximal border of the patella (Callaway et al., 1988).
- *For distal thigh*: until it is just proximal to the femoral epicondyles (Callaway et al., 1988) (see Figure 1.9).

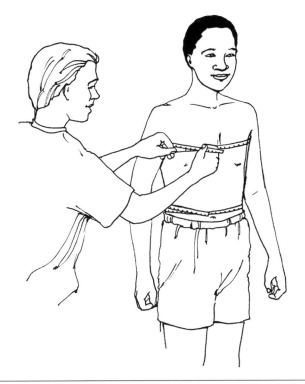

Figure 1.8 Measurement technique for chest and waist girths.

Calf Girth

This is the maximum circumference of the calf when the subject is positioned as for the thigh circumference (see Figure 1.9). The tape is manipulated horizontally up and down the leg to obtain the maximal girth measure.

Ankle Girth

This is the minimum circumference of the lower leg, just proximal to the malleoli (see Figure 1.9). The tape is manipulated horizontally up and down the leg to obtain the minimal girth measure, maintaining the perpendicular orientation of the tape to the long axis of the tibia.

TECHNIQUES FOR MEASURING SKINFOLD THICKNESS

A skinfold is raised by a pinching and rolling action of the measurer's left thumb and index finger. The fold is raised firmly and held throughout the measurement.

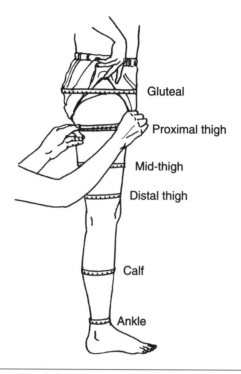

Figure 1.9   Measurement technique for gluteal and lower limb girths.

The caliper is applied at right angles to the fold so that the pressure plates are 1 cm from the thumb and index finger holding the fold (see Figure 1.10). The reading is taken from the dial approximately 2 sec after releasing of the caliper's trigger to permit the instrument's full pressure onto the fold. Measurements are recorded to the nearest 0.1 cm or 0.5 cm depending on the caliper being used.

The Harpenden skinfold caliper (British Indicators, Ltd., Victoria Rd., Burgess Hill, West Sussex, England, RH15 9LB) is the more commonly used instrument of this type in North America. This caliper accommodates a thickness of 50 mm. It has a dial indicator that is calibrated in 0.2 mm intervals, and readings may be interpolated to the nearest 0.1 mm. Figure 1.10 shows the measurement techniques for a number of skinfolds using the Harpenden calipers. Other instruments, such as the Holtain/Tanner–Whitehouse caliper (Holtain Ltd., Crosswell, Crymmtch, Dyfed, Wales, SA41 3UF), the Lange caliper (OWL Instruments Ltd., 177 Idema Rd., Markham, Ontario, Canada, L3R 1A9), and the plastic Slimguide caliper (Creative Health Products, 5148 Saddle Ridge Rd., Plymouth, MI 48170), may be used with similar reliability in the hands of a thoroughly trained measurer. Handling of the Slimguide calipers is shown in Figure 1.11.

The standard requisite for a skinfold caliper is constant pressure of the jaw surface (10 g/mm^2) over the range of jaw opening, although this may be acquired through various pairings of jaw area and spring tension. As a result, there is a tendency for lighter springed calipers (such as the Lange) to produce higher readings, particularly when being used by unskilled measurers (Greuber, Pollock, Graves, Colvin, & Braith, 1990; Sloan & Shapiro, 1972). Correction for systematic error must be made when using calipers that do not coincide with the above standard, especially if the resulting measurements are to be compared with previously established norms.

Triceps Skinfold

The measurer raises a vertical fold at the marked mid-acromiale–radiale line on the posterior surface of the arm. The caliper pressure plates are applied 1 cm distal to the measurer's thumb and index finger (see Figure 1.10).

Biceps Skinfold

The caliper is applied 1 cm distally from the vertical fold raised at the marked mid-acromiale–radiale line on the anterior surface of the arm (see Figure 1.10).

Subscapular Skinfold

The subscapular site is located by palpating the scapula to locate the inferior angle. The fold is picked up just inferior to the inferior angle, along the natural diagonal cleavage of the skin. The caliper pressure plates are applied 1 cm infero–lateral to the measurer's thumb and index finger (Harrison et al., 1988; Ross & Marfell-Jones, 1991) (see Figure 1.10).

Midaxial Skinfold

A horizontal skinfold is grasped at the level of the xyphoid process along the midaxillary line. The caliper pressure plates are applied 1 cm inferior to the thumb and index finger of the measurer (see Figure 1.10).

Iliac Crest Skinfold

To measure the iliac crest skinfold, frequently called the suprailiac skinfold (Harrison et al., 1988; Weiner & Lourie, 1981), the measurer grasps an oblique skinfold 1 cm posterior to the midaxillary line, immediately superior to the anterior superior iliac spine (iliac crest). The caliper pressure plates are applied along this diagonal fold, at the midaxillary line (see Figure 1.10).

Supraspinale Skinfold

Ross and Marfell-Jones (1991) uniquely identify this anterior skinfold as separate from the suprailiac or iliac crest site. A fold is raised about 7 cm superior to the iliospinale along a trajectory from the spinale to the anterior axillary border. This

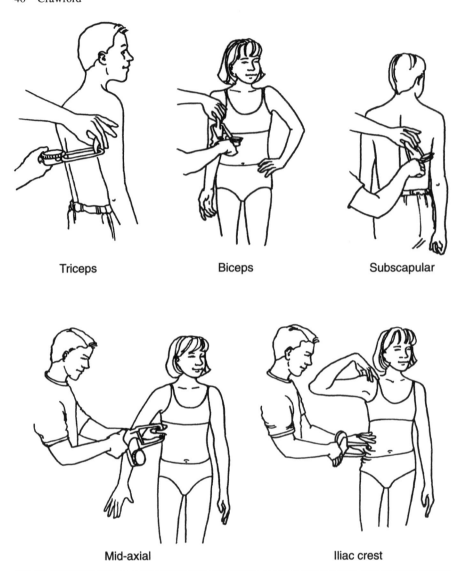

Triceps   Biceps   Subscapular

Mid-axial   Iliac crest

Figure 1.10   Measurement techniques for skinfold thickness using Harpenden calipers.

follows the oblique natural cleavage of the skin medially at about a 45° angle from the horizontal (see Figure 1.11).

Abdominal Skinfold

A vertical fold is raised 5 cm laterally at the level of the umbilicus. The pressure plates of the caliper are applied 1 cm inferiorly to the measurer's thumb and index finger. There is no current agreement on the correct measurement site or the appropriate direction of the fold (vertical or horizontal) for this skinfold (Harrison et al., 1988; Ross & Marfell-Jones, 1991) (see Figure 1.11).

Anterior Midthigh Skinfold

The subject's leg is flexed at a 90° angle at the knee by placing the foot on a raised

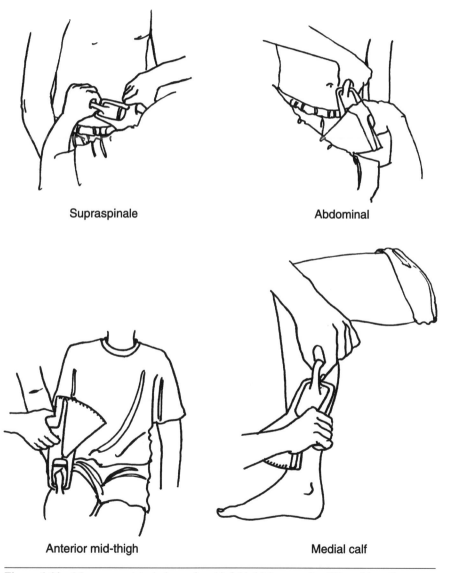

Figure 1.11   Measurement techniques for skinfold thickness using Slimguide calipers. Adapted from MacDougall, Wenger, and Green (1991).

surface. The skinfold is raised on the anterior thigh along the long axis of the femur, midway between the inguinal crease and the proximal border of the patella. The pressure plates of the caliper are applied 1 cm inferiorly to the measurer's thumb and index finger. This can be a difficult skinfold to raise and can be assisted by supporting the underside of the thigh, either by having the subject sit with the thigh relaxed on a horizontal surface or by having the subject grasp the underside of the thigh and raise it as far as possible without moving the leg out of position. Another alternative is to have an assistant grasp folds both proximal and distal to the measurement sight to allow the application of the calipers between the two (see Figure 1.11).

Medial Calf Skinfold

This skinfold is easiest to measure if the subject is standing with the leg flexed, usually by placing the foot on a box. A vertical fold is raised on the relaxed medial calf at the level of estimated greatest circumference. The pressure plates of the caliper are applied 1 cm distally to the measurer's thumb and index finger (see Figure 1.11).

TECHNIQUES FOR MEASURING BREADTHS

Breadths and depths of the axial skeleton are usually measured with an anthropometer assembled to serve as a sliding beam caliper and/or a wide-spreading caliper (Siber–Hegner #106). Smaller (15 cm) sliding engineering calipers, such as the Siber–Hegner #104, can be used directly or adapted to serve as bone calipers for the measurement of humerus, femur, and wrist widths. Adaptations include removing the inside diameter arms and extending the branches with round pressure plates for more complete contact with epicondylar surfaces. The vernier scale on these bone calipers can be read to the nearest .01 cm or .1 mm (Ross & Marfell-Jones, 1991). The Mitutoyo Digimatic caliper (capable to .01mm) can be similarly adapted and is recommended for its ease of calibration and measurement reading.

Biacromial Breadth

This is the distance between the most lateral points on the acromion processes (the most superior lateral point of the acromion process identified by palpation along the crest of the scapular spine). The subject stands erect with the arms hanging loosely at the sides. The measurer stands behind the subject, holding the sliding beam caliper with the thumb and forefingers, palpating the landmarks with the remaining digits. The branches of the caliper are applied upward at an angle of about 45° from the horizontal processes. The sliding branch is brought in firm contact with the bony landmarks, and the reading is taken (see Figure 1.12a).

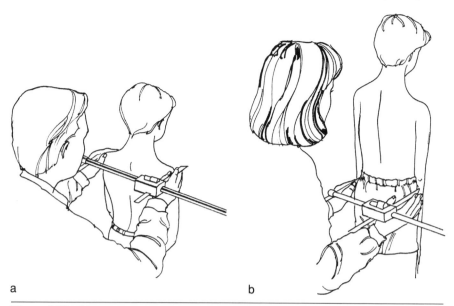

Figure 1.12   Measurement technique for (a) biacromial and (b) biiliocristal breadths.

Biiliocristal Breadth

Also known as the pelvic diameter and transverse pelvic breadth (Wilmore et al., 1988), this is the width between the most lateral points on the superior border of the iliac crest. The subject stands erect with the feet together. The anthropometrist may stand either behind (Weiner & Lourie, 1981; Wilmore et al.) or in front of the subject (Ross & Marfell-Jones, 1991). The measurer holds the instrument in the same manner as for the biacromial breadth (see Figure 1.12b). The branches of the sliding beam caliper are placed so that they encompass the maximum diameter, and firm pressure is applied to ensure that soft tissue contributes minimally to the measure. Ross and Marfell-Jones (1991) suggest that the caliper branches should point upward at a 45° angle from the horizontal, whereas Wilmore et al. describe a technique in which the caliper branches are applied at a 45° angle downward.

Transverse Chest Breadth

This is the diameter of the thorax in the midaxillary line on the most lateral aspect of the sixth ribs (Wilmore et al., 1988). From the anterior aspect, this corresponds to the level of the fourth sternocostal joints. Either the sliding beam or widespreading calipers can be used. In both instances the instrument is held in the same manner as that described for the above measures (see Figure 1.12). The subject can be seated (Ross & Marfell-Jones, 1991) or standing erect (Wilmore et al.), although the latter is the preferred position when measuring children. This is one of the few measures where the anthropometrist stands directly in front of the subject. The most common technique ensures that the caliper branches are applied in a horizontal plane (Weiner & Lourie, 1981; Wilmore et al., 1988). However, Ross and Marfell-Jones (1991) have suggested that in order to avoid both the pectoral and the latissimus dorsi muscle contours, the caliper branches be applied at an angle of about 30° downward from the horizontal. The caliper is applied with light pressure, and as with chest circumference the measurement is read at the end of normal expiration.

Anterior–Posterior Chest Depth

This is the depth of the chest at mesosternale level, which is the fourth condro–sternal joint. This landmark is located by alternating the thumb and index fingers of both hands from the clavicle to each intercostal space until the third space is reached, the next ribs being followed medially to their articulation with the sternum. Anterior–posterior chest depth is usually measured with a wide-spreading caliper or a sliding beam caliper with curved branches. The caliper is applied over the subject's right shoulder, in a downward direction. The relative heights of the measurer and the subject will determine whether the latter should be seated or standing. The olive tip of the caliper branch is held at the marked mesosternale by the thumb and index finger of the measurer's right hand. The opposing branch is placed on the spinous process of the vertebra in the same plane as the anterior landmark (see Figure 1.13). Once again, the measurement is taken at the end of a normal expiration.

Humerus Width

Sometimes referred to as the elbow width (Wilmore et al., 1988), this is the distance between the medial and lateral epicondyles of the humerus. With the subject's arm raised forward to horizontal, with the forearm flexed to 90° at the elbow, the measurer palpates the medial and lateral epicondyles and applies the sliding bone caliper pointing upward, bisecting the right angle formed at the elbow (see Figure 1.14). The medial epicondyle is distal to the lateral epicondyle. Consequently, the caliper is held slightly oblique to the epicondyles.

Wrist Width

This is the distance between the most lateral aspect of the radial styloid and the most medial aspect of the ulnar styloid. The subject's arm is flexed so that the forearm is horizontal facing forward, and the dorsum of the hand is towards the measurer. The caliper is held by the measurer in the same manner as described in Figure 1.14.

Figure 1.13   Measurement technique for anterior–posterior chest depth.

Femur Width

The femur or knee width is the distance between the medial and lateral epicondyles of the femur. The subject is seated and the leg is flexed at the knee to form a 90° angle with the thigh. Palpating the epicondyles with the third and fourth digits, the measurer applies the bone caliper pointing downward, bisecting the right angle formed at the knee (see Figure 1.15). It is important to apply the pressure plates of the caliper branches firmly to minimize the inclusion of soft tissue in this measure.

CONCLUSION

Assessment of physique using anthropometry can serve many purposes in both the study and practice of pediatric exercise and sport. Beyond estimation of body composition, anthropometry is an important tool for the evaluation of growth and maturation, which in turn will influence physiological parameters, strength, and movement mechanics. Tracking such measures in tandem with growth-related changes in physique will provide information regarding the effects of training or

Figure 1.14   Measurement technique for humerus width.

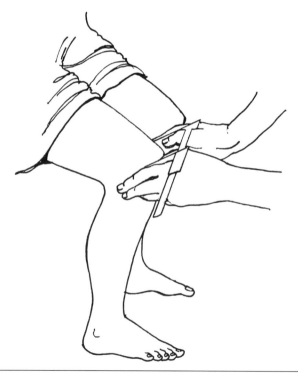

Figure 1.15   Measurement technique for femur width.

detraining of children beyond those normally anticipated with growth. Similarly, the development of more equitable assessments of performance and safer systems of sport participation for children could be based on physique characteristics of maturational status rather than on chronological age alone.

Wherever comparative data are used, it is important that there be an understanding of the limitations of the anthropometric methodologies, including the degree of error inherent in each technique, and the specific landmarks employed. Systematic error can be minimized by thorough training of those involved in measurement to ensure strict and consistent adherence to identified techniques. Random anthropometric error may be more likely in pediatric populations than among adult subjects and can be reduced by controlling the measurement environment, ensuring the full cooperation of subjects, and conducting repeated measurements at each site.

National Center for Health Statistics Norms of Weight-for-Height, Height-for-Age, and Weight-for-Age for Girls and Boys

Weight by age percentiles for boys aged 2 to 18 years

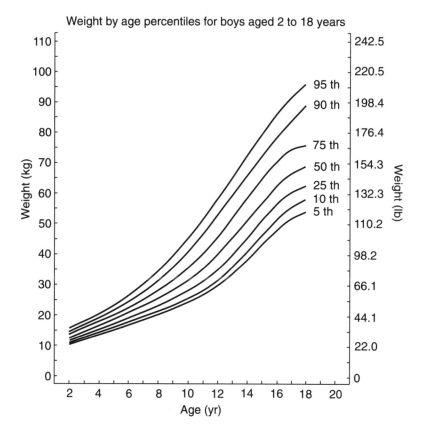

Stature by age percentiles of boys aged 2 to 18 years

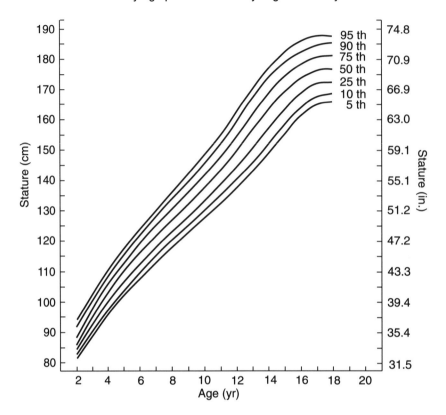

Weight by stature percentiles for prepubescent boys

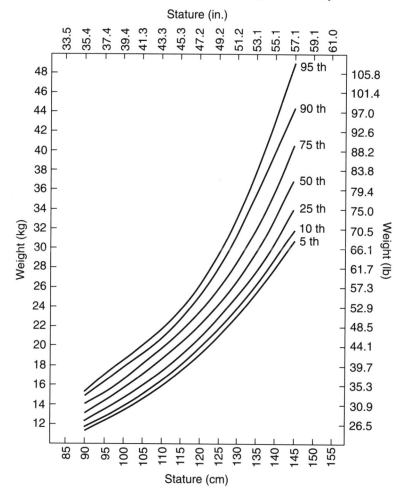

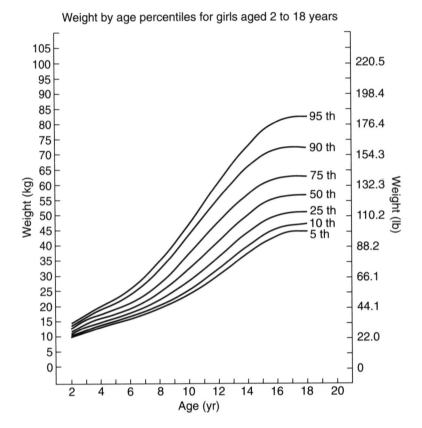

Weight by age percentiles for girls aged 2 to 18 years

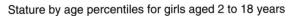

Stature by age percentiles for girls aged 2 to 18 years

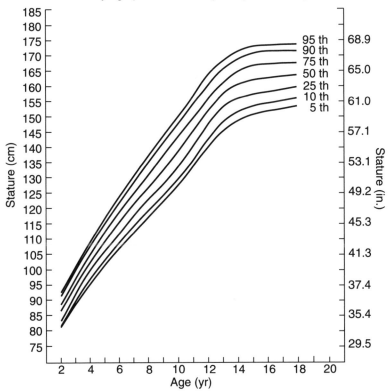

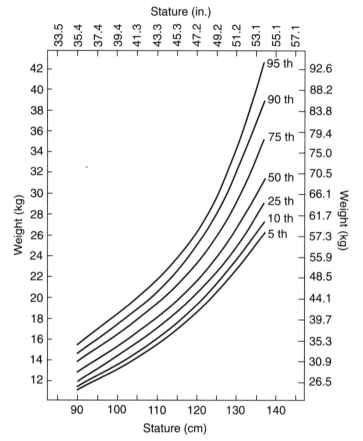

Weight by stature percentiles for prepubescent girls

Appendix 1.2

Normative Anthropometric Data for Boys and Girls

Sitting Height in Centimeters for Children 4 to 18 Years of Age

Age (years)	N	Mean	SD	Percentiles						
				5	10	25	50	75	90	95
				Males						
4	154	57.9	(2.8)	54.2	54.3	55.9	58.0	59.8	61.8	62.3
5	130	60.8	(3.0)	55.1	56.3	59.1	60.7	62.9	64.6	65.2
6	126	63.1	(2.6)	58.7	59.9	61.4	62.7	65.2	66.5	66.8
7	153	65.3	(2.3)	61.6	62.4	64.1	65.0	66.5	68.4	69.4
8	159	68.3	(3.1)	64.0	64.5	66.0	68.0	69.7	72.6	74.6
9	132	70.6	(4.4)	64.3	64.5	67.5	69.7	75.0	75.4	78.4
10	159	73.0	(3.5)	67.5	68.3	70.9	73.0	75.0	78.5	78.5
11	173	73.6	(3.0)	69.5	69.8	71.3	73.4	76.3	77.0	78.3
12	182	77.9	(4.8)	71.9	72.3	74.6	78.2	80.1	82.0	88.8
13	171	79.8	(4.6)	73.4	74.1	76.6	80.0	83.5	85.7	87.7
14	157	82.2	(4.5)	75.2	77.2	78.5	81.5	85.2	89.4	89.5
15	158	85.3	(4.1)	77.9	78.2	83.5	86.0	87.9	90.2	92.9
16	172	89.0	(4.4)	81.6	83.5	85.9	89.1	92.8	93.1	95.3
17	121	91.1	(3.9)	83.6	86.0	88.8	91.1	94.0	95.5	97.7
18	108	90.4	(3.4)	85.7	86.0	88.2	90.3	93.5	94.1	95.6
				Females						
4	118	57.5	(2.1)	54.3	54.8	56.1	57.9	58.7	60.1	60.7
5	140	59.7	(2.9)	54.6	55.4	57.8	60.4	61.2	63.4	64.7
6	125	61.3	(4.2)	51.5	55.8	58.9	62.1	63.7	64.8	66.2
7	132	63.2	(3.6)	56.2	58.5	60.7	63.5	66.3	68.2	68.9
8	142	67.7	(3.7)	61.8	63.0	65.1	67.7	70.0	70.6	73.5
9	139	69.3	(3.5)	63.5	65.8	66.5	69.5	71.0	72.0	74.1
10	147	72.6	(3.2)	66.9	68.2	71.2	72.9	74.5	76.0	77.3
11	157	75.5	(4.6)	69.4	70.1	73.2	75.5	76.3	80.8	86.5
12	167	77.9	(4.3)	71.1	72.6	75.5	77.5	81.3	83.4	84.7
13	195	82.0	(4.2)	75.7	77.7	78.8	81.7	84.8	88.3	89.0
14	185	82.5	(4.0)	75.2	77.0	79.5	83.3	85.1	87.6	88.5
15	160	84.2	(2.6)	80.4	81.1	83.0	83.6	85.7	87.7	88.6
16	160	85.5	(3.2)	80.6	81.5	83.3	85.8	87.2	89.5	90.7
17	134	85.1	(2.8)	80.5	81.7	83.7	84.6	86.8	88.6	90.5
18	135	85.1	(3.2)	77.7	81.4	83.4	86.1	87.0	88.9	89.3

Reprinted from Jetté (1982).

Subischial Length in Centimeters for Children 6 to 17 Years of Age

Age (years)	n	Mean	SD	Percentiles						
				5	10	25	50	75	90	95
				Boys						
6	489	53.6	3.24	48.5	49.6	51.5	53.3	55.7	57.8	59.4
7	551	57.2	3.53	51.6	53.1	55.0	57.1	59.2	61.9	63.7
8	537	60.3	3.44	54.5	55.9	58.2	60.3	62.5	64.7	65.7
9	525	63.9	4.52	57.3	59.1	61.3	64.1	66.6	69.0	70.3
10	509	66.9	4.33	60.2	61.6	64.3	67.0	69.7	72.2	73.7
11	542	70.1	4.43	63.0	64.8	67.5	70.1	73.1	75.4	77.0
12		74.1	4.97	63.5	67.7	70.7	74.3	77.4	79.9	81.8
13		77.9	4.97	69.8	71.6	74.7	77.9	81.4	84.4	86.5
14		81.2	4.74	73.8	75.3	77.8	81.3	84.7	87.2	88.4
15		82.9	4.52	75.2	77.2	78.0	82.9	85.6	88.3	90.2
16		84.0	4.35	77.2	78.4	81.3	83.9	86.5	89.9	91.2
17		84.3	4.61	76.4	78.3	81.2	84.4	87.7	90.0	91.6
				Girls						
6	461	53.5	3.47	48.2	49.3	51.1	53.5	55.7	57.7	59.1
7	512	57.0	3.81	51.1	52.4	54.8	56.9	59.3	61.3	62.7
8	498	60.5	4.29	54.5	56.0	58.2	60.5	63.2	65.6	67.0
9	494	64.0	4.32	57.4	59.0	61.4	63.7	66.7	70.1	71.2
10	505	67.3	4.32	60.5	61.7	64.2	67.1	70.3	73.1	74.5
11	477	70.9	5.21	63.8	65.6	68.3	70.9	73.8	76.6	77.8
12		74.3	4.50	66.2	68.4	71.6	74.4	77.1	80.0	81.7
13		75.7	4.40	68.4	70.3	72.7	75.6	78.8	81.4	82.9
14		76.7	4.12	70.3	71.4	73.8	76.6	79.3	81.8	83.5
15		76.9	4.57	69.8	71.0	73.9	76.6	80.0	82.9	84.5
16		76.6	4.42	69.4	71.0	73.8	76.6	79.4	82.4	84.0
17		76.6	4.31	70.3	71.3	73.7	76.4	79.8	81.8	83.8

Adapted from Malina, Hamill, and Lemeshow (1974) and Roche and Malina (1983).

Upper Arm Length in Centimeters for Children 6 to 17 Years of Age

Age (years)	n	Mean	SD	Percentiles						
				5	10	25	50	75	90	95
				Boys						
6	489	23.7	1.31	21.5	22.1	22.7	23.6	24.6	25.6	25.9
7	551	25.0	1.37	22.6	23.2	24.1	25.1	25.9	26.7	27.4
8	537	26.2	1.39	23.9	24.4	25.3	26.3	27.2	28.1	28.7
9	525	27.6	1.60	25.1	25.5	26.4	27.5	28.6	29.8	30.5
10	509	28.6	1.66	25.8	26.4	27.6	28.7	29.8	30.8	31.4
11	542	30.0	1.85	27.2	27.7	28.8	30.1	31.2	32.3	33.0
12		28.2	1.89	25.3	25.9	26.9	28.2	29.4	30.6	31.5
13		29.8	2.11	26.4	27.0	28.3	29.7	31.2	32.5	33.6
14		31.2	2.05	27.7	28.7	29.8	31.1	32.5	33.8	34.3
15		32.1	2.01	29.1	29.8	30.8	32.1	33.4	34.6	35.2
16		32.7	1.88	29.5	30.4	31.6	32.8	33.9	35.3	36.0
17		33.1	2.21	29.8	30.7	31.6	33.1	34.4	35.6	36.2
				Girls						
6	461	23.4	1.41	21.2	21.5	22.5	23.5	24.5	25.3	25.8
7	512	24.6	1.41	22.3	22.8	23.6	24.6	25.7	26.5	26.8
8	498	26.1	1.57	23.5	24.2	25.2	26.2	27.2	28.3	29.0
9	494	27.5	1.61	25.1	25.4	26.4	27.5	28.6	29.7	30.4
10	505	28.8	1.88	25.9	26.5	27.5	28.8	30.1	31.3	31.8
11	477	30.4	1.88	27.4	28.2	29.2	30.4	31.8	32.9	33.6
12		28.6	1.98	25.3	26.2	27.4	28.6	29.8	31.1	31.9
13		29.4	1.81	26.5	27.1	28.3	29.3	30.5	31.7	38.3
14		29.9	1.68	27.4	27.8	28.9	29.8	31.0	32.0	32.8
15		30.2	1.88	27.1	27.7	28.9	30.1	31.3	32.5	33.2
16		30.2	1.79	27.4	28.1	29.2	30.2	31.4	32.5	33.1
17		30.1	1.63	27.5	28.1	29.1	30.2	31.2	32.2	32.8

Adapted from Malina, Hamill, and Lemeshow (1974) and Roche and Malina (1983).

Forearm Length in Centimeters for Children 6 to 17 Years of Age

Age (years)	n	Mean	SD	Percentiles						
				5	10	25	50	75	90	95
Boys										
6	489	18.2	0.97	16.5	17.0	17.4	18.2	18.8	19.6	19.9
7	551	19.2	1.11	17.4	17.8	18.4	19.2	19.8	20.7	21.1
8	537	20.0	1.15	18.1	18.5	19.3	20.1	20.8	21.6	21.9
9	525	21.1	1.22	19.1	19.4	20.2	21.1	21.8	22.7	23.3
10	509	21.8	1.24	19.7	20.2	21.1	21.8	22.8	23.6	23.9
11	542	22.8	1.40	20.5	21.1	22.0	22.8	23.7	24.7	25.3
12		22.0	1.67	19.2	20.0	21.0	22.0	23.1	24.0	24.8
13		23.0	1.76	20.3	20.9	21.8	23.1	24.2	25.2	26.0
14		24.2	1.72	21.4	22.1	23.2	24.3	25.3	26.2	27.0
15		24.9	1.95	22.2	22.8	23.9	24.9	26.0	27.0	27.7
16		25.2	1.60	22.4	23.1	24.1	25.3	26.3	27.4	27.9
17		25.5	2.18	22.7	23.4	24.4	25.6	26.7	27.7	28.6
Girls										
6	461	17.7	1.02	16.0	16.3	17.1	17.7	18.5	19.1	19.6
7	512	18.7	1.16	17.0	17.3	18.0	18.6	19.5	20.2	20.7
8	498	19.7	1.15	17.7	18.2	18.8	19.7	20.6	21.4	21.7
9	494	20.7	1.21	18.8	19.2	19.8	20.6	21.6	22.5	22.9
10	505	21.7	1.35	19.5	20.1	20.7	21.7	22.7	23.6	24.0
11	477	22.9	1.44	20.5	21.1	21.9	22.8	23.8	24.8	25.4
12		22.0	1.62	19.4	20.0	20.9	22.0	23.0	24.0	24.5
13		22.4	1.50	20.0	20.5	21.5	22.4	23.3	24.3	24.8
14		22.8	1.53	20.5	20.9	21.8	22.8	23.9	24.7	25.2
15		23.0	1.59	20.6	21.0	22.0	23.0	23.9	25.1	25.8
16		23.0	1.51	20.6	21.2	22.0	23.0	23.9	24.8	25.3
17		22.9	1.42	20.6	21.1	22.0	22.8	23.9	24.8	25.3

Adapted from Malina, Hamill, and Lemeshow (1974) and Roche and Malina (1983).

Hand Length in Centimeters for Children 6 to 18 Years of Age

Age (years)	n	Mean	SD	Percentiles						
				5	10	25	50	75	90	95
				Boys						
6	489	12.9	0.68	11.7	12.1	12.4	13.1	13.6	13.9	16.5
7	551	13.5	0.71	12.2	12.4	13.1	13.5	14.0	14.6	14.3
8	537	14.1	0.81	12.5	13.1	13.5	14.2	14.7	15.3	14.8
9	525	14.6	0.78	13.2	13.5	14.2	14.6	15.2	15.7	15.6
10	509	15.1	0.82	13.7	14.1	14.5	15.1	15.7	16.3	15.9
11	542	15.7	0.87	14.2	14.4	15.1	15.6	16.3	16.8	17.3
12	154	16.2	1.0	14.5			16.0			17.8
13	152	16.9	1.1	15.1			16.7			18.7
14	153	17.8	1.2	15.9			17.7			19.4
15	130	18.2	1.0	16.3			18.2			19.7
16	99	18.9	1.0	17.3			18.9			20.4
17	104	18.9	0.9	17.2			18.8			20.1
18	88	19.2	0.9	17.4			19.1			20.5
				Girls						
6	461	12.8	0.70	11.4	11.8	12.2	12.7	13.4	13.8	14.2
7	512	13.3	0.76	12.1	12.3	12.8	13.4	13.8	14.4	14.7
8	498	13.9	0.76	12.4	13.0	13.3	13.8	14.5	14.9	15.4
9	494	14.6	0.77	13.2	13.4	14.1	14.5	15.1	15.7	16.0
10	505	15.1	0.86	13.5	14.0	14.4	15.2	15.7	16.4	16.7
11	477	15.9	0.91	14.3	14.6	15.2	15.8	16.6	17.2	17.6
12	133	16.3	1.0	14.6			16.2			17.7
13	160	16.9	1.0	15.1			16.9			18.4
14	116	17.0	0.9	15.6			16.9			18.4
15	132	17.3	0.9	15.8			17.2			18.8
16	98	17.2	0.9	15.5			17.1			18.6
17	117	17.1	0.9	15.6			17.1			18.4
18	68	17.3	0.8	15.7			17.3			18.5

Reprinted from Malina, Hamill, and Lemeshow (1974) and Snyder, Schneider, Owings, Reynolds, Golomb, and Schork (1977).

Thigh Length (Spinale Height Minus Tibiale Height) for Children 6 to 18 Years of Age

Age (years)	n	Mean	SD	Percentiles						
				5	10	25	50	75	90	95
				Males						
6	18	32.14	2.55	—	29.07	30.88	31.60	33.60	36.23	—
7	23	34.18	2.11	30.90	31.50	32.50	33.80	35.60	37.80	38.36
8	22	36.17	2.44	30.95	32.01	34.73	36.55	37.50	39.73	40.30
9	28	37.20	2.99	31.45	33.55	35.70	36.60	39.13	42.64	43.00
10	22	41.03	3.24	35.16	37.20	38.28	40.55	43.55	45.66	46.84
11	28	42.19	2.44	38.95	39.00	40.35	41.45	44.35	45.93	46.81
12	31	43.46	2.66	38.52	39.14	41.90	43.60	45.00	47.88	48.28
13	36	47.17	2.61	43.71	44.28	45.23	47.10	48.40	50.91	53.14
14	76	48.28	2.68	43.96	44.71	46.53	48.45	50.15	51.42	52.26
15	75	50.06	3.22	44.80	45.98	47.70	50.00	52.50	54.04	55.92
16	57	51.11	3.23	45.31	46.40	48.95	51.40	53.55	54.98	56.32
17	40	51.67	2.91	46.35	47.25	50.35	51.45	54.10	55.64	56.57
18	22	52.23	4.08	44.96	46.55	48.88	53.00	54.23	58.90	59.37
				Females						
6	23	31.92	1.91	29.24	29.64	30.20	31.50	33.20	34.70	36.46
7	23	33.84	2.51	28.26	30.70	31.80	34.00	35.30	37.12	39.04
8	16	35.73	1.84	—	33.00	34.03	35.85	37.18	38.09	—
9	28	38.13	2.48	33.70	34.15	36.60	37.75	39.95	40.72	43.27
10	22	42.04	3.28	36.28	37.57	39.70	41.40	44.68	47.29	48.10
11	24	42.89	2.63	38.58	39.50	40.80	42.95	44.80	46.35	48.23
12	33	45.24	2.38	41.16	42.34	43.55	44.60	46.95	48.86	49.54
13	37	47.25	2.66	41.57	42.94	45.75	47.50	48.70	50.90	50.28
14	67	47.42	2.55	42.64	44.44	46.10	47.20	49.10	50.62	51.54
15	67	47.59	3.17	42.14	44.40	45.80	47.50	49.90	51.82	53.56
16	51	48.01	2.73	43.14	44.20	46.00	48.10	50.00	51.08	53.00
17	46	48.40	2.85	43.88	44.44	45.88	48.90	50.30	52.65	53.43
18	10	49.15	3.34	—	44.02	46.00	49.05	51.60	54.60	—

Adapted from Ross, Drinkwater, Whittingham, and Faulkner (1980).

Tibiale Height for Children 6 to 18 Years of Age

Age (years)	n	Mean	SD	Percentiles						
				5	10	25	50	75	90	95
					Males					
6	18	29.13	1.89	—	26.79	27.70	28.60	30.18	32.50	—
7	23	31.06	1.63	28.54	28.74	29.70	31.20	32.70	33.42	34.06
8	22	33.30	1.91	30.73	30.93	31.68	32.85	34.50	36.62	37.06
9	28	34.87	3.37	30.17	30.50	32.53	34.40	37.18	38.51	42.45
10	22	37.20	2.80	32.51	33.70	35.15	36.95	39.00	41.72	42.84
11	28	38.45	2.41	34.46	34.99	36.43	38.85	40.10	41.48	43.08
12	31	40.10	2.70	35.34	36.56	37.60	40.20	42.30	43.96	44.40
13	37	43.45	2.72	39.54	40.17	41.60	43.35	45.43	47.14	48.81
14	76	44.42	2.91	39.23	41.04	42.63	44.50	46.38	47.80	49.82
15	75	45.56	2.92	40.92	41.90	43.30	45.80	47.90	49.16	49.70
16	57	45.66	2.26	42.30	42.60	44.15	45.60	47.10	49.06	49.82
17	40	45.42	2.37	41.62	42.22	43.25	45.75	47.08	48.78	49.68
18	22	46.58	3.19	40.95	41.92	44.15	46.85	48.70	50.71	53.27
					Females					
6	23	28.75	2.10	26.04	26.20	27.20	28.80	29.70	32.18	33.34
7	23	31.10	1.42	28.64	29.12	30.00	31.30	31.70	33.10	34.46
8	17	33.00	1.46	—	30.22	32.30	33.30	33.80	34.60	—
9	28	35.06	2.37	31.36	31.89	33.33	35.15	36.48	38.48	40.43
10	22	37.58	3.03	33.44	34.35	35.28	37.10	40.05	43.28	44.26
11	25	38.11	2.58	35.90	34.20	36.13	38.30	40.23	40.80	42.73
12	33	41.09	2.22	37.52	38.58	39.60	40.60	43.00	44.00	44.75
13	37	42.43	2.24	38.34	38.82	49.90	42.60	43.85	46.02	46.41
14	67	42.49	2.01	39.18	39.66	41.30	42.50	43.50	45.06	46.30
15	67	42.32	2.26	38.46	39.60	41.00	42.30	43.90	45.42	45.82
16	51	42.83	1.79	40.00	40.22	40.50	43.10	44.10	45.18	45.64
17	46	42.57	2.64	39.18	39.81	40.78	41.95	44.50	45.95	46.47
18	10	42.44	3.59	—	36.29	40.70	42.60	44.70	47.28	—

Adapted from Ross, Drinkwater, Whittingham, and Faulkner (1980).

Foot Length in Centimeters for Children 6 to 17 Years of Age

Age (years)	Mean	SD	Percentiles						
			5	10	25	50	75	90	95
			Boys						
6	17.9	1.01	16.2	16.5	17.2	17.8	18.6	19.4	19.8
7	18.8	1.05	17.1	17.4	18.1	18.8	19.6	20.4	20.8
8	19.6	1.20	17.7	18.1	18.7	19.6	20.5	21.3	21.7
9	20.7	1.23	18.5	19.1	19.9	20.6	21.5	22.4	22.8
10	21.4	1.30	19.2	19.7	20.4	21.4	22.4	23.2	23.7
11	22.3	1.34	20.1	20.4	21.3	22.3	23.2	24.1	24.7
12	23.5	1.51	21.0	21.4	22.4	23.6	24.6	25.6	26.2
13	24.5	1.52	22.0	22.4	23.4	24.5	25.6	26.6	27.0
14	25.4	1.59	23.0	23.5	24.4	25.4	26.4	27.1	27.6
15	25.7	1.28	23.4	24.1	24.8	25.7	26.6	27.4	27.8
16	25.9	1.26	23.6	24.2	25.1	25.8	26.7	27.6	28.0
17	26.0	1.29	24.0	24.3	25.2	25.9	26.8	27.6	28.0
			Girls						
6	17.7	1.07	15.7	16.2	17.1	17.7	18.5	19.2	19.6
7	18.5	1.06	16.6	17.1	17.7	18.5	19.3	19.9	20.5
8	19.4	1.14	17.4	18.1	18.6	19.5	20.3	21.0	21.5
9	20.3	1.20	18.2	18.6	19.5	20.4	21.1	21.9	22.5
10	21.1	1.33	19.1	19.4	20.3	21.2	22.1	22.8	23.3
11	22.0	1.27	20.0	20.3	21.1	21.9	22.9	23.7	24.2
12	23.0	1.20	21.1	21.4	22.2	22.9	23.7	24.5	24.8
13	23.1	1.16	21.2	21.5	22.3	23.2	23.9	24.7	25.1
14	23.3	1.18	21.4	21.8	22.4	23.3	24.2	24.9	25.5
15	23.3	1.26	21.3	21.6	22.4	23.3	24.2	25.0	25.6
16	23.4	1.31	21.2	21.7	22.5	23.4	24.3	25.1	25.6
17	23.4	1.16	21.3	21.8	22.5	23.4	24.2	24.9	25.5

Adapted from Roche and Malina (1983).

Head Girth in Centimeters for Children 4 to 18 Years of Age

Age (years)	N	Mean	SD	Percentiles		
				5th	50th	95th
			Males			
4	118	50.7	1.3	48.7	50.4	52.9
5	142	51.2	1.3	48.6	50.9	53.6
6	108	51.6	1.6	48.7	51.7	53.9
7	104	51.9	1.6	48.9	51.9	54.5
8	95	52.6	1.5	49.9	52.5	54.9
9	114	52.6	1.7	49.7	52.8	54.9
10	124	52.9	1.4	50.5	52.8	55.1
11	141	53.6	1.5	51.1	53.4	55.9
12	154	53.8	1.7	51.1	53.6	56.6
13	154	54.3	1.7	51.8	54.2	57.3
14	155	54.8	1.9	51.9	54.7	58.0
15	131	55.4	1.7	52.4	55.4	57.9
16	100	56.5	1.9	52.6	56.6	59.6
17	104	56.7	1.7	53.5	56.7	59.3
18	88	57.2	1.6	54.5	57.1	59.4
			Females			
4	108	49.7	1.4	47.3	49.6	51.9
5	120	50.2	1.5	47.5	50.2	52.5
6	111	50.5	1.4	48.4	50.4	52.9
7	120	51.1	1.5	48.6	51.0	53.5
8	93	51.8	1.6	49.0	51.7	54.1
9	136	52.0	1.6	49.3	52.0	54.3
10	125	52.7	1.7	49.4	52.6	55.4
11	139	52.8	1.9	49.8	52.8	56.2
12	131	53.1	1.6	50.4	53.1	55.6
13	157	53.7	1.8	50.7	53.6	56.3
14	116	54.0	1.5	51.5	53.8	56.6
15	130	54.3	1.8	51.7	54.1	57.7
16	96	54.2	1.6	52.0	54.1	56.8
17	116	54.6	1.6	51.8	54.5	57.3
18	66	54.3	1.4	51.9	54.3	56.4

Reprinted from Snyder, Schneider, Owings, Reynolds, Golomb, and Schork (1977).

Neck Girth in Centimeters for Children 4 to 18 Years of Age

Age (years)	N	Mean	SD	Percentiles 5th	50th	95th
			Males			
4	37	24.6	1.3	21.5	24.6	26.2
5	58	25.3	1.3	23.6	25.3	27.1
6	39	25.8	1.3	23.4	25.8	28.0
7	40	26.2	1.4	23.4	26.1	27.8
8	36	27.1	1.7	24.4	26.8	29.0
9	42	27.8	1.9	24.2	27.6	31.1
10	40	28.1	1.6	25.4	28.2	30.9
11	40	28.1	1.2	26.0	28.1	30.1
12	55	29.5	1.6	27.1	29.4	31.9
13	58	30.3	1.8	27.6	30.0	33.3
14	49	32.2	1.9	29.1	32.3	35.1
15	42	32.8	1.9	29.4	32.9	35.7
16	38	35.2	2.7	30.7	34.9	39.6
17	28	35.8	2.0	31.6	36.0	38.1
18	38	36.6	2.5	32.3	36.6	40.5
			Females			
4	41	24.0	1.3	22.0	23.9	26.3
5	35	24.5	1.4	22.2	24.3	26.6
6	41	25.7	1.5	23.2	25.3	27.8
7	44	26.0	1.7	23.8	25.9	28.4
8	32	27.0	1.9	23.7	26.7	29.6
9	49	27.5	1.6	25.5	27.3	29.8
10	45	27.6	2.2	24.2	27.6	32.0
11	43	28.5	2.2	25.5	28.0	31.9
12	42	29.3	1.8	26.4	29.0	32.4
13	50	29.7	1.6	27.5	29.4	32.5
14	41	30.2	1.8	27.7	29.8	33.3
15	39	30.8	1.4	28.2	30.8	32.9
16	41	30.8	1.5	28.4	30.7	33.7
17	39	31.4	1.6	28.8	31.0	33.7
18	25	31.4	1.7	28.9	31.2	34.2

Reprinted from Snyder, Schneider, Owings, Reynolds, Golomb, and Schork (1977).

Midarm Girth in Centimeters for Children 7 to 18 Years of Age

Age (years)	N	Mean	SD	Percentiles						
				5	10	25	50	75	90	95

					Males					
7	171	18.648	2.228	16.100	16.600	17.300	18.200	19.400	21.000	23.460
8	230	19.595	2.387	16.555	17.200	18.175	19.200	20.700	22.590	24.190
9	212	20.344	2.388	17.500	17.900	18.700	19.900	21.425	23.540	25.800
10	224	21.111	2.523	17.600	18.200	19.400	20.950	22.300	24.000	25.800
11	211	22.108	3.154	18.160	18.600	20.100	21.600	23.300	26.080	27.800
12	221	22.783	2.880	18.820	19.700	20.900	22.500	24.150	26.280	28.180
13	216	23.735	2.847	19.500	20.670	21.625	23.500	25.200	27.230	28.830
14	209	25.439	3.317	20.650	21.200	23.300	24.900	27.000	29.900	32.050
15	209	26.851	3.239	21.900	23.500	24.950	26.500	28.450	30.600	34.150
16	191	27.551	2.766	23.140	24.520	25.800	27.200	29.200	31.100	32.240
17	206	28.367	2.951	23.600	24.640	26.475	28.200	30.300	32.190	33.430
18	168	29.490	2.749	25.300	26.480	27.700	29.500	31.100	32.710	34.210
					Females					
7	181	18.944	2.167	16.000	16.600	17.500	18.500	19.950	22.180	22.800
8	186	19.830	2.447	16.535	16.800	18.200	19.500	21.025	22.990	24.500
9	168	20.372	2.300	17.190	17.590	18.800	19.950	21.800	23.910	24.610
10	224	21.852	2.970	18.000	18.600	19.525	21.700	23.175	25.850	27.200
11	224	21.807	2.657	18.125	18.650	19.800	21.500	23.600	25.200	26.300
12	207	23.187	2.798	18.680	19.740	21.200	23.000	24.900	26.700	28.080
13	207	24.356	3.070	19.500	20.460	22.200	24.300	26.200	28.000	29.360
14	190	25.111	2.880	20.555	22.000	23.200	24.850	26.700	28.790	30.425
15	198	25.390	2.783	20.990	21.900	23.500	25.050	27.425	29.040	30.810
16	205	25.612	2.779	21.530	22.600	23.800	25.200	27.000	29.400	30.110
17	177	25.949	3.028	21.500	22.300	23.800	25.600	27.500	29.820	32.410
18	154	26.276	3.088	22.550	23.000	23.900	25.800	28.200	30.400	31.550

Adapted from Canada Fitness Survey (1981).

Forearm Girth in Centimeters for Children 6 to 17 Years of Age

Age (years)	Mean	SD	Percentiles						
			5	10	25	50	75	90	95
					Boys				
6	17.4	1.32	15.4	16.0	16.6	17.4	18.2	18.9	19.8
7	18.0	1.40	16.0	16.3	17.2	18.0	18.8	19.8	20.6
8	18.7	1.59	16.3	16.9	17.6	18.6	19.6	20.8	21.6
9	19.4	1.74	16.9	17.3	18.3	19.3	20.4	21.7	22.8
10	19.9	1.61	17.4	18.0	18.7	19.7	20.9	22.1	22.9
11	20.8	1.83	18.2	18.7	19.6	20.6	21.8	23.5	24.3
12	22.0	1.99	19.1	19.5	20.6	21.8	23.3	24.9	25.7
13	23.2	2.18	20.1	20.7	21.7	23.1	24.7	26.1	26.8
14	24.5	2.29	21.1	21.7	23.1	24.5	26.0	27.6	28.6
15	25.6	1.95	22.4	23.2	24.3	25.5	26.8	28.0	29.2
16	26.1	1.91	23.2	24.0	24.9	26.1	27.4	28.6	29.5
17	26.8	1.95	23.6	24.3	25.4	26.8	28.1	29.3	30.3
					Girls				
6	17.1	1.30	15.1	15.5	16.3	17.1	17.8	18.8	19.6
7	17.5	1.42	15.5	16.1	16.6	17.5	18.5	19.5	20.1
8	18.3	1.47	16.1	16.5	17.4	18.3	19.3	20.4	21.2
9	19.0	1.78	16.4	17.1	17.9	18.8	20.2	21.5	22.4
10	19.7	1.91	17.1	17.4	18.4	19.7	20.9	22.1	22.9
11	20.5	1.90	17.5	18.2	19.1	20.4	21.8	23.1	23.9
12	21.6	1.96	18.6	19.3	20.4	21.5	22.8	24.3	25.3
13	22.2	1.76	19.5	20.2	21.1	22.3	23.5	24.7	25.4
14	22.8	1.82	20.2	20.6	21.6	22.6	23.8	25.2	25.8
15	23.3	1.96	20.4	21.1	22.0	23.1	24.5	25.8	26.8
16	23.4	1.99	20.6	21.1	22.1	23.2	24.5	25.7	26.8
17	23.2	1.67	20.8	21.3	22.2	23.2	24.2	25.2	26.2

Adapted from Roche and Malina (1983).

Wrist Girth in Centimeters for Children 4 to 18 Years of Age

Age (years)	N	Mean	SD	Min	5th	50th	95th	Max
						Percentiles		
Males								
4	37	11.6	0.9	10.1	10.2	11.4	13.0	13.4
5	58	11.8	0.8	10.3	10.6	11.6	13.1	14.1
6	39	12.2	0.8	10.3	10.5	12.1	13.4	14.1
7	40	12.4	0.8	10.9	11.0	12.3	13.9	14.4
8	36	12.7	1.0	11.0	11.1	12.5	14.4	16.0
9	42	13.1	1.1	10.8	11.5	13.1	14.7	17.1
10	40	13.5	1.2	11.7	11.8	13.3	15.3	17.1
11	40	13.4	0.9	11.4	11.6	13.4	14.7	15.7
12	55	14.3	1.2	12.2	12.4	14.1	16.1	17.2
13	57	14.7	1.2	12.3	12.7	14.4	16.6	17.5
14	49	15.7	1.2	12.2	13.8	15.5	17.4	17.8
15	42	15.7	1.1	13.3	13.5	15.8	17.1	17.8
16	38	16.7	1.4	12.5	14.1	16.8	18.8	19.5
17	28	16.6	1.3	13.1	13.4	16.7	18.1	18.8
18	38	17.2	1.5	13.3	14.8	16.8	19.8	21.0
Females								
4	40	11.4	0.9	9.2	10.1	11.4	12.9	13.4
5	35	11.7	0.9	10.0	10.3	11.6	13.2	13.3
6	41	12.2	0.8	10.9	11.0	12.1	13.2	14.3
7	46	12.4	1.1	10.4	10.5	12.3	14.3	14.7
8	32	13.0	1.0	11.3	11.4	12.8	14.8	15.6
9	49	13.3	1.1	11.0	11.2	13.2	14.7	15.8
10	45	13.5	1.5	10.8	11.1	13.3	16.1	19.0
11	45	13.6	1.4	11.5	11.5	13.2	16.1	16.9
12	42	14.1	1.2	12.1	12.4	14.0	15.8	17.6
13	50	14.5	1.1	13.0	13.1	14.2	16.6	17.4
14	41	14.8	0.9	13.2	13.5	14.7	16.1	17.0
15	38	15.1	1.0	12.5	13.4	15.0	16.5	17.2
16	41	15.2	1.1	13.1	13.2	15.2	16.6	16.8
17	39	15.0	1.2	11.8	13.0	14.8	16.7	17.7
18	25	15.0	1.3	12.1	12.3	15.1	16.6	17.3

Reprinted from Snyder, Schneider, Owings, Reynolds, Golomb, and Schork (1977).

Chest Girth in Centimeters for Children 7 to 18 Years of Age

Age (years)	N	Mean	SD	Percentiles						
				5	10	25	50	75	90	95

Males

Age	N	Mean	SD	5	10	25	50	75	90	95
7	171	62.018	3.875	55.930	57.600	59.500	61.700	63.900	66.160	69.640
8	230	65.008	4.525	58.500	59.600	62.400	64.900	67.025	70.570	72.735
9	212	67.592	5.384	61.265	62.200	64.025	66.650	69.500	74.140	77.740
10	224	69.560	5.191	62.625	63.600	66.000	69.200	71.850	75.550	78.875
11	211	72.414	5.736	63.960	65.820	68.700	71.400	75.400	80.960	84.100
12	221	74.909	6.323	66.210	67.260	70.700	74.600	78.300	82.160	86.990
13	216	78.056	6.566	68.595	70.400	73.725	77.950	81.725	85.740	89.400
14	209	83.897	7.806	72.100	74.300	78.500	83.000	88.550	94.600	98.650
15	209	87.135	7.309	76.700	79.500	82.750	87.100	91.050	96.300	99.600
16	191	89.574	6.109	79.560	81.220	86.200	89.400	92.700	97.500	101.600
17	206	91.369	6.148	81.355	83.500	87.500	91.300	95.525	99.500	101.930
18	168	93.665	6.042	84.945	86.770	89.425	92.950	97.350	101.230	130.950

Females

Age	N	Mean	SD	5	10	25	50	75	90	95
7	181	62.031	9.164	55.120	56.340	58.350	60.800	63.550	67.080	71.700
8	186	64.077	5.347	56.305	57.970	60.200	63.950	66.925	71.030	73.495
9	168	66.054	5.688	57.890	59.200	62.200	65.600	69.700	73.480	75.900
10	224	70.334	6.447	62.050	63.000	65.500	69.400	74.900	77.850	83.350
11	224	71.692	6.300	63.200	65.000	66.700	70.850	75.000	80.300	83.825
12	207	76.134	6.825	64.880	68.080	71.500	75.900	80.600	84.720	87.280
13	207	79.705	6.404	69.740	71.600	76.000	79.500	82.800	87.900	90.000
14	190	82.225	5.770	73.400	75.000	78.350	81.850	85.800	89.780	91.635
15	198	82.391	5.406	74.490	75.500	78.600	82.400	85.500	89.810	91.015
16	205	82.867	5.947	74.680	76.200	79.750	82.000	86.000	90.020	92.610
17	177	83.432	6.028	74.500	76.400	79.500	82.700	86.750	90.760	94.010
18	154	84.273	6.177	75.325	77.150	80.000	83.650	87.825	93.100	94.825

Adapted from Canada Fitness Survey (1981).

Waist Girth in Centimeters for Children 7 to 18 Years of Age

Age (years)	N	Mean	SD	Percentiles						
				5	10	25	50	75	90	95
Males										
7	171	55.813	4.135	50.180	51.500	53.100	55.300	57.500	61.320	63.940
8	230	58.358	5.291	51.810	53.100	55.375	57.850	60.925	64.460	67.790
9	212	60.050	5.914	52.930	54.330	56.500	59.150	62.575	66.420	70.815
10	224	61.790	5.766	55.100	56.000	58.000	61.000	64.200	67.850	72.200
11	211	63.960	6.304	56.120	57.500	59.500	62.800	66.900	72.080	76.800
12	221	65.393	6.154	56.500	58.420	61.600	64.900	68.050	72.120	77.790
13	216	67.652	6.226	59.255	61.000	63.450	67.250	70.150	75.120	79.205
14	209	71.182	7.561	61.400	63.100	66.150	70.100	74.600	81.400	85.750
15	209	73.463	7.115	65.000	66.200	68.650	72.300	76.350	82.500	87.100
16	191	74.638	7.190	65.820	67.260	70.200	73.400	77.600	84.580	88.740
17	206	75.739	6.600	66.640	68.370	71.200	75.200	78.500	85.530	89.220
18	168	77.814	7.132	69.745	70.890	73.200	76.500	81.000	85.000	89.655
Females										
7	181	54.850	4.702	48.610	49.800	51.750	54.000	57.250	60.680	64.190
8	186	56.703	5.711	49.235	50.770	52.800	55.550	59.600	63.720	66.665
9	168	57.798	5.781	49.690	51.680	54.000	57.300	60.875	65.470	67.975
10	224	61.019	6.965	52.500	54.200	56.400	59.650	64.075	69.400	76.650
11	224	61.311	6.504	53.275	54.550	56.725	60.000	64.000	69.400	74.225
12	207	63.671	6.499	55.080	57.300	59.500	62.400	67.300	72.720	74.260
13	207	66.204	6.907	56.840	58.300	61.600	65.500	69.000	74.800	78.480
14	190	67.769	6.714	59.360	60.820	63.575	66.400	70.850	76.470	80.970
15	199	67.974	6.131	59.500	61.400	63.500	67.000	71.800	76.400	79.000
16	205	68.110	6.866	59.620	61.120	64.000	67.200	70.400	76.120	80.350
17	177	68.783	7.021	60.000	60.900	64.050	67.800	72.150	76.960	83.390
18	154	70.112	8.111	60.575	61.350	64.575	68.350	73.650	81.350	84.550

Adapted from Canada Fitness Survey (1981).

Gluteal Girth in Centimeters for Children 7 to 18 Years of Age

Age (years)	N	Mean	SD	Percentiles 5	10	25	50	75	90	95
						Males					
7	168	63.873	4.820	57.225	58.500	60.850	63.300	66.375	69.000	73.030
8	228	67.183	5.363	59.745	61.000	63.725	66.550	70.325	73.910	77.310
9	209	69.744	6.286	61.350	63.100	65.900	68.900	73.100	77.300	82.800
10	222	72.391	6.266	64.345	66.060	68.475	71.600	75.575	80.100	83.385
11	209	75.632	6.689	66.100	68.100	71.000	74.500	79.250	86.600	88.500
12	218	78.118	6.517	68.795	70.590	73.975	78.050	81.600	86.200	90.730
13	214	81.820	7.172	71.650	73.650	77.200	81.350	86.125	89.400	93.625
14	207	86.337	7.332	75.440	77.580	80.500	86.300	91.000	96.260	99.280
15	208	89.917	6.996	80.435	82.400	85.800	89.050	93.175	98.600	102.655
16	190	91.621	5.903	82.255	84.620	87.975	90.800	94.500	100.380	102.835
17	206	92.118	5.790	83.045	85.340	88.500	92.200	94.850	99.500	102.905
18	168	93.584	7.038	85.335	87.850	90.000	93.150	96.475	101.320	103.310
						Females					
7	176	65.009	5.084	58.670	60.210	62.000	64.150	66.925	72.030	73.905
8	183	67.788	5.872	60.200	61.640	63.500	67.300	71.500	75.940	78.660
9	165	70.704	6.415	61.530	63.500	66.200	70.000	74.550	78.300	82.770
10	222	75.382	7.041	65.630	67.000	70.150	75.000	79.325	83.910	87.710
11	222	77.117	7.267	67.030	68.700	71.975	76.400	81.400	86.440	91.500
12	203	82.147	7.193	71.240	73.440	77.200	81.500	86.900	92.500	94.180
13	203	86.977	7.534	74.560	77.240	83.000	87.200	91.300	95.360	98.500
14	190	90.278	6.780	80.265	83.000	85.975	89.900	94.200	98.970	100.390
15	196	91.035	5.992	81.155	84.000	86.725	90.850	94.875	98.560	100.650
16	202	91.143	6.552	81.515	83.630	86.975	90.700	94.125	98.710	101.685
17	177	92.104	6.669	82.120	84.360	87.750	91.200	95.750	100.400	105.010
18	151	93.184	6.915	83.840	85.080	88.500	92.000	96.900	130.000	106.200

Adated from Canada Fitness Survey (1981).

Thigh Girth in Centimeters for Children 7 to 18 Years of Age

Age (years)	N	Mean	SD	Percentiles						
				5	10	25	50	75	90	95
					Males					
7	171	35.908	3.916	30.960	32.040	33.800	35.400	37.200	40.500	41.880
8	229	38.051	3.910	32.900	33.700	35.600	37.500	40.500	43.000	45.350
9	210	39.890	4.401	34.155	35.400	37.275	39.150	42.125	45.580	49.335
10	218	41.781	4.384	35.985	37.000	38.800	41.200	44.300	47.000	49.510
11	209	43.764	6.011	36.050	37.900	40.200	43.00	46.400	51.100	52.300
12	219	45.242	5.600	37.400	39.000	41.800	45.000	48.000	51.100	53.500
13	214	46.899	4.920	40.350	41.100	43.500	46.600	49.125	52.700	55.700
14	205	49.571	5.624	41.300	42.520	45.950	49.200	52.600	56.400	59.810
15	209	51.503	5.418	43.850	45.700	48.150	50.600	54.100	58.300	63.200
16	190	52.452	4.593	45.410	47.200	49.400	52.100	55.000	58.670	61.245
17	206	52.906	5.258	45.940	47.170	49.775	52.700	55.525	58.000	61.255
18	165	54.405	5.142	47.720	49.600	51.400	53.500	56.500	59.440	62.150
					Females					
7	179	37.854	4.065	32.500	33.400	35.500	37.100	39.700	43.100	45.200
8	184	39.957	4.533	34.400	34.750	36.600	39.450	42.700	46.100	48.325
9	168	41.346	4.817	35.180	35.900	38.225	40.650	44.475	46.820	49.000
10	223	44.637	5.327	37.420	38.560	40.500	43.800	47.700	51.400	54.180
11	223	45.139	5.045	37.920	39.300	41.200	44.400	48.500	52.060	54.140
12	204	48.306	5.483	39.575	41.100	44.750	47.850	51.850	55.500	56.850
13	206	51.328	5.661	41.875	44.140	47.850	51.450	54.800	58.030	60.290
14	186	53.162	4.983	45.435	47.480	49.400	53.000	56.525	58.800	61.065
15	197	53.517	4.856	45.190	47.180	50.300	53.900	56.800	59.000	61.500
16	203	53.689	4.747	45.680	48.600	50.900	53.200	56.300	59.420	62.300
17	175	54.178	5.066	46.300	48.320	50.900	53.800	57.200	60.920	64.820
18	154	54.842	5.171	48.100	49.100	50.600	54.250	57.925	62.300	64.850

Adapted from Canada Fitness Survey (1981).

Calf Girth in Centimeters for Children 7 to 18 Years of Age

Age (years)	N	Mean	SD	Percentiles						
				5	10	25	50	75	90	95

Males

Age (years)	N	Mean	SD	5	10	25	50	75	90	95
7	171	24.692	1.947	21.960	22.500	23.500	24.500	25.500	27.000	28.180
8	230	26.094	2.297	22.965	23.500	24.700	26.000	27.400	29.100	30.000
9	212	27.201	2.713	24.000	24.530	25.425	26.500	28.300	30.570	32.700
10	223	28.298	2.501	25.200	25.600	26.600	28.000	29.400	31.200	33.100
11	211	29.287	2.769	25.360	26.000	27.400	29.000	31.000	32.580	34.680
12	221	30.295	3.149	25.910	26.700	28.650	30.100	31.900	33.700	35.050
13	216	31.813	3.128	27.085	28.210	29.900	31.600	33.400	35.500	36.700
14	209	33.669	3.380	28.250	29.700	31.300	33.600	35.600	37.700	39.200
15	208	34.809	2.956	30.500	31.270	32.700	34.600	36.400	38.900	39.955
16	191	35.201	2.965	30.860	31.800	33.500	35.000	37.100	38.700	39.620
17	206	35.418	2.453	31.300	32.400	33.775	35.400	37.100	38.430	39.295
18	168	36.269	2.821	32.045	33.280	34.200	35.900	37.800	39.410	40.555

Females

Age (years)	N	Mean	SD	5	10	25	50	75	90	95
7	179	25.381	2.453	22.400	23.000	23.800	24.900	26.500	28.000	29.200
8	186	26.388	3.163	23.100	23.670	24.675	26.200	27.500	29.120	31.790
9	168	27.002	2.597	23.445	24.000	25.225	26.700	28.675	30.010	31.255
10	224	29.095	3.022	24.850	25.700	27.100	28.900	30.675	32.550	34.325
11	224	29.548	2.849	25.525	26.050	27.400	29.100	31.275	33.200	34.975
12	206	31.199	3.068	26.035	27.470	29.100	31.000	33.325	35.160	36.130
13	207	32.686	3.071	27.740	28.880	30.700	32.600	34.400	36.620	37.960
14	190	33.797	2.870	29.400	30.500	31.975	33.500	35.350	37.500	39.490
15	198	33.886	2.777	29.595	30.400	32.175	33.850	35.500	37.000	38.020
16	203	34.080	3.099	29.520	30.500	32.500	33.800	35.500	38.000	39.420
17	176	34.326	3.074	30.255	30.970	32.500	34.200	35.600	38.350	39.600
18	153	34.588	3.023	30.370	31.000	32.650	34.200	36.150	38.300	40.410

Adapted from Canada Fitness Survey (1981).

Ankle Girth in Centimeters for Children 4 to 18 Years of Age

Age (years)	N	Mean	SD	Min	Percentiles			Max
					5th	50th	95th	
				Males				
4	37	15.0	0.8	13.4	13.6	14.9	16.2	17.1
5	58	15.4	0.9	12.9	13.8	15.3	17.0	17.5
6	39	15.8	1.2	13.4	14.1	15.8	17.5	20.0
7	40	16.5	1.2	14.5	14.5	16.2	18.5	20.0
8	36	17.1	1.4	15.1	15.3	16.9	19.6	21.5
9	42	17.6	1.5	15.0	15.4	17.5	19.7	23.3
10	40	18.3	1.7	15.6	15.8	18.4	21.6	22.2
11	40	18.2	1.2	15.7	15.9	18.2	19.7	21.7
12	55	19.7	1.7	16.1	16.6	19.6	22.2	24.2
13	58	20.4	1.9	17.2	17.6	20.1	23.3	25.3
14	49	21.7	1.8	17.0	18.1	21.7	24.4	24.7
15	42	21.2	1.6	17.7	18.0	21.2	23.6	24.9
16	38	22.5	1.9	17.1	18.9	22.5	25.4	27.5
17	28	22.5	1.4	18.8	19.2	22.7	24.2	24.5
18	38	22.8	2.0	18.4	19.1	22.6	26.6	27.7
				Females				
4	40	14.9	1.1	13.0	13.3	14.6	16.9	17.8
5	35	15.5	0.9	13.9	14.0	15.3	17.0	17.3
6	41	16.1	1.1	14.4	14.6	15.9	18.0	19.9
7	46	16.8	1.5	13.6	14.3	16.5	19.2	20.7
8	32	17.6	1.3	15.5	15.6	17.4	19.8	21.2
9	49	18.1	1.4	14.9	15.4	18.0	20.4	20.9
10	45	18.7	2.0	14.9	15.5	18.7	20.8	27.8
11	45	18.8	1.8	15.2	15.6	18.7	21.4	23.6
12	42	19.3	1.6	16.0	16.5	19.3	21.4	24.0
13	50	20.4	1.6	17.0	17.7	20.0	22.9	24.5
14	41	20.8	1.4	18.3	18.4	20.7	23.2	23.9
15	39	21.0	1.4	17.1	18.4	21.1	23.2	24.7
16	41	21.2	1.5	18.3	18.8	20.8	23.7	24.7
17	39	20.8	1.5	17.3	18.5	20.5	24.0	24.6
18	25	21.0	1.6	18.2	18.3	20.7	23.8	24.4

Reprinted from Snyder, Schneider, Owings, Reynolds, Golomb, and Schork (1977).

Midaxial Skinfold in Millimeters for Children 6 to 17 Years of Age

Age (years)	n	Mean	SD	Percentiles						
				5	10	25	50	75	90	95
				Boys						
6	575	4.1	2.01	2.5	3.0	3.0	4.0	4.0	5.0	6.5
7	632	4.4	3.18	3.0	3.0	3.0	4.0	4.5	6.0	8.0
8	618	4.8	2.97	3.0	3.0	3.0	4.0	5.0	7.0	9.0
9	603	5.5	3.91	3.0	3.0	3.5	4.0	6.0	9.0	14.0
10	576	5.6	3.84	3.0	3.0	3.5	4.0	6.0	10.0	14.0
11	628	6.3	4.57	3.0	3.0	4.0	4.5	7.0	13.0	18.0
12	540	6.5	5.01	3.0	3.2	3.8	4.8	6.8	14.2	19.6
13	542	6.8	5.57	3.2	3.3	4.1	5.0	7.1	13.8	19.5
14	526	6.9	5.92	3.2	3.5	4.2	5.2	7.1	14.3	19.8
15	525	7.2	5.84	3.4	3.8	4.4	5.5	7.6	13.4	19.7
16	496	7.0	5.01	3.5	4.0	4.5	5.6	7.5	13.2	18.3
17	416	7.8	5.65	3.6	4.1	4.6	5.8	8.3	15.1	22.4
				Girls						
6	536	4.9	2.86	3.0	3.0	3.5	4.0	5.0	7.0	9.0
7	609	5.3	2.86	3.0	3.0	4.0	4.0	6.0	9.0	11.0
8	613	6.2	3.96	3.0	3.0	4.0	5.0	7.0	11.0	15.0
9	581	7.0	4.65	3.0	3.5	4.0	5.5	8.0	14.0	18.0
10	584	7.4	4.98	3.0	3.5	4.0	6.0	8.0	15.0	20.0
11	564	7.9	4.97	3.5	4.0	4.5	6.0	10.0	15.0	19.0
12	454	8.6	5.91	3.6	4.2	5.1	6.6	10.6	16.8	23.5
13	490	9.4	6.33	4.0	4.5	5.7	7.5	11.5	18.2	23.3
14	484	10.3	6.28	4.4	5.1	6.4	8.4	12.8	20.1	23.2
15	424	11.1	7.13	4.6	5.2	6.5	8.7	13.4	22.5	27.4
16	441	11.4	7.06	4.8	5.6	6.9	9.5	13.7	21.6	28.2
17	393	11.1	7.11	4.6	5.4	6.7	8.8	13.8	21.1	26.2

Adapted from Johnson, Hamill, and Lemeshow (1972, 1974).

Supraspinale Skinfold for Children 6 to 18 Years of Age

| Age (years) | n | Mean | SD | \multicolumn{7}{c}{Percentiles} |
				5	10	25	50	75	90	95
\multicolumn{11}{c}{Males}
6	12	4.57	3.24	—	2.93	3.10	3.65	4.27	11.73	—
7	23	5.57	3.46	2.88	3.32	3.90	4.70	5.90	8.74	17.78
8	22	5.63	4.35	2.85	3.10	3.30	4.40	5.45	10.60	20.97
9	28	5.68	4.99	3.00	3.09	3.40	4.25	5.70	11.35	20.99
10	22	3.73	4.92	3.42	3.56	3.88	4.80	7.68	15.97	22.10
11	28	7.36	6.04	3.49	3.87	4.60	5.35	6.75	14.54	26.55
12	31	11.13	8.01	3.50	3.62	4.90	7.60	16.60	26.02	27.60
13	37	8.61	6.27	4.03	4.36	4.60	6.50	10.05	16.80	28.31
14	76	8.03	5.18	3.79	4.34	5.00	6.20	10.00	12.83	19.44
15	75	7.94	5.68	3.90	4.36	4.70	5.80	7.90	16.00	21.04
16	57	8.08	5.52	3.69	4.20	4.95	6.10	8.25	15.04	22.80
17	40	7.56	5.42	3.51	3.61	5.03	5.95	9.10	11.58	20.57
18	22	6.25	1.63	4.03	4.35	4.95	5.90	7.50	9.08	9.71
\multicolumn{11}{c}{Females}
6	20	5.45	2.48	2.73	3.35	4.07	4.70	5.78	11.00	12.74
7	23	6.16	3.09	3.22	3.34	3.80	4.80	7.30	11.36	12.92
8	17	5.53	1.70	—	3.68	4.10	4.80	7.10	8.20	—
9	28	6.51	2.95	3.45	3.77	4.50	5.70	7.85	11.63	14.05
10	22	9.45	6.00	4.12	4.23	5.00	7.10	12.70	20.90	24.95
11	25	9.99	5.32	4.16	5.12	6.50	8.80	12.00	19.88	24.15
12	33	10.78	5.29	4.17	4.92	6.20	10.40	14.00	20.28	21.83
13	37	11.10	5.06	5.20	6.85	6.90	8.80	14.60	23.92	27.46
14	67	12.31	5.88	4.96	6.08	8.40	10.60	15.70	22.30	26.76
15	67	11.72	5.14	6.00	6.80	7.50	10.00	14.60	19.60	22.32
16	51	11.74	5.47	5.18	6.52	8.00	10.90	13.30	19.28	25.52
17	46	11.15	3.99	6.14	6.34	8.58	10.55	12.73	16.81	20.55
18	10	11.71	4.43	—	6.70	7.68	10.30	15.83	19.17	—

Adapted from Ross, Drinkwater, Whittingham, and Faulkner (1980).

Abdominal Skinfold in Millimeters for Children 6 to 18 Years of Age

Age (years)	n	Mean	SD	Percentiles						
				5	10	25	50	75	90	95
				Males						
6	12	4.56	3.24	—	2.93	3.10	3.65	4.28	11.73	—
7	23	7.73	3.49	3.74	4.74	5.30	6.80	9.00	12.86	17.94
8	22	7.26	5.11	3.42	3.53	4.05	5.25	8.43	16.22	23.21
9	28	7.58	6.30	3.43	3.79	4.53	5.85	7.18	14.65	27.15
10	22	9.81	8.85	3.52	3.69	4.60	7.10	9.43	28.39	34.88
11	28	10.17	8.91	4.14	4.39	5.20	6.55	11.43	30.70	35.17
12	31	15.07	11.41	3.94	4.50	5.80	10.00	23.80	33.12	38.32
13	37	12.20	9.81	4.76	5.28	6.35	8.60	13.45	30.88	40.18
14	76	11.19	7.40	4.56	5.31	6.60	8.55	14.78	20.92	29.92
15	75	11.12	8.16	4.80	5.34	6.30	7.80	13.00	22.62	32.88
16	57	11.24	8.71	4.98	5.52	6.10	7.80	11.20	27.22	34.07
17	40	11.25	7.06	4.61	4.95	6.33	9.30	13.63	19.28	33.78
18	22	10.37	3.62	6.05	6.42	7.83	8.45	13.88	16.20	17.99
				Females						
6	20	7.82	3.90	4.01	4.24	5.10	7.10	8.63	13.34	20.35
7	23	8.01	4.66	3.82	3.90	4.60	5.80	8.80	16.74	19.90
8	17	6.45	1.88	—	4.50	4.80	5.80	8.10	9.68	—
9	28	8.24	3.19	3.76	4.47	6.05	7.85	10.13	12.17	16.31
10	22	12.00	8.32	3.88	4.39	5.68	8.55	16.28	24.71	32.79
11	25	13.69	6.33	5.45	5.80	8.70	12.20	18.05	20.88	29.07
12	33	13.02	6.82	4.89	5.30	6.70	12.00	16.70	23.92	28.71
13	37	14.53	7.89	4.99	6.28	8.45	11.20	18.00	29.86	31.50
14	67	16.90	8.10	7.34	7.84	10.50	14.50	21.20	29.44	34.80
15	67	16.17	6.89	7.08	8.44	11.00	15.20	21.70	26.44	29.64
16	51	16.34	8.51	6.18	7.76	10.00	14.50	21.80	25.62	34.94
17	46	15.00	5.54	7.78	8.99	10.23	14.25	19.05	22.73	24.37
18	10	15.84	4.41	—	9.73	11.65	17.00	19.83	21.19	—

Adapted from Ross, Drinkwater, Whittingham, and Faulkner (1980).

Front Thigh Skinfold in Millimeters for Children 6 to 18 Years of Age

Age (years)	n	Mean	SD	Percentiles 5	10	25	50	75	90	95
						Males				
6	12	12.60	4.41	—	7.52	10.80	11.50	14.35	21.78	—
7	23	15.57	4.85	10.16	10.48	11.00	15.40	18.60	21.88	28.56
8	22	15.00	4.70	7.14	8.59	9.78	12.90	17.55	29.48	36.37
9	28	15.06	6.81	7.35	7.40	10.25	13.85	18.05	23.53	33.32
10	22	18.36	8.18	10.80	10.86	13.30	16.30	20.40	31.85	41.78
11	28	17.55	8.01	10.14	10.98	13.50	15.70	18.10	27.10	43.30
12	31	21.82	11.85	9.10	9.84	13.10	18.40	30.80	43.56	46.08
13	37	16.20	7.57	9.88	10.00	11.65	14.50	17.40	26.44	37.60
14	76	14.76	6.20	5.99	8.10	10.05	13.10	19.25	23.92	26.92
15	75	13.98	7.36	7.36	8.00	9.30	11.50	15.30	23.24	32.64
16	57	12.99	7.23	6.52	7.20	8.30	10.70	14.65	24.78	28.44
17	40	12.34	5.87	6.61	6.93	8.15	10.65	15.20	20.98	23.89
18	22	12.65	4.06	7.12	7.83	8.55	12.90	16.03	18.92	20.25
						Females				
6	20	17.99	7.52	9.66	10.82	12.65	15.55	21.18	32.13	—
7	23	16.47	5.61	9.04	9.68	12.40	14.20	21.50	24.64	27.80
8	17	16.52	6.39	—	7.90	13.45	16.40	18.10	26.56	—
9	28	18.58	6.89	8.20	8.92	13.60	17.60	22.95	27.78	33.90
10	22	22.00	9.95	11.63	12.93	13.95	19.20	26.53	42.61	46.47
11	25	23.68	7.92	11.58	13.20	18.85	23.20	27.40	36.92	42.34
12	33	23.82	9.34	12.01	14.20	17.40	23.60	26.30	36.82	46.15
13	37	21.48	7.77	10.93	13.60	15.85	19.20	26.80	34.86	37.58
14	67	23.30	7.63	10.48	13.38	18.60	22.20	28.40	33.72	36.88
15	67	24.74	7.28	15.54	16.16	18.90	23.00	29.80	36.56	38.04
16	51	24.17	7.24	12.28	13.44	19.20	24.40	27.80	34.72	36.24
17	46	25.79	7.37	14.70	16.68	20.93	25.10	29.23	36.49	39.80
18	10	24.85	6.63	—	13.78	20.80	24.75	28.25	37.22	—

Adapted from Ross, Drinkwater, Whititngham, and Faulkner (1980).

Biacromial Breadth in Centimeters for Children 4 to 18 Years of Age

Age (years)	N	Mean	SD	\multicolumn{7}{c}{Percentiles}

Age (years)	N	Mean	SD	5	10	25	50	75	90	95
\multicolumn{11}{c}{Males}
4	154	22.4	1.5	19.7	20.9	21.7	22.5	23.5	23.8	24.2
5	130	23.9	1.5	21.2	21.4	23.2	24.2	25.0	25.5	25.8
6	126	25.5	2.5	23.0	23.5	24.2	25.1	26.0	27.1	27.6
7	153	25.8	1.6	22.7	24.0	24.7	25.6	26.9	28.2	28.4
8	159	27.2	1.5	24.9	25.4	26.3	27.0	28.1	28.7	29.5
9	132	28.4	2.1	25.3	25.3	26.9	28.5	30.5	30.9	31.7
10	159	29.5	2.1	26.1	26.1	28.1	29.6	31.0	31.8	32.8
11	173	30.2	1.5	27.3	28.0	29.2	30.4	31.1	32.0	32.5
12	182	31.9	2.5	28.9	29.6	30.4	31.4	33.1	35.3	36.9
13	172	32.9	1.8	30.0	30.4	31.2	33.4	34.0	34.7	35.9
14	157	33.9	2.5	30.8	31.1	31.7	33.2	35.9	37.5	38.8
15	158	35.8	2.9	31.4	33.2	34.2	35.9	37.2	39.8	40.0
16	172	37.4	2.6	33.0	34.3	35.7	37.1	39.4	40.0	41.0
17	121	38.5	2.4	34.3	35.4	36.9	38.8	40.2	40.9	41.8
18	108	38.9	2.0	35.7	36.7	37.2	39.0	40.5	41.6	42.3
\multicolumn{11}{c}{Females}
4	118	22.4	1.2	20.7	21.1	21.5	22.1	23.3	24.2	24.4
5	140	23.3	1.5	21.0	21.2	22.5	23.3	24.0	25.1	25.4
6	125	24.7	1.5	22.2	23.3	23.8	24.8	25.4	26.3	27.0
7	132	25.0	2.2	22.6	23.0	24.0	25.0	26.5	27.2	27.9
8	142	26.5	1.9	24.0	24.6	25.4	27.0	27.9	28.5	28.5
9	139	28.2	1.8	25.4	26.3	27.2	28.0	29.8	30.0	30.5
10	148	29.6	1.5	27.0	27.2	28.5	29.7	30.8	31.4	31.6
11	157	30.4	1.8	27.7	28.3	29.3	30.3	31.5	32.7	33.0
12	167	31.5	2.1	27.9	29.0	30.1	31.5	32.7	34.5	34.9
13	195	33.0	1.9	29.5	30.3	32.0	33.2	33.9	35.6	36.1
14	185	33.3	1.8	30.2	30.8	31.6	33.5	34.4	35.5	36.2
15	160	33.7	2.6	29.8	32.0	32.3	34.3	35.1	36.2	37.1
16	160	34.2	1.8	31.0	31.8	33.0	34.5	35.5	36.3	36.9
17	134	34.2	1.6	32.0	32.3	33.4	34.0	35.2	36.5	36.8
18	135	34.9	1.9	31.2	31.5	33.8	35.2	35.9	36.8	37.4

Reprinted from Jetté (1982).

Biiliocristal Breadth in Centimeters for Children 4 to 18 Years of Age

Age (years)	N	Mean	SD	Percentiles						
				5	10	25	50	75	90	95
Males										
4	154	16.9	1.3	14.8	15.4	16.3	17.0	17.6	18.4	19.0
5	130	17.5	1.2	15.9	16.0	16.6	17.4	18.4	19.0	19.1
6	126	18.2	1.1	16.7	17.0	17.5	18.2	19.2	19.6	20.0
7	153	18.7	1.1	17.3	17.6	18.1	18.5	19.5	20.2	20.6
8	159	19.8	1.5	17.3	18.3	19.0	19.7	20.5	22.0	22.4
9	131	20.4	2.3	15.3	18.0	19.0	20.4	21.7	22.3	25.4
10	159	21.0	1.9	18.7	18.8	19.9	20.9	22.3	24.0	24.7
11	173	21.9	1.6	19.6	19.7	20.9	21.7	22.9	24.0	24.5
12	182	23.3	1.8	20.5	21.2	21.9	23.4	24.6	25.4	26.1
13	172	24.1	1.9	20.9	21.6	22.6	24.0	25.5	27.2	27.6
14	157	25.0	2.1	21.7	22.2	23.6	25.2	26.5	27.3	29.7
15	158	25.8	1.9	23.3	23.6	24.6	25.4	26.5	28.1	29.5
16	172	27.2	2.2	23.8	24.3	25.9	26.9	28.9	29.3	31.0
17	121	27.8	2.4	24.4	25.5	26.3	27.4	29.4	29.8	31.8
18	108	27.4	2.1	24.2	24.2	26.1	27.2	28.5	30.8	31.5
Females										
4	118	16.3	1.0	14.6	15.2	15.7	16.2	17.0	17.4	17.8
5	140	17.1	1.3	15.3	15.5	16.2	17.0	18.0	18.8	18.9
6	125	18.5	1.4	16.6	16.9	17.7	18.4	19.1	19.4	20.2
7	132	18.6	1.4	16.5	17.1	17.6	18.5	19.2	20.0	20.6
8	142	19.7	1.7	17.5	18.3	18.9	19.8	20.6	21.4	21.7
9	139	20.8	2.0	18.2	19.2	19.7	20.5	21.2	22.6	24.5
10	148	21.4	1.8	19.4	19.8	20.7	21.4	22.5	24.7	25.3
11	157	22.7	1.9	19.8	20.1	21.2	22.5	23.8	24.9	26.9
12	167	23.6	2.4	20.3	20.8	22.0	23.7	24.7	26.1	28.1
13	195	24.8	2.1	21.4	22.2	23.2	24.7	25.9	27.7	28.7
14	185	25.5	2.6	21.6	22.9	24.2	25.1	26.5	27.9	29.4
15	160	25.9	1.6	23.9	24.3	24.7	25.3	27.0	28.1	29.1
16	160	26.9	2.1	24.1	24.6	25.3	26.7	28.2	29.0	29.5
17	134	26.9	2.0	24.2	24.6	25.7	27.2	28.0	29.4	29.9
18	134	27.7	1.8	24.6	25.4	26.3	28.0	28.3	30.2	31.0

Reprinted from Jetté (1982).

Transverse Chest Breadth in Centimeters for Children 4 to 18 Years of Age

Age (years)	N	Mean	SD	Percentiles						
				5	10	25	50	75	90	95
				Males						
4	153	16.9	1.0	15.4	15.6	16.2	16.9	17.5	18.2	18.5
5	129	17.6	1.0	15.8	16.2	17.0	17.6	18.4	18.7	19.3
6	126	18.2	1.1	16.7	17.1	17.6	18.2	18.8	19.1	19.3
7	153	18.3	1.0	16.5	17.1	17.4	18.1	19.0	19.6	20.0
8	159	19.2	1.2	17.3	17.8	18.2	19.2	20.1	20.6	21.0
9	132	20.3	1.4	18.1	18.3	19.2	20.4	21.1	21.8	22.3
10	159	20.7	1.6	18.2	18.5	19.4	20.5	21.7	22.9	22.9
11	173	20.9	1.7	16.7	19.4	20.0	21.1	21.7	22.6	23.3
12	182	22.3	1.7	20.0	20.3	21.1	22.0	23.2	24.2	25.4
13	172	23.1	2.1	20.6	20.8	21.7	23.0	23.9	25.6	26.8
14	157	23.9	2.0	20.6	21.2	22.1	24.1	25.0	26.3	27.2
15	158	25.2	2.0	22.1	23.3	23.9	24.6	26.2	28.4	28.8
16	171	26.0	2.1	22.8	23.6	24.7	25.6	27.3	28.6	30.5
17	121	26.9	1.8	24.5	25.1	25.6	26.6	28.1	28.6	30.0
18	108	27.4	2.5	24.1	24.1	24.8	27.6	28.9	31.1	31.9
				Females						
4	118	16.4	0.8	15.1	15.4	15.8	16.5	17.0	17.5	17.6
5	140	16.9	1.1	15.4	15.6	16.1	17.0	17.6	18.2	18.7
6	125	17.7	1.2	16.3	16.6	16.9	17.7	18.2	18.7	19.3
7	132	18.1	1.9	15.7	16.7	17.1	17.6	18.6	19.5	20.4
8	142	18.9	1.2	17.0	17.5	18.0	18.8	19.7	20.3	21.3
9	139	19.6	1.5	17.8	18.0	18.5	19.2	20.8	21.4	21.7
10	148	20.4	1.5	18.4	18.4	19.2	20.0	21.8	22.2	23.3
11	157	21.0	1.4	18.9	19.3	19.9	20.9	21.9	22.6	22.9
12	167	22.0	2.0	18.6	19.2	20.4	22.2	23.4	25.0	25.5
13	196	23.1	1.9	20.0	20.5	21.6	23.2	24.2	25.7	26.4
14	185	23.1	1.5	20.9	21.0	22.0	23.0	24.1	25.0	25.7
15	160	24.0	1.5	22.2	22.5	23.2	23.6	24.7	26.2	26.7
16	160	24.2	1.8	21.7	22.1	23.2	23.9	25.2	26.5	27.5
17	134	24.2	1.8	21.6	21.6	23.0	24.5	25.2	26.2	27.7
18	135	24.3	2.4	20.5	21.8	22.7	24.2	25.1	26.9	28.2

Reprinted from Jetté (1982).

Antero–Posterior Chest Depth in Centimeters for Children 4 to 18 Years of Age

Age (years)	N	Mean	SD	Percentiles						
				5	10	25	50	75	90	95
				Males						
4	154	12.1	1.1	10.9	11.0	11.4	11.8	12.5	13.3	14.3
5	130	12.3	0.9	11.0	11.2	11.5	12.2	13.0	13.4	13.6
6	126	12.6	0.9	10.9	11.5	12.0	12.5	13.1	14.0	14.1
7	153	13.2	1.0	11.9	12.0	12.4	13.1	14.0	14.6	14.8
8	159	13.4	1.0	11.6	12.3	12.5	13.2	14.1	14.8	14.9
9	132	14.1	1.6	12.3	12.6	12.9	13.7	15.2	15.6	17.2
10	159	14.1	1.2	12.4	12.5	13.4	14.3	14.6	16.0	16.0
11	173	14.6	1.1	13.1	13.4	14.0	14.6	14.9	16.2	16.6
12	181	15.2	1.3	13.4	13.6	14.5	15.1	16.0	16.8	17.6
13	172	15.7	1.4	13.6	14.0	14.6	15.5	16.7	17.7	18.2
14	157	16.5	1.6	14.0	14.4	15.3	16.4	17.7	18.7	19.1
15	158	17.0	1.5	14.4	15.1	16.2	17.0	17.8	18.9	19.8
16	171	17.8	1.6	15.5	15.9	16.6	17.7	18.3	19.8	20.8
17	121	18.4	1.7	16.3	16.6	16.8	18.4	20.1	20.5	21.0
18	108	18.5	1.6	16.8	16.8	17.5	18.2	19.2	20.3	22.2
				Females						
4	118	11.6	0.7	10.4	10.8	11.0	11.5	12.0	12.5	12.7
5	140	12.3	0.8	11.1	11.3	11.6	12.2	12.8	13.2	13.5
6	125	12.4	1.3	10.8	11.0	11.6	12.1	13.0	13.6	14.0
7	132	12.6	1.0	11.2	11.5	11.9	12.4	13.3	13.7	14.3
8	142	13.1	1.2	11.4	11.7	12.3	13.0	13.7	14.1	14.4
9	139	13.7	1.7	12.0	12.2	12.9	13.5	14.1	15.0	15.7
10	148	13.9	1.5	11.0	11.9	13.0	13.7	14.9	16.0	16.2
11	157	14.2	1.5	12.5	12.9	13.1	14.0	14.8	16.3	16.9
12	167	15.3	1.5	12.3	13.5	14.5	15.1	16.4	17.1	17.5
13	195	15.7	1.5	13.3	13.7	14.4	15.9	16.9	17.7	18.3
14	185	15.6	1.6	12.0	12.9	15.1	15.9	16.5	17.4	17.8
15	160	16.0	1.7	13.3	14.0	14.7	15.8	17.0	17.9	19.0
16	160	16.6	1.4	14.5	14.6	15.6	16.7	17.4	18.4	19.0
17	134	16.5	1.4	14.5	15.0	15.2	16.3	17.7	18.3	18.5
18	135	16.3	1.4	13.9	14.7	15.6	16.2	17.0	18.3	18.9

Reprinted from Jetté (1982).

Wrist Breadth in Centimeters for Children 4 to 18 Years of Age

Age (years)	N	Mean	SD	Percentiles						
				5	10	25	50	75	90	95
Males										
4	154	3.8	0.3	3.2	3.5	3.6	3.8	3.9	4.0	4.1
5	130	3.9	0.3	3.4	3.5	3.7	3.9	4.0	4.2	4.4
6	126	4.0	0.3	3.6	3.7	3.9	4.0	4.2	4.3	4.4
7	153	4.1	0.3	3.7	3.7	3.8	4.1	4.3	4.4	4.5
8	159	4.3	0.3	3.9	4.0	4.1	4.2	4.5	4.7	4.7
9	132	4.5	0.4	3.9	4.0	4.3	4.5	4.8	4.8	4.9
10	159	4.6	0.3	4.0	4.2	4.4	4.5	4.7	5.0	5.2
11	173	4.6	0.3	3.8	4.1	4.5	4.7	4.8	5.0	5.0
12	182	4.9	0.4	4.3	4.4	4.7	4.9	5.1	5.4	5.4
13	172	5.1	0.4	4.5	4.6	4.8	5.1	5.4	5.6	5.8
14	157	5.3	0.4	4.8	4.9	5.1	5.3	5.6	5.8	5.9
15	158	5.5	0.5	4.8	5.0	5.2	5.4	5.7	5.8	6.0
16	172	5.6	0.3	5.1	5.2	5.4	5.5	5.8	6.0	6.1
17	121	5.7	0.2	5.3	5.4	5.6	5.7	5.9	6.0	6.1
18	108	5.7	0.3	5.2	5.2	5.3	5.7	5.9	6.1	6.2
Females										
4	118	3.6	0.2	3.0	3.3	3.4	3.6	3.7	3.9	3.9
5	140	3.7	0.3	3.1	3.2	3.5	3.7	3.9	4.0	4.1
6	125	3.9	0.3	3.4	3.5	3.7	3.9	4.0	4.1	4.3
7	132	3.9	0.4	3.5	3.6	3.7	3.8	4.1	4.2	4.4
8	142	4.1	0.3	3.6	3.7	3.9	4.2	4.4	4.4	4.5
9	139	4.3	0.3	3.9	3.9	4.1	4.3	4.4	4.6	4.6
10	148	4.4	0.3	4.0	4.1	4.2	4.5	4.6	4.7	4.9
11	157	4.6	0.3	4.0	4.3	4.4	4.6	4.7	4.9	5.1
12	167	4.7	0.3	4.0	4.3	4.5	4.8	5.0	5.1	5.1
13	195	4.9	0.3	4.3	4.4	4.6	4.9	5.1	5.2	5.3
14	185	4.8	0.3	4.4	4.5	4.6	4.8	5.0	5.2	5.3
15	160	4.8	0.3	4.3	4.3	4.6	4.8	4.9	5.2	5.2
16	160	5.0	0.5	4.5	4.6	4.8	4.9	5.1	5.3	5.3
17	134	4.9	0.3	4.2	4.5	4.8	4.9	5.0	5.2	5.2
18	135	4.9	0.3	4.5	4.6	4.7	5.0	5.1	5.2	5.5

Reprinted from Jetté (1982).

REFERENCES

Attalah, N.L. (1980). *Growth of the limbs and their segments during childhood and adolescence: A photogrammetric study.* Unpublished doctoral dissertation, London University.

Bailey, D.A., Malina, R.M., & Mirwald, R.L. (1986). Physical activity and growth of the child. In F. Falkner & J.M. Tanner (Eds.), *Human growth: A comprehensive treatise* (pp. 147-170). New York: Plenum Press.

Bailey, S.M. (1991). Theoretical considerations in the measurement and interpretation of change in adult dimensions. In J. H. Himes (Ed.), *Anthropometric assessment of nutritional status* (pp. 51-82). New York: Wiley–Liss.

Birrer, R.B., & Levine, R. (1987). Performance parameters in children and adolescent athletes. *Sports Medicine,* **4,** 211-227.

Bookstein, F.L. (1978). *The measurement of biological shape and shape change.* New York: Springer–Verlag.

Borms, J. (1986). The child and exercise: An overview. *Journal of Sports Sciences,* **4,** 3-20.

Callaway, C.W., Chumlea, W.C., Bouchard, C., Himes, J.H., Lohman, T.G., Martin, A.D., Mitchell, C.D., Mueller, W.H., Roche, A.F., & Seefeldt, V.D. (1988). Circumferences. In T.G. Lohman, A.F. Roche, & R. Martorell (Eds.), *Anthropometric standardization reference manual* (pp. 39-54). Champaign, IL: Human Kinetics.

Cameron, N. (1984). *The measurement of human growth.* London: Croom Helm.

Cameron, N. (1986). The methods of auxological anthropometry. In F. Falkner & J.M. Tanner (Eds.), *Human growth—A comprehensive treatise,* New York: Plenum Press.

Cameron, N., Tanner, J.M., & Whitehouse, R.H. (1982). A longitudinal analysis of the growth of limb segments in adolescence. *Annals of Human Biology,* **9**(3), 211-220.

Carter, J.E.L. (1978). Prediction of outstanding athletic ability: The structural perspective. In F. Landry & W. Orban (Eds.), *Exercise physiology* (pp. 29-42) Miami, FL: Symposia Specialists.

Carter, J.E.L. (1980). *The Heath–Carter somatotype method.* San Diego, CA: San Diego State University Press.

Carter, J.E.L. (Ed.) (1984). *Physical structure of Olympic athletes, Part II: Kinanthropometry of Olympic athletes.* Basel: Karger.

Carter, J.E.L. (1985). Morphological factors limiting human performance. In D.H. Clarke & H.M. Eckert (Eds.), *Limits of human performance* (pp. 106-117). Champaign, IL.: Human Kinetics.

DeRose, E.H., Crawford, S.M., Kerr, D.A., Ward, R., & Ross, W.D. (1989). Physique characteristics of Pan American Games lightweight rowers. *International Journal of Sports Medicine,* **10**(4), 292-297.

Gibson, R.S. (1990). *Principles of nutritional assessment.* New York: Oxford University Press.

Greuber, J.L., Pollock, M.L., Graves, J.E., Colvin, A.B., & Braith, R.W. (1990). Comparison of Harpenden and Lange calipers in predicting body composition. *Research Quarterly in Exercise and Sport,* **61**(2), 184-190.

Habicht, J.-P., Yarbrough, C., & Martorell, R. (1979). Anthropometric field methods: Criteria for selection. In D.B. Jelliffe & E.F.P. Jelliffe (Eds.), *Nutrition and growth* (pp. 365-388). New York: Plenum Press.

Hamill, P.V.V., Drizid, T.A., Johnson, C.L., Reed, R.B., & Roche, A.F. (1977). NCHS growth curves for children birth-18 years: United States. In NCHS, *Vital and Health Statistics* (Series 11), (Publication No. PHS 78-1650). Washington, DC: DHEW.

Hamill, P.V.V., Drizid, T.A., Johnson, C.L., Reed, R.B., & Roche, A.F. (1979). Physical growth: National Center for Health Statistics percentiles. *American Journal of Clinical Nutrition, 32*, 607-629.

Harrison, G.G., Buskirk, E.R., Carter, J.E.L., Johnston, F.E., Lohman, T.G., Pollock, M.L., Roche, A.F., & Wilmore, J. (1988). Skinfold thicknesses and measurement technique. In T. G. Lohman, A. F. Roche, & R. Martorell (Eds.), *Anthropometric standardization reference manual* (pp. 55-70). Champaign, IL: Human Kinetics.

Hauspie, R.C. (1979). Adolescent growth. In F.E. Johnston, A.F. Roche, & C. Susanne (Eds.), *Human physical growth and maturation: Methodologies and factors* (pp. 161-176). New York: Plenum Press.

Haywood, K.M. (1986). *Life span motor development.* Champaign, IL: Human Kinetics.

Healy, M.J.R., & Tanner, J.M. (1981). Size and shape in relation to growth and form. *Symposia of the Zoolgical Society of London, 46*, 19-35.

Hebbelinck, M., Ross, W.D., Carter, J.E.L., & Borms, J. (1980). Anthropometric characteristics of female Olympic rowers. *Canadian Journal of Applied Sport Sciences, 5*, 255-262.

Houlsby, W. T. (1986). Functional aerobic capacity and body size. *Archives of Diseases of Childhood, 61*(4), 388-393.

Hughson, R., Albinson, J., Bar-Or, O., Bishop, P., Bouchard, C., Cumming, G.R., Cunnigham, D.A., Jackson, J., Kozey, J., Marteniuk, R., & Stanish, B. (1986). Children in competitive sports—A multi-disciplinary approach. *Canadian Journal of Sport Sciences, 11*(4), 162-172.

Jensen, R.K. (1981). The effect of a 12 month growth period on the body moments of inertia of children. *Medicine and Science in Sports and Exercise, 13*, 238-242.

Jensen, R.K. (1987). Growth of estimated segment masses between four and sixteen years. *Human Biology, 59*, 173-189.

Lohman, T.G. (1987). The use of skinfolds to estimate body fatness in children and youth. *Journal of Physical Education, Recreation, and Dance,* Nov-Dec, 98-102.

Lohman, T.G., Roche, A.F., & Martorell, R. (1988). *Anthropometric standardization reference manual.* Champaign, IL: Human Kinetics.

Malina, R.M., Hamill, P.V.V., & Lemeshow, S. (1973). Selected body measurements of children 6-11 years: United States. NCHS, *Vital and Health Statistics* (Series 11, Vol. 123), Washington, DC: DHEW.

Malina, R.M., Hamill, P.V.V., & Lemeshow, S. (1974). Body dimensions and proportions, white and negro children 6-11 years: United States. NCHS, *Vital and Health Statistics* (Series 11 Vol. 143), Washington, DC: DHEW.

Marks, G.C., Habicht, J.-P., & Mueller, W.H. (1989). Reliability, dependability, and precision of anthropometric measurements. *American Journal of Epidemiology, 130*(3), 578-587.

Martin, A.D., Carter, J.E.L., Hendy, K.C., & Malina, R.M. (1988). Segment lengths. In T.G. Lohman, A.F. Roche, & R. Martorell (Eds.), *Anthropometric standardization reference manual* (pp. 9-26.). Champaign, IL: Human Kinetics.

Martorell, R., Mendoza, F., Mueller, W.H., & Pawson, I.G. (1988). Which side to measure: Right or left? In T.G. Lohman, A.F. Roche, & R. Martorell (Eds.), *Anthropometric standardization reference manual* (pp. 87-91). Champaign, IL: Human Kinetics.

Mueller, W.H., & Martorell, R. (1988). Reliability and accuracy of measurement. In T. G. Lohman, A. F. Roche, & R. Martorell (Eds.), *Anthropometric standardization reference manual* (pp. 83-86). Champaign, IL: Human Kinetics.

Neumann, C.G. (1979). Reference data. In D.B. Jelliffe & E.F.P. Jelliffe (Eds.), *Nutrition and growth* (pp. 299-328). New York: Plenum Press.

86   Crawford

Roche, A.F., & Himes, J.H. (1980). Incremental growth charts. *American Journal of Clinical Nutrition*, **33**, 2041-2052.

Roche, A.F., & Malina, R.M. (1983). *Manual of physical status and performance in childhood.* New York: Plenum Press.

Ross, W.D., De Rose, E.H., & Ward, R. (1988). Anthropometry applied to sports medicine. In A. Dirix, H. G. Knuttgen, & K. Tittel (Eds.), *The Olympic book of sports medicine* (pp. 233-265). London: Blackwell Scientific.

Ross, W.D., Drinkwater, D.T., Bailey, D.A., Marshall, G.H. & Leahy, R.M. (1980). Kinanthropometry: Traditions and new perspectives. In M. Ostyn, G. Beunen, & J. Simons (Eds.), *Kinanthropometry II* (pp. 1-27). Baltimore: University Park Press.

Ross, W.D., Drinkwater, D.T., Whittingham, N.O., & Faulkner, R.A. (1980). Anthropometric prototypes: Ages six to eighteen years. In K. Berg & B. O. Eriksson (Eds.), *Children and exercise IX* (pp. 3-12). Baltimore: University Park Press.

Ross, W.D., & Marfell-Jones, M.J. (1991). Kinanthropometry. In J.D. MacDougall, H.A. Wenger, & H.J. Green (Eds.), *Physiological testing of the high-performance athlete* (pp. 223-308). Champaign, IL: Human Kinetics.

Ross, W.D., & Ward, R. (1986). Scaling anthropometric data for size and proportionality. In T. Reilly, J. Watson, & J. Borms (Eds.), *Kinanthropometry III* (pp. 203-220). London: E & FN Spon.

Ross, W. D., & Wilson, N. C. (1974). A stratagem for proportional growth assessment. *Acta Pediatrica Belgica* **28**, (Suppl.), 169-182.

Rutenfranz, J., Lange Andersen, K., Seliger, V., Ilmarinen, J., Klimmer, F., Kylian, H., Rutenfranz, M., & Ruppel, M. (1982). Maximal aerobic power affected by maturation and body growth during childhood and adolescence. *European Journal of Pediatrics*, **139**(2), 106-112.

Sloan, A.W., & Shapiro, M. (1972). A comparison of skinfold measurements with three standard calipers. *Human Biology*, **44**(1), 29-36.

Sullivan, K.M., & Gorstein, J. (1990). *ANTHRO. Software for calculating pediatric anthropometry.* Atlanta: Centers for Disease Control, Center for Chronic Disease Prevention and Health Promotion.

Tanner, J.M. (1977). Human growth and constitution. In Harrison, G. A., Weiner,J.S., Tanner,J.M., and Barnicott,N.A. (Eds.), *Human biology* (pp. 301-385). Oxford: Oxford University Press.

Tanner, J.M. (1986). Use and abuse of growth standards. In F. Falkner & J. M. Tanner (Eds.), *Human growth—A comprehensive treatise* (Vol. 3, pp. 95-109). New York: Plenum Press.

Tanner, J.M., & Davies, P.S.W. (1985). Clinical longitudinal standards for height and height velocity for North American children. *Journal of Pediatrics*, **107**(3), 317-329.

Waterlow, J.C., Buzina, R., Keller, W., Lane, J.M., Nichman, M.Z., & Tanner, J.M. (1977). The presentation and use of height and weight data for comparing the nutritional status of groups of children under the age of 10 years. *Bulletin of the WHO*, **55**, 489-98.

Weiner, J.S., & Lourie, J.A. (1981). *Practical human biology.* New York: Academic Press.

Wilmore, J.H., Frisancho, R.A., Gordon, C.C., Himes, J.H., Martin, A.D., Martorell, R., & Seefeldt, V.D. (1988). Body breadth equipment and measurement techniques. In T. G. Lohman, A. F. Roche, & R. Martorell (Eds.), *Anthropometric standardization reference manual* (pp. 27-38). Champaign, IL: Human Kinetics.

2

Alan D. Martin
Richard Ward

Body Composition

Traditionally the term *body composition* has almost always referred to the estimation of body fatness, based on the simple partition of the body into two components: the fat mass and the fat-free mass. The relative amount of fat in the body (%fat) is by far the most common measure of body composition in adults and children, because of the well-established relationship between obesity and a variety of diseases and risk factors, and the relationship between fatness, fitness, and athletic performance. However, the measurement of fatness alone has some drawbacks. Many recent studies have shown that the distribution of fat on the body is a better predictor of health risk than overall fatness in both men (Larsson et al., 1984) and women (Lapidus et al., 1984). Specifically, an increased amount of fat in the abdominal region is associated with elevated risk for cardiovascular disease, stroke, and diabetes (Krotkiewski, Björntorp, Sjöstrom, & Smith, 1983). Little research has been done on fat distribution in children, though it is clearly important to know how a child's fat distribution pattern changes during growth, so that both healthy and unhealthy patterns can be followed. Even the important question of whether overall fatness level in a child is predictive of adult fatness is not clear. Genetic factors probably account for less than 20% of adult obesity, and leanness in neonates bears little relationship to adult leanness. However, fatter children and children with obese parents are more likely to be fat as adults; hence the importance of assessing fatness in children (Freedman et al., 1987).

PROBLEMS WITH TRADITIONAL ASSESSMENT METHODS

The traditional emphasis on fatness overlooks other important aspects of body composition. Over the years of physical maturation of a typical male, muscle mass increases from less than 1 kg to about 28 kg, and skeletal mass increases from a similarly low value to about 10 kg. The quantities of these tissues have important implications for health, nutritional status, and physical performance and should therefore be estimated along with the degree of fatness. Unfortunately, few methods exist for estimating muscle and bone masses even in adults. In the absence of such methods, various indexes can be used to reflect changes in these tissue masses even though their masses cannot be estimated directly. For example, skinfold-corrected limb girths are a useful indicator of muscularity, and bone dimensions, such as wrist breadth and elbow breadth, can be used as indicators of skeletal mass. Thus any comprehensive assessment of body composition in children should include measures of overall fatness, fat distribution, muscle, and bone.

Models of body composition fall into two general categories: chemical and anatomical. The chemical models subdivide the body into chemically defined constituents, in particular, water, lipid, protein, and minerals. Thus, the two-component model of fat and fat-free mass is the simplest of the chemical models. Despite its almost universal use, this model has important limitations. It is nonphysiological and nonanatomical, because its fat component is an amalgamation of all of the body's lipid regardless of its location or function. Also, because of the wide range of variability, particularly evident in children, the assumptions implicit in the model may lead to unacceptable error in individual predictions of body fat (Martin & Drinkwater, 1991). However, because of its prevalence, the two-component model will be discussed in some detail later. It is important to appreciate that the fat component is lipid and not adipose tissue. Adipose tissue is a storage site for lipid and as such is composed of adipocytes and supporting matrix and contains water, protein, and minerals, as well as stored lipid. The anatomical model divides the body into components such as adipose tissue, skeletal muscle, bone, and organs. Although it is self-evident that such a model is more appropriate when considering matters of health and physical performance, few anatomical models currently exist.

A further general problem of all techniques of body composition analysis is the lack of validation. Validation of any method requires comparison with a true, or criterion, value. In the case of body composition, these criterion measures can only come from direct dissection of the body (Level I). The validation of in vivo techniques has been limited in almost all cases to intercomparisons of different indirect methods. In this sense, *indirect* means that they measure some parameter other than fat and estimate fatness by making one or more quantitative assumptions about the relationship between the measured quantity and the amount of fat, for example, densitometry and total body water (Level II). Another classification is that of the doubly indirect methods (Level III), whereby estimation equations are derived from one of the indirect methods, most commonly densitometry (Martin & Drinkwater, 1991). As an example, the estimation of percentage body fat using skinfold measures requires a regression equation based on a densitometric criterion and is, therefore, deemed to be a doubly indirect method.

With increasing demand for measures of body composition, there has been a proliferation of innovative methods that have again focused on the fat–nonfat model. These generally fall into the doubly indirect methods as they require calibration with a Level II method, typically underwater weighing, the most common densitometric method. By their nature these regression equations are sample-specific because the relationship of total body lipid to the measure or measures used in the particular method varies according to the unique characteristics of the sample upon which the regression equation is based. As a result there are over 100 equations for estimating percent fat from skinfolds, reflecting the influence of factors including age, gender, genetic differences, and level and type of habitual activity (Lohman, 1981). The vast majority of these equations are based on adult samples. Because of the lack of appreciation of the sample-specificity of these equations, adult-derived equations are frequently applied to children. Children are not small adults and exhibit great variation in body form and composition, leading to large errors when inappropriate equations are applied.

Data collected as part of the 1981 Canada Fitness Survey on children aged 6 to 18 are tabulated by gender and age in Appendix 2.1, for comparative purposes.

TECHNIQUES FOR ESTIMATING FATNESS

Over the last 50 years, many methods have been developed for estimating the amount of fat in the body. Some of these, such as total body electrical conductivity, are of limited usefulness and will not be discussed here.

Hydrostatic (Underwater) Weighing

All measures of body fat are based on the two-component chemical model consisting of a fat component with density d_f and a fat-free component whose density is d_{ffm}. If D is the whole body density, then a simple mathematical analysis for this model yields the following equation for %fat (F):

$$F = \left[\frac{100 d_f d_{ffm}}{d_{ffm} - d_f}\right] \frac{1}{D} - \left[\frac{100\ d_f}{d_{ffm} - d_f}\right] \qquad (1)$$

The standard approach to solving this equation is to assume values for d_{ffm} and d_f and then to measure D, typically by underwater weighing and the application of Archimedes' principle.

The most common assumptions for the densities of the fat and fat-free masses are 0.900 g/ml and 1.100 g/ml, respectively. Putting these values into equation (1) leads to the Siri (1956) equation for percent fat from body density (D):

$$\%\text{fat} = \frac{495}{D} - 450$$

Whole body density is then measured, typically by underwater weighing. The subject is weighed first in air and then totally immersed after maximal expiration from the lungs. The air remaining in the lungs is termed the *residual volume* (RV) and is measured independently. The volume of the body is determined using Archimedes' principle as the loss in weight of the body upon immersion divided by the density of water at that temperature. Because density equals weight divided by volume, density can then be determined using the following equation:

$$D = \frac{W_{air}}{\dfrac{W_{air} - W_{water}}{d_{water}} - (RV + 0.100)} \tag{2}$$

where D is whole body density in g/ml, W_{air} is weight in air in kg, W_{water} is weight in water in kg, d_{water} is the density of water in g/ml at the temperature of the water in the tank, and RV is the residual volume of the lungs in liters. The constant, 0.100, is an estimated correction (in liters) for the amount of gas in the gastrointestinal tract. For example, if measurements on a 14-year-old boy show that $W_{air} = 50.0$ kg, $W_{water} = 0.95$ kg, and $RV = 1.10$ liters, then equation (2) gives $D = 1.045$ g/ml. Putting this value into Siri's equation then gives %fat = 23.7%.

A central problem with this approach is that the density of the fat-free mass, as one would expect, is not constant in all individuals, particularly children. Any difference between the assumed value and the true value of fat-free density in an individual will result in an error in prediction of percentage body fat. The standard deviation of the density of the fat-free mass in adults has been estimated to be about 0.016 g/ml (Martin & Drinkwater, 1991). This seemingly small variability in fact leads to large errors. The effects of variability in the fat-free density can be calculated by using the true fat-free density in place of the assumed value of 1.100 g/ml in equation (1). By way of example, if a person has a whole body density of 1.07 g/ml, the estimated body fat from the Siri equation is 12.6%. If the fat-free density is actually 1.12 g/ml, rather than 1.10 g/ml, then the true fatness is 19.1%. Conversely, if the true fat-free density is 1.08 g/ml then the true fatness is 4.7%. Relative to adults, a child's fat-free mass has a greater water fraction and a lower bone mineral fraction. This will lower the fat-free density and cause over-estimation of percent body fat if the standard adult value for fat-free density is assumed. Fat-free density varies greatly during growth. Estimates range from 1.063 g/ml at birth to 1.100 g/ml for boys at maturity (Lohman, 1985). It should be noted that these are mean values of groups and no mention was made of variability within the group. Two similar equations have been proposed (Haschke, 1983; Lohman, 1984) for the estimation of percent fat from density in children. Lohman's equation for 8- to 12-year-old boys and girls differs from the Siri equation in that the density of the fat-free mass is assumed to be 1.084 g/ml. Putting this value in equation (1) gives:

$$\%\text{fat} = \frac{530}{D} - 489 \qquad \text{(Lohman, 1984)}$$

Note that putting the previous data into this equation results in a %fat value of 18.2%, compared to the value of 23.7% with the standard assumption. Westrate and Deurenberg (1989) estimated that the density of the fat-free mass slowly increased with age from 1.080 g/ml at 7 years of age to 1.100 g/ml at 18 years in both boys and girls, and therefore proposed an equation incorporating age:

$$\%\text{fat} = \frac{[562 - 4.2(\text{age} - 2)]}{D} - [525 - 4.7(\text{age} - 2)], \text{ where age is in years.}$$

Again using the previous data for the 14-year-old boy, this equation gives 21.0% fat. It should be appreciated that using 1.100 g/ml for the fat-free density in children will result in an over-estimation of %fat.

Beyond the assumption of constant densities, there are practical problems associated with underwater weighing of children. The procedure requires considerable subject cooperation; in fact, very young children cannot be measured at all with this method. At the time of weighing, subjects must empty their lungs down to residual volume while submerged. Younger children are reluctant to do this consistently, which results in poor reproducibility for the technique. Deurenberg, Pieters, and Hautvast (1990) reported that the reproducibility of the measurement was about 0.0006 g/ml (0.3% body fat) in adults and about 0.0048 g/ml (2.5% body fat) in children, reflecting the problems in assessment of children.

Two other indirect methods merit discussion here. Whole-body counting is based on the fact that all naturally occurring potassium contains a constant known fraction of the isotope ^{40}K, which emits gamma rays quantified in a whole-body counter. This enables the calculation of total body potassium (Forbes, 1987). If the potassium fraction of the fat-free mass is a known constant, then the fat-free mass can be determined. Fat mass is then obtained as the difference between body mass and fat-free mass. Fat estimation by total body water relies on a similar assumption, namely, that the water fraction of the fat-free mass is constant. Total body water (TBW) is obtained by a dilution technique in which a known amount of a tracer (typically deuterium oxide or tritium oxide that is totally miscible with all body water) is ingested and, after a suitable time period for equilibration, a body fluid (e.g., urine) is sampled. After measuring the volume of the sample and the amount of tracer in it, TBW can be calculated (Sheng & Huggins, 1979). Assuming a value of 73.2% for the water fraction of the fat-free mass allows for the determination of the fat-free mass and, hence, by subtraction from body mass, the fat mass and %fat. However, the value of 73.2% is by no means constant, even in adults. Estimates suggest that it may be as high as 80% in neonates and declines by the late teens to the adult values of about 71% to 75% (Haschke, 1983). When hydration is higher than the assumed adult value of 73.2%, %fat will be underestimated by this method. Similarly, the potassium fraction of the fat-free mass increases considerably during growth. Thus the changing composition of the fat-free mass during the growth of children can cause serious errors in the assumptions of all three of these methods for estimating %fat: densitometry, total body water, and whole-body counting of the ^{40}K isotope, because they all rely in some way on the constancy of the fat-free mass.

Some researchers have attempted to resolve this problem by measuring other body parameters along with body density. Siri was the first to propose that total body water should be measured, as well as body density, and gave an equation for estimating %fat from D and TBW in adults (Siri, 1956). Currently, researchers are developing equations for %fat that incorporate TBW and some measure of bone mineral density. However, the more variables that an equation requires, particularly those like bone mineral density that require sophisticated and expensive equipment, the less useful it is to those interested in assessing the body composition of children.

Anthropometry: %Fat

By far the most common technique for estimating fatness is the use of skinfold calipers to determine the thickness of a double layer of skin and subcutaneous adipose tissue at selected sites on the body (Martin, Ross, Drinkwater, & Clarys, 1985). Typically, the sum of several skinfolds is entered into an equation for estimating body density that is derived from a regression relationship between skinfolds and density determined by underwater weighing of a sample of children. Then %fat is estimated from the Siri equation or some modified version of it. Even if the individual being measured conforms to the description of those in the originating sample (e.g., in gender, age, general physique), there is considerable potential for error in prediction. The best indicator of predictability is the standard error of estimate (*SEE*) of the regression equation. Lohman (1981) reported that the average *SEE* in an adult sample was about 3.7% body fat. This can be interpreted to mean that in approximately two out of three predictions the true percent body fat will be within ± 3.7% body fat of the estimated value. In children the *SEE* is higher, at around 4.5% body fat (Deurenberg et al., 1990). Thus, in a group of children estimated to be 15% fat, one out of three children will have a true value outside the range of 10.5% to 19.5% body fat. This gives a considerable margin of error within individual predictions.

Because of the inconstancy of the fat-free mass discussed previously, there are many equations for estimating %fat from skinfold thicknesses. Deurenberg and co-workers (1990) have recently reported such equations based on their measurement of 378 boys and girls, divided into prepubertal, pubertal, and postpubertal groups. They used four skinfold sites: biceps, triceps, subscapular, and iliac crest, the sites chosen by Durnin and Womersley (1974) for use in their popular equations for estimating %fat in adults. This iliac crest site is located 1 to 2 cm above the iliac crest on the midaxillary line; a common mistake is to take this measure in a more anterior position, where its value is often considerably smaller. The equations for %fat (Deurenberg et al., 1990) are given in Table 2.1.

Table 2.1   Estimation of %Fat in Children at Three Different Maturation Levels, Based on Four Skinfold Thicknesses

Maturation level	Estimated %fat
Boys	
Prepubertal	%fat = 26.56 (log S_4) − 22.23
Pubertal	%fat = 18.70 (log S_4) − 11.91
Postpubertal	%fat = 18.88 (log S_4) − 15.58
Girls	
Prepubertal	%fat = 29.85 (log S_4) − 25.87
Pubertal	%fat = 23.94 (log S_4) − 18.89
Postpubertal	%fat = 39.02 (log S_4) − 43.49

Note. Where log S_4 is the log to base 10 of the sum of the biceps, triceps, subscapular, and iliac crest skinfolds (in mm).
Adapted from Deurenberg et al. (1990).

Anthropometry: Sum of Skinfolds

The equations of Deurenberg et al. (1990) should be used with caution. Like the Durnin and Womersley (1974) equations used for adults, they reflect only upper body sites and therefore assume that the relationship between upper-body and lower-body fat stores is consistent across individuals. Unfortunately, as is readily apparent, fat storage in the gluteal and thigh regions is not consistently related to upper-body fat storage. The large standard error associated with these equations means that estimates of %fat for many individuals will be subject to large error. The changing composition of the fat-free mass also means that the %fat values are subject to large error. One way to minimize these problems is to use the sum of skinfold thicknesses to reflect total body fat instead of converting this sum to %fat. It should be kept in mind that a sum of skinfolds is only a measure of subcutaneous adipose tissue and to infer total body fat from this means that we are assuming a constant relationship between the amount of subcutaneous adipose tissue and the amount stored internally around the organs. Several researchers have indicated that there is an increase in deposition of internal adipose tissue relative to subcutaneous tissue with advancing years in adults (Borkan, Hults, Gerzof, Robbins, & Silbert, 1983), but little is known about this in children. A further complication of using a sum of skinfolds in children is that with growth there are large and rapid changes in body size. The same set of skinfold thicknesses in two boys who differ in size will not represent the same amount of adipose tissue, either in absolute terms or relative terms. If a larger boy has the same sum of skinfolds as a smaller boy, the larger boy will have more absolute fat mass, but less relative fat. This poses a problem in interpreting skinfold thicknesses around the period of peak height velocity at puberty. Some suggest standardizing skinfold thicknesses to height, based on a geometric similarity system

(Ross & Wilson, 1974). Bearing these limitations in mind, we have presented in Figure 2.1 the means for the sum of five skinfolds (triceps, biceps, subscapular, iliac crest, medial calf) in boys and girls, 7 to 18 years of age, measured as part of the 1981 Canada Fitness Survey. As illustrated in this graph, the growth of the adipose tissue does not conform to a regular curve of growth, such as the sigmoid-like curve of height. Skinfold thicknesses show an undulating pattern of development. In the Canada Fitness Survey data the prepubescent years are associated with an increase in mean thicknesses with advancing age groups. The male and female patterns then diverge as the secondary sexual adipose tissue is laid down in females, accounting for the relatively larger skinfold thicknesses in females for the remainder of the life span (Figures 2.2, a–e).

Anthropometry: Fat Patterning

Although we are recommending the sum of skinfolds as a simple and useful indicator of total body fatness, comparison of the individual skinfold values can yield important information on the distribution of fat around the body. Parizkova (1961) reported a pattern of relatively greater deposition of adipose tissue on trunk sites relative to limb sites with advancing age in both boys and girls, with girls showing a relatively greater limb-to-trunk deposition than boys. In Canadian children measured as a part of the Canada Fitness Survey (Figures 2.2, a–e), a sexual dimorphism is apparent at all five sites, with the greater thickness in females being more marked after 12 years of age.

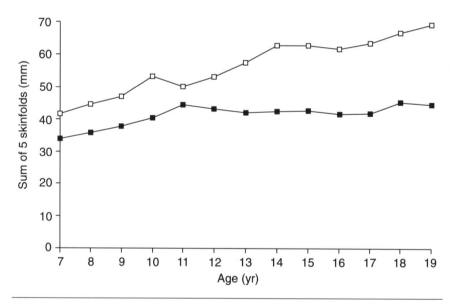

Figure 2.1   Mean sum of five skinfolds (triceps, biceps, subscapular, iliac crest, medial calf) for boys and girls by age group (girls: open squares, boys: solid squares). Data from Canada Fitness Survey (1981).

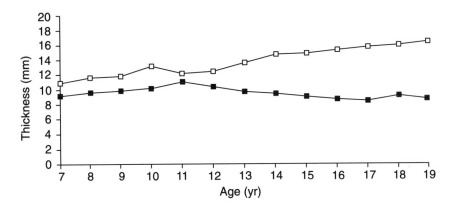

Figure 2.2a   Mean triceps skinfold thickness for boys and girls by age group (girls: open squares, boys: solid squares). Data from Canada Fitness Survey (1981).

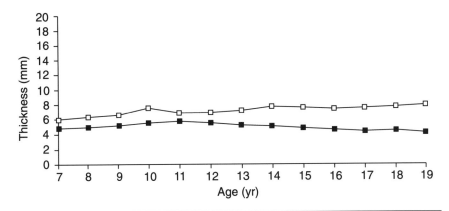

Figure 2.2b   Mean biceps skinfold thickness for boys and girls by age group (girls: open squares, boys: solid squares). Data from Canada Fitness Survey (1981).

Figure 2.3 (p. 97) shows means of a ratio of trunk–limb skinfold thicknesses [ratio = (subscapular + iliac crest) / (triceps + medial calf)] used as an indicator of the trunk-to-limb dysplasia in adipose tissue deposition (Canada Fitness Survey data). In boys the shift in dominance from limb- to trunk-deposition is dramatically evident. However, in girls this phenomenon is masked by the relatively greater increase in limb sites occurring at puberty with the deposition of secondary sexual adipose tissue on the upper arms and in the gluteal and thigh regions. This has been quantified recently using magnetic resonance imaging by de Ridder et al. (1992) who showed that in late female puberty, adipose tissue is stored predominantly in the gluteal, and not the abdominal, region. It is of interest to note that the medial calf skinfold reflects this changing secondary sexual pattern in females. Although

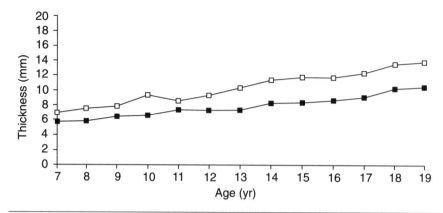

Figure 2.2c   Mean subscapular skinfold thickness for boys and girls by age group (girls: open squares, boys: solid squares). Data from Canada Fitness Survey (1981).

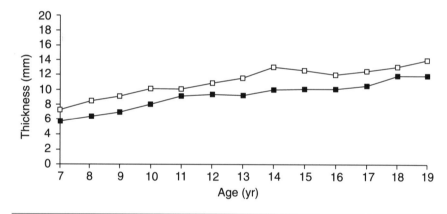

Figure 2.2d   Mean iliac crest skinfold thickness for boys and girls by age group (girls: open squares, boys: solid squares). Data from Canada Fitness Survey (1981).

the thigh skinfold is thought to be the best indicator of this pattern in the lower limb, our experience has been that changes in the thigh skinfold are reflected in the medial-calf skinfold. Figure 2.4 (p. 98) shows differences between means of individual skinfold thicknesses of boys and girls at each age group in the Canadian sample. Strikingly, the medial calf skinfold shows the same pattern of development as the triceps skinfold, whereas the iliac crest does not show a dramatic change in dimorphism after 12 years of age. The conclusion must be, therefore, that the medial calf site is also a site of deposition of secondary sexual adipose tissue, along with the triceps and front thigh. With medial calf being an easier skinfold to measure than the front thigh skinfold, yet showing similar changes, we would recommend the use of the medial calf site where it is not feasible to measure the front thigh.

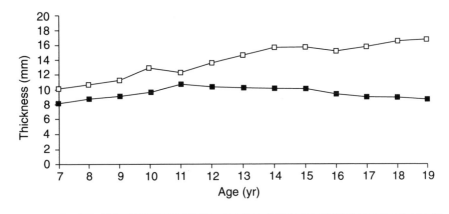

Figure 2.2e   Mean medial calf skinfold thickness for boys and girls by age group (girls: open squares, boys: solid squares). Data from Canada Fitness Survey (1981).

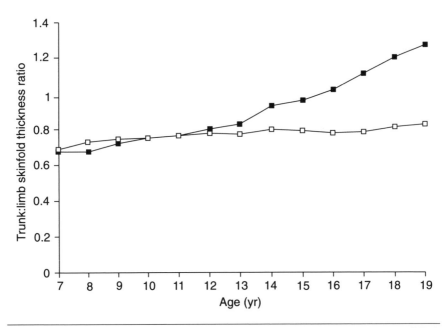

Figure 2.3   Mean ratio of sum of trunk skinfolds (subscapular, iliac crest) to sum of limb skinfolds (triceps, medial calf) for boys and girls by age group (girls: open squares, boys: solid squares). Data from Canada Fitness Survey (1981).

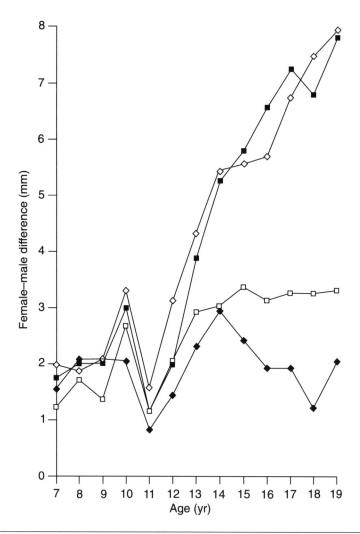

Figure 2.4   Difference between male and female mean skinfold thicknesses at four sites (difference = female mean–male mean). Solid squares = triceps; open squares = subscapular; solid diamonds = iliac crest; open diamonds = medial calf. Data from Canada Fitness Survey (1981).

Bioelectrical Impedance and Infrared Interactance

The observation by Hoffer, Meador, and Simpson (1969) of the high correlation in adults between fat-free mass and the body's electrical resistance, specifically the resistive index (height squared divided by resistance), has been confirmed by many others. It is now the basis of the common bioelectrical impedance analysis (BIA) method for assessing body composition in adults. However, the equations inherent in BIA instruments are derived from studies on adults and thus reflect the relationship between the resistive index and fat-free mass found in adult samples. As we have seen, the composition of the fat-free mass in children differs from that of adults, and as a result, several groups have reported that using instruments based on adult equations results in the over-estimation of fat-free mass in children (Eston et al., 1990; Kay-Covington, Kluka, & Love, 1990). There is currently not enough information on BIA and children to provide a scientific basis for its use. If BIA equations for children are calibrated against densitometrically determined %fat with allowances made for the lower fat-free density of children, then BIA may prove to be a useful technique in the future.

Infrared interactance involves the use of a beam of near infrared radiation applied to a selected skinfold site and the measurement of the intensity and pattern of reflected radiation. The resulting optical densities obtained at two frequencies are combined in a densitometrically based equation that also includes height, weight, and a measure of the subject's level of physical activity. Typically, the instrument is applied at an upper arm site. A recent study concluded that the use of this instrument had little or no advantage over fat estimations based on simple anthropometry (height and weight or skinfolds) or BIA (Elia, Parkinson, & Diaz, 1990). No studies have been reported for children, but because the technique is calibrated against densitometry, it is likely to be less reliable in children than in adults.

Body Mass Index

In recent years the old Quetelet Index (weight/height^2), now renamed the body mass index (BMI), has been used frequently as a measure of fatness, both in adults and children. The origin of this use is in epidemiological studies where fatness is of interest, but the only anthropometric data available are height and weight. However, its use has spread widely, and it is now accepted by many as a valid indicator of obesity. It should be immediately clear that the BMI cannot distinguish between those who are heavy because they are fat and those who are heavy because of musculoskeletal dominance. From this it follows that BMI will only be a useful estimator of fatness in populations in which overweight is due to excess fat. In a sample of nearly 20,000 Canadian adults (Ross et al., 1988), BMI showed about the same correlation coefficient with adiposity (0.50) as it did with measures of muscularity (0.58) and bone breadths (0.51). Because of its low correlation with fatness, BMI has no validity as a predictor of fatness in individual adults. The simultaneous changes in fatness, muscularity, and bone mass seen during growth also preclude the use of BMI as a measure in children. Its role should be confined exclusively to epidemiological studies.

TECHNIQUES FOR ESTIMATING MUSCULARITY

It is unfortunate that the estimation of muscle mass has not been given the importance it deserves in body composition assessment. Measures of %fat do not clearly separate athletes in different sports, because leanness is a prerequisite for most sporting performances. Whereas distance runners, gymnasts, sprinters, and body-builders are all typically below about 10% fat, they differ greatly in muscularity. The traditional method for estimating muscle mass has been the use of urinary creatinine excretion. This is based on the assumptions that all excreted creatinine results from muscle metabolism and that the amount excreted is proportional to muscle mass. However, this method requires an assumption regarding the number of kilograms of muscle that correspond to a gram of excreted creatinine (Forbes, 1987). At best this gives only an approximate estimate of muscularity. Medical imaging techniques, such as computed tomography and magnetic resonance imaging, give accurate measures of muscle cross-sectional areas, but have limited use because of their invasive nature or high cost.

In the absence of expensive imaging equipment, the best approach to measuring muscularity is to estimate limb muscle girths by correcting the limb girth for the thickness of the skinfold in that region. In this method both the muscle and limb cross-sections are assumed to be circular and concentric. The thickness of the adipose tissue layer is taken to be half the skinfold thickness. It is then easy to derive a general expression for the muscle girth (Martin, Spenst, Drinkwater, & Clarys, 1990):

$$\text{muscle girth} = \text{limb girth} - \pi \text{ (skinfold)}$$

Specifically,

$$\text{arm muscle girth} = \text{arm girth} - \pi \text{ (triceps skinfold)}$$
$$\text{thigh muscle girth} = \text{thigh girth} - \pi \text{ (front thigh skinfold)}$$
$$\text{calf muscle girth} = \text{calf girth} - \pi \text{ (medial calf skinfold)}$$

These indicators of muscularity can be used independently or summed, like skinfolds, to give an index of total muscularity. In older men these measures have been compared to dissected muscle mass, resulting in the only cadaver-validated equation for estimating muscle mass (Martin et al., 1990). This equation is not available for children and there is no way to estimate their absolute muscle mass. The Canada Fitness Survey data included arm and calf girths with the corresponding skinfolds; the estimated muscle girths are shown plotted in Figures 2.5 and 2.6. There are no gender differences in either of these muscularity indicators until about 12 years of age, after which girls' muscle growth flattens off while the boys' values steadily increase.

TECHNIQUES FOR ESTIMATING SKELETAL SIZE

As with muscularity few attempts have been made to produce equations for estimating skeletal mass. Matiegka (1921) used the sum of selected bone breadths (wrist, elbow, knee, and ankle) in his equation, but cautioned that the equation had not been validated against cadaver dissection. Subsequently, von Döbeln (1964) used an equation based on right- and left-side wrist and knee breadths. We recommend

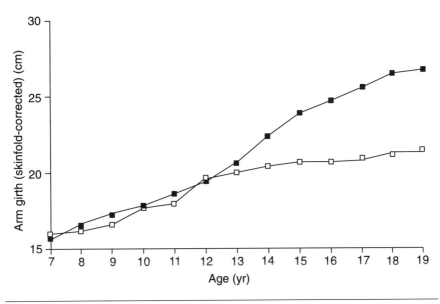

Figure 2.5   Mean skinfold-corrected arm girth for boys and girls by age group (girls: open squares, boys: solid squares). Data from Canada Fitness Survey (1981).

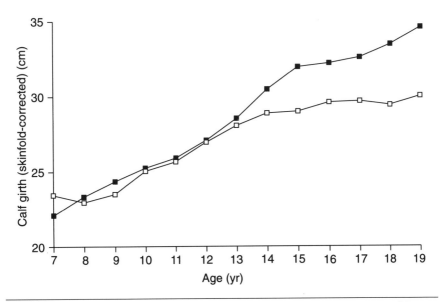

Figure 2.6   Mean skinfold-corrected calf girth for boys and girls by age group (girls: open squares, boys: solid squares). Data from Canada Fitness Survey (1981).

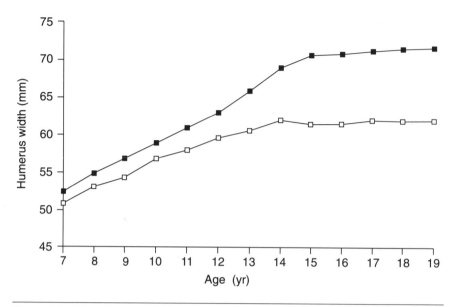

Figure 2.7   Mean humerus width for boys and girls by age group (girls: open squares, boys: solid squares). Data from Canada Fitness Survey (1981).

the use of wrist, elbow, and knee breadths. The Canada Fitness Survey data included elbow (humerus) and knee (femur) breadths, and these are shown plotted against the age groups for boys and girls in Figures 2.7 and 2.8. It can be seen that boys have greater bone breadths at all ages than girls, and the difference is greatly increased around 12 to 13 years of age.

COMPREHENSIVE PHYSIQUE ASSESSMENT

Although there are many national standards for individual anthropometric variables such as height, weight, triceps skinfold, relaxed arm girth, or skinfold corrected arm girth, there is limited availability of comprehensive anthropometric standards. The 1981 Canada Fitness Survey was used to update the Canadian Standardised Test of Fitness (Fitness Canada, 1987). In the physique-assessment portion of the test, age- and sex-specific percentile distributions for four indexes were displayed as a profile.

The four indexes are as follows:

1. sum of five skinfolds—SOS (triceps+biceps+subscapular+iliac crest+medial calf)
2. waist-to-hip girth ratio—WHR (waist/hip girth)
3. sum of trunk skinfolds—SOTS (subscapular+iliac crest)
4. body mass index—BMI (weight/height^2)

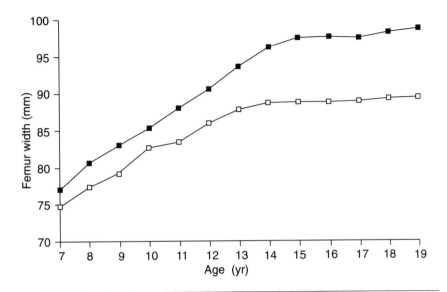

Figure 2.8   Mean femur width for boys and girls by age group (girls: open squares, boys: solid squares). Data from Canada Fitness Survey (1981).

Unfortunately, the tables start at 15 years of age and, therefore, have limited application to youth. In practice, the individual subject is rated on each index, and interpretations are made from this differential comparison. One of the problems with this design is that each of these indexes derives its justification from epidemiological studies as a measure of "fatness." If a subject gets different ratings for each index, how should this be interpreted? Another cause for concern is the use of the BMI, whose limitations have been discussed previously.

The O-SCALE system arose out of a need to provide a more satisfactory system for individual physique assessment than that afforded by weight/height tables or the densitometric-based estimations of % body fat. The O-SCALE system does not require the assumption of any biological constants. Featuring the use of inexpensive anthropometric instruments, the sophistication of the system is in the computerized resolution and display features. The advanced O-SCALE system requires the measurements of weight, height (stretch stature), 8 skinfolds, 10 girths (body perimeters), and 2 bone widths (Ross & Ward, 1989). The system may be used in an abbreviated form with only height, weight, and 6 skinfolds being measured. There are two levels of description of physique. A general description is facilitated by two ratings, one of adiposity and the other of proportional weight. The second level of analysis is a detailed description utilizing comparisons to age- and gender-specific norms for both size and proportionality scores. This level of analysis requires the use of the IBM-compatible microcomputer software (available from Kinemetrix, Inc., Burnaby, British Columbia). The practical application of this system to the assessment of children can be seen by examining the O-SCALE print-outs for two individuals.

O-SCALE rating for: Overweight boy
Date: 12/6/95

Age (decimal years)	: 12.2
Height (centimeters)	: 161.9
Weight (kilograms)	: 56.5
Sum of 6 skinfolds (millimeters)	: 50.8
Proportional sum of 6 skinfolds (mm)	: 53.4
Proportional weight (kilograms)	: 65.6

```
        1 . . 2 . . 3 . . 4 . . 5 . . 6 . . 7 . . 8 . . 9 .
A                         •
W                                             •
        4%. . 11%. . 23%. . 40%. . 60%. . 77%. .89%. .96%.
```

Size profile

Male age 12.2	Present	Norm percentiles 4%	50%	96%
Weight	56.5	30.5	44.9	64.8
Height	161.9	139.0	155.8	175.5
Skinfolds				
Triceps	7.4	5.8	9.3	26.5
Subscapular	6.4	4.4	6.4	28.7
Supraspinale	5.8	3.5	6.0	27.6
Abdominal	8.6	4.3	7.5	35.9
Front thigh	11.8	8.3	14.5	44.4
Medial calf	10.8	5.0	9.3	28.1
Girths				
Arm (relaxed)	25.9	19.2	23.2	30.2
Forearm (maximum)	26.7	19.7	23.1	27.2
Calf (maximum)	35.4	26.7	31.5	37.7

Widths
Humerus   7.4   5.5   6.4   7.5
Femur   10.0   8.1   9.3   10.5

Corrected girths
Arm   23.6   17.1   20.1   24.0
Calf   32.0   24.2   28.1   32.9

Proportionality profile

Your measurements are scaled to a common stature and then plotted relative to your age and sex norms.

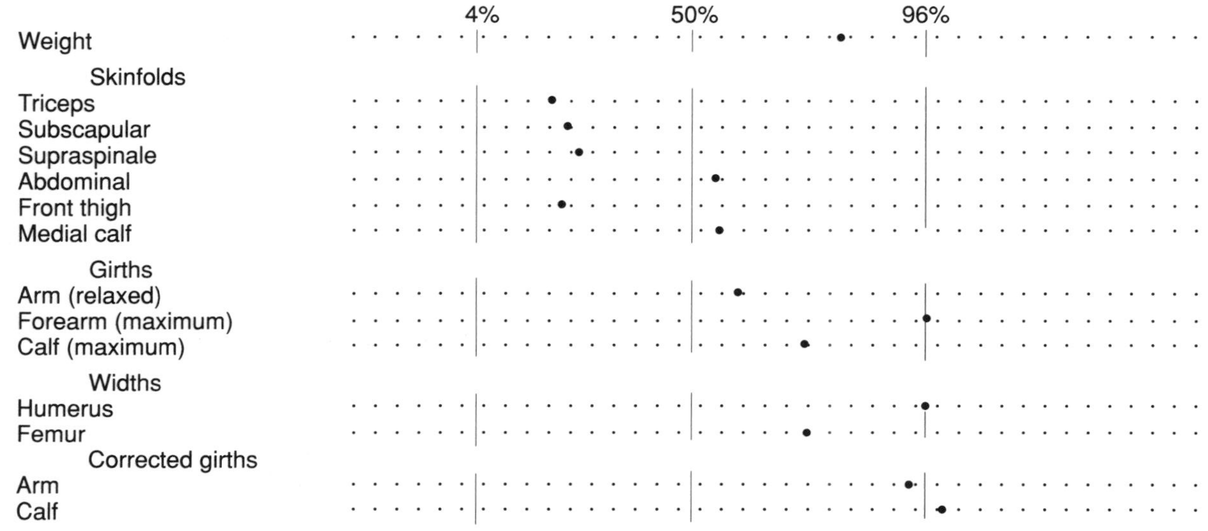

4%   50%   96%

Weight

Skinfolds
Triceps
Subscapular
Supraspinale
Abdominal
Front thigh
Medial calf

Girths
Arm (relaxed)
Forearm (maximum)
Calf (maximum)

Widths
Humerus
Femur

Corrected girths
Arm
Calf

Figure 2.9   The short O-SCALE system print-out for an overweight 12-year-old boy.

O-SCALE rating for: Dieting girl
Date: 23/06/95   : 27/11/95

4/6/95			27/11/95
12.0	:	Age (decimal years)	12.5
150.8	:	Height (centimeters)	152.8
45.5	:	Weight (kilograms)	43.5
83.5	:	Sum of 6 skinfolds (millimeters)	68.3
94.2	:	Proportional sum of 6 skinfolds (mm)	76.1
65.4	:	Proportional weight (kilograms)	60.1

```
      1 . . 2 . . 3 . . 4 . . 5 . . 6 . . 7 . . 8 . . 9
A    |_____●____○_____|
W    |_____●_____○_____|
     4% . 11% . 23% . 40% . 60% . 77% . 89% . 96%
```

Size profile

Female age 12.5	Present	Comparison	Norm percentiles 4%	50%	96%
Weight	43.5	45.5	31.2	46.0	69.5
Height	152.8	150.8	138.0	158.1	169.8
Skinfolds					
Triceps	12.0	13.5	7.5	12.8	23.6
Subscapular	8.0	11.0	5.0	9.3	27.2
Supraspinale	7.3	7.5	4.9	10.1	27.1
Abdominal	11.0	15.5	5.0	13.3	31.7
Front thigh	18.0	20.0	11.1	22.2	42.0
Medial calf	12.0	16.0	6.8	12.8	25.1

Girths					
Arm (relaxed)	24.6	25.8	19.2	23.1	29.2
Forearm (maximum)	22.0	22.8	19.2	22.2	25.2
Calf (maximum)	31.8	33.0	27.2	31.2	37.5
Corrected girths					
Arm	20.8	21.6	16.2	19.2	23.5
Calf	28.0	28.0	24.0	27.2	33.0

Proportionality profile

Your measurements are scaled to a common stature and then plotted relative to your age and sex norms.

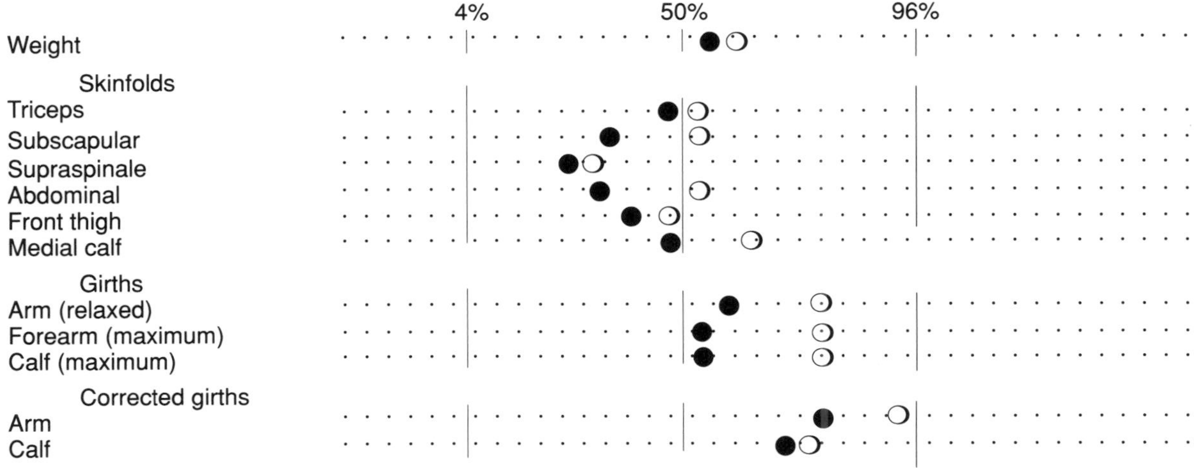

4%   50%   96%

Weight

Skinfolds
Triceps
Subscapular
Supraspinale
Abdominal
Front thigh
Medial calf

Girths
Arm (relaxed)
Forearm (maximum)
Calf (maximum)

Corrected girths
Arm
Calf

Figure 2.10 The short O-SCALE system print-out of repeat measurements for an overweight 12-year-old girl before and after a period of caloric restriction.

Figure 2.9 shows the short print-out for a 12-year-old boy who was classified as obese based upon the criterion of being above the 80th percentile in comparison to national weight-for-height tables (see pages 104-105). The proportional weight rating (W) for the boy of 7 on the 9-point scale indicates that the boy is rated around the 80th percentile in weight-for-height. However, the adiposity (A) ("fatness") rating of 4 on the scale indicates that he is between the 23rd and 40th percentiles for this measure in comparison to other 12-year-old boys. The inference is that it is not the adipose tissue that leads to the high weight-for-height rating, but presumably the musculo-skeletal development. This is confirmed in the second part of the print-out that displays the size listing of the variables in comparison to the 4th, 50th and 96th percentiles for the same age- and sex-norm group. The most powerful part of the analysis is displayed as the proportionality profile on the lower part of the page. This profile shows higher ratings for muscle (as indicated by skinfold-corrected girths) than for any of the skinfolds. This detailed appraisal of physique thus confirms the inference of the difference between the A and W ratings, in that the boy indeed has good muscular development, which therefore explains the higher weight-for-height rating.

The O-SCALE sytem software has a feature that compares data collected on two measurement occasions. This feature was invoked to produce a print-out of analysis on the data before and after a 5-month period of caloric restriction with little change in the habitual physical activity level of a 12-year-old girl (Fig. 2.10; pp. 106-107). The initial measurement occasion is indicated by the open circles. The A and W ratings have both dropped by one, indicating a loss in adiposity and a commensurate loss in weight. The proportionality profile shows a loss of adipose tissue in all the skinfolds, which is accompanied by a loss in relative muscularity rating, particularly in the arm. This approach has proved particularly successful in elucidating the changes in body composition that accompany dietary and exercise interventions.

ANTHROPOMETRIC PROFILE ANALYSIS

A limitation of the O-SCALE system is the complex analysis required and, therefore, the requirement for a computer program. In this text we have supplied a profile assessment package based upon the Canada Fitness Survey data (1981) to allow for appraisals of physique without the requirement of computer analysis (Appendix 2.1). To illustrate its use we present the profile analysis of a 12-year-old boy, who in contrast to the two individuals already shown in the O-SCALE analyses, has relatively low muscle development and high ratings for skinfold thicknesses. The first step is to locate the table in Appendix 2.1 that is appropriate for the age and gender of the child of interest. A column is provided on the left of the 5th percentile column for entry of the subject's measurements. A circle is then made around the closest percentile value for each variable. This produces a visual comparison of the child to the same age- and sex-norm group and a rapid comprehensive appraisal of body composition status (Figure 2.11).

Boys 12 years of age	Name:	Overweight boy										
						Percentiles						
		5	10	20	30	40	50	60	70	80	90	95
Height (cm)	146.0	138.9	142.5	145.2	146.5	148.1	150.1	151.8	154.0	157.0	160.6	163.6
Weight (kg)	42.0	31.9	32.4	35.6	37.7	39.4	41.0	42.7	44.5	48.0	51.5	56.9
Sum of 5 skinfolds (mm)	79.5	24.7	26.1	29.0	31.1	34.0	37.8	42.1	46.2	54.2	63.2	89.3
Skinfolds (mm)												
Triceps	14.8	5.8	6.4	7.2	7.8	8.7	9.6	10.8	11.9	13.8	16.5	19.3
Biceps	10.0	2.8	3.1	3.5	4.0	4.3	4.7	5.1	5.8	7.0	9.3	11.1
Subscapular	17.7	4.5	4.8	5.0	5.5	5.8	6.2	6.7	7.3	8.3	10.7	14.8
Iliac crest	18.8	3.9	4.5	5.2	5.9	6.8	8.0	8.6	10.2	12.0	17.1	22.5
Medial calf	18.2	5.0	5.6	6.6	7.5	8.2	9.4	10.8	11.6	13.0	17.0	21.1
Muscle girths (cm)												
Relaxed arm (skinfold-corrected)	19.9	16.3	16.9	17.7	18.1	18.6	19.1	19.6	20.4	21.2	22.2	22.8
Calf (skinfold-corrected)	25.5	23.5	24.4	25.2	25.8	26.4	26.9	27.4	28.1	29.0	30.0	31.1
Bone widths (cm)												
Humerus	62.5	56.1	58.0	60.0	61.1	61.9	63.1	64.0	65.0	66.1	67.9	69.1
Femur	90.0	82.0	84.3	86.7	88.0	89.5	90.4	91.9	93.3	94.9	97.0	98.7

Figure 2.11   Profile analysis of an overweight 12-year-old boy.

It can be seen that the 12-year-old boy is rated around the 30th percentile for height but at the 60th percentile for weight. The relative ratings of the weight and height can be used in combination as a weight-for-height rating. If the weight rating is displaced to the right of the height column then the child is larger in proportional weight, whereas a displacement to the right of height for the weight rating infers a more linear physique. This particular boy, therefore, has a relatively high weight-to-height ratio. This is explained by the very high skinfold ratings (80th percentile and above). The muscularity as indicated by the skinfold-corrected girths is relatively low. The conclusion therefore is that this boy is overweight because of adipose tissue deposition rather than muscular development. Late maturation may contribute to this situation. The two bone widths can be used as an indicator of frame size, with this child being rated around the 50th percentile for both measures. It is important to point out that this does not involve any of the proportionality scaling that is used in the O-SCALE system, but is purely an appraisal of the size of each of the variables. However, it can be a useful field method when more sophisticated analyses are not available.

CONCLUSION

When assessing the body composition of children, the most sophisticated or expensive methods are not necessarily the best. Because children are not small adults most of the adult assumptions are not valid. We advocate the use of anthropometry, with careful attention to technique definitions, to assess fatness, muscularity, and skeletal size. Comparison with norms for the individual or group of interest can be simply done using percentiles. We have provided Canadian norms for a selection of measures (Appendix 2.1). The closest values to the age and gender of the child of interest can be found in the table to give a quick and accurate visual assessment of body composition.

Appendix 2.1

Percentile Tables for Anthropometric Variables

Boys 7 Years of Age

					Percentiles						
	5	10	20	30	40	50	60	70	80	90	95
Height (cm)	113.5	116.0	118.2	120.4	122.1	123.4	125.2	126.4	128.6	131.6	134.0
Weight (kg)	19.6	20.5	21.7	22.8	23.8	24.3	25.0	25.6	26.7	29.7	32.3
Sum of 5 skinfolds (mm)	22.6	23.7	24.8	27.1	28.4	31.3	32.7	35.5	39.4	46.6	58.7
Skinfolds (mm)											
Triceps	5.9	6.3	6.7	7.3	8.2	8.6	9.1	10.0	11.0	12.2	14.9
Biceps	2.9	3.1	3.4	3.6	4.0	4.3	4.6	5.0	5.4	6.6	9.6
Subscapular	4.0	4.2	4.4	4.6	4.8	5.1	5.3	5.6	6.3	7.6	10.1
Iliac crest	3.3	3.6	4.0	4.4	4.7	5.3	5.5	6.0	7.0	8.6	13.1
Medial calf	4.6	5.1	5.8	6.4	6.9	7.4	8.3	8.9	9.8	12.0	15.2
Muscle girths (cm)											
Relaxed arm (skinfold-corrected)	13.6	14.0	14.5	15.0	15.2	15.4	15.7	16.2	16.8	17.6	18.3
Calf (skinfold-corrected)	20.0	20.2	21.0	21.3	21.7	22.1	22.3	22.7	23.2	24.0	24.5
Bone widths (mm)											
Humerus	48.0	48.9	50.0	51.0	52.0	52.1	53.0	53.7	54.8	56.0	57.3
Femur	70.7	72.0	74.0	75.1	76.0	76.8	77.8	79.0	80.0	81.9	84.0

Boys 8 Years of Age

					Percentiles						
	5	10	20	30	40	50	60	70	80	90	95
Height (cm)	120.9	123.3	125.3	127.5	129.0	130.2	131.0	132.7	134.6	136.2	138.5
Weight (kg)	22.3	23.0	24.6	25.9	26.8	27.6	28.7	30.1	31.5	34.1	37.5
Sun of 5 skinfolds (mm)	21.5	22.8	25.6	27.6	29.1	31.0	33.5	37.4	42.8	52.2	69.5
Skinfolds (mm)											
Triceps	5.6	6.0	7.0	7.5	8.3	8.9	9.6	10.4	11.8	13.8	16.7
Biceps	2.8	3.1	3.4	3.7	4.0	4.3	4.7	5.1	6.0	7.1	8.8
Subscapular	4.0	4.2	4.4	4.6	4.9	5.2	5.4	6.0	6.3	8.1	11.0
Iliac crest	3.0	3.5	4.1	4.4	4.8	5.2	5.6	6.6	7.7	11.3	16.2
Medial calf	4.7	5.1	5.9	6.5	7.3	7.8	8.5	9.7	10.8	14.2	16.3
Muscle girths (cm)											
Relaxed arm (skinfold-corrected)	14.3	14.7	15.2	15.7	16.1	16.4	16.6	17.0	17.4	18.5	19.4

Calf (skinfold-corrected)	20.9	21.3	22.1	22.5	22.8	23.2	23.7	24.1	24.7	25.5	26.2
Bone widths (mm)											
Humerus	49.5	50.1	52.0	53.0	53.8	54.8	55.5	56.5	58.0	59.5	60.6
Femur	72.6	74.8	77.0	79.0	79.8	81.0	82.0	83.0	84.3	85.9	87.8

Boys 9 Years of Age

					Percentiles						
	5	10	20	30	40	50	60	70	80	90	95
Height (cm)	124.8	126.8	129.5	131.2	133.2	135.0	136.9	138.4	139.8	142.8	146.3
Weight (kg)	24.7	25.6	26.5	28.1	29.0	30.1	31.3	32.7	35.2	39.3	42.7
Sum of 5 skinfolds (mm)	21.7	23.8	26.3	28.0	30.7	33.0	34.8	38.7	47.4	60.5	76.0
Skinfolds (mm)											
Triceps	5.9	6.4	7.2	7.8	8.3	9.0	10.0	11.0	12.1	14.9	16.6
Biceps	2.7	3.1	3.4	3.7	4.2	4.5	5.0	5.4	6.4	8.2	10.0
Subscapular	4.0	4.2	4.5	4.8	5.1	5.4	5.8	6.2	7.4	10.4	13.9
Iliac crest	3.2	3.7	4.2	4.6	5.0	5.4	6.2	7.1	8.6	13.3	17.8
Medial calf	4.6	5.2	6.0	6.8	7.3	7.9	8.7	10.5	11.8	14.0	17.9
Muscle girths (cm)											
Relaxed arm (skinfold-corrected)	15.0	15.3	16.0	16.3	16.6	17.0	17.3	17.7	18.2	19.4	20.5
Calf (skinfold-corrected)	21.8	22.3	22.9	23.2	23.7	24.1	24.4	25.0	25.6	26.6	27.7
Bone widths (mm)											
Humerus	51.1	52.0	53.5	54.5	55.5	56.5	57.7	58.5	60.0	62.2	63.9
Femur	74.5	77.0	79.0	80.1	81.0	82.4	83.7	85.4	87.6	89.7	93.2

Boys 10 Years of Age

					Percentiles						
	5	10	20	30	40	50	60	70	80	90	95
Height (cm)	129.2	130.3	134.2	136.6	138.0	139.7	141.1	142.9	145.2	147.7	149.2
Weight (kg)	27.2	27.9	29.8	31.0	32.0	33.2	34.2	36.3	38.3	42.0	45.7
Sum of 5 skinfolds (mm)	22.9	25.2	28.0	29.6	31.9	35.2	37.8	42.0	48.4	61.4	77.6
Skinfolds (mm)											
Triceps	5.4	6.3	7.2	8.0	8.7	9.4	10.0	11.2	12.3	15.3	17.7
Biceps	2.9	3.2	3.6	3.9	4.4	4.7	5.1	5.9	6.8	8.2	10.1

(continued)

	5	10	20	30	40	Percentiles 50	60	70	80	90	95
Subscapular	4.2	4.4	4.6	5.1	5.3	5.7	6.2	6.9	7.8	9.7	14.5
Iliac crest	3.6	4.0	4.5	5.0	5.5	6.5	7.4	8.8	10.1	14.9	21.0
Medial calf	4.7	5.4	6.3	7.2	7.8	8.7	9.3	10.5	11.8	15.8	19.5
Muscle girths (cm)											
Relaxed arm (skinfold-corrected)	15.3	15.8	16.3	16.8	17.3	17.7	18.1	18.6	19.0	20.0	20.5
Calf (skinfold-corrected)	22.6	23.2	23.9	24.3	24.5	24.9	25.4	25.8	26.4	27.3	28.2
Bone widths (mm)											
Humerus	52.1	54.0	55.5	57.0	57.9	58.5	59.5	60.9	61.8	63.8	65.6
Femur	77.4	79.9	81.3	83.0	84.0	85.3	86.5	87.7	89.1	91.8	93.4

Boys 11 Years of Age

	5	10	20	30	40	Percentiles 50	60	70	80	90	95
Height (cm)	134.0	136.8	140.3	142.2	143.3	145.0	147.0	148.2	150.9	153.7	156.0
Weight (kg)	28.9	30.1	32.7	34.4	35.8	37.0	38.5	40.6	42.8	49.3	53.3
Sum of 5 skinfolds (mm)	21.7	23.7	29.1	32.7	35.1	37.6	42.1	49.6	57.5	70.4	89.2
Skinfolds (mm)											
Triceps	5.5	6.5	7.6	8.8	9.3	10.1	11.0	12.4	14.3	16.9	20.6
Biceps	2.8	3.1	3.6	4.2	4.5	4.9	5.6	6.3	7.6	9.1	11.0
Subscapular	4.2	4.4	4.8	5.3	5.6	6.1	6.6	7.6	8.5	12.3	16.4
Iliac crest	3.7	4.0	4.7	5.4	6.1	7.6	8.7	10.3	13.1	16.3	20.9
Medial calf	4.6	5.2	6.6	7.6	8.3	9.7	11.0	12.1	14.5	17.2	20.3
Muscle girths (cm)											
Relaxed arm (skinfold-corrected)	15.7	16.1	16.8	17.3	17.9	18.4	18.8	19.3	20.0	21.2	22.5
Calf (skinfold-corrected)	23.2	23.6	24.2	24.9	25.3	25.9	26.3	26.8	27.4	28.4	29.5
Bone widths (mm)											
Humerus	55.0	56.3	57.9	59.0	60.1	61.0	61.9	62.9	63.9	65.6	67.0
Femur	80.6	81.2	83.8	85.0	86.2	87.6	88.7	90.0	92.5	94.5	97.5

Boys 12 Years of Age

	Percentiles										
	5	10	20	30	40	50	60	70	80	90	95
Height (cm)	138.9	142.5	145.2	146.5	148.1	150.1	151.8	154.0	157.0	160.6	163.6
Weight (kg)	31.9	32.4	35.6	37.7	39.4	41.0	42.7	44.5	48.0	51.5	56.9
Sum of 5 skinfolds (mm)	24.7	26.1	29.0	31.1	34.0	37.8	42.1	46.2	54.2	63.2	89.3
Skinfolds (mm)											
Triceps	5.8	6.4	7.2	7.8	8.7	9.6	10.8	11.9	13.8	16.5	19.3
Biceps	2.8	3.1	3.5	4.0	4.3	4.7	5.1	5.8	7.0	9.3	11.1
Subscapular	4.5	4.8	5.0	5.5	5.8	6.2	6.7	7.3	8.3	10.7	14.8
Iliac crest	3.9	4.5	5.2	5.9	6.8	8.0	8.6	10.2	12.0	17.1	22.5
Medial calf	5.0	5.6	6.6	7.5	8.2	9.4	10.8	11.6	13.0	17.0	21.1
Muscle girths (cm)											
Relaxed arm (skinfold-corrected)	16.3	16.9	17.7	18.1	18.6	19.1	19.6	20.4	21.2	22.2	22.8
Calf (skinfold-corrected)	23.5	24.4	25.2	25.8	26.4	26.9	27.4	28.1	29.0	30.0	31.1
Bone widths (mm)											
Humerus	56.1	58.0	60.0	61.1	61.9	63.1	64.0	65.0	66.1	67.9	69.1
Femur	82.0	84.3	86.7	88.0	89.5	90.4	91.9	93.3	94.9	97.0	98.7

Boys 13 Years of Age

	Percentiles										
	5	10	20	30	40	50	60	70	80	90	95
Height (cm)	143.9	146.3	151.3	154.1	156.2	157.5	159.7	161.8	164.0	169.3	172.3
Weight (kg)	34.6	37.7	40.2	43.0	45.5	47.4	49.5	51.3	53.1	58.8	63.5
Sum of 5 skinfolds (mm)	23.5	25.8	28.3	31.1	32.8	35.5	39.8	45.2	52.8	67.3	81.9
Skinfolds (mm)											
Triceps	5.5	6.0	6.8	7.5	8.2	9.0	9.8	11.1	12.3	15.9	17.7
Biceps	2.9	3.1	3.5	3.8	4.0	4.3	4.9	5.6	6.9	7.9	9.6
Subscapular	4.4	4.9	5.3	5.6	5.9	6.2	6.8	7.6	8.7	11.0	15.6
Iliac crest	4.2	4.7	5.6	6.1	6.6	7.2	8.5	10:2	12.4	16.7	21.5
Medial calf	4.9	5.6	6.6	7.5	8.1	9.0	10.1	11.3	13.5	17.0	18.7
Muscle girths (cm)											
Relaxed arm (skinfold-corrected)	17.1	18.1	18.8	19.3	19.7	20.5	21.1	21.4	22.1	23.4	24.6

(continued)

	Percentiles										
	5	10	20	30	40	50	60	70	80	90	95
Calf (skinfold-corrected)	24.4	25.4	26.5	27.3	27.8	28.3	28.9	29.7	30.5	31.6	32.6
Bone widths (mm)											
Humerus	59.4	61.2	62.9	64.0	64.7	65.5	66.9	68.0	69.0	71.1	72.8
Femur	84.0	87.4	89.8	90.9	92.0	93.8	95.0	96.4	97.8	99.5	101.7

Boys 14 Years of Age

	Percentiles										
	5	10	20	30	40	50	60	70	80	90	95
Height (cm)	149.2	152.9	158.3	161.5	164.2	166.7	168.6	170.9	174.3	177.9	180.5
Weight (kg)	39.9	41.6	45.8	49.2	53.1	55.5	58.7	61.5	65.5	71.9	78.0
Sum of 5 skinfolds (mm)	24.1	25.7	29.6	32.2	34.2	36.6	38.7	42.9	50.4	67.8	87.6
Skinfolds (mm)											
Triceps	5.4	6.1	6.7	7.1	7.7	8.4	9.1	10.1	11.5	15.2	20.7
Biceps	2.9	3.2	3.4	3.7	3.9	4.1	4.6	5.0	5.9	7.8	11.7
Subscapular	5.0	5.4	5.7	6.2	6.4	6.8	7.4	8.1	9.6	14.1	18.6
Iliac crest	4.0	4.7	6.1	6.7	7.2	8.0	8.9	11.1	12.9	16.1	25.9
Medial calf	5.2	5.8	6.6	7.3	8.1	8.8	9.6	11.4	12.8	16.1	19.2
Muscle girths (cm)											
Relaxed arm (skinfold-corrected)	18.2	19.1	20.4	21.1	21.7	22.0	22.8	23.5	24.6	26.2	26.9
Calf (skinfold-corrected)	25.7	26.7	28.2	28.9	29.6	30.4	31.1	32.0	32.6	34.0	35.6
Bone widths (mm)											
Humerus	61.0	62.0	64.8	66.3	67.9	69.1	70.3	71.9	73.0	74.8	77.1
Femur	86.8	88.5	91.4	93.0	94.2	95.9	97.3	99.0	100.8	103.7	105.4

Boys 15 Years of Age

	Percentiles										
	5	10	20	30	40	50	60	70	80	90	95
Height (cm)	160.5	162.4	165.8	168.4	169.9	171.5	173.4	175.5	177.8	181.2	183.4
Weight (kg)	47.9	49.1	52.8	56.2	58.4	61.1	63.6	66.2	69.8	75.1	81.5

Sum of 5 skinfolds (mm)	24.8	26.8	28.3	30.7	33.4	35.9	39.6	42.9	51.8	69.6	86.0
Skinfolds (mm)											
Triceps	5.0	5.5	6.1	6.6	7.5	7.9	8.5	9.9	11.7	14.8	19.3
Biceps	2.7	3.0	3.4	3.6	3.8	4.1	4.4	4.9	5.5	7.3	9.7
Subscapular	5.3	5.5	5.9	6.3	6.8	7.4	7.7	8.3	9.2	12.1	16.1
Iliac crest	4.8	5.3	6.2	6.6	7.2	8.3	9.1	10.5	13.8	17.9	25.9
Medial calf	5.1	5.4	6.1	7.0	7.8	8.8	9.3	10.5	12.7	16.4	21.0
Muscle girths (cm)											
Relaxed arm (skinfold-corrected)	19.9	21.0	22.0	22.7	23.3	23.8	24.6	25.1	26.0	26.8	28.2
Calf (skinfold-corrected)	28.1	28.7	29.6	30.3	31.0	31.6	32.2	32.7	33.6	34.6	36.0
Bone widths (mm)											
Humerus	63.6	65.3	67.5	68.5	69.6	70.5	71.5	72.4	74.0	76.1	78.0
Femur	89.1	91.0	92.6	94.8	95.8	97.3	98.5	100.0	101.7	103.9	106.4

Boys 16 Years of Age

						Percentiles					
	5	10	20	30	40	50	60	70	80	90	95
Height (cm)	160.9	165.5	168.3	170.6	172.5	173.6	175.7	177.4	180.0	183.4	185.6
Weight (kg)	51.0	53.8	57.0	59.5	61.1	63.3	65.8	69.5	73.8	77.0	82.7
Sum of 5 skinfolds (mm)	23.9	26.5	29.7	31.6	33.9	36.7	39.2	44.3	51.5	61.2	78.1
Skinfolds (mm)											
Triceps	4.9	5.2	6.0	6.8	7.3	8.0	8.8	9.9	11.4	13.7	16.3
Biceps	2.8	3.0	3.2	3.4	3.7	4.0	4.2	4.7	5.4	6.5	8.1
Subscapular	5.6	5.9	6.5	6.9	7.3	7.6	8.1	8.9	9.7	11.9	16.4
Iliac crest	4.6	5.1	6.0	6.8	7.5	8.4	9.5	11.1	13.6	18.3	
Medial calf	5.0	5.6	6.3	6.6	7.5	8.2	9.2	10.5	11.8	15.9	18.1
Muscle girths (cm)											
Relaxed arm (skinfold-corrected)	20.7	22.1	23.0	23.6	24.1	24.6	25.2	25.9	26.7	27.5	28.6
Calf (skinfold-corrected)	27.8	28.9	30.3	31.3	31.9	32.2	32.9	33.6	34.4	35.7	36.2
Bone widths (mm)											
Humerus	64.8	66.1	67.7	69.0	70.0	71.0	71.8	72.6	74.0	75.5	76.7
Femur	89.7	91.4	93.5	95.0	96.6	97.4	98.8	100.0	101.6	104.1	105.3

continued

Boys 17 Years of Age

						Percentiles					
	5	10	20	30	40	50	60	70	80	90	95
Height (cm)	164.6	166.3	169.5	171.9	173.7	175.5	176.4	178.0	179.7	182.1	185.1
Weight (kg)	53.4	55.5	58.1	61.0	64.0	66.0	68.4	70.7	74.0	78.7	84.3
Sum of 5 skinfolds (mm)	25.9	27.3	29.8	31.3	33.0	35.7	39.2	43.3	51.8	64.2	83.9
Skinfolds (mm)											
Triceps	4.9	5.4	5.9	6.4	6.9	7.6	8.6	9.6	11.5	14.2	17.7
Biceps	2.8	3.0	3.2	3.4	3.5	3.7	4.0	4.4	5.2	7.0	8.3
Subscapular	5.8	6.3	6.8	7.0	7.7	8.3	8.6	9.5	10.5	13.1	16.9
Iliac crest	4.8	5.5	6.2	7.0	8.1	8.8	9.7	11.0	14.3	19.6	25.0
Medial calf	4.5	4.9	5.8	6.4	7.0	7.6	8.6	9.9	11.3	14.3	18.0
Muscle girths (cm)											
Relaxed arm (skinfold-corrected)	21.8	22.4	23.6	24.5	25.0	25.4	26.1	26.7	27.7	28.6	29.8
Calf (skinfold-corrected)	28.7	29.9	30.5	31.4	32.1	32.7	33.3	33.9	34.5	35.5	36.4
Bone widths (mm)											
Humerus	65.2	67.1	68.4	69.4	70.1	71.0	71.9	73.0	73.9	75.9	77.4
Femur	90.8	92.0	93.5	94.8	96.0	97.0	98.0	99.2	101.0	104.1	106.6

Boys 18 Years of Age

						Percentiles					
	5	10	20	30	40	50	60	70	80	90	95
Height (cm)	164.6	168.8	170.7	172.2	174.2	175.4	176.7	178.5	180.4	183.1	184.9
Weight (kg)	56.7	58.3	62.3	64.3	66.4	67.8	69.8	73.8	77.8	82.4	86.8
Sum of 5 skinfolds (mm)	26.6	28.3	30.0	33.3	35.9	39.2	42.5	46.6	54.9	73.0	93.9
Skinfolds (mm)											
Triceps	4.6	5.5	6.0	6.7	7.3	7.9	8.9	10.1	12.1	16.6	19.7
Biceps	2.8	2.9	3.2	3.3	3.6	3.8	4.0	4.4	5.3	7.4	9.0
Subscapular	6.3	6.7	7.3	7.7	8.5	9.0	9.6	10.4	12.0	15.6	21.1
Iliac crest	5.1	5.9	6.9	7.6	8.6	10.0	11.1	12.9	16.0	20.4	28.4
Medial calf	4.8	5.1	5.7	6.3	7.1	7.9	8.6	9.9	11.5	14.8	18.6
Muscle girths (cm)											
Relaxed arm (skinfold-corrected)	23.0	24.1	24.7	25.4	25.9	26.4	27.0	27.8	28.4	29.2	29.8

	5	10	20	30	40	50	60	70	80	90	95
Calf (skinfold-corrected)	29.4	30.5	31.5	32.1	32.7	33.2	33.9	34.4	35.6	36.4	37.0
Bone widths (mm)											
Humerus	65.4	66.3	68.4	70.0	71.0	71.9	72.5	73.0	74.1	75.5	77.9
Femur	90.3	91.9	93.9	95.8	96.3	97.3	99.0	100.1	102.0	104.7	106.8

Girls 7 Years of Age

						Percentiles					
	5	10	20	30	40	50	60	70	80	90	95
Height (cm)	114.0	116.2	119.2	120.9	122.4	123.8	125.1	126.9	128.6	131.8	133.7
Weight (kg)	19.9	20.4	21.8	22.8	23.4	24.2	24.9	26.2	28.2	30.6	32.8
Sum of 5 skinfolds (mm)	25.3	27.2	30.7	33.0	34.4	37.3	40.9	43.5	47.3	65.7	78.0
Skinfolds (mm)											
Triceps	7.0	7.6	8.6	9.3	9.7	10.2	11.1	11.6	12.7	14.9	17.6
Biceps	3.3	3.7	4.2	4.5	4.8	5.2	5.6	6.1	7.2	9.1	11.2
Subscapular	4.2	4.4	4.8	5.1	5.4	5.8	6.3	7.2	8.3	11.2	15.0
Iliac crest	3.2	3.8	4.6	5.0	5.4	5.9	6.5	7.5	9.0	14.6	18.8
Medial calf	5.6	6.2	7.3	8.3	9.0	9.4	10.3	11.3	12.3	15.2	17.2
Muscle girths (cm)											
Relaxed arm (skinfold-corrected)	13.3	13.7	14.3	14.7	15.0	15.3	15.6	16.0	16.7	17.6	18.7
Calf (skinfold-corrected)	19.6	20.3	20.9	21.3	21.6	21.8	22.4	23.0	23.7	24.4	25.1
Bone widths (mm)											
Humerus	45.8	47.0	48.2	49.0	49.9	51.0	51.8	52.6	53.9	55.0	55.9
Femur	68.1	69.5	71.3	72.3	73.6	74.7	75.2	76.5	78.0	79.7	83.0

Girls 8 Years of Age

						Percentiles					
	5	10	20	30	40	50	60	70	80	90	95
Height (cm)	117.8	120.9	124.0	125.5	127.4	129.1	130.2	132.6	135.2	138.4	140.8
Weight (kg)	21.7	22.6	23.9	25.1	26.2	26.8	28.4	30.3	31.6	34.2	36.9
Sum of 5 skinfolds (mm)	25.4	27.2	30.5	33.5	35.7	39.5	42.7	49.7	54.5	70.4	85.4

(continued)

						Percentiles					
	5	10	20	30	40	50	60	70	80	90	95
Skinfolds (mm)											
Triceps	6.8	7.5	8.2	9.3	10.0	11.3	12.1	13.1	14.3	17.5	18.6
Biceps	3.4	3.8	4.3	4.6	5.0	5.4	6.1	6.9	8.1	10.3	11.7
Subscapular	4.3	4.6	5.0	5.5	5.9	6.2	6.9	8.1	9.2	12.9	16.3
Iliac crest	3.7	4.1	4.7	5.3	6.0	6.7	7.6	9.0	11.7	17.7	20.5
Medial calf	5.5	6.1	7.3	8.2	8.8	9.8	11.0	11.8	13.3	16.5	18.8
Muscle girths (cm)											
Relaxed arm (skinfold-corrected)	13.8	14.2	14.8	15.2	15.6	15.9	16.3	16.7	17.3	18.2	19.1
Calf (skinfold-corrected)	20.6	21.2	21.7	22.0	22.3	22.8	23.2	23.8	24.3	24.8	25.4
Bone widths (mm)											
Humerus	47.2	49.0	50.5	51.5	52.0	53.0	54.0	54.9	55.6	57.0	58.2
Femur	70.0	72.1	73.3	74.7	75.7	77.2	78.5	79.3	81.1	83.3	84.7

Girls 9 Years of Age

						Percentiles					
	5	10	20	30	40	50	60	70	80	90	95
Height (cm)	124.0	126.0	129.0	131.2	133.0	135.1	137.1	138.7	140.2	143.8	147.5
Weight (kg)	23.6	24.4	25.7	27.2	28.7	30.3	31.4	33.3	35.8	38.8	41.7
Sum of 5 skinfolds (mm)	25.8	29.8	32.6	35.3	39.7	43.3	47.5	51.7	58.9	66.0	85.4
Skinfolds (mm)											
Triceps	7.0	7.9	8.7	9.5	10.6	11.3	12.2	13.2	15.1	16.6	18.4
Biceps	3.7	4.0	4.4	4.9	5.6	6.1	6.7	7.4	8.0	9.8	12.5
Subscapular	4.4	4.7	5.2	5.7	6.2	6.7	7.3	8.2	9.8	12.3	15.2
Iliac crest	3.5	4.3	5.3	5.8	6.7	7.8	8.6	10.4	12.0	17.1	20.5
Medial calf	6.0	6.9	8.0	8.8	9.7	10.5	11.8	12.6	14.0	16.3	19.0
Muscle girths (cm)											
Relaxed arm (skinfold-corrected)	14.4	14.8	15.2	15.6	16.1	16.5	16.9	17.4	17.9	18.9	19.5
Calf (skinfold-corrected)	20.2	21.3	22.0	22.5	22.9	23.5	23.8	24.3	25.1	25.8	26.8
Bone widths (mm)											
Humerus	48.7	50.0	51.1	52.3	53.3	54.0	55.4	56.2	57.3	59.5	61.0
Femur	71.9	73.0	75.1	76.5	77.7	78.7	80.5	81.6	83.0	84.9	87.2

Girls 10 Years of Age

					Percentiles						
	5	10	20	30	40	50	60	70	80	90	95
Height (cm)	130.4	132.8	135.1	137.1	139.1	140.5	142.1	143.9	146.3	150.8	152.4
Weight (kg)	26.9	27.6	30.0	31.4	33.2	34.9	36.8	39.5	41.1	45.3	49.7
Sum of 5 skinfolds (mm)	28.5	31.4	34.7	39.7	44.3	47.8	52.5	59.0	70.6	81.7	92.6
Skinfolds (mm)											
Triceps	7.1	8.0	9.4	10.2	11.6	12.3	13.4	15.2	16.9	19.9	21.7
Biceps	3.6	4.3	4.9	5.2	5.9	6.5	7.4	8.3	9.8	11.9	13.6
Subscapular	4.7	5.1	5.6	6.2	6.9	7.6	8.4	9.9	12.3	16.3	21.7
Iliac crest	4.1	4.7	5.4	6.3	7.2	8.3	10.0	11.8	14.8	19.9	21.6
Medial calf	6.2	7.0	8.6	9.9	11.2	12.3	13.3	15.0	16.7	19.4	22.0
Muscle girths (cm)											
Relaxed arm (skinfold-corrected)	15.0	15.4	16.0	16.5	17.0	17.4	17.9	18.4	19.1	20.3	21.9
Calf (skinfold-corrected)	21.6	22.5	23.3	23.7	24.2	24.7	25.3	26.0	26.8	27.6	28.7
Bone widths (mm)											
Humerus	50.9	51.9	53.4	55.0	55.9	57.0	58.0	59.0	59.9	61.8	63.8
Femur	73.9	76.6	78.5	80.0	81.0	82.0	83.1	84.5	87.0	90.0	92.0

Girls 11 Years of Age

					Percentiles						
	5	10	20	30	40	50	60	70	80	90	95
Height (cm)	134.1	136.9	139.6	141.9	144.0	145.6	147.0	149.7	153.2	156.9	159.9
Weight (kg)	28.5	29.7	31.1	33.1	34.9	37.1	39.1	41.5	44.5	49.5	52.6
Sum of 5 skinfolds (mm)	27.9	30.3	33.7	37.3	39.8	43.3	46.4	55.2	66.0	83.2	93.8
Skinfolds (mm)											
Triceps	7.0	8.0	8.7	9.6	10.3	11.1	12.1	13.9	15.4	18.4	20.6
Biceps	3.6	4.0	4.5	4.9	5.3	5.9	6.5	7.7	9.2	11.5	13.0
Subscapular	4.8	5.1	5.5	6.2	6.5	7.0	7.6	8.6	10.7	14.6	18.8
Iliac crest	4.4	4.7	5.5	6.5	7.0	7.8	9.3	10.8	14.1	20.1	23.6
Medial calf	6.3	7.2	8.2	9.1	10.0	11.4	12.6	14.2	16.0	18.6	20.5
Muscle girths (cm)											
Relaxed arm (skinfold-corrected)	15.4	15.8	16.4	16.8	17.2	17.8	18.2	18.9	19.4	20.3	21.2

(continued)

	Percentiles										
	5	10	20	30	40	50	60	70	80	90	95
Calf (skinfold-corrected)	22.5	23.0	23.7	24.5	25.0	25.6	26.0	26.6	27.4	28.3	29.4
Bone widths (mm)											
Humerus	51.9	53.2	55.1	55.9	57.0	58.0	58.6	60.1	61.2	62.8	64.1
Femur	74.1	77.5	79.7	81.0	81.9	83.2	84.3	85.6	87.6	89.9	92.4

Girls 12 Years of Age

	Percentiles										
	5	10	20	30	40	50	60	70	80	90	95
Height (cm)	139.8	143.6	147.4	149.3	151.4	153.1	154.9	157.4	160.0	163.3	165.6
Weight (kg)	30.9	34.1	37.7	40.2	41.8	43.9	46.1	48.1	52.3	56.7	60.9
Sum of 5 skinfolds (mm)	29.5	33.6	38.3	41.0	43.9	48.3	51.6	57.8	68.6	80.8	95.7
Skinfolds (mm)											
Triceps	7.0	7.8	9.1	10.3	10.9	11.7	12.8	13.9	16.0	18.4	20.2
Biceps	3.4	3.9	4.7	5.2	5.8	6.3	7.0	7.6	8.2	11.1	12.3
Subscapular	5.1	5.5	6.6	7.1	7.7	8.2	8.9	9.9	11.8	14.4	18.1
Iliac crest	5.1	5.6	6.5	7.4	8.4	9.3	10.3	12.0	14.8	19.7	23.5
Medial calf	6.9	7.7	8.6	10.2	11.1	12.0	13.8	15.5	17.6	20.7	24.6
Muscle girths (cm)											
Relaxed arm (skinfold-corrected)	16.3	16.6	17.6	18.3	18.7	19.3	19.6	20.1	20.8	21.8	22.5
Calf (skinfold-corrected)	23.4	24.0	25.0	25.6	26.5	27.1	27.9	28.3	28.9	29.6	30.9
Bone widths (mm)											
Humerus	53.4	55.2	57.0	58.1	59.2	60.0	60.5	61.2	62.5	64.0	65.1
Femur	77.0	79.0	81.2	84.0	85.4	86.7	87.7	89.0	90.2	91.5	92.8

Girls 13 Years of Age

	Percentiles										
	5	10	20	30	40	50	60	70	80	90	95
Height (cm)	143.6	148.2	152.5	155.1	156.8	158.4	160.3	162.2	164.2	167.1	168.5
Weight (kg)	36.8	38.9	42.3	44.7	47.6	49.9	52.4	54.0	57.5	61.4	65.3

Sum of 5 skinfolds (mm)	31.9	34.7	40.0	43.6	46.4	52.2	58.6	64.6	76.3	86.5	95.8
Skinfolds (mm)											
Triceps	7.2	8.1	9.8	10.6	11.5	13.1	14.4	15.6	18.3	20.7	23.4
Biceps	3.7	4.3	4.7	5.2	6.1	6.4	7.0	7.9	9.1	11.1	13.2
Subscapular	5.4	6.2	7.0	7.5	8.3	8.9	10.0	10.9	13.2	17.1	20.3
Iliac crest	5.0	5.5	6.8	7.8	9.0	10.1	11.3	13.3	16.6	19.3	23.2
Medial calf	7.3	8.2	9.9	11.3	12.4	13.5	14.4	16.2	19.2	22.2	25.4
Muscle girths (cm)											
Relaxed arm (skinfold-corrected)	17.0	17.5	18.3	18.9	19.4	20.0	20.5	21.0	21.6	22.5	23.3
Calf (skinfold-corrected)	24.1	25.1	26.0	26.9	27.4	28.0	28.6	29.3	30.1	30.9	32.1
Bone widths (mm)											
Humerus	53.2	55.5	57.6	59.0	60.0	60.6	61.6	62.6	63.7	65.3	66.4
Femur	80.1	81.2	83.7	85.0	86.5	88.1	89.0	90.2	91.8	93.7	96.0

Girls 14 Years of Age

						Percentiles					
	5	10	20	30	40	50	60	70	80	90	95
Height (cm)	151.6	153.0	156.2	157.8	159.8	161.2	163.3	165.2	167.3	169.0	171.5
Weight (kg)	42.6	44.0	47.5	49.7	51.5	53.5	55.7	57.4	61.0	66.2	69.4
Sum of 5 skinfolds (mm)	33.4	36.9	41.7	47.5	54.3	59.6	66.1	70.9	77.1	93.3	106.9
Skinfolds (mm)											
Triceps	8.1	8.8	10.2	11.9	13.3	14.5	15.3	17.0	18.7	21.7	24.9
Biceps	3.7	4.2	5.0	5.8	6.4	7.1	7.8	8.7	10.0	12.1	14.7
Subscapular	6.2	6.7	7.4	8.4	9.3	9.9	10.9	12.3	14.2	18.4	21.7
Iliac crest	5.4	6.3	7.5	8.5	9.8	11.6	13.4	15.6	18.1	22.1	25.1
Medial calf	8.0	8.8	10.3	12.0	13.8	14.8	16.0	17.6	19.6	23.6	27.3
Muscle girths (cm)											
Relaxed arm (skinfold-corrected)	17.6	17.9	18.8	19.4	20.1	20.5	20.9	21.2	21.7	22.6	23.7
Calf (skinfold-corrected)	25.5	26.0	26.9	27.7	28.2	28.8	29.5	30.1	30.9	31.7	32.5
Bone widths (mm)											
Humerus	55.8	57.1	59.0	60.0	61.0	61.8	62.3	63.5	64.9	67.2	68.8
Femur	79.9	82.2	84.9	86.0	87.3	88.6	89.5	90.6	92.8	95.5	97.1

(continued)

Girls 15 Years of Age

					Percentiles						
	5	10	20	30	40	50	60	70	80	90	95
Height (cm)	151.3	153.7	156.3	158.6	160.9	162.1	164.1	165.5	167.1	169.5	172.0
Weight (kg)	43.9	44.6	48.3	51.1	52.8	54.7	57.6	59.7	61.7	65.3	68.3
Sum of 5 skinfolds (mm)	34.6	37.3	43.7	50.0	54.1	59.4	64.3	71.8	79.2	95.0	101.9
Skinfolds (mm)											
Triceps	8.5	9.3	10.9	11.9	13.5	14.8	16.0	17.4	19.2	21.6	22.9
Biceps	3.8	4.2	4.9	5.4	6.2	6.8	7.6	8.7	9.8	11.9	13.6
Subscapular	6.4	6.8	7.9	8.5	9.5	10.7	12.0	13.3	15.4	19.0	20.5
Iliac crest	5.7	6.2	7.5	8.5	9.7	11.2	12.4	14.8	17.2	21.9	24.6
Medial calf	7.4	8.7	11.0	12.4	13.5	14.6	15.9	18.3	20.0	23.0	25.6
Muscle girths (cm)											
Relaxed arm (skinfold-corrected)	17.5	18.3	19.2	19.5	20.0	20.4	21.0	21.4	22.2	23.3	24.1
Calf (skinfold-corrected)	25.6	26.1	27.1	27.5	28.4	29.0	29.7	30.3	31.0	31.8	32.4
Bone widths (mm)											
Humerus	55.3	57.0	58.7	60.0	61.0	62.0	62.4	63.0	64.0	65.9	67.1
Femur	80.4	82.6	84.8	86.5	87.6	88.5	89.8	91.2	92.4	95.0	96.8

Girls 16 Years of Age

					Percentiles						
	5	10	20	30	40	50	60	70	80	90	95
Height (cm)	151.9	154.4	157.2	159.1	160.8	162.1	163.8	165.0	166.1	169.8	172.6
Weight (kg)	44.9	46.7	49.4	51.4	52.6	54.6	55.8	58.3	61.6	66.4	69.2
Sum of 5 skinfolds (mm)	36.7	39.3	45.3	50.2	52.7	55.3	61.0	66.6	78.1	89.7	106.0
Skinfolds (mm)											
Triceps	9.3	10.5	11.5	12.6	13.9	14.8	16.0	17.4	18.6	21.5	24.5
Biceps	3.9	4.3	5.0	5.5	6.2	6.7	7.4	8.2	9.3	11.2	13.9
Subscapular	6.8	7.3	8.5	9.0	9.6	10.4	11.8	13.0	14.2	17.9	20.2
Iliac crest	5.2	6.7	7.5	8.8	9.6	10.9	11.7	13.4	16.0	20.8	23.4
Medial calf	7.4	8.7	10.0	11.4	12.9	13.9	15.4	17.0	19.1	23.0	27.1

Muscle girths (cm)

Relaxed arm (skinfold-corrected)	18.1	18.7	19.2	19.6	20.2	20.5	20.9	21.5	22.0	23.1	23.7
Calf (skinfold-corrected)	25.8	26.3	27.4	28.1	28.8	29.2	29.6	30.2	30.8	32.3	33.7

Bone widths (mm)

Humerus	55.7	56.9	58.9	60.0	60.5	61.5	62.4	63.4	64.4	65.2	67.0
Femur	80.6	82.0	84.5	85.6	87.0	88.3	89.6	91.0	92.4	95.5	99.8

Girls 17 Years of Age

					Percentiles						
	5	10	20	30	40	50	60	70	80	90	95
Height (cm)	151.9	154.2	157.2	159.5	161.3	162.5	164.5	166.6	169.0	172.0	174.2
Weight (kg)	44.5	46.1	49.1	51.4	53.3	55.9	57.8	59.7	63.7	67.5	72.8
Sum of 5 skinfolds (mm)	37.1	39.9	45.8	50.9	55.0	58.8	63.1	69.2	76.2	93.3	106.7

Skinfolds (mm)

Triceps	9.2	10.0	11.5	12.5	14.0	15.0	16.0	18.2	19.8	22.5	26.6
Biceps	4.0	4.5	5.0	5.5	6.1	6.9	7.7	8.4	9.9	11.9	14.4
Subscapular	6.9	7.4	8.4	9.2	10.3	11.1	12.6	13.8	15.1	17.9	23.3
Iliac crest	5.5	6.3	7.4	8.8	10.1	11.0	12.0	14.6	17.0	21.0	24.5
Medial calf	8.2	9.2	10.7	12.6	13.6	14.9	15.9	17.7	19.7	22.7	27.1

Muscle girths (cm)

Relaxed arm (skinfold-corrected)	18.0	18.4	19.1	19.7	20.5	20.9	21.5	21.9	22.4	23.1	24.6
Calf (skinfold-corrected)	25.8	26.3	27.5	27.8	28.6	29.0	29.6	30.4	31.1	32.1	33.1

Bone widths (mm)

Humerus	56.7	58.0	59.6	60.7	61.3	62.0	63.0	63.7	64.6	65.9	67.2
Femur	81.4	83.1	85.0	86.7	87.5	88.3	89.1	90.6	93.0	95.2	97.1

Girls 18 Years of Age

					Percentiles						
	5	10	20	30	40	50	60	70	80	90	95
Height (cm)	150.4	154.5	157.2	159.1	161.0	162.6	165.1	166.5	168.4	170.3	173.2
Weight (kg)	45.7	47.4	50.2	52.7	54.6	56.3	58.0	61.4	64.1	72.4	77.9
Sum of 5 skinfolds (mm)	35.6	41.9	46.8	51.9	56.8	62.9	67.8	72.3	79.5	105.2	114.9

(continued)

					Percentiles						
	5	10	20	30	40	50	60	70	80	90	95
Skinfolds (mm)											
Triceps	9.4	10.1	11.5	12.4	13.8	15.7	17.1	19.3	21.1	24.2	27.1
Biceps	3.8	4.1	5.0	5.5	6.4	7.0	7.5	8.3	10.2	12.2	15.0
Subscapular	7.4	8.1	9.1	10.2	11.2	12.0	12.4	14.6	16.2	21.3	26.8
Iliac crest	5.3	6.2	7.9	9.1	10.4	11.7	13.3	15.0	18.3	21.8	25.7
Medial calf	7.9	9.2	10.8	12.3	13.9	15.9	17.0	19.0	21.2	25.6	27.7
Muscle girths (cm)											
Relaxed arm (skinfold-corrected)	17.6	18.4	19.3	20.1	20.3	21.0	21.5	22.0	22.9	24.3	24.8
Calf (skinfold-corrected)	24.3	26.5	27.7	28.4	29.0	29.8	30.2	30.7	31.2	32.3	33.5
Bone widths (mm)											
Humerus	56.9	57.9	58.8	59.8	60.8	61.9	62.5	63.5	64.8	66.4	67.6
Femur	81.3	82.6	84.7	85.6	87.9	89.0	90.1	91.3	92.8	95.0	99.1

The information in these tables is compiled from the public-use database of the 1981 Canada Fitness Survey. Copies of the database can be purchased from Canadian Fitness and Lifestyle Research Institute, 185 Somerset West, Suite 201, Ottawa, ON K2P 0J2. The Canada Fitness Survey was conducted in 1981 by "Canada Fitness Survey," a nongovernmental organization incorporated under the name of Canadian Fitness and Lifestyle Research Institute in December 1985. Funding for the survey came from Fitness Canada, a former federal department now merged with Health Canada and known as the Fitness Directorate.

REFERENCES

Borkan, G.A., Hults, D.E., Gerzof, S.G., Robbins, A.H., & Silbert, C.K. (1983). Age changes in body composition revealed by computed tomography. *Journal of Gerontology*, **38**, 673-677.

de Ridder, C.M. , de Boer, R.W. , Seidell, J.C., Nieuwenhoff, C.M., Jeneson, J.A.L., Bakker, C.J.G., Zonderland, M., & Erich, W.B.M. (1992). Body fat distribution in pubertal girls quantified by magnetic resonance imaging. *International Journal of Obesity*, **16**, 443-449.

Deurenberg, P., Pieters, J.J.L., & Hautvast, J.G. (1990). The assessment of the body fat percentage by skinfold thickness in childhood and young adolescence. *British Journal of Nutrition*, **63**, 293-303.

Durnin, J.V. & Womersley, J. (1974). Body fat assessed from total body density and its estimation from skinfold thickness: Measurements on 481 men and women aged from 16 to 72 years. *British Journal of Nutrition*, **32**, 77-97.

Elia, M., Parkinson, S.A., & Diaz, E. (1990). Evaluation of near infra-red interactance as a method for predicting body composition. *European Journal of Clinical Nutrition*, **44**, 113-121.

Eston, R.G., Kreitzman, S., Lamb, K.L., Brodie, D.A., Robson, S., & Carney, J. (1990). Assessment of fat-free mass by hydrodensitometry, skinfolds, infra-red interactance and electrical impedance in boys and girls aged 11-12 years. *Journal of Sports Science*, **8**, 174-185.

Fitness Canada. (1987). *Canadian standardised test of fitness: Operations manual* (3rd ed.). Ottawa, ON: Fitness and Amateur Sport.

Forbes, G.B. (1987). *Human body composition*. New York: Springer-Verlag.

Freedman, D.S., Shear, C.L., Burke, G.L., Webber, L.S., Harsha, D.W., & Berenson, G.S. (1987). Persistence of juvenile-onset obesity over eight years: The Bogalusa heart study. *American Journal of Public Health*, **77**, 588-592.

Haschke, F. (1983). Body composition of adolescent males. Part II. Body composition of male reference adolescents. *Acta Paediatrica Scandinavica*, **307**(Suppl.), 13-23.

Hoffer, E.T., Meador, C.K., & Simpson, D.C. (1969). Correlation of whole body impedance with total body water. *Journal of Applied Physiology*, **27**, 531-534.

Kay-Covington, N., Kluka, D.A., & Love, P.A. (1990). Relationship between bioelectric impedance and anthropometric techniques to determine body fat in a black pediatric population. *Pediatric Exercise Science*, **2**, 140-148.

Krotkiewski, M., Björntorp, P., Sjöstrom, L., & Smith, U. (1983). Impact of obesity on metabolism in men and women: Importance of regional adipose tissue distribution. *Journal of Clinical Investigation*, **72**, 1150-1162.

Lapidus, L., Bergtsson, C., Larsson, B., Pennert, K., Rybo, E., & Sjostrom, L. (1984). Distribution of adipose tissue and risk of cardiovascular disease and death: A 12 year follow up of participants in the population study of women in Gothenburg, Sweden. *British Medical Journal*, **289**, 1257-1261.

Larsson, B., Svardsudd, K., Welin, L., Wilhelmsen, L., Björntorp, P., & Tibblin, G. (1984). Abdominal adipose tissue distribution, obesity, and risk of cardiovascular disease and death: 13 years follow up of participants in the study of men born in 1913. *British Medical Journal*, **288**, 1401-1404.

Lohman, T.G. (1981). Skinfolds and body density and their relation to body fatness: A review. *Human Biology*, **53**, 181-225.

Lohman, T.G. (1984). Research progress in validation of laboratory methods of assessing body composition. *Medicine and Science in Sports and Exercise*, **16**, 596-603.

Lohman, T.G. (1985). Research relating to assessment of skeletal status. In A.F. Roche (Ed.), *Body composition assessment in youth and adults, Report on the sixth Ross conference on medical research* (pp. 38-41). Columbus, Ohio: Ross Laboratories.

Martin, A.D., & Drinkwater, D.T. (1991). Variability in the measures of body fat, assumptions or technique? *Sports Medicine*, **11**, 277-288.

Martin, A.D., Ross, W.D., Drinkwater, D.T., & Clarys, J.P. (1985). Prediction of body fat by skinfold caliper: Assumptions and cadaver evidence. *International Journal of Obesity*, **9**(Suppl. 1), 31-39.

Martin, A.D., Spenst, L.F., Drinkwater, D.T., & Clarys, J.P. (1990). Anthropometric estimation of muscle mass in men. *Medicine and Science in Sports and Exercise*, **22**, 729-733.

Matiegka, J. (1921). The testing of physical efficiency. *American Journal of Physical Anthropology*, **4**, 223-230.

Parizkova, J. (1961). Total body fat and skinfold thickness in children. *Metabolism*, **10**, 794-807.

Ross, W.D., Crawford, S.M., Kerr, D.A., Ward, R., Bailey, D.A., & Mirwald, R.M. (1988). Relationship of the body mass index with skinfolds, girths, and bone breadths in Canadian men and women aged 20-70 years, *American Journal of Physical Anthropology*, **77**, 169-173.

Ross, W.D., & Ward, R. (1989). *The advanced O-scale physique assessment system.* Burnaby, BC: Kinemetrix.

Ross, W.D., & Wilson, N.C. (1974). A stratagem for proportional growth assessment. *Acta Paediatrica Belgica, 28*(Suppl.), 169-182.

Sheng, H.P., & Huggins, R.A., (1979). A review of body composition studies with emphasis on total body water and fat. *American Journal of Clinical Nutrition, 32,* 630-647.

Siri, W.E. (1956). The gross composition of the body. In C.A. Tobias & J.H. Lawrence (Eds.), *Advances in biological and medical physics* (Vol. 4, pp. 239-280). New York: Academic Press.

von Döbeln, W. (1964). Determination of body constituents. In G. Blix (Ed.), *Occurrences, causes, and prevention of overnutrition* (pp. 103-106). Upsala: Almquist and Wiksell.

Westrate, J.A., & Deurenberg, P. (1989). Body composition in children, proposal for a method for calculating body fat percentage from total body density or skinfold thickness measurements. *American Journal of Clinical Nutrition, 50,* 1104-1115.

3

Robert A. Faulkner

Maturation

The terms *growth* and *maturation*, although sometimes used interchangeably, refer to distinct biological activities. Growth refers to an increase in the size of the body as a whole or the size attained by specific parts of the body, and maturation refers to the tempo and timing of progress toward the mature biological state. Growth focuses on size, and maturation focuses on the progress of attaining size (Malina & Bouchard, 1991).

Chronological age is a poor marker of biological maturity. At any given age maturational differences cause children to differ greatly in work capacity and motor competence (Rowland, 1990). These differences create many problems when studying the effects of physical training in children or in assessing exercise or sport performance in children. Techniques which estimate biological age are thus important in understanding the effects of physical activity on physiological function in children and in understanding performance of children and adolescents in sport and physical activity.

Techniques for estimating maturity vary depending on the biological system being assessed. Commonly used systems include skeletal maturation, sexual maturation, and somatic (physique) maturation. Dental maturation is also used, but is not as common.

This chapter describes the above methods, but focuses primarily on field techniques such as the assessment of sexual maturation. Skeletal-age assessment techniques are very complex, and a full description is beyond the scope of this chapter. Special concerns and considerations in using the various procedures are discussed.

GROWTH AND MATURATIONAL CHARACTERISTICS OF CHILDREN AND YOUTH

The principal physical events of puberty include the adolescent growth spurt and the development of reproductive organs and secondary sex characteristics. Changes also occur in body composition and in the cardiorespiratory system. Skeletal age is the only maturational indicator that can be applied over the entire growth period, but as discussed in a later section, it is generally not a good predictor of pubertal events. Using pubertal events as indicators of maturation level is by definition limited to the adolescent period.

There is not much difference in growth or growth rates between boys and girls until adolescence. The time during adolescence where maximum gains in stature are attained is defined as peak height velocity (PHV). The relationship of PHV to other key pubertal events is illustrated in Figure 3.1. There is considerable variation among children in the age of onset, intensity, and duration of biological maturity events.

Data from North American and European studies show that peak height (stature) velocity occurs at about 12 years of age in girls and at about 14 years of age in boys; the normal variation ranges from about 9.3 to 15 years for girls and from about 12 to 16 years for boys (Largo, Gasser, Prader, Stuetzle, & Huba, 1978; Malina, 1989; Preece & Baines, 1978). The absolute PHV value may vary considerably among children, ranging from about 7 to 12 cm/year in boys and from about 6 to 11 cm/year in girls (Marshall & Tanner, 1986). Girls on average are advanced in maturity compared to boys; their advancement is evident in the onset of secondary sex characteristics. There is greater sex difference in the age of PHV than in the onset of the secondary sex characteristics. For example, on average, girls' PHV is about 2 years ahead of boys, but boys' genitalia development begins only about 6 months later than the onset of girls' breast development (Marshall & Tanner, 1970).

In general these characteristics proceed in the order shown in Figure 3.1, although the order of onset and the duration of the development may vary considerably in normal healthy children; for example, in some children pubic hair may precede genital or breast development (Malina & Bouchard, 1991). The onset of the first menstrual cycle (menarche) in girls is a late maturational event that occurs (on average) about one year after PHV, but the normal range is from 0 to 2.5 years after PHV (Danker-Hopfe, 1986; Marshall & Tanner, 1969). Less than 1% of girls experience menarche prior to PHV (Marshall & Tanner, 1986). Breast development in girls may begin anywhere between 8 and 13 years of age. Some girls will have reached adult status in breast development by age 13, but others may not reach full development until age 19 (Marshall & Tanner, 1969). Adult pubic hair distribution is usually obtained between 12 and 17 years of age (Marshall & Tanner, 1986). In boys genitalia development may begin as early as 9 years of age or as late as 14 or 15 years, and pubic hair development may begin as early as 11 or as late as 15 years of age (Largo & Prader, 1983; Marshall & Tanner, 1970; Taranger, Lichtenstein, & Svennberg-Redegren, 1976).

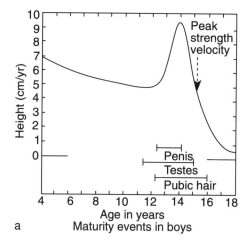

a   Maturity events in boys

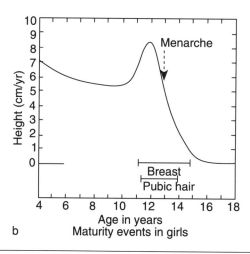

b   Maturity events in girls

Figure 3.1   Sequence of maturational events in boys (a) and girls (b).
Note. The solid bars indicate the period of accelerated development in the biological
marker. Testicular development generally is the first sign of puberty in boys. The spurt in
height (PHV) and penis and pubic hair growth begin about 1 year later. There is a peak
gain in strength about .5-1 year after PHV. Breast budding is usually the first physical
sign of puberty in girls; this occurs just after the onset of the growth spurt in height. Menarche generally comes later, occurring after PHV. In both boys and girls the whole sequence of events may normally occur 2 or more years earlier or later than average.
Reprinted from Ross, Brown, Faulkner, Vajda, and Savage (1976).

Other less commonly used markers of secondary sex characteristics are axillary hair, facial hair, and voice change. Although there are not extensive data on these indicators, the available data suggest that these are relatively late maturational events that usually occur near or shortly after PHV (Neyzi, Alp, Yalcindag, Yakacikli, & Orhon, 1975; Taranger et al., 1976).

Gradients in Growth

Peak gains in growth occur for body dimensions other than height and weight. It is beyond the scope of this chapter to discuss the other dimensions, but in general the peak velocities follow a pattern similar to height (although the timing may be different). A comprehensive analysis of other dimensions, such as widths, tissue masses, and segmental lengths, has been presented by Marshall and Tanner (1986) and Malina and Bouchard (1991). During puberty trunk length generally increases at a greater rate than leg length does in both boys and girls (Eveleth, 1978). Girls, however, gain relatively more height in the trunk, while boys gain relatively more height in the legs (compared to girls). In the lower limbs peak gains occur first in the feet; in the upper limbs peak velocities occur first in the hands, followed by the forearms, and finally the upper arms (Cameron, Tanner, & Whitehouse, 1982). Peak gains in shoulder and hip breadths usually coincide with peak velocity in trunk length (Tanner, Whitehouse, Marubini, & Rebele, 1976). Peak growth velocity for weight (PWV) generally occurs after PHV. Peak weight velocity is (on average) greater in boys than girls and usually occurs sooner after PHV in boys (0.2-0.4 years after PHV in boys and 0.3-0.9 years after PHV in girls). There are also differences in tissue growth between girls and boys. Boys put on greater muscle tissue during puberty, and girls put on more fat tissue. Peak muscle mass gains occur shortly after PHV in boys (Rasmussen, Faulkner, Mirwald, & Bailey, 1990). Most boys also experience a peak gain in strength about 0.5 to 1 year after PHV (Beunen et al., 1992; Carron & Bailey, 1974; Rasmussen et al., 1990; Stolz & Stolz, 1951). Peak gains in strength are more variable in girls than in boys, but generally occur near PHV (Faust, 1977). Many girls actually have a decline in strength after PHV.

Both absolute and relative (to size) heart and lung volumes increase during puberty. In boys there is a testosterone-induced increase in hemoglobin concentration (Krabbe, Christensen, Worm, Christiansen, & Transbol, 1978); thus boys have a greater oxygen carrying capacity and subsequent advantage in endurance exercise compared to girls.

Variations in Growth Parameters and Maturity

The criteria for classifying children into maturity categories based on different maturation assessments have been suggested by Malina and Bouchard (1991). In applying skeletal age (SA) techniques, children assessed as ±1 year or less of their chronological age would be classified as "average" maturers, children whose SA is delayed by more than 1 year would be classified as "late" maturers, and those whose SA is advanced by more than 1 year would be classified as "early" maturers. Similar systems are also used with other maturation indicators, such as age of menarche or PHV; that is, children within ±1 year of the "average" values for these criteria would be classified as "average" maturers, those advanced by more than 1 year would be classified as "early" maturers, and those delayed by more than 1 year would be classified as "late" maturers.

Maturity-related physique differences among children are most evident when comparing early to late maturers. In reviewing data from a variety of sources (Clarke, 1971; Dupertuis & Michael, 1953; Johnston & Malina, 1966; Lindgren, 1978; Reynolds, 1946; Shuttleworth, 1939; Zuk, 1958), Malina and Bouchard (1991) noted the following: Early maturers tend to be heavier and taller (at all ages) when they are compared to late maturers. Final adult stature, however, is generally similar. Early maturers tend to have broader hips and relatively narrower shoulders when compared to late maturers, and late maturers tend to have relatively greater leg lengths and relatively shorter trunks compared to early maturers. In terms of body shape (somatotype), late maturers tend to be more ectomorphic, and early maturers more endomorphic and mesomorphic. As would be expected, early maturing boys tend to have greater muscle mass at any given age, but when controlling for size differences there is generally not much maturity-associated difference. The exception is at the upper ends of muscularity where early maturers tend to have greater muscularity even when controlling for size differences. Early maturing boys have more fat tissue at all ages, but there is not much difference in final adult values between early and late maturers. In contrast, early maturing girls have greater fat mass at all ages compared to late maturers, and this difference remains in post-adolescence.

Maturity Events and Performance

Data from several studies show an adolescent spurt in performance tasks in boys but not in girls. Beunen et al. (1988) analyzed performance data in a longitudinal study on boys in Belgium. Spurts in muscular strength and endurance tasks generally began about 1.5 years prior to PHV and reached peak gains about 0.5 to 1 year after PHV. In contrast peak gains in speed and flexibility tasks occurred prior to PHV. Beunen's data also showed a positive velocity in motor tasks during the adolescent growth spurt in stature. According to Malina and Bouchard (1991), this result indicates that, on average, there is no "period of awkwardness" during adolescence, as has been suggested in the growth and development literature. Malina and Bouchard caution, however, that some boys do show negative velocities in performance during adolescence; therefore, as is the case with many aspects of growth, individual variation must be recognized.

There is no data directly relating PHV to motor performance in girls, but Espenschade (1940) investigated the relationship of menarche (which occurs after PHV) to motor-performance skills. In general no specific trends were found, and changes in motor performance over the span of 1.5 years prior to menarche to 3.5

years after menarche were relatively small. Girls do not exhibit the definite peak strength gain that is seen in boys.

Absolute maximal aerobic power ($L \cdot min^{-1}$) begins to increase several years prior to PHV, and peak gains occur close to or just after PHV (Mirwald & Bailey, 1986). Boys in general have greater gains in absolute maximal aerobic power than do girls. The increase in absolute $\dot{V}O_2max$ reflects the growth-induced increase in body mass and the greater oxygen carrying capacity secondary to increased hemoglobin concentration. Relative maximal aerobic power ($ml \cdot kg^{-1} \cdot min^{-1}$) actually begins to decline about 1 year prior to PHV and may continue to decline for several years after PHV. Similar declines in relative $\dot{V}O_2max$ in post-menarcheal girls also have been shown (Malina & Bouchard, 1991). The decline in relative $\dot{V}O_2max$ is attributable to the rapid increase in body mass during the adolescent growth spurt. The increased fat mass associated with sexual maturation in girls has a major impact on the decline in relative $\dot{V}O_2max$. The results of data using relative $\dot{V}O_2max$ should be treated with caution, as simply dividing absolute $\dot{V}O_2$ by body mass may be misleading because this ratio does not adequately account for growth-related size changes (Winter, 1992).

In summary, boys in general show peak gains in a variety of motor tasks during the adolescent growth period, whereas girls generally do not exhibit peak gains. In general there are few gender differences in performance in preadolescence, although when biological age is considered boys on average perform better (Bailey, Malina, & Mirwald, 1986). The gender differences increase markedly during adolescence however. It may be that other factors (e.g., social and personal considerations) influence girls to be physically active and to perform physical tasks (Malina & Bouchard, 1991); however, these factors are difficult to quantify.

Maturity Status and Performance

Maturity status is related to performance in skills requiring strength, motor performance, aerobic, or anaerobic power.

Strength.   Malina and Bouchard (1991) (based on data from Jones, 1949, on grip and push strength) reported early maturing boys to be generally stronger at all ages compared to normal and late maturers; no consistent differences appeared among maturation groups in girls. In boys the strength differences among maturation groups remained after controlling for body weight and stature; this difference likely reflects an increase in muscle mass associated with the adolescent growth spurt. In contrast, the late maturing girls were actually stronger than the early maturers when controlling for body weight, and there were no differences when adjusting for stature. This result is explained by the relative tissue mass changes during adolescence in girls; that is, there is a relative increase in fat tissue and a relative decrease in lean tissue.

Motor Performance.   Beunen, Ostyn, Simons, Renson, and Van Gerven (1980) compared several motor tasks among early-, average-, and the late-maturing boys and girls 11 to 18 years of age. Early-maturing boys, in general, performed better than average- or late-maturing boys even when performance was controlled for body size. By 18 years of age, however, there was no difference between average and early maturers, while the performance of late maturers equalled the other groups in some tasks. The variation among maturity groups in girls was inconsistent across tasks and age. Early-maturing girls performed better in an arm-pull exercise, but there was no difference when controlling for body weight. Later maturers performed better in tasks requiring body mass movement during early adolescence, but did not differ from early or average maturers by age 14 and 15. These differences in early adolescence are explained by the relative increase in fat tissue during puberty in girls (the early maturers gain fat tissue earlier than the later maturers).

Aerobic Power.   Early-maturing boys and girls have, on average, greater absolute $\dot{V}O_2$max than late maturers (Kemper, Vershuur, & Ritmeester, 1987; Mirwald & Bailey, 1986). The differences are greater for boys than girls. In contrast, late maturing boys and girls have greater relative $\dot{V}O_2$max (ml-kg$^{-1} \cdot$ min^{-1}) than early maturers. As pointed out by Malina and Bouchard (1991), the difference in relative aerobic power in girls is likely explained by the relatively greater fat mass in early maturing girls. In boys the difference likely reflects the rapid increase in overall body mass during adolescence as well as the increased heart and lung volumes and higher hemoglobin levels associated with the adolescent growth period.

Anaerobic Power.   Early maturers are at an advantage in performing anaerobic activities. Preadolescent children are not mature in their capacity to derive energy from the anaerobic lactate pathway; this is due to lower glycogen stores and lower concentrations of PFK, a glycolytic rate-limiting enzyme (Bailey et al., 1986).

Application to Sport and Physical Activity

The most common age range for youth sports is generally from 11 to 16 years, the period of greatest variation among adolescents in maturity status. On average, advanced-maturing boys and girls are bigger and stronger than their less advanced peers. Earlier-maturing boys (at any chronological age) have greater muscle mass and typically are stronger than later maturers. Young male athletes in baseball, football, track, swimming, and rowing (i.e., sports where size may be an advantage) tend to be more advanced maturationally (Bailey et al., 1986). As adolescence proceeds, the size and performance of late maturers tend to "catch-up" to the early maturers. In contrast, young figure skaters and gymnasts (sports where greater size can be a disadvantage) tend to be delayed maturers (Malina, Meleski, & Shoup, 1982; Ross, Brown, & Faulkner, 1977). Late maturing girls often perform better than their more advanced peers, and the performance advantage tends to persist throughout adolescence and into early adulthood. This difference is related to the increased fat mass associated with the onset of secondary sex characteristics in girls. This extra mass is a detriment in skills that require moving body mass through space; thus female track athletes, gymnasts, figure skaters, and ballet dancers tend to be delayed maturationally. Conversely, young female swimmers tend to be advanced maturationally.

Finally, it is important to emphasize that many factors contribute to success in sport and other physical-activity skills; these include motivation, accessibility, coaching, and social environment, as well as physical ability. Maturation level is simply one more factor that may contribute to this complex phenomenon.

ASSESSING SKELETAL AGE

Skeletal maturation is thought to be the best method for assessing biological age or maturity status, and it is the only method that spans the entire growth period—from birth to adulthood (Malina & Bouchard, 1991). The skeleton develops from cartilage in the prenatal period to fully developed bone in early adulthood. Skeletal age assessment is based on the fact that a more mature child will have more bone development and less cartilage than a less advanced child has. X-rays are used to determine the amount of bone development and how close the shape and contours of the bones are to adult status. The assessment of skeletal maturity is based on recognition of maturity indicators; these radiographically visible features assist the determination of the maturity level of a bone (Roche, 1980). The indicators reflect the development of calcified or ossified areas of bone and the external contour changes that result from bone growth and ossification (Roche, 1986). To be useful an indicator must occur during the maturation of every child (Hoerr, Pyle, & Francis, 1962), The hand-wrist area of the left hand is the site most often used as indicator. It is an ideal area because it is distanced from the gonads (reducing the risk of X-ray exposure), there are many bones to assess in the area, and it is reasonably typical of the skeleton as a whole. A typical hand-wrist X-ray for an 8-year-old boy is illustrated in Figure 3.2.

Three methods used to evaluate skeletal development are Greulich-Pyle (Greulich & Pyle, 1959), Tanner-Whitehouse (Tanner, Whitehouse, Marshall, Healy, & Goldstein, 1975; Tanner et al., 1983), and Fels (Roche, Chumlea, & Thissen, 1988). The systems are complex and require extensive experience to be used accurately and reliably; therefore, only a brief explanation of each system follows.

Greulich-Pyle Method

The Greulich-Pyle method (GP) involves matching a child's X-ray to a standard plate in an *atlas*. The standards were derived from a high socioeconomic status white population in Cleveland, Ohio. The radiograph of the hand-wrist is compared to age-standard plates from the atlas until a match is found. The atlas plates are based on yearly intervals from birth to 19 years; there are separate plates for boys and girls. An example of a standard plate for a 14-year-old girl is shown in Figure 3.3. Often it is necessary and/or desirable to interpolate between the standards. This is done by assessing bone-specific ages of the individual bones based on descriptions of the maturity indicators for each bone in the hand-wrist X-ray. An example of a maturity indicator for the distal radius is shown in Figure 3.4. Usually, subjective

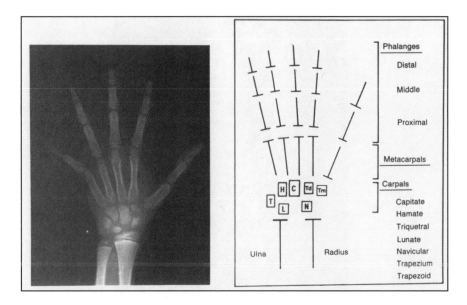

Figure 3.2 A hand–wrist X-ray of a boy showing the specific bones that are used to assess skeletal age.
Reprinted from Malina and Bouchard (1991).

impressions of each bone or a combination of certain bones (depending on the stage of development and the purpose of the assessment) are used to determine the specific bone age. The accuracy of the GP method is not known, but inter- and intratester reliability has been reported to ± 0.5 years in 95% of cases (Greulich and Pyle, 1959).

The atlas method is attractive because it provides vivid visual guides for matching X-rays, but it has several limitations. The GP method rates maturity on an age scale which is more than 30 years old. The matching process gives the most likely chronological age for the child being matched, as judged from the X-ray. Matching children at the extreme age groups is thus difficult; more importantly, the relationship between actual age and maturity is not necessarily constant across populations or over time within a single population (Tanner et al., 1975). For example, the hand-wrist plates in the atlas are generally in advance of the mean levels of maturation in American children (Roche, 1986).

Tanner-Whitehouse (TW2-20; TW2-RUS; TW2-Carpal Method)

Three systems, based on similar procedures, have been developed by Tanner et al. (1975, 1983). The systems are based on assigning numerical scores based on written criteria to bones depending on their levels of maturity. The systems use either eight or nine (depending on the bone assessed) stages (A to H or I): Stage A always

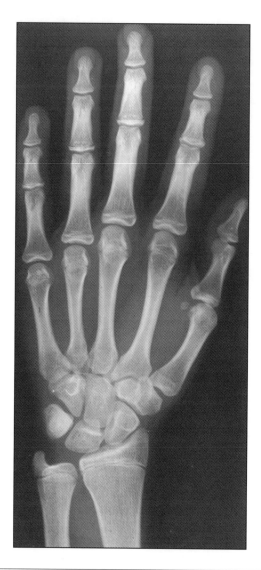

Figure 3.3 Greulich-Pyle reference plate for skeletal age 14 for girls. The epiphyseal cartilage plates of the radius and ulna are now appreciably reduced in thickness. The fusion
of the epiphysis of the first metacarpal with its shaft is now completed, although the line
of fusion is still distinct. Epiphyseal–diaphyseal fusion is well under way, also, in the second, third, fourth, and fifth metacarpals. Fusion is now almost complete in the proximal
phalanges of the second, third, and fourth fingers, and it is completed in the fifth. This
process is almost completed in the middle phalanx of the second finger, and it is well advanced in the middle phalanges of the third, fourth, and fifth fingers.
Reprinted from Greulich and Pyle (1959).

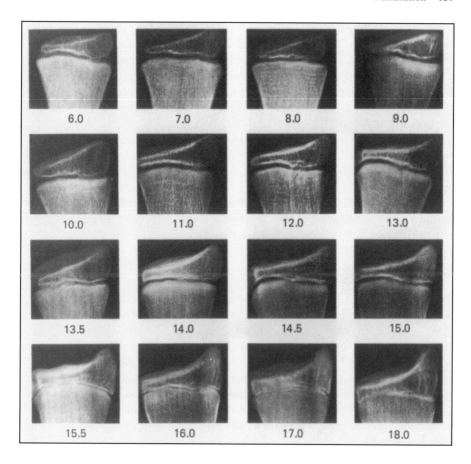

Figure 3.4 Example of a maturity indicator for the distal radius in boys aged 6 to 18 years. The value below each insert is the Greulich-Pyle skeletal age (years) for the stage of development.
Reprinted from Roche (1986).

indicates absence of bone formation, and Stage H or Stage I represents adult bone status. Each bone is given a weighted value, and the total value for all the bones evaluated for the specific method is summarized as an overall maturity score.

The TW2-20 system entails matching 20 individual bones in the hand and wrist to a set of written criteria. Many of the bones of the hand and wrist have been found to give nearly the same information about maturity; the carpal bones have been found to give different (and perhaps less accurate) information about the maturity process than the information from the long bones (Tanner et al., 1975). In order to allow for these possible confounders, the RUS and Carpal systems were developed. The RUS system includes the radius, ulna, and the finger bones; and the Carpal system includes only the carpal bones (see Figure 3.2). The partitioning of the bones is particularly useful in adolescence, because the carpals often attain maturity by about age 13, while the radius, ulna, and finger bones are still maturing (Malina & Bouchard, 1991). An example of a 9-year-old boy assessed by the three systems is shown in Table 3.1. As indicated in Table 3.1 the three systems are not interchangeable, because the bone age ranges from 9.5 years to 10.6 years. It is therefore imperative that researchers and clinicians identify the specific system used in any assessment.

The bone maturity scores can be interpreted by relating them to a set of standards. For example, a centile (Figure 3.5) can be used directly to state where a given child is in relation to the standard; for example, a child might be rated at the 25th centile for a RUS score, etc.

Reliability of the TW2 system is thought to be slightly greater than the GP; repeat measures on the same radiograph are less than 0.5 years in 95% of the cases (Tanner et al., 1975).

Fels Method

The Fels Method (FM) is the newest technique. As with the other methods, the technique involves matching criteria measures to the X-ray of the hand and wrist. As with the TW2 system, the X-ray is matched to specific criteria for each bone. The FM is unique in calculating a standard error for the skeletal age estimate, and the calculations have been programmed for a microcomputer (Roche et al., 1988). Specific indicators of the various bones are given a weighted value depending on the child's age. For example, complete union of the epiphysis of the radius may occur over several years, but the appearance of a specific maturity indicator of another bone may be present only for a brief period; therefore, the radius would be given less weighting and the other bone more weighting in the calculation. The reference sample for the Fels method is from American children studied between 1932 and 1972 as part of the Fels Longitudinal Study.

Comparing the Methods

The strengths and weaknesses of the different methods must be taken into account in determining a method of choice. All three methods (GP, TW2, FM) yield a skeletal age that corresponds to the level of skeletal maturity attained by a child relative to a reference sample, but the methods cannot be used interchangeably (Malina, 1989). They differ in scoring systems, are based on different reference samples, and the skeletal ages derived are not equivalent (Malina & Bouchard, 1991).

Skeletal age (SA) can be expressed relative to the child's chronological age (CA). For example a child who has a CA age of 11 and a SA of 13 is maturationally advanced by 2 years; conversely, a child with a CA of 13 and a SA of 11 would be classified as delayed by 2 years.

Skeletal age assessment has many strengths, but the techniques require expensive equipment and highly trained technicians, and involve exposure to X-ray dosage; SA is therefore primarily limited to research and clinical applications.

Table 3.1   An Example of Assigning Maturity Scores for a 9-Year-Old Boy, Showing the Centile Score and the Bone Age Score Derived from the TW2 Standards

Bone	Rating	29-bone score	RUS score	Carpal score
Radius	F	48	59	
Ulna	E	39	40	
Metacarpal I	E	19	21	
III	F	16	19	
V	F	17	18	
Proximal phalanx I	E	15	17	
III	E	13	15	
V	E	13	15	
Middle phalanx III	E	13	15	
V	E	14	15	
Distal phalanx I	E	14	17	
III	F	16	18	
V	F	16	18	
Capitate	H	116		214
Hamate	G	81		159
Triquetral	G	45		102
Lunate	F	36		84
Scaphoid	E	30		71
Trapezium	E	28		66
Trapezoid	F	32		77
20-bone score		621	—	—
RUS score		—	287	—
Carpal score		—	—	773
20-bone centile		85	—	—
RUS centile		—	75	—
Carpal centile		—	—	95
20-bone bone age		10.2	—	—
RUS bone age		—	9.5	—
Carpal bone age	—	—	—	10.6

Reprinted from Tanner, Whitehouse, Marshall, Healy, and Goldstein (1975).

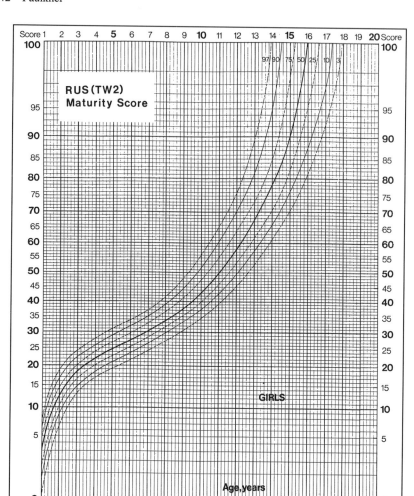

Figure 3.5 Standards for TW2-RUS skeletal maturity score for girls. The bone age can be indirectly derived from the curve (i.e., bone age is the age at which the 50th centile child has the score of the given child) or directly from tables of bone age corresponding to the given maturity scores.
Reprinted from Tanner, Whitehouse, Marshall, Healy, and Goldstein (1975).

ASSESSING SEXUAL MATURATION

Sexual maturation is highly related to the overall process of physiological maturation, and therefore sexual-maturation assessment methods can be useful in estimating biological maturation. These methods are also the most practical; they can be used to assess maturity status at any age, they do not require longitudinal assessment, and they are relatively easy to administer. Assessing sexual maturation is based on the evaluation of secondary sex characteristics, such as breast development and age of menarche in girls, genital development in boys, and pubic hair development in both boys and girls. Other maturity indicators that can be used include the development of axillary (arm pit) hair in boys and girls and facial hair and voice change in boys.

Age of menarche (the first menstrual, or sexual, cycle) is an important biological landmark in girls and is the most commonly used maturity indicator. There are three methods to assess age of menarche. The best way is to ask girls at regular intervals about their menstrual status; this method has limitations because it requires collection of longitudinal data beginning at about age 10 and may continue until age 15. Normative values for a population can be estimated by the status-quo method. This involves gathering cross-sectional data on a large sample of girls over a broad age range to estimate mean age of menarche and the expected variance for the population. The status-quo method is of no value for individual assessment. The third method (recall method) is useful in assessing menarche in postpubertal girls (if longitudinal assessment has not been done). This method simply asks girls to recall, to the best of their ability, the date of their first menstrual cycle. The recall accuracy may be as high as 80% if the interview is done carefully (Ross & Marfell-Jones, 1991). Bergsten-Brucefors (1976) reported a correlation of 0.81 between actual date of menarche and recalled age 4 years later, but only 63% of girls could accurately recall the date of menarche (within 3 months). Damon, Damon, Reed, & Valadian (1969) found a correlation of 0.78 between actual date and recalled date of menarche 19 years after the event.

In any recall questionnaires, girls should be asked if they have had a period, the age when they first started menstruating, the month and year when they first started, and the number of days since their last period. Simply asking for subjects to indicate age can bias the results considerably; for example if a girl actually started her first cycle at 11.7 years of age, she may simply respond that her age was 11. Premenarcheal girls also may be influenced to bias their response if most other girls in the sample are postmenarcheal (Marshall & Tanner, 1986); these limitations should be kept in mind if using a recall method.

In the first and last methods, age of menarche can be ascertained by a questionnaire or in a private interview with a trained technician. It is imperative that this data be collected in a private environment and that the girl understands that results are confidential. We generally use an interview format and have had no difficulty in obtaining this valuable information. Age of menarche data is quite reliable if it is collected prospectively at regular intervals; most girls can distinctly recall this event.

A rating system for the development of breast (B), genital (G), and pubic hair (PH) was originally developed by Tanner (1962). In this system each characteristic is rated on a 5-point scale: Stage 1 indicates the prepubertal stage; Stage 2 indicates initial development of the characteristic; Stage 3 and Stage 4 indicate continued development; and Stage 5 represents the adult or mature development of the characteristic. A description of these scales is presented in Figures 3.6 to 3.9. In girls breast budding (Stage B2) is most often the first sign of sexual maturation; therefore, a girl noted as Stage PH2, but at Stage B2 would be considered as just entering puberty. In boys the first sign of sexual maturation is genital development; therefore, a boy at Stage 2 for genital development would be considered as just beginning puberty, even though PH development may be at Stage 1.

The stages of development in the rating system are somewhat arbitrary, and it is imperative to remember that the development of secondary sex characteristics is a continuous process. The stages of development are also specific to the criteria; that is, it is not correct to average ratings from two different criteria to get an overall rating of maturation. The child's rating on the specific indicators (e.g., B3, G3, PH2, etc.) should be clearly stated. Professional interrater correlations for the rating scales range from 0.86 to 0.96 for boys and from 0.70 to 0.98 for girls (Nicolson & Hanley, 1971).

Other systems based on the original descriptions of Tanner are also used. Ross and Marfell-Jones (1991) recommend a 6-point scale for pubic hair development and a 5-point scale for breast and genital development. Genital development in boys can be measured more precisely using a prader orchidometer to directly measure testicular volume. This technique requires direct manipulation of the testicles and is therefore not practical outside a clinical setting.

A more detailed assessment of adolescent development, intended for clinicians with a comprehensive understanding of secondary sex characteristics, has been suggested by Johnson, Moore, and Jeffries (1978). This system incorporates detailed information from physical and biochemical secondary sex characteristics to classify the child into one of six maturity stages.

Ratings to determine stages of secondary sex characteristic development have been done most often by direct visual observation, or in some cases by assessing standardized photographs. These approaches are appropriate for a clinical setting, but pose many problems for the general assessment of children in a field situation. There are ethical concerns in applying invasive techniques, and many adolescents (and their parents) may feel uncomfortable about the assessment and not give consent. Self-assessment technqiues have been developed in order to reduce these concerns. It has been demonstrated that children and adolescents can rate their own sexual development accurately and reliably (Duke, Litt, & Gross, 1980; Matsudo & Matsudo, 1993; Morris & Udry, 1980; Peterson, Tobin-Richards, & Boxer, 1983). For example, Duke et al. reported kappa coefficients between physician and self-rating scores of 0.81, 0.91, and 0.88 for B and PH (females), and PH and G (males) respectively. Matsudo and Matsudo reported coefficients of association between physician and self-ratings ranging from 60% for genitalia to 71% for pubic hair. An example of self-assessment scales for breast development in girls and genitalia development in boys is shown in Figures 3.10 and 3.11. We have adapted original work by Morris and Udry in utilizing self-assessment methods in our lab. We have found the use of drawings (as opposed to actual photos) and limiting the assessment to PH development to be less threatening to subjects, schools, and parents and to be well-accepted. The procedure basically involves the children rating their PH development by comparing themselves to the illustrations shown in Figures 3.12 and 3.13. In our lab a trained technician explains the procedures to each subject individually and emphasizes the confidentiality of results. The subject is then left

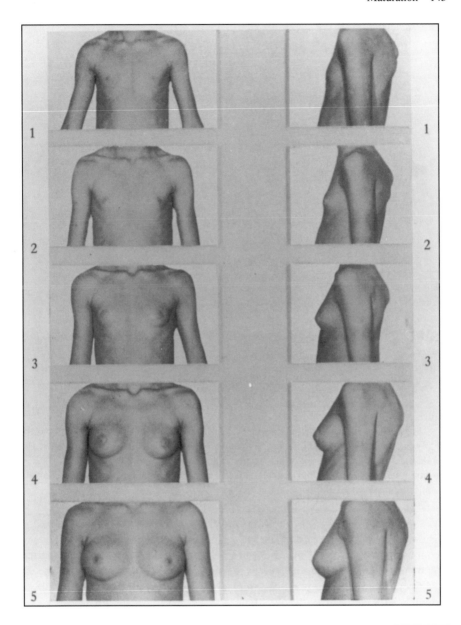

Figure 3.6   Stages of breast development in girls.
Note. Stage 1: Breasts are preadolescent. There is elevation of the papilla only. Stage 2: Breast bud stage. A small mound is formed by the elevation of the breast and papilla. The areolar diameter enlarges. Stage 3: There is further enlargement of breasts and areola with no separation of their contours. Stage 4: There is a projection of the areola and papilla to form a secondary mound above the level of the breast. Stage 5: The breasts resemble those of a mature female.
Reprinted from Tanner (1962).

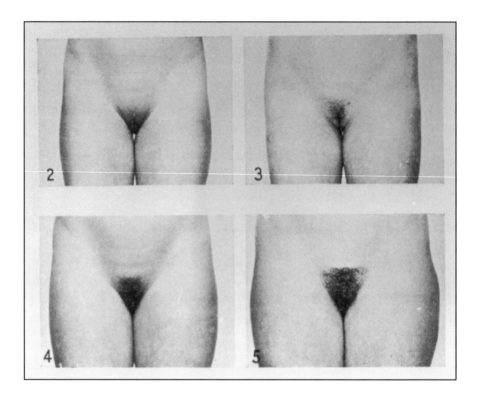

Figure 3.7   Stages of pubic hair development in girls.
Note. Stage 1 (not shown): There is no pubic hair. Stage 2: There is sparse growth of long slightly pigmented hair, primarily along the labia. Stage 3: The hair is darker, coarser, and more curled than Stage 1 and spreads sparely over the junction of the pubes. Stage 4: The hair resembles adult quality, but covers a smaller area than in the adult. Stage 5: The hair is adult in quantity and quality.
Reprinted from Tanner (1962).

alone in a private room to complete the self-assessment. Once the self-assessment is complete, the child places the results in a sealed envelope. The subject is identified only by subject number; this also helps reassure the children of confidentiality. We have found this system to work exceptionally well—and have had no difficulty in obtaining information from any children.

Self-assessment techniques are not the methods of choice in a clinical setting, and there is still need for ongoing studies to verify the validity and reliability of the methods in large samples (Marshall and Tanner, 1986). Nevertheless, for nonclinical applications where a general maturity status of the child is desired, self-assessment techniques can be very useful.

Other indicators such as voice change or facial and axillary hair, although not as good as indicators as others, can be used. These are particularly worthwhile if other markers cannot be assessed due to practical or ethical concerns. The following are

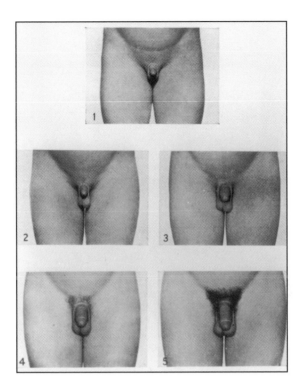

Figure 3.8   Stages of genitalia development in boys.
Note. Stage 1: The penis, testes, and scrotum are childhood size. Stage 2: The scrotum and testes are enlarged, but the penis is not. The scrotum skin reddens in color. Stage 3: There is further growth of the testes and scrotum, and the penis has begun to enlarge (mainly in length). Stage 4: There is further growth of the testes and scrotum and increased size (especially breadth) of the penis. Stage 5: The genitalia are adult in size and shape.
Reprinted from Tanner (1962).

suggested criteria for these markers according to Malina and Bouchard (1991). Axillary hair can be rated on a 3-stage scale in both sexes: 1 = none present; 2 = slight growth; 3 = adult distribution. The growth pattern in girls can be determined even if the hair is shaved. Facial hair in boys can be rated: 1 = none; 2 = increase in length, with pigmentation at corners of upper lip, spreading medially to complete moustache; 3 = hair on the upper part of the cheeks and in the midline just below the lower lip; 4 = hair on the sides and lower border of the chin. Voice change in boys: 1 = unbroken; 2 = signs of breaking; 3 = definitely broken or adult quality.

The assessment of secondary sex characteristics is best determined from longitudinal data, in which children are tested at regular intervals. Ideally this would occur every 3 or 4 months, as changes in secondary sexual characteristics can occur rapidly, but in practice this may be difficult.

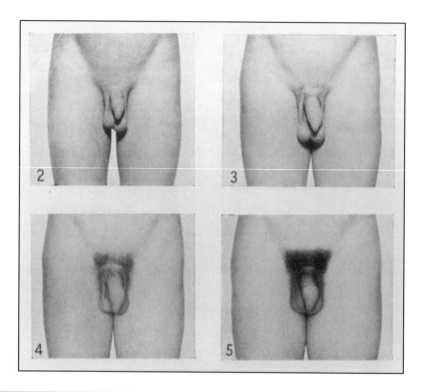

Figure 3.9   Stages of pubic hair development in boys.
Note. Stage 1 (not shown): There is no pubic hair. Stage 2: There is sparse growth of long, slightly pigmented, straight (or slightly curled) hair, primarily at the base of the penis. Stage 3: The hair is darker, coarser, and more curled. The hair spreads sparsely over the junction of the pubes. Stage 4: The hair is adult in type, but covers a smaller area than in the adult. Stage 5: The hair is adult in quantity and quality.
Reprinted from Tanner (1962).

In order to understand the rating systems for secondary sex characteristics it is necessary to appreciate the interrelationships among the various indicators. As discussed previously, there is considerable variation among children in the onset and duration of any pubertal event. In boys the degree of pubic hair and genitalia may not be at the same developmental stage, and PHV may be reached at different stages of genitalia or pubic-hair development. Studies comparing pubic-hair and genitalia development have shown anywhere from 51% to 85% of boys classified as PH2 to be in either the second or third stage of genitalia development (Marshall & Tanner, 1970; Taranger et al., 1976). In girls menarche usually occurs by B2 or B3, but in some girls it may occur as early as B1 (Billewicz, Fellowes, & Thomson, 1981). Although most girls reach PHV during B3, as many as 30% to 40% will reach PHV during B2, and about 10% will not achieve PHV until B4 (Marshall & Tanner, 1986).

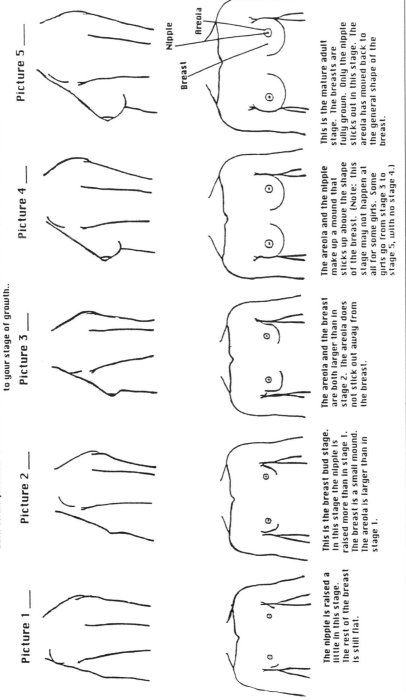

Figure 3.10   Self-assessment of breast development for girls.
Reprinted from Morris and Udry (1980).

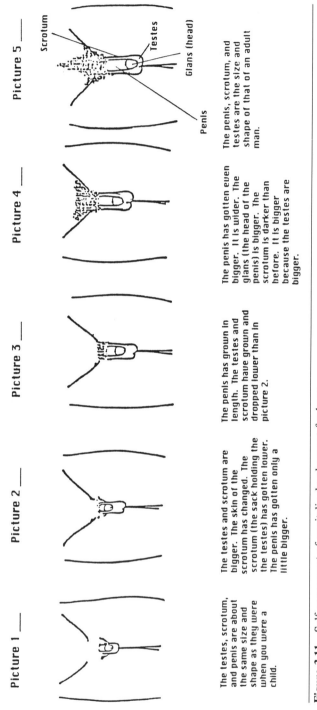

The pictures on this page show different stages of growth of the testes, scrotum, and penis. A boy goes through each of the 5 stages as shown. Please look at each of the pictures. Read the sentences. Put an x on the line above the picture which is closest to your stage of growth.

Do not look at pubic hair growth!

Picture 1 _____   Picture 2 _____   Picture 3 _____   Picture 4 _____   Picture 5 _____

Scrotum

Testes

Glans (head)

Penis

The testes, scrotum, and penis are about the same size and shape as they were when you were a child.

The testes and scrotum are bigger. The skin of the scrotum has changed. The scrotum (the sack holding the testes) has gotten lower. The penis has gotten only a little bigger.

The penis has grown in length. The testes and scrotum have grown and dropped lower than in picture 2.

The penis has gotten even bigger. It is wider. The glans (the head of the penis) is bigger. The scrotum is darker than before. It is bigger because the testes are bigger.

The penis, scrotum, and testes are the size and shape of that of an adult man.

Figure 3.11   Self-assessment of genitalia development for boys.
Reprinted from Morris and Udry (1980).

The drawings on this page show <u>different amounts of female pubic hair.</u>
Please look at each of the drawings and read the sentences under the drawings.
Then check the drawing that is <u>closest</u> to your stage of hair development.

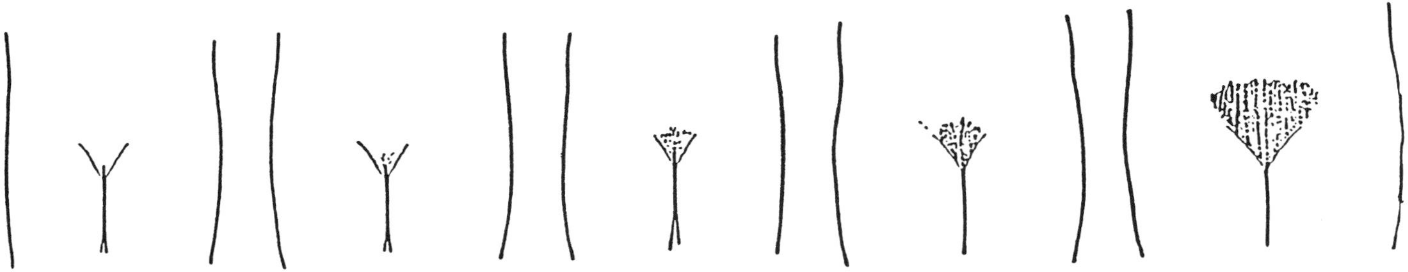

Picture 1 ___	Picture 2 ___	Picture 3 ___	Picture 4 ___	Picture 5 ___
There is no pubic hair at all.	There is a small amount of long, lightly colored hair. This hair may be straight or a little curly	There is hair that is darker, curlier and thinly spread out to couer a somewhat larger area than in stage 2.	The hair is thicker and more spread out, couering a larger area than in stage 3.	The hair now is widely spread couering a large area, like that of an adult female.

Figure 3.12 Self-assessment of pubic hair development for girls.

Note. The following introduction (written and/or verbal) is given to the child prior to the assessment.

"As you keep growing over the next few years, you will see changes in your body. These changes happen at different ages for different children, and you may already be seeing some changes. Others may have already gone through some changes. Sometimes it is important to know how a person is growing without having a doctor examine them. It can be hard for a person to describe herself or himself in words, so doctors have drawings of stages that all children go through. Five drawings of pubic hair growth are attached for you to look at.

"We want to know how well you can select your stage of growth from the set of drawings. All you need to do is pick the drawing that looks like you do now. Put a check mark above the drawing that is closest to your stage of development, then put the sheet in the envelope and seal it so your answer will be kept private."
Reprinted from Morris and Udry (1980).

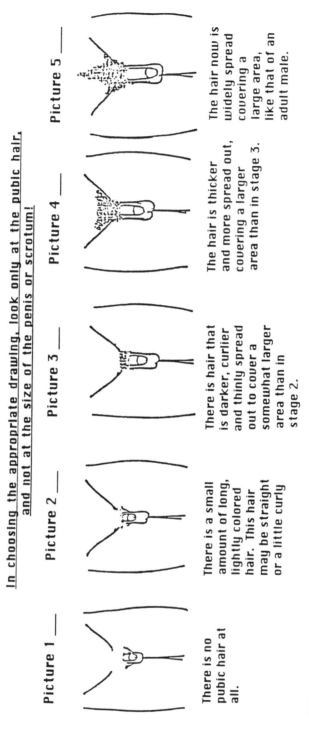

Figure 3.13 Self-assessment of pubic hair development for boys.
Reprinted from Morris and Udry (1980).

Axillary hair development generally does not begin in boys until genitalia development is well advanced and about 1 or 2 years after the first sign of pubic hair development (Neyzi et al., 1975; Taranger et al., 1976). As is the case with the other markers, there may be sizeable variation among children, and occasionally the axillary hair may appear before pubic hair. The relationship between facial hair and axillary hair is also variable, and hair may appear in both sites at the same age (Marshall & Tanner, 1986). Axillary hair development in girls usually appears by B3 or B4.

ASSESSING SOMATIC MATURATION

Using physique measurements as indicators of maturity status requires longitudinal data; therefore, the applicability of these techniques is limited. Somatic maturation is most useful in classifying children retrospectively into maturity groups for analyzing growth data. Age at PHV is the most common somatic maturity indicator. It is derived from fitting data (gathered over the course of a child's growth period) to a growth curve and determining mathematically where the peak gains in stature occurred. Peak height velocity is an important indicator and serves as a standard landmark for assessing other growth parameters, including secondary sex characteristics.

Accurate estimates of the percentage of final adult stature attained at any given age require longitudinal data and, therefore, are not of great utility. The exception is when parental height is available. In this instance adult stature might be estimated for the child based on parental values, and some indication of the child's stature relative to the estimated adult stature (based on parental values) can be used as a maturity marker. For example, a child who has obtained 80% of estimated adult value (at a given chronological age) would be considered more mature than a child who has achieved 70% of predicted height. The potential range of error using this approach is substantial; therefore, it does not have widespread application.

Prediction of maturity status from various anthropometric variables or indexes is attractive because the measures are relatively easy to take and are less invasive than other indicators. However, an accepted system for this methodology has yet to be developed.

ASSESSING BIOCHEMICAL MARKERS

Measurement of the adrenal hormone dehydroepiandrosterone sulfate (DHEAS) has recently been used as a maturity marker in boys (Arquitt, Stoecker, Hermann, & Winterfeldt, 1991). Plasma DHEAS rises with secondary sex development and is positively related to bone age (Babalola & Ellis, 1985; Katz, Hodiger, Zemel, & Parks, 1985). Reference values for plasma DHEAS have been established for children

(Babalola & Ellis, 1985). The necessity of taking blood samples and the need for laboratory analysis of the samples restrict the applicability of the technique.

ASSESSING DENTAL AGE

Techniques have been developed to assess maturity based on dental age (Demerjian, 1986; Demerjian, Goldstein, & Tanner, 1973). The simplest assessment of dental age up to about age 13 is documentation of the time or age of eruption of the deciduous (baby) and permanent teeth. After age 13 more sophisticated techniques, based on principles similar to skeletal maturity assessment, can be used. Scores are given according to the developmental stage of the tooth (from the beginning of calcification to the formation of the root). The mandibular permanent teeth are rated in a specific order: first molar, second premolar, first premolar, canine, lateral incisor, central incisor. The rating is assigned by following written criteria and by comparing the developmental status of each tooth to standardized X-rays. Each tooth is then given a rating from A (beginning of calcification) to H (complete development). Once the ratings are assigned, each stage is given a numerical score, and the sum of these scores provides an estimate of an individual's dental maturity on a scale from 0 to 100 (Demirjian). As with skeletal age assessments, these techniques are limited because of technical requirements and the necessity for X-ray exposure. They also are more applicable for population groups as there is a high probability of misclassification in individual children (Demerjian).

INTERRELATIONSHIPS AMONG ASSESSMENT TECHNIQUES

Data from several studies show skeletal, sexual, and somatic maturity indicators to be positively interrelated, although the correlation values are not exceptionally high. For example there is no clear relationship between skeletal age and the development of the secondary sex characteristics in normal children (Marshall, 1974); therefore, skeletal age cannot be used as a method to predict when pubertal events will occur.

The landmarks most closely related are skeletal age and age of menarche, whereas dental maturity is not highly related to the other methods (Tanner, 1990). In general, however, a child classified as early, average, or delayed in maturity by one method will likely be classified similarly by the other methods. Based on an analysis of several maturity indicators done by Bielicki (1975) and Bielicki, Koniarek & Malina (1984), Malina and Bouchard (1991) suggest that there is a general maturity factor that underlies the maturation process during adolescence and that this factor places individuals into early, average or late maturity groups. They also point out, however, that there is variation within and among the various maturity assessment techniques, suggesting that no single system will provide a complete description of an individual child's tempo of growth and maturation.

Combining several indicators into an overall maturity rating has been applied by some investigators. For example, McKay, Bailey, Wilkinson, and Houston (1994) derived a maturity rating of prepubescent, early pubescent, or late pubescent for children based on pubic hair self-assessment, height velocity (assessed from four measurements over two years), menarcheal status for girls, and axillary hair rating for boys.

CONCLUSION

There is no single gold standard of maturity status against which to validate the various assessment methods. The method of choice will likely depend on the specific situation; for example, some methods are more feasible for field work, and others are restricted to clinical or laboratory environments. Skeletal age assessment is thought to be the best method for determining biological maturity status, but its application is limited due to cost, technical, and ethical factors. Somatic assessment techniques are generally limited to longitudinal data, and usually can only be applied retrospectively. The most appropriate methods for general application are thus secondary sex characteristic assessment techniques. These techniques also have limitations due to variation in the timing, tempo, and duration of their indicators. Thus, it is imperative that the specific characteristic(s) being utilized to assess maturity status be clearly identified. It is also important to maintain privacy and confidentiality when assessing secondary sex charateristics. Self-assessment of secondary sex characteristics can alleviate many of the personal concerns of adolescents and their parents, and has been shown to be an accurate and reliable method of data gathering.

REFERENCES

Arquitt, A.B., Stoecker, B.J., Hermann, J.S., & Winterfeldt, E.A. (1991) Dehydroepiandrosterone sulfate, cholesterol, hemoglobin, and anthropometric measures related to growth in male adolescents. *Journal of the American Dietetic Association*, **91**, 575-579.

Babalola, A.A. & Ellis, G. (1985). Serum dehydroepiandrosterone sulfate in a normal pediatric population. *Clinical Biochemistry*, **18**, 184-189.

Bailey, D.A., Malina, R.M., & Mirwald, R.L. (1986). Physical activity and growth of the child. In F. Falkner & J.M. Tanner (Eds.), *Human growth: A comprehensive treatise*, (Vol. 2, pp. 147-170), New York: Plenum Press.

Bergsten-Brucefors, A. (1976). A note on the accuracy of recalled age at menarche. *Annals of Human Biology*, **3**, 71-73.

Beunen, G.P., Malina, R.M., Renson, R., Simons, J., Ostyn, M., Lefevre, J. (1992). Physical activity and growth, maturation and performance: A longitudinal study. *Medicine and Science in Sports and Exercise*, **24**, 576-585.

Beunen, G.P., Malina, R.M., Van't Hof, M.A., Simons, J., Ostyn, M., Renson, R., & Van Gerven, D. (1988). *Adolescent growth and motor performance: A longitudinal study of Belgian boys*. Champaign, IL: Human Kinetics.

Beunen, G., Ostyn, M., Simons, J., Renson, R., & Van Gerven, D. (1980). Motorische vaardigheid somatische ontwikkeling en biologische maturiteit [Motor ability, somatic development and biological maturity]. *Geneeskunde en Sport*, **13**, 36-42.

Bielicki, T. (1975). Interrelationships between various measures of maturation rate in girls during adolescence. *Studies in Physical Anthropology*, **1**, 51-64.

Bielicki, T., Koniarek, J., & Malina, R.M. (1984). Interrelationships among certain measures of growth and maturation rate in boys during adolescence. *Annals of Human Biology*, **11**, 201-210.

Billewicz, W.Z., Fellowes, H.M., & Thomson, S.M. (1981). Menarche in Newcastle-upon-Tyne girls, *Annals of Human Biology*, **8**, 313-320.

Cameron, N., Tanner, J.M., & Whitehouse, R.H. (1982). A longitudinal analysis of growth of limb segments in adolescence. *Annals of Human Biology*, **9**, 211-220.

Carron, A.V., & Bailey, D.A. (1974). Strength development in boys from 10 through 16 years. *Monographs of the Society for Research in Child Development*, **39** (Serial No. 157).

Clarke, H.H. (1971). *Physical and motor tests in the Medford Boys' Growth Study*. Englewood Cliffs, NJ: Prentice Hall.

Damon, A., Damon, S.T., Reed, R.B., & Valadian, I. (1969). Age at menarche of mothers and daughters, with a note on accuracy of recall. *Human Biology*, **41**, 161-175.

Danker-Hopfe, H. (1986). Menarcheal age in Europe. *Yearbook of Physical Anthropology*, **29**, 81-112.

Demerjian, A. (1986). Dentition. In F. Faulkner, & J.M. Tanner (Eds.), *Human growth: A comprehensive treatise* (Vol. 2, pp. 269-298). New York: Plenum Press.

Demerjian, A., Goldstein, H., & Tanner, J.M. (1973). A new system of dental age assessment. *Human Biology*, **45**, 211-227.

Duke, P.M., Litt, I.F., & Gross, R.T. (1980). Adolescents' self-assessment of sexual maturation. *Pediatrics*, **66**, 918-920.

Dupertuis, C.W., & Michael, N.B. (1953). Comparison of growth in height and weight between ectomorphic and mesomorphic boys. *Child Development*, **24**, 203-214.

Espenschade, A. (1940). Motor performance in adolescence, including the study of relationships with measures of growth and maturity. *Monographs of the Society for Research in Child Development*, **5** (Serial No. 24).

Eveleth, P.B. (1978). Differences between populations in body shape of children and adolescents. *American Journal of Physical Anthropology*, **49**, 373-382.

Faust, M.S. (1977). Somatic development of adolescent girls. *Monographs of the Society for Research in Child Development*, **42** (Serial No. 169).

Greulich, W.W., & Pyle, S.I. (1959). *Radiographic atlas of skeletal development of the hand and wrist* (2nd ed.). Stanford, CA: Stanford University Press.

Hoerr, N.L., Pyle, S.I., & Francis, C.C. (1962). *Radiographic atlas of skeletal development of the foot and ankle, a standard of reference*, Springfield, IL: Charles C. Thomas.

Johnson, T.R., Moore, W.M., & Jeffries, J.E. (1978). *Children are different: Developmental physiology* (2nd ed.). Columbus, OH: Ross Laboratories.

Johnston, F.E., & Malina, R.M. (1966). Age changes in the composition of the upper arm in Philadelphia children. *Human Biology*, **38**, 1-21.

Jones, H.E. (1949). *Motor performance and growth: A developmental study of static dynamometric strength*. Berkely, CA: University of California Press.

Katz, S.H. Hediger, M.L., Zemel, B.S., & Parks, J.S. (1985). Adrenal androgens, body fat, and advanced skeletal age in puberty: New evidence for the relationship of andrenarche and gonadarche in males. *Human Biology*, **57**, 401-413.

Kemper, H.C.G., Verschuur, R., & Ritmeester, J.W. (1987). Longitudinal development of growth and fitness in early and late maturing teenagers. *Pediatrician*, **14**, 219-225.

Krabbe, S., Christensen, T., Worm, J., Christiansen, C., & Transbol, I. (1978). Relationship between haemoglobin and serum testosterone in normal children and adolescents and in boys with delayed puberty. *Acta Paediatrica Scandinavia*, **67**, 655-658.

Largo, R.H., Gasser, T., Prader, A., Stuetzle, W., & Huber, P.J. (1978). Analysis of the adolescent growth spurt using smoothing spline functions. *Annals of Human Biology*, **5**, 421-434.

Largo, R.H., & Prader, A. (1983). Pubertal development in Swiss boys. *Helvetia Paediatrica Acta*, **38**, 211-228.

Lindgren, G. (1978). Growth of schoolchildren with early, average and late ages of peak height velocity. *Annals of Human Biology*, **5**, 253-267.

Malina, R.M. (1989). Growth and maturation: Normal variation and the effects of training. In C.V. Gisolfi & D.R. Lamb (Eds.), *Perspectives in exercise science and sports medicine, Vol. 2: Youth, Exercise, and Sport* (pp. 223-265). Indianapolis: Benchmark Press.

Malina, R.M. & Bouchard, C. (1991). *Growth, maturation and physical activity*. Champaign, IL: Human Kinetics.

Malina, R.M., Meleski, B.W., & Shoup, H.F. (1982). Anthropometric, body composition and maturity characteristics of selected school-aged athletes. *Pediatric Clinics of North America*, **29**, 1305-1323.

Marshall, W.A. (1974). Interrelationships of skeletal maturation, sexual development and somatic growth in man. *Annals of Human Biology*, **1**, 29-40.

Marshall, W.A. & Tanner, J.M. (1969). Variations in the pattern of pubertal changes in girls. *Archives of Disease in Childhood*, **44**, 291-303.

Marshall, W.A. & Tanner, J.M. (1970). Variations in the pattern of pubertal changes in boys. *Archives of Disease in Childhood*, **45**, 13-23.

Marshall, W.A. & Tanner, J.M. (1986). Puberty. In F. Falkner & J.M. Tanner (Eds.) *Human growth: A comprehensive treatise* (Vol. 2, pp. 171-209). New York: Plenum Press.

Matsudo, S.M. & Matsudo, V.R. (1993). Validity of self-evaluation on determination of sexual maturation level. In A.C. Claessens, J. Lefevre, & B. Vanden Eynde (Eds.), *World wide variation in physical fitness* (pp. 106-109). Leuven: Institute of Physical Education.

McKay, H.A., Bailey, D.A., Wilkinson, A.A., & Houston, C.S. (1994). Familial comparison of bone mineral density at the proximal femur and lumbar spine. *Bone and Mineral*, **24**, 95-107.

Mirwald, R.L. & Bailey, D.A. (1986). *Maximal aerobic power*. London, ON: Sports Dynamics.

Morris, N.M., & Udry, J.R. (1980). Validation of a self-administered instrument to assess stage of adolescent development. *Journal of Youth and Adolescence*, **9**, 271-280.

Neyzi, O., Alp, H., Yalcindag, A., Yakacikli, S., & Orhon, A. (1975). Sexual maturation in Turkish boys. *Annals of Human Biology*, **2** 251-259.

Nicolson, A. & Hanley, C. (1971). Indices of physiological maturity: Derivation and interrelationships. In M.C. Jones, N. Bayley, & J.W. McFarlane (Eds.), *The course of human development* (p. 42). Toronto: John Wiley & Sons.

Petersen, A.C., Tobin-Richards, M. & Boxer, A. (1983). Puberty: Its measurement and its meaning. *Journal of Early Adolescence*, **3**, 47-62.

Preece, M.A. & Baines, M.J. (1978). A new family of mathematical models describing the human growth curve. *Annals of Human Biology*, **5**, 1-24.

Rasmussen, R.L., Faulkner, R.A., Mirwald, R.L., & Bailey, D.A. (1990). A longitudinal analysis of structure/function related variables in 10-16 year old boys. In G. Beunen, J.

Ghesquiere, T. Reybrouck, & A.L. Claessens (Eds.), *Children and exercise* (pp. 27-33). Stuttgart: Ferdinand-Enke-Verlag.

Reynolds, E.L. (1946). Sexual maturation and the growth of fat, muscle and bone in girls. *Child Development*, **17**, 121-144.

Roche, A.F. (1980). The measurement of skeletal maturation. In F.E. Johnston, A.F. Roche, & C. Susanne (Eds.), *Human physical growth and maturation: Methodologies and factors* (pp. 61-82). New York: Plenum Press.

Roche, A.F. (1986). Bone growth and maturation. In F. Falkner & J.M. Tanner (Eds.), *Human growth: A comprehensive treatise* (Vol. 2, pp. 25-60), New York: Plenum Press.

Roche, A.F., Chumlea, W.C., & Thissen, D. (1988). *Assessing the skeletal maturity of the hand-wrist: Fels method*. Springfield, IL: Charles C. Thomas.

Ross, W.D., Brown, S.R., & Faulkner, R.A. (1977). Age of menarche in Canadian skaters and skiers. *Canadian Journal of Applied Sport Sciences*, **1**, 191-193.

Ross, W.D., Brown, S.R., Faulkner, R.A., Vajda, A.S., & Savage, M.V. (1976). Monitoring growth in young skaters. *Canadian Journal of Applied Sport Sciences*, **1**, 163-167.

Ross, W.D., & Marfell-Jones, M.J. (1991). Kinanthropometry. In J.D. MacDougall, H.A. Wenger, & H.J. Green (Eds.). *Physiological testing of the high-performance athlete* (pp. 224-305). Champaign, IL: Human Kinetics.

Rowland, T.W. (1990). *Exercise and chidlren's health*. Champaign, IL: Human Kinetics.

Shuttleworth, F.K. (1939). The physical and mental growth of girls and boys age six to nineteen in relation to age at maximum growth. *Monographs of the Society for Research in Child Development*, **4** (Serial No. 22).

Stolz, H.R., & Stolz, L.M. (1951). *Somatic development of adolescent boys*. New York: Macmillan.

Tanner, J.M. (1962). *Growth of adolescents* (2nd ed.). Oxford, UK: Blackwell Scientific.

Tanner, J.M. (1990). *Foetus into man*. Cambridge MA: Harvard University Press.

Tanner, J.M., Whitehouse, R.H., Cameron, N., Marshall, W.A., Healy, M.J.R., & Goldstein, H. (1983). *Assessment of skeletal maturity and prediction of adult height (TW2 method)* (2nd ed.). London: Academic Press.

Tanner, J.M., Whitehouse, R.H., Marshall, W.A., Healy, M.J.R., & Goldstein, H. (1975). *Assessment of skeletal maturity and prediction of adult height (TW2 method)*. London: Academic Press.

Tanner, J.M., Whitehouse, R.H., Marubini, E., & Resele, F. (1976). The adolescent growth spurt of boys and girls of the Harpenden Growth Study. *Annals of Human Biology*, **3**, 109-126.

Taranger, J., Lichtenstein, H., & Svennberg-Redegren, I. (1976). The somatic development of children in a Swedish urban community: VI. Somatic pubertal development. *Acta Paediatrica Scandinavia (Supplement)*, **258**, 121-135.

Winter, E.M. (1992). Scaling: Partitioning out differences in size. *Pediatric Exercise Science*, 296-301.

Zuk, G.H. (1958). The plasticity of the physique from early adolescence through adulthood. *Journal of Genetic Psychology*, **92**, 205-214.

II

PHYSIOLOGICAL ASSESSMENT

The physiological response of children to exercise and physical activity has received considerable interest in recent years, from the acute response to single bouts of activity to the chronic response from training programs. Most studies have monitored some aspect of aerobic or anaerobic performance. Fewer studies have assessed strength and power in children. It is difficult to compare performance across studies since different testing protocols and modes of activity are often employed. The chapters on anaerobic and aerobic performance (by Oded Bar-Or and Luc Léger, respectively) provide a review of the different tests and protocols that have been used to assess children and conclude with some recommendations related to standardizing procedures. Obviously the specific purposes of the study and unique characteristics of the subjects dictate the choice of test and protocol. However, whenever possible, there would appear to be many advantages in using protocols that are widely used with perhaps identification of a single protocol that is generally recommended.

Measurement of muscular strength and endurance, especially in a laboratory setting, is not common in studies of children. In fact, there appears to be a need for studies that describe the developmental changes in muscular force and power during the circumpubertal years. Catherine Gaul's chapter on muscular strength and endurance (chapter 6) presents the various methods for the assessment of strength using isokinetic, isotonic, and isometric modes of testing. The chapter includes a discussion about differentiating between the neurogenic and myogenic components of force generation. Such differentiation should be useful in monitoring developmental changes as well as the response to strength training programs.

4

Oded Bar-Or

Anaerobic Performance

The term *anaerobic task* assumes that the biochemical pathways for the generation of adenosine triphosphate (ATP) during the task do not require oxygen (O_2). However, even when a task is very intense and of a brief duration, there is still some aerobic contribution to its execution (Bar-Or, 1987; Vandewalle, Pérès, Heller, & Monod, 1987). This aerobic contribution is greater among children than among adults (Hebestreit, Mirmura, & Bar-Or, 1993). Nevertheless, activities of supramaximal intensities (i.e., above the lowest power that is produced in order to elicit maximal O_2 uptake) and of a short duration (from less than 1 s to 30-60 s) have been termed *anaerobic* and are the focus of this chapter. Although most of the literature on the testing of anaerobic performance is related to adults, the growing body of knowledge on children and adolescents is the basis for this chapter.

A variety of tests have been suggested for the assessment of a person's anaerobic characteristics. Some tests (e.g., maximal levels of O_2 deficit, O_2 debt, blood lactate, and base excess; or the accumulated oxygen demand method) are based on metabolic or biochemical criteria. Other tests (sprinting ability, step-running, vertical jump, monoarticular extension–flexion, and cycling tests) are based on physical performance. A description of metabolic and biochemical tests is provided in textbooks of exercise physiology, as well as in a recent book on the testing of athletes (Bouchard, Taylor, Simoneau, & Dulac, 1991). The use of the *accumulated oxygen demand* method with children has been described by Carlson and Naughton (1993). To review the testing of anaerobic power in adults see Bar-Or (1987) and Vandewalle et al. (1987). A description of some of the more common anaerobic field tests in children is available in a recent chapter by Van Praagh (1995).

Both in the training and the clinical literature, *mechanical power* has often been used erroneously as a synonym for strength. It is important therefore to realize that, whereas *strength* is a measure of force, *power* is work × time^{-1} and represents the product of force and velocity. This chapter will address laboratory tests that measure or assess mechanical power of children and adolescents. In keeping with the general intent of this book, the focus will be on those tests that are feasible for use with children and are affordable for most exercise laboratories.

GROWTH CHARACTERISTICS
OF ANAEROBIC PERFORMANCE

Children's performance in anaerobic sports events such as high jump, swim sprints, or 200m running is distinctly lower than in adults. This, at least in part, reflects children's lower ability to generate mechanical energy from chemical energy sources through anaerobic pathways. Whether expressed in absolute power units, per kg body mass, or per kg lean body mass, anaerobic performance is lower in children than in adolescents and adults (Bar-Or, 1983; Blimkie, Roche, Hay, & Bar-Or, 1988; Davies, Barnes, & Godfrey, 1972; Davies & Young, 1984; di Prampero & Cerretelli, 1969; Evans, Eckerson, Housh, & Johnson, 1993; Falgairette, Bedu, Fellmann, Van Praagh, & Coudert, 1991; Inbar, 1985; Inbar & Bar-Or, 1986; Kurowski, 1977; Mercier, Mercier, Granier, LeGallais, & Préfaut, 1992; Paterson, Cunningham, & Bumstead, 1986; Saavedra, Logassé, Bouchard, & Simoneau, 1991; Weijiang & Juxiang, 1988). Anaerobic performance continuously increases throughout the various growth and maturation stages (Blimkie et al., 1988; Inbar & Bar-Or, 1986; Kurowski 1977), reaching peak levels in the second or third decade of life (di Prampero & Cerretelli, 1969; Inbar & Bar-Or).

Although it is not clear whether there are any specific developmental stages at which the transition from a childhood pattern to an adulthood pattern is at its fastest, some major changes occur during puberty. This has been shown in a longitudinal study of 11- to 15-year-old boys (Paterson et al., 1986), in a recent mixed-longitudinal study of circumpubertal boys (Falk & Bar-Or, 1993), and in cross-sectional studies on 48 pre-, mid- and late-pubertal boys (Suei, McGillis, Falk, Blimkie, & Bar-Or, 1991), and 144 6- to 15-year-old boys (Falgairette, Bedu, Fellmann, Van Praagh, & Coudert, 1991) . The latter study is particularly important, because pubertal status was assessed through salivary testosterone (which had been shown to be strongly correlated with plasma free-testosterone concentration). Both peak power ($r = 0.45$) and mean anaerobic power ($r = 0.47$) were significantly correlated with salivary testosterone. Even though the authors did not partial out the effect of body size in the above relationships, their conclusion that a major increase in the anaerobic performance of boys occurs during puberty is valid.

There are very few data which compare the anaerobic performances of girls with boys (Blimkie et al., 1988; Docherty & Gaul, 1991; Van Praagh, Fellmann, Bedu, Falgairette, & Coudert, 1990; Weijiang & Juxiang, 1988). In general, girls score lower than boys of identical chronological age. The difference is apparent also when values are normalized for body mass, but the difference disappears when power per lean mass is calculated. One exception is a study from China (Weijiang & Juxiang, 1988), in which 14- to 18-year-old girls had significantly lower mean power and peak power per kg lean body mass (Wingate Anaerobic Test) when compared with boys.

Even though anaerobic performance during growth is strongly correlated with lean body mass and the mass of the exercising muscle, peak power and mean anaerobic power increase during adolescence, even when expressed per kg lean body mass or per kg muscle mass (Blimkie et al., 1988; Mercier et al., 1992). Recent data on rats (Lodder, de Haan, & Sargeant, 1991) confirm that the lower performance in the growing muscle is not merely a reflection of muscle size, but of qualitative changes.

The exact qualitative characteristics that are responsible for the relatively low anaerobic performance of the prepubescent child are not clear. One possibility is that the rate of anaerobic glycolysis is limited in children (Eriksson & Saltin, 1974) because of the low concentration of the rate-limiting enzyme phosphofructokinase in their muscles (Eriksson, Gollnick, & Saltin, 1973; Fournier, Ricci, Taylor, Ferguson, Montpetit, & Chaitman, 1982). This is manifested by a low maximal lactate concentration in blood (Åstrand, 1952; Duché et al., 1992; Matejkova, Koprivova, & Placheta, 1980; Rutenfranz et al., 1981) and muscle (Eriksson et al., 1973), and by a lower acidosis in blood following maximal aerobic exercise (Kinderman, Huber, & Keul, 1975; Matejkova et al., 1980). The possible effect of testosterone on the rate of glycolysis has been investigated. In some animals, anaerobic capability is related to the level of circulating testosterone (Dux, Dux, & Guba, 1982). However, even though a positive relationship has been found between maximal blood lactate and salivary testosterone level of 41 boys, the correlation was only 0.39 (Fellmann et al., 1988). Furthermore, changes in testosterone activity cannot explain the puberty-related increase in anaerobic performance among females.

MEASUREMENT TECHNIQUES AND REPRESENTATIVE VALUES

Anaerobic tests, which use mechanical power as their criterion, are divided into two categories: (a) those that measure or assess the highest mechanical power that a muscle or a group of muscles can generate over a brief period (ranging from less than 1 s to approximately 10 s), and (b) those that measure or assess the ability of the muscles to sustain a high power over time (usually 15-60 s). The former have been referred to as tests of *peak power*, whereas the latter reflect local muscle endurance, often referred to as *anaerobic capacity*.

Table 4.1 summarizes anaerobic tests that measure or assess mechanical power and have been used with children and adolescents in the laboratory. These are classified according to the criterion of anaerobic performance that they measure (peak power or local muscle endurance), the exercise task, its duration, and the required apparatus. Each of the tests summarized in Table 4.1, and described below, represents a particular category. Other versions within each category have been developed and used with adults, or with children and youth, but their detailed description is beyond the scope of this chapter.

Each of the following sections describes an anaerobic test listed in Table 4.1 and, whenever available, provides a graph with representative values for children and adolescents. This author would have liked to present normative data for each of the tests. However, to obtain true norms, it is necessary to test sufficiently large representative samples of various age groups in the child and adolescent population. Such norms—which may differ among countries, socioeconomic, and nutritional groups—are not available. Figures 4.2, 4.3, and 4.5 through 4.10 are presented merely to summarize represantative values as reported in the literature. None of the

Table 4.1   Laboratory Tests That Measure or Assess Mechanical Power as an Index of Anaerobic Performance

Name of test	Performance index	Task	Duration s	Apparatus
Force–Velocity	PP	5-8 bouts of all-out cycling	5-7 each	Constant force, isokinetic cycle
Margaria step running	PP	Sprinting upstairs	~1	Regular stairs, timer
Vertical jump–Sargent	PP (height)	Vertical jump from a stationary position, reaching maximal height	<1	Vertical ruler on a wall
Vertical jump–force platform	PP	Vertical jump from a stationary position	<1	Force platform
Sprint running–motorized treadmill	LME (time)	Sprinting to exhaustion	10-30	Motorized treadmill
Sprint running—nonmotorized treadmill	LME	Sprinting to exhaustion	10-30	Nonmotorized treadmill with a body harness and force sensors
Isokinetic cycling	PP, LME	All-out cycling	15-60	Isokinetic cycle ergometer
Isokinetic–monoarticular	PP, LME	Single or multiple maximal knee extensions, flexions	<1-30	Isokinetic dynamometer
Wingate	PP, LME	All-out cycling or arm cranking	30 s	Fixed-resistance cycle ergometer

PP = peak power; LME = local muscle endurance

studies in these figures was designed to yield bona fide norms. Only one of them (Figure 4.4) is related to females, which reflects the paucity of information regarding anaerobic performance of girls.

FORCE VELOCITY (F-V) CYCLING TEST

The test, as shown in Figure 4.1, is intended to identify peak power during short-term cycling or arm cranking. It is comprised of several (typically 5-8) "all-out" 5- to 7-s cycling bouts, each performed against a different, but constant, braking force. As expected, the higher the force, the lower the peak velocity (determined as pedaling rate) attained in each bout. Although the relationship between force and velocity in a contracting muscle is curvilinear, it is quite linear in adults (Sargeant, Hoinville, & Young, 1981) and in girls and boys (Van Praagh et al., 1990) during cycling at pedaling rates of 50 rpm to 150 rpm. By extrapolation, the highest force that the subject can work against can be determined (i.e., at zero velocity; Fo in Figure 4.1) and likewise the highest velocity at which the subject can pedal (i.e., against zero force; Vo). Because power is the product of force and velocity, it is possible to calculate the highest power performed in each of these bouts and then plot it against the respective braking force. The resulting parabola enables calculation, by interpolation, of peak power for each subject, as well as the force that is needed to achieve peak power. This force is approximately 50% of Fo (Vandewalle, Pérès, Heller, & Monod, 1985).

This test was developed originally for adults (Pirnay & Crielaard, 1979; Sargeant et al., 1981; Vandewalle et al., 1985) and subsequently adapted for children (Bedu et al., 1991; Mercier et al., 1992; Van Praagh, Falgairette, Bedu, Fellman, & Coudert, 1989). It is currently used in the author's laboratory to test children with neuromuscular disability. The F-V test can be used with an isokinetic (Sargeant et al., 1981) or a constant-force (Falgairette et al., 1991; Van Praagh et al., 1989) ergometer.

Because of the fast recovery of children following high-intensity exercise (Hebestreit et al., 1993), a 2-min rest period between consecutive bouts is sufficient to achieve full recovery. To safeguard against fatigue effects, however, the testing protocol in the author's laboratory and elsewhere calls for 5-min rest periods. The total time required for completion of the F-V test is therefore 30 min to 40 min. This is much longer than the time required for completion of other anaerobic tests, but because of the very brief duration of each bout, the procedure is physically less fatiguing than protocols such as all-out treadmill running or the Wingate Anaerobic Test (WAnT).

The F-V Test has other advantages: (a) peak power achieved by it is closer to a person's "real" peak cycling power than measured by the WAnT or other cycling protocols; (b) force–velocity relationships can be monitored during cycling or arm cranking, particularly if the test is done with an isokinetic ergometer (even though, unlike monoarticular tasks, angular velocity at the joint keeps changing during each cycle); and (c) the F-V test can be used as a means for identifying the optimal braking force for the WAnT (see related section below).

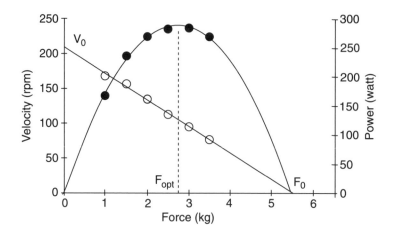

Figure 4.1   The Force–Velocity Test. A 10-year-old male performed six cycling sprints, each against a different braking force. The velocity–force regression line (open circles) is extrapolated to determine the force at zero velocity (F_o), which is the highest possible force, and the velocity against zero force (V_o), which is the highest possible cycling velocity. Power values (black circles), calculated for each of the sprints, are plotted against force. The highest power, determined by interpolation, would be elicited at an optimal force (F_{opt}), which is approximately 50% of F_o.

No data are available to this author about the reliability and reproducibility of the F-V Test. There is, however, a high correlation ($r = 0.93$) between peak power obtained by it and that obtained by the WAnT (Van Praagh et al., 1990). Figure 4.2 is a summary of representative peak power values in boys, as measured by the F-V test.

MARGARIA STEP-RUNNING TEST

In 1966 a laboratory test was introduced to assess peak mechanical power of a person who sprints up stairs (Margaria, Aghemo, & Rovelli, 1966). The subject is required to run up stairs at maximal speed, taking two steps at a time, after a few steps of running on the flat. The time (t) that it takes to make two strides (i.e., from the time that one foot takes off until it lands again four steps higher) is registered, using mechanical microswitches or photocells. The vertical height (h) of the stairs is measured, as is the body mass of the subject (m). Mechanical power (P) is calculated using the equation

$$P(kgm \cdot s^{-1}) = m(kg) \; 9.81 \; h(m) \; t^{-1}(s)$$

Some investigators, including Kalamen (1968), have modified the protocol to running three, instead of two, stairs at a time. Davies et al. (1972) used one step at a time

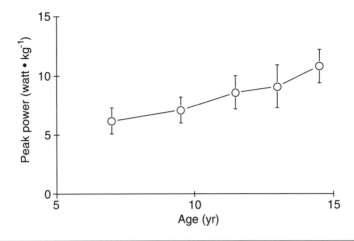

Figure 4.2   Representative values of peak power (per kg body mass) of legs in males who performed the Force–Velocity Cycling Test. Means ± 1*SD*. Data on 144 boys, based on Falgairette et al. (1991).

with young children. Other modifications have included a longer run on the flat and a mix of two and three stairs at a time. The test acquired popularity during the 1960s and 1970s, mostly due to its simplicity and the inexpensive equipment. It has been used in children and adults of a wide age range (Davies et al., 1972; Di Prampero & Cerretelli, 1969; Kurowski, 1977; Margaria et al., 1966). In fact, the first data that showed the lower ability of children to perform anaerobic exercise were derived from the Margaria step-running test (Margaria et al., 1966).

One disadvantage of the step-running test is that various muscle groups in the upper and lower limbs, as well as the trunk, contribute to step running. Because people differ in their style of sprinting up stairs, it is difficult to tell how much each of these muscle groups contributes to the task. Furthermore, the skill of step sprinting may be age dependent.

Figures 4.3 and 4.4 summarize peak power values for boys and girls, respectively, who performed the Margaria step-running test.

VERTICAL JUMP TESTS

The task of the suject in this test is to jump as high as possible, from a stationary position, using both legs for take off.

Sargent Jump

More than seven decades ago, Sargent (1921) introduced the first test that was intended to assess performance that is related to a person's muscle power. In

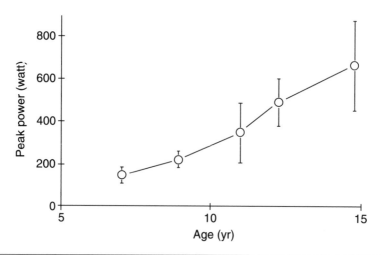

Figure 4.3 Representative values of peak power in males who performed the Margaria Step-Running Test. Means ± 1*SD*. Data on 47 boys.
Adapted from Davies et al. (1972).

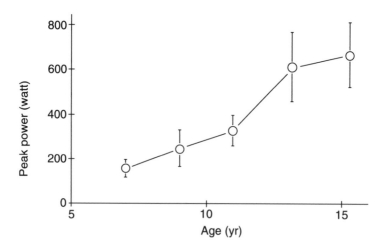

Figure 4.4 Representative values of peak power in females who performed the Margaria Step-Running Test. Means ± 1*SD*. Data on 45 girls.
Adapted from Davies et al. (1972).

preparation for the jump, the subject is allowed to crouch momentarily and then be helped by a swing forward with the arms. The maximal vertical elevation is determined by the highest point that is reached by the fingers, with the arms extended. This is compared to the height reached by the fingers when the subject is standing erect, with arms extended upwards. There are various ways of recording the achieved height, ranging from having the subject hold a piece of chalk and strike a board with it at peak height to the use of electronic pressure sensors that are spread on the board. Scoring is usually recorded as net vertical elevation, which is a function of the instantaneous power exerted at take off.

The test is easily learned by children and can be administered under both field and laboratory conditions. Test–retest reliability following three to four practice trials is high (0.92 among adults) (Glencross, 1966). As reported by Davies and Young (1984), a correlation of 0.92 was found between scores in the Sargent jump and those achieved by a vertical jump from a force platform. Validity of the Sargent jump as a test of muscle power was evaluated in the author's laboratory by comparing the scores with *peak power* in the WAnT. The r value in 48 adolecent boys was 0.77, suggesting a fair-to-good validity.

Using a Force Platform

When the takeoff in a vertical jump is done from a force platform, peak power can be calculated by measuring the instantaneous force exerted just before takeoff and multiplying it by the respective vertical velocity (as calculated from the height of the jump). Using this method with ten 11.8 ± 0.4-year-old boys and 11.7 ± 0.4-year-old girls, Davies and Young (1984) found that peak power in the vertical jump was 45% lower than that obtained during the first 5 s of all-out cycling. This difference resulted from a lower force, rather than a lower velocity, in the vertical jump. As a group, the peak power of these children during the jump was only 30% of that obtained by 22.7 ± 1.5-year-old adults. This difference could not be explained fully by the larger body mass of the adults.

SPRINT RUNNING TESTS

The ability to sustain high-speed running depends, in part at least, on anaerobic performance. Thus, the time that can be maintained at a speed requiring supramaximal energy expenditure can be used as an index of local muscle endurance. An alternative index has been the calculated mechanical power output, as derived from body mass, velocity, and treadmill slope.

Motorized Treadmill

Several authors have used sprint running on a motorized treadmill as an anaerobic performance test in adults (Cunningham & Faulkner, 1969) and in children (Paterson et al., 1986). Such a test taxes many muscle groups and, as such, can yield information about the "total" anaerobic capacity of an individual. One shortcoming, however, is that the calculation of power during a running task is based on assumptions that may not be valid for supramaximal effort. Another potential problem is that some subjects—paticularly the young, untrained ones—may terminate their run prematurely because of fear, rather than as a result of having reached a "real" anaerobic capacity. When performed by trained boys, the test–retest reliability of a running task that required 20% more than maximal O_2 uptake was $r = 0.76$ at age 10 and $r = 0.84$ at age 15 (Paterson et al.). These are considerably lower reliability coefficients than those reported for cycling tasks such as the F-V test and the WAnT.

Nonmotorized Treadmill

Lakomy (1987) described a sprint test on a nonmotorized treadmill in which anaerobic performance can be measured in adults. Van Praagh (1995) used this test with children. His protocol lasts less than 10 s, during which the subject attempts to develop maximal speed while connected at the waist to a horizontal belt. The belt, in turn, is connected to gauges that monitor vertical displacement and horizontal traction forces. These together with the treadmill speed allow one to calculate potential and kinetic energy and power. As reported by Lakomy (1987) the reliability of this test in adults (unreported sample size) was 0.93.

There are no published reliability data for children. Nor are there representative data to illustrate the relationship between anaerobic performance and age during sprint running on a treadmill.

ISOKINETIC ANAEROBIC CYCLING TESTS

Even though anaerobic cycling tests with a constant braking force have been used in various laboratories, a protocol in which the pedaling velocity is constant can yield important information about muscle power and especially muscle fatigability. The rationale is that, based on force–velocity principles, there is an optimal velocity at which the highest power is obtained (Wilkie, 1960). This optimum is approximately 110-pedaling rpm for children and adults alike (Dotan & Bar-Or, 1983; Sargeant, 1989; Sargeant & Dolan, 1986; Sargeant, Dolan, & Thorne, 1984). By definition, the velocity in constant-resistance anaerobic tests is progressively reduced as the muscle fatigues. As a result, a person's highest possible power at the latter stages of, for example, a 30-s test will be underestimated. Cycling protocols done at a constant velocity are intended to correct for the above shortcoming.

An isokinetic cycle ergometer has been developed by Sargeant et al. (1981). By use of strain gauges, force is measured at the pedals, and the power is continuously monitored for each leg throughout the pedal revolution. Protocols can vary from a single pedal revolution, through a F-V test, to tasks that last 60 s or more. This ergometer has been used with children (Sargeant et al., 1984) and adults (McCartney,

Heigenhauser, Sargeant, & Jones, 1983; Sargeant et al., 1981). Modification of the ergometer offers measurement of eccentric as well as concentric cycling tasks.

The isokinetic approach can yield basic *in situ* information on muscle contraction characteristics, particularly the relationships among force, velocity, and power. Its disadvantage, however, is that an appropriate ergometer is markedly more expensive than ergometers suitable for constant-force testing. In fact, the studies introduced by the groups of Sargeant (1981) and McCartney (1983) were all done using a prototype ergometer and, to the best of this author's knowledge, there are no commercial isokinetic ergometers that reach its level of sophistication.

ISOKINETIC MONOARTICULAR ANAEROBIC TESTS

Isokinetic dynamometers, such as Cybex and Kin Com, measure torque during a movement across a single joint (e.g., knee extension, elbow flexion), and their main use has been to assess muscle strength. However, by knowing the torque and the angular velocity, it is also possible to determine mechanical power. The advantage of this approach over cycling, jumping, or running protocols is that characteristics of a single muscle group can be measured under well-controlled conditions that keep other body joints stable and immobilized. There is also a need to standardize the location of the tested joint versus the axis of the lever arm of the machine.

Most testing protocols with these dynamometers require a single maximal motion at each angular velocity. This allows the study of torque-velocity and power-velocity relationships. These protocols are discussed in chapter 6.

Some protocols are available that assess muscle fatigability through repetition of maximal contractions over time. Thorstenson, Grimby, & Karlsson (1976), for example, have administered to adults a protocol of alternating 50-times-maximal knee extensions and passive knee flexions, at an angular velocity of 180° per s. This, combined with muscle biopsies, identified biochemical and histochemical correlates of anaerobic performance in the quadriceps muscle (Inbar, Kaiser, & Tesch, 1981; Thorstenson et al., 1976). Saavedra et al. (1991), using a modified Hydra-Gym machine, conducted 10-, 30-, and 90-s tests of total work output during repeated knee extensions and flexions in 9- to 19-year-old girls and boys. The authors reported an excellent reliability and validity for these measurements. However, the source that they are quoting (Lagassé et al., 1989) refers to single contractions, rather than repeated contractions over time, which does not provide a validation of the 10- to 90-s tasks as tests of local muscle endurance.

An isokinetic, monoarticular muscle endurance test was recently developed in the author's laboratory for children and adolescents, using the Kin Com dynamometer. This McMaster Muscle Endurance Test (McMET) yields information about power and fatigue characteristics in the knee extensors and the knee flexors. The subject performs 25 maximal knee extensions and flexions at an angular velocity of 180° per s. Each cycle takes 1.1 s to 1.2 s, and the total duration of the test is 27 s to 30 s (depending on the time interval taken by the subject to switch from maximal flexion to maximal extension, and vice versa). Possible uses of the McMET include a comparison of left- and right-thigh muscles or of upper and lower limbs. The test was found feasible for children and adolescents (Calvert, Bar-Or, McGillis, & Suei, 1993). Its validity was evaluated, using the WAnT as a gold standard. In 48 pre-, mid-, and late-pubescent boys, correlation between total work of the extensors in the McMET and total work in the WAnT was 0.94. The respective r value for knee flexors was 0.92. When values were corrected for body mass, r value for knee extensors was 0.79, suggesting that the above strong association does not merely reflect body size.

THE WINGATE ANAEROBIC TEST (WAnT)

The WAnT was developed in the mid-1970s at the Wingate Institute in Israel (Ayalon, Inbar, & Bar-Or, 1974), based on a 30-s cycling test previously suggested by Cumming (1973). It has since gained recognition and is now the most popular test of anaerobic performance. The characteristics of the WAnT (feasibility, reliability, and validity), when used with children, adolescents, and adults, have been explored by various groups. Its test-retest reliability in able-bodied children ranges between 0.92 and 0.97 (Bar-Or, 1987). Intraindividual coefficient of variation among 6- to 12-year-old girls and boys is 7.3% and 6.8% for peak power and mean power, respectively (Naughton, Carlson, & Fairweather, 1992). It has been found to be feasible and informative when used in children with a neuromuscular disability (Emons & Van Baak, 1993; Parker, Carriere, Hebestreit, & Bar-Or, 1992; Tirosh, Rosenbaum, & Bar-Or, 1990; Van Mil, Schoeber, Calvert, & Bar-Or, in press).

Protocol

The WAnT requires 30-s cycling or arm cranking at maximal velocity against a constant braking force (determined individually for each subject). Most laboratories use a brief (2-3 s) flying start against "zero" resistance to overcome the initial inertia of the flywheel. The required resistance is then applied. To obtain the child's best performance, it is essential to emphasize the importance of pedaling "*as fast as possible*" throughout the test. It should be further explained that the task is "very hard, but it takes only 30 seconds, so that when you feel tired you know that there are only a few more seconds to go."

The test is preceded by 3 to 5 min of warm-up cycling and then 1 to 2 min of rest (sitting on the ergometer). The warm-up should be at a moderate intensity, raising the heart rate to 150 to 160 beats per min. Warming-up has been shown to increase performance of peak power and mean power in children (Inbar & Bar-Or, 1975). Another use of the warm-up period is to practice sprint cycling. This is achieved by three to four sprints (2-3 s each) at maximal speed, against a braking force that is a little lower than that used in the test itself.

Required Equipment

Any ergometer with a fixed braking force (i.e., independent of pedaling rate) is suitable. If a mechanical ergometer is used, it is best to apply the resistance by hanging weights (e.g., Fleisch-Metabo ergometer), rather than by a pendulum (e.g., Monark ergometer). Electronically braked ergometers must have a constant-force mode (as in the newly developed WATSYSTEM), so that power output will be fully dependent on pedaling rate. Whichever ergometer is used, pedaling rate must be be monitored continuously. This can be done by a variety of counting and recording devices, which differ in sophistication. In the author's laboratory, a photo-sensitive cell is activated 18 times at each pedal revolution, with the impulse fed into a personal computer. Online analysis by a computer has also been described by others (Cabrera, Lough, Doershuk, & DeRivera, 1993). A much simpler, yet accurate, method is to count the revolutions by a mechanical or electromagnetic microswitch and feed the impulse to a chart recorder (Docherty & Gaul, 1991) or the marker channel of a one-channel ECG. By running the paper strip throughout the 30-s test, one can then obtain a permanent record.

The WAnT is tolerated easily by children, but some adolescents (and adults), especially if they are tall and heavy, may feel light-headed and even nauseated a few minutes after the test. This can be prevented in most cases by pedaling for an additional 2 to 3 min against a very low resistance once the test has been completed and then lying down on a mat for another 3 to 4 min. This procedure is seldom needed for children younger than 12 years.

It has recently been shown (Hebestreit et al., 1993) that children recover following the WAnT much faster than adults: While young men needed a 10-min recovery to repeat their full performance a second time, prepubescent boys fully recovered within 2 min. A practical implication is that if, for whatever reason, the WAnT has to be repeated, a rest period for children need not exceed 5 to 10 min. (This time factor may be different for children who have a muscle disease or other disabilities, but specific data are not available.) For more information about the WAnT and its characteristics, see Inbar, Bar-Or, & Skinner (in press).

Performance Indexes

With a fixed braking force, the child produces the highest power during the first few s, and then there is a decline in power, which reflects local muscle fatigue. As shown in Figure 4.5, two indexes of performance can be derived from the power-time curve: peak power, which is the highest mechanical power (expressed in kpm per min or in Watt) obtained at any time during the test, and mean power, which is the average power throughout the 30 s. The latter can be described also as total work (expressed in kpm or in joules). Some authors have also been monitoring a fatigue index, expressed as the percentage of drop in power from peak to the lowest point. In adults, the fatigue index is highly correlated with the preponderance of fast-twitch muscle fibers (Bar-Or et al., 1980). Such information requires a muscle biopsy that, for ethical reasons, is not likely to be done with children.

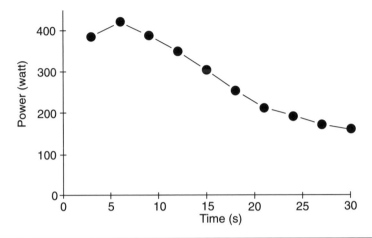

Figure 4.5   The Wingate Anaerobic Test. A typical power vs time curve in a 10-year-old male, assuming power is averaged every 3 s. In this example peak power is 422 W, mean power is 287 W, and total work is 8610 joule.

Originally it was assumed that peak power reflects alactic performance. It has subsequently been shown, however, that after the first few s of the test, there is a dramatic surge in lactate concentration in the *vastus lateralis* of young adults (Jacobs, Tesch, Bar-Or, Karlsson, & Dotan, 1983). It is, therefore, doubtful whether peak power can be considered an *alactic index* of performance. It is better to refer to it as the highest mechanical power generated during a cycling or arm-cranking motion. Mean power (or total work) is an index of local muscle endurance. It was originally assumed to reflect anaerobic capacity (Bar-Or, 1983). This, however, is untrue because protocols longer than 30 s (Katch, Weltman, Martin, & Gray, 1977) can yield more anaerobic work than does the WAnT. It is not clear whether the fatigue index reflects anaerobic performance.

Choice of Optimal Braking Force

Because power is the product of force and velocity, each combination of braking force and pedaling rate may yield a different power. An important methodological consideration is, therefore, to choose a braking force that would elicit the highest power performance for each subject. Dotan and Bar-Or (1983) reported that in 13- to 14-year-old girls and boys the optimal braking force for mean power, when using the Monark ergometer, is 67 and 70 g per kg body weight, respectively. Using a Fleisch ergometer (in which one pedal revolution moves the perimeter of the flywheel 10 m), the corresponding forces are 40 g and 42 g per kg body weight. Irrespective of the ergometer used, the optimal force in these girls and boys is equivalent to 3.92 and 4.13 joule per kg body weight, respectively, for each pedal revolution. Optimal forces for adults are 20% to 25% higher. It is quite possible that children

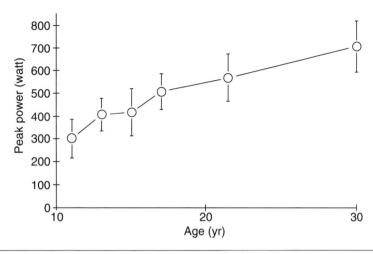

Figure 4.6 Representative values of peak power of legs in males, using the Wingate Anaerobic Test (WAnT). Means ± 1*SD*. Data on 164 boys and men, based on Inbar (1985).

younger than 13 years of age may need lower optima. More reseach is needed to establish the specific optimal forces for various age groups. Optimal forces to elicit the highest possible peak power are higher than those needed for the highest mean power (Dotan & Bar-Or, 1983; Vandewalle et al., 1987), but there are no specific data for children regarding the optima for peak power.

Ideally, an optimal force should be chosen according to the muscle mass of the limbs that perform the test. Because this is impractical, body mass is usually used. The author's laboratory is now developing alternative approaches to determine optimal forces in children who are obese, very lean, or have a neuromuscular disability. One such alternative is to use the optimal force determined during the F-V test (see Figure 4.1 and related text), as the optimal force for mean power in the WAnT. This approach has been suggested previously (Vandewalle et al., 1985; Van Praagh et al., 1990). Its validity has been reported for healthy adults (Vandewalle et al.) and for children with neuromuscular disabilities (Van Mil et al., in press).

Representative values for peak power of the legs and the arms are shown in Figures 4.6 and 4.7, respectively. Values for mean power of the legs are presented in absolute power units (Figure 4.8), as well as per kg body mass (Figure 4.9). Absolute mean power values for the arms are summarized in Figure 4.10.

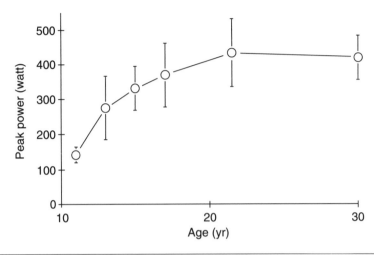

Figure 4.7   Representative values of peak power of arms in males, using the Wingate Anaerobic Test (WAnT). Means ± 1*SD*. Data on 110 boys, based on Inbar (1985).

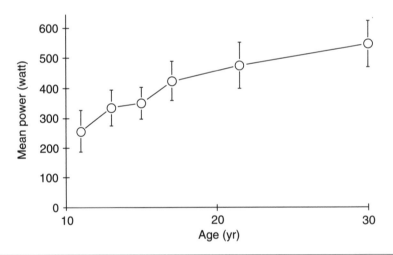

Figure 4.8   Representative values of mean power of legs in males, using the Wingate Anaerobic Test (WAnT). Means ± 1*SD*. Data on 164 boys and men, based on Inbar (1985).

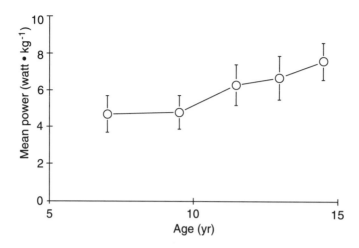

Figure 4.9   Representative values of mean power (per kg body mass) of legs in males, using the Wingate Anaerobic Test (WAnT). Means ± 1*SD*. Data on 144 boys, based on Falgairette et al. (1991).

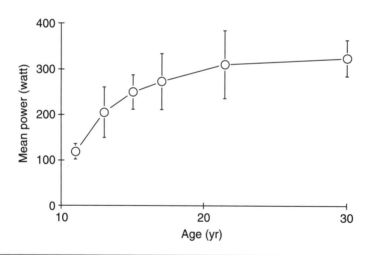

Figure 4.10   Representative values of mean power of arms in males, using the Wingate Anaerobic Test (WAnT). Means ± 1*SD*. Data on 110 boys and men, based on Inbar (1985).

CONCLUSION

Among tests that assess peak power, the Sargent jump is the least expensive. However, several assumptions have to be made about the actual force and velocity in this ballistic task. Furthermore, the style of the jump is hard to standardize, which makes it hard to determine the exact muscle groups that contribute to the jump. By incorporating a force platform into the vertical jump protocol, it is possible to determine mechanical forces and their direction. The Margaria step-running test, while still inexpensive, is easier to standardize than the Sargent jump. In this test it is still difficult to determine the exact muscle groups that contribute to performance. The force–velocity test is the method of choice for determining peak power, as well as force–velocity relationships, during cycling. Such relationships can best be determined during isokinetic contractions, but suitable ergometers are still prohibitively expensive for most laboratories. With proper standardization, using an isokinetic dynamometer, single monoarticular contractions would best determine peak power (as well as force–velocity relationships) of a single muscle group.

Among tests that assess local muscle endurance, treadmill sprinting would yield the highest total work, because of the large muscle mass used during running. This method, however, requires several assumptions to calculate mechanical power, and it is hard to determine which muscles contribute to the task. The main disadvantage of this method, particularly with children, is that subjects are often afraid to push themselves to full capacity, because they fear tripping. The use of a nonmotorized treadmill may alleviate this fear, but the equipment is expensive; more research is needed to assess the validity of this method.

The tests of choice to determine both peak power and anaerobic capacity are cycling protocols that last 30 s to 60 s. Among these an isokinetic protocol would yield the most valid information regarding force–velocity relationships. The required ergometer, however, is very expensive. The Wingate Test can be done with much less sophisticated equipment. By increasing sampling frequency of pedal motion in this test, a near-instantaneous peak power can be measured. The Wingate Test has been evaluated more extensively than any other anaerobic performance test, in both able-bodied participants and in disabled populations, and found to be highly reliable and valid. One disadvantage of the Wingate Test is that a 30-s cycling task is too short to extract all muscular anaerobic work. Longer protocols would yield more work, but also require a greater percentage of aerobic contribution and may have low subject compliance.

REFERENCES

Åstrand, P.O. (1952). *Experimental studies of physical working capacity in relation to sex and age* (pp. 85-392). Copenhagen: Munksgaard.

Ayalon, A., Inbar, O., & Bar-Or, O. (1974). Relationships among measurements of explosive strength and anaerobic power. In R.C. Nelson & C.A. Morehouse (Eds.), *International series on sport sciences* (Vol. 1. Biomechanics IV) (pp. 572-577). Baltimore: University Park Press.

Bar-Or, O. (1983). *Pediatric sports medicine for the practitioner: From physiologic principles to clinical applications.* New York: Springer.

Bar-Or, O. (1987). The Wingate anaerobic test, an update on methodology, reliability and validity. *Sports Medicine*, **4**, 381-394.

Bar-Or, O., Dotan, R., Inbar, A., Rotshtein, A., Karlsson, J., & Tesch, P. (1980). Anaerobic capacity and muscle fiber type distribution in man. *International Journal of Sports Medicine*, **1**, 89-92.

Bedu, M., Fellmann, N., Spielvogel, H., Falgairette, G., Van Praagh, E., & Coudert, J. (1991). Force-velocity and 30s Wingate tests in boys at high and low altitudes. *Journal of Applied Physiology*, **70**, 1031-1037.

Blimkie, C.J.R., Roche, P., Hay, J.T., & Bar-Or, O. (1988). Anaerobic power of arms in teenage boys and girls: Relationship to lean tissue. *European Journal of Applied Physiology*, **57**, 677-683.

Bouchard, C., Taylor, A.W., Simoneau, J.-A., & Dulac, S. (1991). Testing anaerobic power and capacity. In J.D. MacDougall, H.A. Wegner, & H.J. Green (Eds.), *Physiological testing of the high-performance athlete* (pp.175-221). Champaign, IL: Human Kinetics.

Cabrera, M.E., Lough, M.D., Doershuk, C.F., & DeRivera, G.A. (1993). Anaerobic performance—assessed by the Wingate test—in patients with cystic fibrosis. *Pediatric Exercise Science*, **5**, 78-87.

Calvert, R.E., Bar-Or, O., McGillis, L.A., & Suei, K. (1993). Total work during an isokinetic and Wingate endurance tests in circumpubertal males. *Pediatric Exercise Science*, **5**, 398.

Carlson, J.S., & Naughton, G.A. (1993). An examination of the anaerobic capacity of children using maximal accumulated oxygen deficit. *Pediatric Exercise Science*, **5**, 60-71.

Cumming, G.R. (1973). Correlation of athletic performance and aerobic power in 12-17 year-old children with bone age, calf muscle, total body potassium, heart volume and two indices of anaerobic power. In O. Bar-Or (Ed.), *Pediatric work physiology* (pp. 109-134). Tel Aviv: Wingate Institute.

Cunningham, D.A., & Faulkner, J.A. (1969). The effect of training on aerobic and anaerobic metabolism during a short exhaustive run. *Medicine & Science in Sports*, **1**, 65-69.

Davies, C.T.M., Barnes, C., & Godfrey, S. (1972). Body composition and maximal exercise performance in children. *Human Biology*, **44**, 195-214.

Davies, C.T.M., & Young, K. (1984). Effects of external loading on short-term power output in children and young male adults. *European Journal of Applied Physiology*, **52**, 351-354.

Di Prampero, P.E., & Cerretelli, P. (1969). Maximal muscular power (aerobic and anaerobic) in African natives. *Ergonomics*, **12**, 51-59.

Docherty, D., & Gaul, C.A. (1991). Relationship of body size, physique, and composition to physical performance in young boys and girls. *International Journal of Sports Medicine*, **12**, 525-532.

Dotan, R., & Bar-Or, O. (1983). Load optimization for the Wingate anaerobic test. *European Journal of Applied Physiology*, **51**, 409-417.

Duché, P., Falgairette, G., Bedu, M., Fellmann, N., Lac, G., Robert, A., & Coudert, J. (1992). Longitudinal approach of bioenergetic profile in boys before and during puberty. In J. Coudert, & E. Van Praagh (Eds.), *Pediatric work physiology* (pp. 43-45).Paris: Masson.

Dux, L., Dux, E., & Guba, F. (1982). Further data on the androgenic dependency of the skeletal musculature. The effect of pre-pubertal castration on the structural development of skeletal muscle. *Hormone and Metabolism Research*, **14**, 191-194.

Emons, H.J.G., & Van Baak, M.A. (1993). Effect of training on aerobic and anaerobic power and mechanical efficiency in spastic cerebral palsied children. *Pediatric Exercise Science*, **5**, 412.

Eriksson, B.O., Gollnick, P.D., & Saltin, B. (1973). Muscle metabolism and enzyme activities after training in boys 11-13 years old. *Acta Physiologica Scandinavica*, **87**, 485-497.

Eriksson, B.O., & Saltin, B. (1974). Muscle metabolism during exercise in boys aged 11 to 16 years compared to adults. *Acta Paediatrica Belgica*, **28**(Suppl.), 257-265.

Evans, S.A., Eckerson, J.M., Housh, T.J., & Johnson, G.O. (1993). Muscular power of arms in high school wrestlers. *Pediatric Exercise Science*, **5**, 72-77.

Falgairette, G., Bedu, M., Fellmann, N., Van Praagh, E., & Coudert, J. (1991). Bio-energetic profile in 144 boys aged from 6 to 15 years with special reference to sexual maturation. *European Journal of Applied Physiology*, **62**, 151-156.

Falk, B., & Bar-Or, O. (1993). Longitudinal changes in peak mechanical power (aerobic and anaerobic) of circum-pubertal boys. *Pediatric Exercise Science*, **5**, 318-331.

Fellmann, N., Bedu, M., Spigelvogel, H., Falgairette, G., Van Praagh, E., Jarrige, J.-F., & Coudert, J. (1988). Anaerobic metabolism during pubertal development at high altitude. *Journal of Applied Physiology*, **64**, 1382-1386.

Fournier, M., Ricci, J., Taylor, A.W., Ferguson, R., Monpetit, R., & Chaitman, B. (1982). Skeletal muscle adaptation in adolescent boys: sprint and endurance training and detraining. *Medicine & Science in Sports & Exercise*, **14**, 453-456.

Glencross, D.J. (1966). The nature of the vertical jump test and the standing broad jump. *Research Quarterly*, **37**, 353-359.

Hebestreit, H. Mimura, K., & Bar-Or, O. (1993). Recovery of anaerobic muscle power following 30-s supramaximal exercise: Comparison between boys and men. *Journal of Applied Physiology*, **74**, 2875-2880.

Inbar, O. (1985). *The Wingate anaerobic test—Characteristics, applications and norms* (in Hebrew). Natanya, Israel: Wingate Press.

Inbar, O., & Bar-Or, O. (1975). The effects of intermittent warm-up on 7-9 year-old boys. *European Journal of Applied Physiology*, **34**, 81-89.

Inbar, O., & Bar-Or, O. (1986). Anaerobic characteristics in male children and adolescents. *Medicine & Science in Sports & Exercise*, **18**, 264-269.

Inbar, O., Bar-Or, & Skinner, J.S. (in press). *The Wingate Anaerobic Test: Development, characteristics, and application.* Champaign, IL: Human Kinetics.

Inbar, O., Kaiser, P., & Tesch, P. (1981). Relationships between leg muscle fiber type distribution and leg exercise performance. *International Journal of Sports Medicine*, **2**, 154-159.

Jacobs, I., Tesch, P.A., Bar-Or, O., Karlsson, J., & Dotan, R. (1983). Lactate in human skeletal muscle after 10 and 30 s of supramaximal exercise. *Journal of Applied Physiology*, **55**, 365-367.

Kalamen, J. (1968). *Measurement of maximum muscular power in man.* Unpublished doctoral dissertation, Ohio State University.

Katch, V., Weltman, A., Martin, R., & Gray, L. (1977). Optimal test characteristics for maximal anaerobic work on the bicycle ergometer. *Research Quarterly*, **48**, 319-327.

Kindermann, V.W., Huber, G., & Keul, J. (1975). Anaerobe Kapazität bei Kindern und Jugendlichen in Beziehung zum Erwachsenen. *Sportartz und Sportmedizin*, **6**, 112-115.

Kurowski, T.T. (1977). *Anaerobic power of children from ages 9 through 15 years.* Unpublished M.Sc. thesis, Florida State University.

Laggassé, P.-P., Katch, F.I., Katch, V.L., & Roy, M.-A. (1989). Reliability and validity of the Omnitron hydraulic resistance exercise and testing device. *International Journal of Sports Medicine*, **10**, 455-458.

Lakomy, H. (1987). The use of a non-motorized treadmill for analysing sprint performance. *Ergonomics*, **30**, 627-638.

Lodder, M.A.N., de Haan, A., & Sargeant, A.J. (1991). The effect of growth on specific tetanic force in the skeletal muscle of the unanaesthetized rat. *Journal of Physiology*, **438**, 151P.

Margaria, R., Aghemo, P., & Rovelli, E. (1966). Measurement of muscular power (anaerobic) in man. *Journal of Applied Physiology*, **21**, 1662-1664.

Matejkova, J., Koprivova, Z., & Placheta, Z. (1980). Changes in acid-base balance after maximal exercise. In Z. Placheta (Ed.), *Youth and physical activity* (pp. 191-199). Brno: Purkyne University.

McCartney, N., Heigenhauser, G.J.F., Sargeant, A.J., & Jones, N.L. (1983). A constant velocity cycle ergometry for the study of muscle function. *Journal of Applied Physiology*, **55**, 212-217.

Mercier, B., Mercier, J., Granier, P., Le Gallais, D., & Préfaut, C. (1992). Maximal anaerobic power: Relationship to anthropometric characteristics during growth. *International Journal of Sports Medicine*, **13**, 21-26.

Naughton, G., Carlson, J., & Fairweather, I. (1992). Determining the variability of performance on Wingate aerobic tests in children aged 6-12 years. *International Journal of Sports Medicine*, **13**, 512-517.

Parker, D.F., Carriere, L., Hebestreit, H., & Bar-Or, O. (1992). Anaerobic endurance and peak muscle power in children with cerebral palsy. *American Journal for Diseases of Children*, **146**, 1069-1073.

Paterson, D.H., Cunningham, D.A., & Bumstead, L.A. (1986). Recovery O_2 and blood lactic acid: longitudinal analysis in boys aged 11 to 15 years. *European Journal of Applied Physiology*, **55**, 93-99.

Pirnay, F, & Crielaard, J.M. (1979). Mesure de la puissance anaérobie alactique. *Medicine du Sport*, **53**, 13-16.

Rutenfranz, J., Andersen, K.L., Seliger, V. Klimmer, F., Ilmarinen, J., Ruppel, M., & Kylian, H. (1981). Exercise ventilation during the growth spurt period: Comparison between two European countries. *European Journal of Pediatrics*, **136**, 135-142.

Saavedra, C., Lagassé, Bouchard, C., & Simoneau, J-A. (1991). Maximal anaerobic performance of the knee extensor muscles during growth. *Medicine & Science in Sports & Exercise*, **23**, 1083-1089.

Sargeant, A.J. (1989). Short-term muscle power in children and adolescents. In O. Bar-Or (Ed.), *Advances in pediatric sports sciences* Vol. 3 (pp. 41-63). Champaign, IL: Human Kinetics.

Sargeant, A.J., & Dolan, P. (1986). Optimal velocity of muscle contraction for short-term power output in children and adults. In J. Rutenfranz, R. Mocellin & F. Klimt (Eds.), *Children and exercise XII* (pp. 39-42). Champaign, IL: Human Kinetics.

Sargeant, A.J., Dolan, P., & Thorne, A. (1984). Isokinetic measurement of maximal leg force and anaerobic power output in children. In J. Ilmarinen & I. Välimäki (Eds.), *Children and sport* (pp. 93-98). Berlin: Springer.

Sargeant, A.J., Hoinville, E., & Young, A. (1981). Maximum leg force and power output during short-term dynamic exercise. *Journal of Applied Physiology*, **51**, 1175-1182.

Sargent, D.A. (1921). The physical test of a man. *American Physical Education Review*, **26**, 188-194.

Suei, K., McGillis, L.A., Falk, B., Blimkie, C.J.R., & Bar-Or, O. (1991). Relationships among muscle endurance, power and strength in circum-pubertal boys. *Medicine & Science in Sports & Exercise*, **23**, S32.

Thorstenson, A., Grimby, G., & Karlsson, J. (1976). Fatigability and fiber composition of human skeletal muscle. *Acta Physiologica Scandinavica*, **98**, 318-322.

Tirosh, E., Rosenbaum, P., & Bar-Or, O. (1990). A new muscle power test in neuromuscular disease: feasibility and reliability. *American Journal for Diseases of Children*, **144**, 1083-1087.

Vandewalle, H., Pérès, G., Heller, J., & Monod, H. (1985). All out anaerobic capacity test on cycle ergometers. *European Journal of Applied Physiology*, **54**, 222-229.

Vandewalle, H., Pérès, G., Heller, J., & Monod, H. (1987). Standard anaerobic exercise tests. *Sports Medicine*, **4**, 268-289.

Van Mil, G.A.H., Schoeber, N., Calvert, R.E., & Bar-Or, O. (in press). Optimization of braking force in the Wingate test for children and adolescents with a neuromuscular disease. *Medicine and Science in Sports and Exercise*.

Van Praagh, E. (1995). Testing of anaerobic performance. In O. Bar-Or (Ed.), *Encyclopedia of sport medicine: The child and adolescent athlete* (pp. 602-616). London: Blackwell.

Van Praagh, E., Falgairette, G., Bedu, M., Fellmann, N., & Coudert, J. (1989). Laboratory and field tests in 7-year-old boys. In S. Oseid & K-H. Carlsen (Eds.), *Children and exercise XIII* (pp. 11-17). Champaign, IL: Human Kinetics.

Van Praagh, E., Fellmann, N., Bedu, M., Falgairette, G., & Coudert, J. (1990). Gender difference in the relationship of anaerobic power output to body composition in children. *Pediatric Exercise Science*, **2**, 336-348.

Weijiang, D., & Juxiang, Q. (1988). Anaerobic performance of Chinese untrained and trained 11- to 18-year-old boys and girls. In Q. Mianuya, & Y. Changlong (Eds.), *China's sports medicine. Medicine and sports science*, (Vol. 28, pp. 52-60). Basel: Karger.

Wilkie, D.R. (1960). Man as a source of mechanical power. *Ergonomics*, **3**, 1-8.

5

Luc Léger

Aerobic Performance

To cover the topic of assessment of aerobic performance in children, I first describe the concept of aerobic fitness and its main components ($\dot{V}O_2$max, efficiency, and endurance) and describe the change of each of these components during growth. Then the units used to quantify aerobic fitness components are covered extensively because they directly affect the concepts behind these components. This groundwork puts us in a good position to describe the methods used to test the aerobic fitness components and underline their advantages and disadvantages.

GROWTH CHARACTERISTICS OF AEROBIC FITNESS

Aerobic fitness is the capacity to accomplish endurance performance that mainly depends on aerobic metabolism. Middle-distance and long-distance events are typical sports that require a high level of aerobic fitness. Aerobic fitness also appears to be related to health status, particularly in relation to cardiovascular health.

Aerobic fitness has three components:

1. Maximal aerobic power (MAP) or maximal oxygen consumption ($\dot{V}O_2$max)
2. Mechanical efficiency or economy of aerobic energy processes
3. Aerobic endurance or aerobic capacity or anaerobic threshold

Maximal Aerobic Power

Maximal aerobic power corresponds to the maximal exercise intensity that can be sustained in steady state aerobiosis. From a practical point of view, MAP coincides with a plateau in oxygen consumption level ($\dot{V}O_2$) as the exercise intensity increases in a discontinuous multistage protocol. This plateau ($\dot{V}O_2$max) is not always seen in continuous multistage tests, particularly with children (Armstrong, Williams, Balding, & Kirby, 1991; Freedson, & Goodman, 1993; Massicotte, Gauthier, & Markon, 1985; Vaccaro & Mahon, 1987); the highest $\dot{V}O_2$ value is then called $\dot{V}O_2$ peak, because it is possible that true $\dot{V}O_2$max was not reached. In general, however, $\dot{V}O_2$ peak values are very close to or equal to $\dot{V}O_2$max values.

Although the plateau phenomenon appears to be less common in children, the reproducibility and test–retest reliability of $\dot{V}O_2$ measurements in children are similar to those found in adults (Vaccaro & Mahon, 1987). Acceptable reliability has also been obtained in 3- to 4-year old children (Shuleva, Hunter, Hester, & Dunawaw, 1990).

High $\dot{V}O_2$max values are important because they reflect good function of the cardiorespiratory system that makes it possible to accomplish submaximal tasks with less fatigue. Compared to adults, young individuals generally have lower $\dot{V}O_2$max when expressed in L · min^{-1} (Figure 5.1). When related to body weight, however, $\dot{V}O_2$max (ml · kg^{-1} · min^{-1}) is relatively stable for boys (50-55 ml · kg^{-1} · min^{-1}) and decreases only slightly for girls (from 50-40 ml · kg^{-1} · min^{-1}) during growth (Figure 5.2). In 3- to 6-year-old children, however, slightly lower values, around 42 ml · kg^{-1} · min^{-1}, have been reported (Shuleva et al., 1990). According to a recent study by Falgairette (1989), who reviewed at least 60 studies on $\dot{V}O_2$max changes during growth, there are large differences among children at any age as well as different trends showing either a decrease or an increase in relative $\dot{V}O_2$max with age. However, separating studies according to the ergometer used for testing (cycle ergometer vs. treadmill) or to the training status considerably reduces the variability (Falgairette, 1989). Such considerations indicate that $\dot{V}O_2$max per kg body weight increases with age instead of staying constant in trained boys, and it stays constant instead of decreasing in trained girls (Figure 5.3). Although these data are based on cross-sectional studies, similar trends were observed with longitudinal data in untrained (Kemper, 1986; Mirwald & Bailey, 1986) (Figure 5.4a and b) and trained children (Jones, 1991).

Because biological age does not coincide exactly with chronological age, evolution of $\dot{V}O_2$max with age is often expressed as a function of peak height velocity (Mirwald and Bailey, 1986; Vanden Eynde, Vienne, Vuylsteke-Wauters, & Van Gerven, 1988). Height does not increase linearly with age. There is a small slowing process at puberty, and this is best seen by taking the derivative of the height–age curve, that is, the height velocity as a function of age. Height velocity clearly peaks at different ages for boys and girls and for individuals reaching puberty at different ages. Thus, in comparing individuals, gender, or data from various countries in which puberty is sometimes reached at a different chronological age, $\dot{V}O_2$max values should be reported according to age before and after puberty (Figure 5.4c and d),

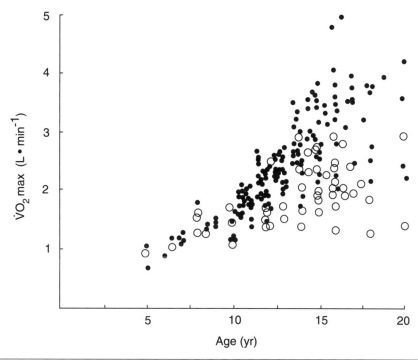

Figure 5.1   Absolute $\dot{V}O_2$max (L · min^{-1}) as a function of age during growth. Each point represents the mean value of a different group (320 groups from 60 studies covering more than 7,000 children tested on the cycle ergometer or treadmill). Open circles = females; closed circles = males.

Adapted from Falgairette (1989).

instead of using absolute chronological age (Figure 5.4a and b). Using this approach results in less variation among $\dot{V}O_2$max-age curves of different countries (Figure 5.4a and b vs. Figure 5.4c and d). This does not mean that chronological age curves are inadequate. It simply means that both chronological age and age according to peak height velocity yield different and valuable information.

All these considerations indicate that it is difficult to suggest international standards. The variation between studies (Figure 5.4) is not only due to different experimental conditions but also to real differences among populations. This is supported by different results obtained by children of two European countries, using the same testing methodology (Rutenfranz et al., 1981).

Mechanical Efficiency

Aerobic fitness is not exclusively related to $\dot{V}O_2$max. If two athletes have the same $\dot{V}O_2$max, the one with the lowest $\dot{V}O_2$ requirement at a given exercise intensity will be the better performer (Daniels & Daniels, 1992; Krahenbuhl, Pangrazie, Stone,

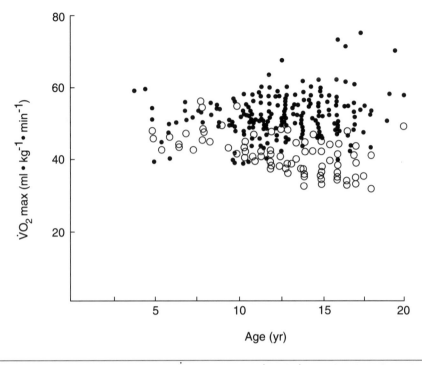

Figure 5.2   Relative-to-body-weight V̇O₂max (ml · kg⁻¹ · min⁻¹) as a function of age during growth (See Figure 5.1). Open circles = females; closed circles = males.
Adapted from Falgairette (1989).

Morgan, & Williams, 1989; Noakes, 1988). Sometimes, two athletes may have the same performance although their V̇O₂max values are different; this means that the one with the lower V̇O₂max is compensating with a higher efficiency (Noakes, 1988). Economy is thus a critical component of aerobic fitness.

This is even more crucial with children and adolescents, particularly in weight-bearing activities (Figure 5.5) for which children systematically consume more energy than adults (Åstrand 1952; Daniels, Oldridge, Nagle, & White, 1978; Léger, Cloutier, & Massicotte, 1986; McDougall, Roche, Bar-Or, & Moroz, 1983; Rowland, Auchinachie, Keenan, & Green, 1987). Among the studies, Léger et al. (1986) attempted to integrate age in a multiple regression model, and they also found a significant age–speed interaction. In other words, the curves of younger subjects were not only above older ones but also exhibited a smaller slope, indicating that younger individuals who are able to achieve high speeds behave like older ones. Adult subjects, who are also less economical, usually exhibit lower slopes (Kearney & Van Handel, 1989). Integrating age in the regression also regularizes the spaces and slopes between curves at any age (Figure 5.5b) in contrast to a series of single regressions for each age group (Figure 5.5a). Space and slope differences between single regressions (Figure 5.5a) are randomly irregular, but expected due to the

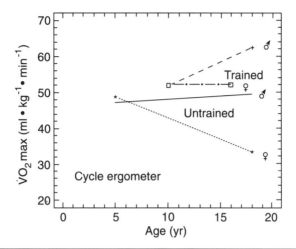

Figure 5.3   Relative-to-body-weight bicycle ergometer $\dot{V}O_2$max (ml · kg^{-1} · min^{-1}) as a function of age, gender, and training status (T = trained; U = untrained). Boys, U, 5-18 yr: $y = 46.4 + 0.15x$, 91 groups: $n = 2648$; T, 10-18 yr: $y = 38.4 + 1.33x$, 33 groups: $n = 330$. Girls, U, 5-18 yr: $y = 54.8 - 1.21x$, 50 groups: $n = 1315$; T, 10-16 yr: $y = 51.6 + 0.027x$, 12 groups: $n = 119$. Similar patterns but higher values are reported for treadmill. Adapted from Falgairette (1989).

sampling process. However, systematic differences associated with the growth spurt would be hidden using the multiple regression approach.

In any event, the treadmill $\dot{V}O_2$ requirement for a specific speed (ml · kg^{-1} · min^{-1}) is definitely higher in younger individuals. Although $\dot{V}O_2$max per unit body weight is relatively stable during growth (Bar-Or, 1983; Krahenbuhl, Skinner, & Kohrt, 1985; Falgairette, 1989) (Figure 5.2), aerobic performance (Figure 5.6) still increases with age during growth (Krahenbuhl et al., 1989; Léger, Lambert, Goulet, Rowan, & Dinelle, 1984). This phenomenon is referred to as the *aerobic reserve* identified by Bar-Or (1983). At the same exercise intensity, older children or adolescents consume less energy and are thus exercising at a lower percentage of their $\dot{V}O_2$max (greater aerobic reserve) because $\dot{V}O_2$max is stable with age. Rowland (1989) and Unnithan and Eston (1990) suggested a similar concept but their %$\dot{V}O_2$max values for any particular speed and age were quite different than those reported by Bar-Or (1983). Analysis of the data from Léger et al. (1986) also showed different values. All studies support the concept of aerobic reserve but the phenomenon needs to be quantitatively reassessed.

The aerobic reserve concept is also valid for activities that are not weight bearing, such as stationary cycling. In activities where the work is done against external resistance, $\dot{V}O_2$max is best expressed in L · min^{-1}. Even though submaximal $\dot{V}O_2$ for a given power output is almost the same at any age during growth, %$\dot{V}O_2$max is much higher (less aerobic reserve) in younger individuals because absolute $\dot{V}O_2$max increases with age (Figure 5.1).

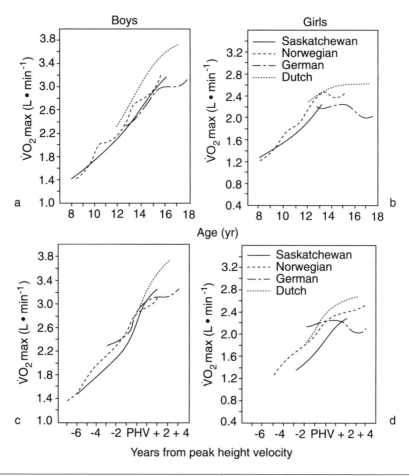

Figure 5.4   Longitudinal evolution of absolute $\dot{V}O_2$max (L · min^{-1}) as a function of chronological age (a,b) and age according to peak height velocity (c,d) in boys (a,c) and girls (b,d).
Reprinted from Mirwald and Bailey (1976).

Due to the relationship between $\dot{V}O_2$max and submaximal $\dot{V}O_2$, the aerobic reserve increases with age in both running and cycling activities. In running, the numerator of the %$\dot{V}O_2$max ratio (i.e., submax $\dot{V}O_2$ in ml · kg^{-1} · min^{-1}) decreases with age, whereas in cycling, the denominator, $\dot{V}O_2$max in L · min^{-1}, increases with age.

The systematic differences between children and adults in the mechanical efficiency of running might be partly linked to a mathematical artifact due to the ml · kg^{-1} · min^{-1} units used to express the energy requirement during running (see next section). It is much more complicated to determine the mechanical work output during running than to determine that value for cycling. Still it is possible to calculate it using sophisticated biomechanical analysis of the translational and rotational

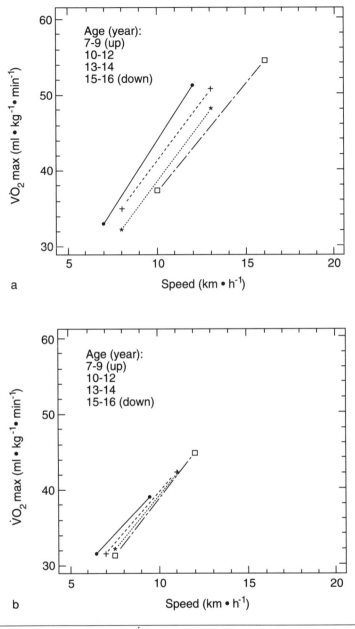

Figure 5.5 Submaximal treadmill V̇O₂ requirement (ml · kg⁻¹ · min⁻¹) as a function of speed (*S*, km · h⁻¹) and age (*A*, yr). Figure 5.5a shows simple regression for different age groups. Figure 5.5b shows a graphical representation of a multiple regression integrating age as one of the predictors.

Figure 5.5a adapted from MacDougall, Roche, Bar-Or, and Moroz (1983). Figure 5.5b adapted from Léger, Cloutier, and Massicotte (1986).

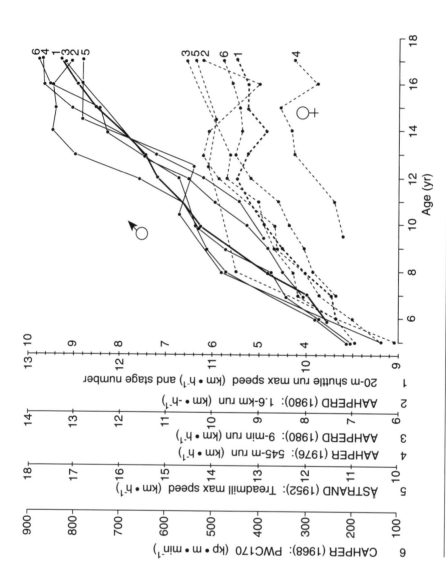

Figure 5.6 Increase in weight-bearing activity performance as a function of age.
Reprinted from Léger, Lambert, Goulet, Rowan, and Dinelle (1984).

kinetic energy of body segments in motion (Ebbeling, Hamill, Freedson, & Rowland, 1992). It was found from a total-work-output–total-energy-input ratio that mechanical efficiency of children increased from 15% to 22% as speed increased and that these values were much lower than those found for adults (30-42%). Thus, there may be differences between adults and children in true mechanical efficiency. On the other hand, in cycling, where $L \cdot min^{-1}$ is the accepted unit, there appears to be no systematic difference between children and adults (Léger et al., 1986). Therefore, any indirect estimation of $\dot{V}O_2$ or $\dot{V}O_2max$ during growth is less subject to systematic errors if the data are obtained on the cycle ergometer rather than the treadmill.

Aerobic Endurance

Aerobic fitness is not exclusively related to $\dot{V}O_2max$ or mechanical efficiency. It has been shown that athletes with similar $\dot{V}O_2max$ and efficiency may be so different, from a performance point of view, that motivation, anaerobic fitness, or both, could not explain these differences. Expressions such as aerobic capacity (Volkov, Shirkovets, & Borilkevich, 1975), aerobic endurance (Péronnet, Thibault, Rhodes, & McKenzie, 1987), and anaerobic threshold (Hollmann, 1985; Wasserman & McIlroy, 1964) have been used to denote the third component of aerobic fitness. Although the importance of the third component is well established, its measurement is not easy, particularly the measurement of anaerobic threshold (Brooks, 1985; Hughson, Weisiger, & Swanson, 1987; Tokmakidis, 1989).

Changes in endurance during growth are not as well documented as changes in $\dot{V}O_2max$ or mechanical efficiency. According to Berthoin (1994), the endurance time at any $\%\dot{V}O_2max$ is relatively stable during growth and similar in children and adults. On the other hand, the $\%\dot{V}O_2max$ corresponding to a lactate concentration of 4 mmol $\cdot$ L^{-1} decreases with age during growth. The decrease is probably an artifact because the lactate value at the inflexion point of the lactate-intensity curve is much lower than 4 mmol $\cdot$ L^{-1} in children compared to adults (Williams & Armstrong, 1991a).

Combination of Aerobic Components

Aerobic fitness depends on three components: (a) the maximal aerobic power, or $\dot{V}O_2max$, (b) the mechanical efficiency, or running economy, and (c) the aerobic endurance at any $\%\dot{V}O_2max$, or the *anaerobic threshold*. Thus, the performance achieved in a long-distance event is a combined measure of these three components. Also, the maximal external power output at $\dot{V}O_2max$ or the maximal speed at $\dot{V}O_2max$ is mostly dependent on $\dot{V}O_2max$ and economy since endurance is less a factor in a multistage test. Thus, even though distance running performance (2.4K run or 12-min run) or the maximal load of a multistage test are often used to predict $\dot{V}O_2max$, such tests are essentially measuring combinations of two or three components of aerobic fitness. In fact, the measurement error of these $\dot{V}O_2max$ predictions is mostly due to the failure to take into consideration the individual economy, and an average value is mistakenly attributed to each individual.

USING $\dot{V}O_2$max TO EXPRESS AEROBIC FITNESS

Whether $\dot{V}O_2$max should be expressed in $L \cdot min^{-1}$ or $ml \cdot kg^{-1} \cdot min^{-1}$ depends on the purpose of testing. Furthermore, the use of ratio units such as $\dot{V}O_2$max $\cdot kg^{-1}$ (body weight) raises some mathematical biases (Buskirk & Longstreet Taylor, 1957; Katch, 1973; Tanner, 1949; Winter, 1992).

Absolute $\dot{V}O_2$max $(L \cdot min^{-1})$

The meaning of absolute $(L \cdot min^{-1})$ changes according to the goal pursued. It can be used as an indicator of growth status, an indicator of aerobic system status, and as an indicator of aerobic performance.

An Indicator of Growth Status.   Absolute $\dot{V}O_2$max is proportional to active muscle mass and thus higher in larger individuals. Absolute $\dot{V}O_2$max increases systematically during growth (Figure 5.1) and may be used as a gross indicator of growth. These observations are in accord with the fact that more mature children (Tanner method) have higher $\dot{V}O_2$ peaks (Armstrong et al., 1991). Height is less affected by change in body composition (fat and lean tissues) than weight and is a better indicator of growth. As demonstrated by Rutenfranz et al. (1990), $\dot{V}O_2$max is linearly related to height until the end of growth (Figure 5.7) when there is an inflexion with age (Figure 5.1). To illustrate possible deviations from the normal growing curve before and after puberty, it may be desirable to express an increase in $\dot{V}O_2$max as a function of age, normalized for puberty (Figure 5.4c and d) instead of chronological age (Figure 5.4a and b). Also, the derivative of the $\dot{V}O_2$max–age curve (i.e., the velocity–age curve) better discloses differences between individuals or gender and shows a clear peak at puberty (Figure 5.8a), suggesting that absolute $\dot{V}O_2$max is an acceptable indicator of the growing status. Furthermore, absolute $\dot{V}O_2$ velocity curves of boys and girls coincide when age is normalized according to peak height velocity (Figure 5.8c), confirming the usefulness of absolute $\dot{V}O_2$max as an indicator of growth status. This is not the case of $\dot{V}O_2$max–age curves relative to body weight; they stay horizontal, or even decrease slightly, with chronological age or when normalized according to peak height–velocity (Figure 5.8b and d).

An Indicator of Aerobic System Status.   Absolute $\dot{V}O_2$max reflects short-term intraindividual changes of the aerobic system (i.e., cardiorespiratory system and oxidative metabolism). However, absolute $\dot{V}O_2$max cannot be used to assess interindividual differences or long-term intraindividual differences in the aerobic system because observed differences may be due to body size rather than the aerobic system.

An Indicator of Aerobic Performance.   Absolute $\dot{V}O_2$max reflects both intra- and interindividual differences in performances against external resistance, such as pedaling on a stationary cycle ergometer, as long as there are not too many interindividual differences in economy and endurance. However, absolute $\dot{V}O_2$max cannot be used as an indicator of performance in weight-bearing activities, such as running

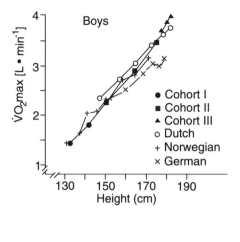

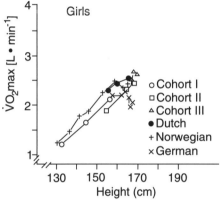

Figure 5.7   Absolute V̇O₂max (L · min⁻¹) as a function of height during growth (8-20 yrs).
Reprinted from Rutenfranz et al. (1990).

or stepping, where the energy requirements are body-weight dependent, thus negating the effect of a large body-weight absolute V̇O₂max.

V̇O₂max Relative to Body Weight

As was the case for absolute V̇O₂max, the meaning of V̇O₂max relative to body weight depends on the purpose of testing. It can be used as an indicator of aerobic system status or an indicator of aerobic performance.

An Indicator of the Aerobic System Status.   Relative-to-body-weight V̇O₂max cannot be used to follow intraindividual changes in the aerobic system (Figure 5.8),

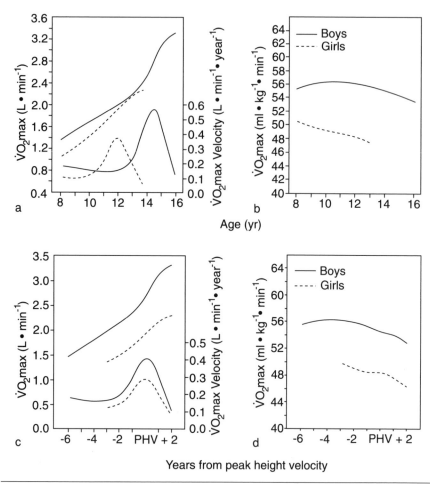

Figure 5.8 Absolute (a,c) and relative to body weight (b,d) V̇O₂max as a function of chronological age (a,b) and peak height velocity age (c,d). Absolute V̇O₂max velocity are also shown (a,c).
Reprinted from Mirwald and Bailey (1986).

because a change in total body weight due solely to body fat would affect relative-to-body-weight V̇O₂max even though the aerobic system has not changed. Intraindividual changes in the aerobic system are better followed with absolute V̇O₂max.

However, absolute V̇O₂max could not be used to compare aerobic systems of individuals of different sizes. Normalizing for size by dividing absolute V̇O₂max by body weight could be misleading because the active muscle mass does not always represent the same proportion of total body mass. Two individuals with the same absolute and active muscle mass will have different relative-to-body-weight V̇O₂max if their % body fat and total body weight are different. This is why interindividual comparisons of the aerobic system are better assessed by relative-to-lean-body-mass

$\dot{V}O_2$max. This may also be one of the reasons why girls, who gradually accumulate more fat than boys, are characterized by a slight decrease in relative-to-body-weight $\dot{V}O_2$max with age while this value is relatively constant in boys (Figure 5.2).

An Indicator of Aerobic Performance.   Because the absolute energy expenditure in weight-bearing activities such as running or stepping is body weight dependent (Cureton et al., 1978; Ryschon, Kemp, Shappart, & Johnson, 1991; Thomas, Weller, & Cox, 1993), relative-to-body-weight $\dot{V}O_2$max is a better predictor of performance in these types of activities than absolute $\dot{V}O_2$max (Buskirk & Longstreet Taylor, 1957). This is true even though relative-to-body-weight $\dot{V}O_2$max could either be affected by the numerator term (the aerobic system) or the denominator term (the body weight) of the ratio. In fact, in performance where individuals have to carry extra equipment loads, it would be better to express $\dot{V}O_2$max relative to total mass or body + carried loads (Cureton et al., 1978). The importance of relative-to-body-weight $\dot{V}O_2$max as a performance predictor is less if there are large interindividual variations in economy and endurance. Whereas economy increases systematically until the end of growth, and whereas biological age does not always parallel chronological age, correlations between $\dot{V}O_2$max and running performance are usually fewer during growth than during adulthood (Léger, Mercier, Gadoury, & Lambert, 1988). The fact that relative-to-body-weight $\dot{V}O_2$max is better correlated to weight-bearing performance than is absolute $\dot{V}O_2$max does not mean that it is the better unit as an indicator of weight-bearing performance.

Dividing absolute $\dot{V}O_2$max by body weight mathematically implies that $\dot{V}O_2$max (and the same is true for $\dot{V}O_2$ at any exercise intensity) is linearly related to body weight and that this relationship passes through the origin of the x-y axes (Katch, 1973; Tanner, 1949; Winter, 1992). Although these conditions are not fully respected (Bergh, Sjodin, Forsberg, & Svedenhag, 1991; Katch; Tanner; Winter), ml · kg^{-1} · min^{-1} is the most common norm used to compare aerobic fitness to individual performance in weight-bearing activities or to compare the energy requirement at any submaximal exercise intensity among such activities.

Krahenbuhl and Williams (1992) do not find any practical advantage of using units other than ml · min^{-1} · kg^{-1} body mass. On the other hand, more and more researchers observe that either submaximal $\dot{V}O_2$, or $\dot{V}O_2$max expressed in ml · kg^{-1} · min^{-1}, are inversely related to body mass (Bergh et al., 1991; Williams, Cavanagh, & Ziff, 1987) (Figure 5.9). Therefore, heavier individuals appear to be more economical in using ml · kg^{-1} · min^{-1} units, and they will perform better with a similar $\dot{V}O_2$max (ml · kg^{-1} · min^{-1}). In general, however, their $\dot{V}O_2$max will also be lower (Figure 5.9), thus negating this advantage. Use of ml · kg^{-1} · min^{-1} units is obviously misleading (Bergh et al.; Katch, 1973; Winter, 1992).

Winter (1992), who recently reviewed the various ways of expressing $\dot{V}O_2$, considers the allometric equations to be the best method to normalize data for children. Hence, $\dot{V}O_2$max (Y) can be related to a power function of body weight (X):

$$Y = aX^b \tag{1}$$

This equation is easily obtained by computing a linear regression with the natural logarithm (ln) of each variable:

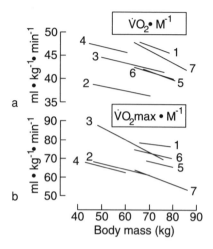

Figure 5.9   Submaximal (a) and maximal (b) V̇O₂max per kg body mass as function of body mass for different groups of athletes. Submaximal values were obtained at 12 km · h⁻¹ for the females (Group 2) and at 14 km · h⁻¹ for the males (other groups). In these groups of athletes with wide body mass variation relative to body mass, V̇O₂ and V̇O₂max (in ml · kg⁻¹ · min⁻¹) decreases with body mass.
Reprinted from Bergh, Sjodin, Forsberg, and Svedenhag (1991).

$$\ln Y = a + b \ln X \tag{2}$$

which is equivalent to

$$Y = e^{(a + b \ln X)} \tag{3}$$

or

$$Y = e^{a} \, e^{b \ln X} \tag{4}$$

or

$$Y = a' \, X^{b} \tag{5}$$

and we are back to equation 1.

Using the allometric approach, Bergh et al. (1991) found that submaximal V̇O₂ and V̇O₂max were related to body mass to the powers of 0.76 and 0.71, respectively. These values were obtained on adult subjects, but Bergh et al. indicate that computation of submaximal V̇O₂ values in children (Åstrand, 1952) yields a power of 0.74. The power value of 0.71 for V̇O₂max agrees also with Andersen, Seliger, Rutenfranz, and Mocellin (1974), who reported that V̇O₂max of boys in L · min⁻¹ increases faster than predicted on the basis of height squared according to the dimensional law (Åstrand & Rodahl, 1970), but is different from the value of 1.0 reported by Cooper (1989).

With respect to this discussion, it should be noted that differences between children and adults in the O_2 cost of running disappear when $\dot{V}O_2$ is expressed in ml · min^{-1} · m^{-2} of body surface area (Rowland, 1989) (Figure 5.10). According to the dimensional law, m^2 is equivalent to $\text{kg}^{0.667}$, which is different than $\text{kg}^{0.75}$. Instead of using the dimensional law, we can use CAHPER height–weight norms (Quinney, Watkinson, Massicotte, Conger, & Gauthier, 1982) and calculate surface area (m^2) with the Dubois–Dubois formula (Consolazio, Johnson, & Pecora, 1963); then the allometric approach indicates that weight (WT, kg) is a function of surface area (SA, m^2) to the power of 1.461 (i.e., $\text{SA}^{1.461}$). It follows that $\text{WT}^{0.75}$ is equivalent to $(\text{SA}^{1.461})^{0.75}$ or $\text{SA}^{1.461} \times^{0.75}$ or $\text{SA}^{1.096}$ and is very close to SA^1, as suggested by Rowland. In general, reporting $\dot{V}O_2$ as a function of height, weight, or surface area should yield results that are equivalent since these three variables are interdependent. On an individual basis, however, it is only logical that the O_2 cost of running is more proportional to weight than to height or surface area. Expressing $\dot{V}O_2$ as a power function of weight is preferred.

Allometric regressions permit the use of the power-function ratio ($\dot{V}O_2$max per mass^b) instead of a simple ratio ($\dot{V}O_2$max per mass^1). According to Winter (1992), the use of such a power ratio erases the differences seen between boys and adults when submaximal $\dot{V}O_2$ is expressed in ml · kg^{-1} · min^{-1}; however, the actual power for body mass was not mentioned. Furthermore, computations on the data of Léger et al. (1986) using a power of 0.75 show an increase in submaximal $\dot{V}O_2$ (ml · $\text{kg}^{-0.75}$ · min^{-1}) with age. Similarly, expressing $\dot{V}O_2$max as it should be, in ml · $\text{kg}^{-0.75}$ · min^{-1} instead of ml · kg^{-1} · min^{-1}, yields a completely different profile of the $\dot{V}O_2$max–age curve. For instance, using the power of 0.75 (or 0.71) to express $\dot{V}O_2$max, it is expected that the $\dot{V}O_2$max of boys will increase until the end of growth instead of being relatively stable as shown with ml · kg^{-1} · min^{-1} units (Figure 5.11). In girls, the $\dot{V}O_2$max per $\text{kg}^{0.75}$ or per $\text{kg}^{0.71}$ will increase in a logarithmic pattern, but at a much slower rate than with boys, and after a plateau is reached, $\dot{V}O_2$max per $\text{kg}^{0.75}$ or per $\text{kg}^{0.71}$ will decrease, instead of decreasing slowly from the beginning, as seen with ml · kg^{-1} · min^{-1} units (Figure 5.11). The age at which this plateau occurs for girls may differ considerably depending on which set of data these observations are based. In a recent abstract, Welsman, Armstrong, Winter, and Kirby (1993) also report that $\dot{V}O_2$max expressed as a power function of body mass behaved differently from $\dot{V}O_2$max per kg body mass during growth, but the power value was not reported. In a more recent review of literature, however, Armstrong & Welsman (1994), reported a value of -0.798 for both males and females of prepubertal, pubertal, and adult ages, a value that is higher than -0.75 or the theoretical value of -0.667. They suggest the difference is the result of the irregular growth process and differential changes that occur in the proportions of body segments. We usually think that running performances increase during growth because the $\dot{V}O_2$max (ml · kg^{-1} · min^{-1}) stays relatively stable while the $\dot{V}O_2$ requirement (ml · kg^{-1} · min^{-1}) decreases. It may be that $\dot{V}O_2$max (ml · $\text{kg}^{-0.75}$ · min^{-1}) increases (Figure 5.11) while the $\dot{V}O_2$ requirement (ml · $\text{kg}^{-0.75}$ · min^{-1}) stays constant. Thus, the functional aerobic capacity pattern is not affected with age, but the patterns of its components, $\dot{V}O_2$max and submaximal $\dot{V}O_2$ requirement, are affected. Also,

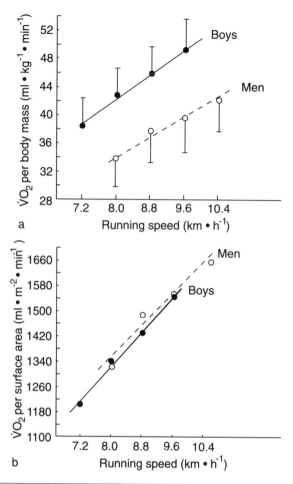

Figure 5.10 $\dot{V}O_2$max per kg body mass (a) and per m^2 of surface area (b) as a function of speed in 10- to 12-year-old boys and in young men. Note that differences between boys and men disappear when $\dot{V}O_2$max is standardized according to surface area.
Reprinted from Rowland, Auchinachie, Keenan, & Green (1987).

on both the treadmill and the cycle ergometer, children and adults will have similar energy requirements, which is more readily acceptable than the actual point of view since there is no a priori reason why children should be less efficient than adults. That would be consistent with similar delta efficiency in children and adults as measured with added vertical or horizontal resistance on the treadmill (Cooke, McDonagh, Nevill, & Davies, 1991).

The similarity in the mechanical efficiency in children and adults does not mean that the energy cost of running is the same at any running speed, whether $\dot{V}O_2$ is expressed in $ml \cdot kg^{-0.75} \cdot min^{-1}$ or in $ml \cdot kg^{-1} \cdot min^{-1}$, because the amount of work being done may not be proportional to the running speed in individuals of different

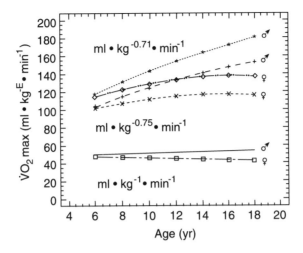

Figure 5.11 $\dot{V}O_2$max per kg, kg$^{0.75}$, and kg$^{0.71}$ as a function of age. Based on data of Falgairette (1989) for treadmill $\dot{V}O_2$max values of untrained children, where $\dot{V}O_2$max per kg = 48.21 + 0.317 age for boys (82 groups, n = 1559) and 49.74 − 0.408 age for girls (44 groups, n = 836).

sizes. For instance, biomechanical analysis of running at three different speeds in children and adults (Ebbeling et al., 1992) reveals that adults are doing approximately 1.8 times more work per kg and per stride than children. Also, with a shorter stride, children have to run at a higher stride frequency in order to achieve the same speed, which further increases their total work output at any speed. Using running speed as the independent variable, scaling for body mass with the allometric approach should resolve all these problems; at the same time it may also explain why the dimensional law does not apply exactly in running. In addition to the difficulty in assessing the work output equivalent to running speed, Rowland (1992) has evoked higher utilization of fatty acid to explain higher $\dot{V}O_2$ requirement per kg of running in children, but data of the same group (Ebbeling et al., 1992) fail to disclose any significant difference between children and adults for the respiratory exchange ratio. That kind of factor, if valid, would also apply to the cycle ergometer data. Another factor that could partly explain the lower efficiency of children while running is that their smaller body mass probably returns less elastic energy. That would be consistent with similar $\dot{V}O_2$ cost (L · min^{-1}) for children and adults on the cycle ergometer, because elastic energy is less important in a continuous angular cycling motion. In support of the elastic argument, Bosco et al. (1987) observed a negative relationship between the energy cost of running and the recoil of elastic energy (r = −0.66) when measured as the ratio of mechanical efficiency of jumping with and without the prestretch preceding the extension of the legs.

Although true age differences in the $\dot{V}O_2$ cost of weight-bearing activities are not totally excluded, the allometric approach should yield a proper unit to express

$\dot{V}O_2$ as a function of the intensity of exercise, as long as the residual error of the model is small and similar over the whole range of body mass.

One of the problems with the allometric approach so far may be the lack of consistency among reported power values (Rowland, 1992). Still, the allometric approach is the approach of choice when comparing individuals of different sizes, which is the case during growth. However, $ml \cdot kg^{-1} \cdot min^{-1}$ units are more practical and may be used within any age category except when there are very large or very small individuals.

$\dot{V}O_2$max Relative to Lean Body Mass

The meaning of $\dot{V}O_2$max relative to lean body mass depends on the purpose of testing. It can be used as either an indicator of aerobic system status or an indicator of aerobic performance.

An Indicator of Aerobic System Status. $\dot{V}O_2$ relative to lean body mass is probably the best unit to assess both intra- and interindividual differences in the status of the aerobic system (Buskirk & Longstreet Taylor, 1957). Because lean body mass is smaller than total body mass, values of $\dot{V}O_2$max ($ml \cdot kg^{-1} \cdot min^{-1}$) relative to lean body mass are higher than the values expressed as relative-to-body-weight using the same units ($ml \cdot kg^{-1} \cdot min^{-1}$). For example, a $\dot{V}O_2$max of 60-ml $\cdot min^{-1} \cdot kg^{-1}$ body weight would correspond to a $\dot{V}O_2$max of 70-ml $\cdot min^{-1} \cdot kg^{-1}$ lean body mass (LBM) for an individual weighing 70 kg with a 60 kg lean body mass.

Lean body mass has been satisfactorily measured in adults using Siri's formula (Siri, 1961) and a density estimate, but only recently has Lohman (1989) provided age-adjusted equations during growth. Caution is recommended when using these relatively new equations with anthropometric estimates of body density.

An Indicator of Aerobic Performance. $\dot{V}O_2$max relative to lean body mass has only limited value in relation to weight-bearing activities since the resistance is proportional to total body weight, including carried equipment. Against external resistance, it is absolute $\dot{V}O_2$max that counts.

EXPRESSING AEROBIC FITNESS THROUGH MECHANICAL EFFICIENCY

Mechanical efficiency differs considerably depending on the ergometer used for testing, and the issue will thus be covered separately for cycle and treadmill ergometers.

Cycle Ergometer

Mechanical efficiency (ME) is the ratio of mechanical power (P) generated by the muscles and the energy rate (E) required to sustain such a power:

$$ME = P \cdot E^{-1} \tag{6}$$

If both power and energy rate are expressed in W, the ratio has no units. For example, at 1200 kg $\cdot$ m $\cdot$ min^{-1} or 196 W on the cycle ergometer, the gross energy cost in a steady state situation where all the energy is aerobically produced is 2.7 L O$_2$ $\cdot$ min^{-1} or 13.1 kcal $\cdot$ min^{-1} (assuming a calorie equivalent of 4.85 kcal $\cdot$ L^{-1}) or 913.8 W and gross mechanical efficiency equals 21.5%.

To obtain net mechanical efficiency, the resting $\dot{V}O_2$ requirement has to be subtracted from the gross $\dot{V}O_2$ requirement before calculating the ratio. This may increase the mechanical efficiency value by 2% to 3%, depending on the subject's resting $\dot{V}O_2$ requirement, which is body-size dependent. However, the body-size effect is small and should not greatly affect mechanical efficiency scores on the cycle ergometer attained during the growth period. This is confirmed by the work of Rowland, Staab, Unnithan, Rambusch, and Siconolfi (1990), who found no difference in the increase of the $\dot{V}O_2$ requirement (delta efficiency) from 65 to 105 W in males between the ages of 10.5 and 21. The authors concluded that the muscles of children and adults do not differ in efficiency of aerobic energy utilization during work on the cycle ergometer.

Computations of work performed on the cycle ergometer do not usually consider the work done to move the legs alone or the resistance of the pedals, chainwheel, and bearings. Thus, actual mechanical efficiency is slightly higher than the measurement based on net external work. The additional work performed has been estimated to be 8% to 9% (Bergh, Kanstrup, & Ekblom, 1976; Winter, 1991), values similar to the ones that could be derived from the study of Hagberg, Giese, Spitznagle, and Mullin (1981). These researchers removed the chains from the bicycles of elite cyclists and required them to pedal at various rpm. The gross $\dot{V}O_2$ requirement (ml $\cdot$ kg^{-1} $\cdot$ min^{-1}) was almost exclusively related to lower limb mobilization without resistance and was related to angular velocity (Va, rpm) as follows:

$$\dot{V}O_2 = 17.2 - 0.332\ Va + 0.0029\ Va^2,\ r = 0.94 \tag{7}$$

This equation is valid only at speeds above 50 rpm. From 50 rpm to 100 rpm, the net cost of freely moving the legs on the pedals increases by 5.51 ml $\cdot$ kg^{-1} $\cdot$ min^{-1}. This cost is expressed in ml $\cdot$ kg^{-1} $\cdot$ min^{-1} because it depends on limb weight, which means that the absolute cost (L $\cdot$ min^{-1}) depends on both body weight and angular velocity. At 50 rpm, a common angular velocity for testing children, the gross $\dot{V}O_2$ of pedaling without resistance is 7.85 ml $\cdot$ kg^{-1} $\cdot$ min^{-1} and corresponds to a net cost of about 4 ml $\cdot$ kg^{-1} $\cdot$ min^{-1}.

Corresponding absolute $\dot{V}O_2$ for body weights 25 kg and 65 kg (i.e., 6 to 18 years of age) are 0.10 and 0.26 L $\cdot$ min^{-1}, respectively. At 100W the total cost is approximately 1.57 L $\cdot$ min^{-1} for an adult (L $\cdot$ min^{-1} = 0.433 + 0.01134 W) (Andersen, Shephard, Denolin, Varnouskas, & Masironi, 1971), which includes 0.26 L $\cdot$ min^{-1} or 16.6% of the total cost for pedaling without resistance and 1.31 L $\cdot$ min^{-1} for pedaling against external resistance. For 6-year-old children weighing 25 kg, the total gross cost is thus equal to 1.41 L $\cdot$ min^{-1}, that is, the sum of external and internal costs (1.31 + 0.1 L $\cdot$ min^{-1}). Based on these data, the cost of pedaling without resistance is much less in a child and only represents 7.1% of the total cost. It is also expected that total energy cost is about 10% less at 100W in a small 6-year-old child versus a heavier adult counterpart. These conclusions are based on a 4 ml · kg^{-1} · min^{-1} cost of pedaling at 50 rpm without resistance. Results would be different at higher angular velocities. Conclusions could also be different if the 2-ml · kg^{-1} · min^{-1} value reported by the American College of Sports Medicine (1986) and Bolen, Rotman, and Laguizamon (1981) were used. With that value the body-weight effect and its significance during growth would be much less. The added cost of moving light or heavy legs could be hidden within interindividual and random error variations and would explain why Rowland et al. (1990) found no signficant difference in the O$_2$ increase (delta efficiency) from 65W to 105W between 10.5- to 21-year-old males. Within the total cost-of-cycling data, body weight does not seem to substantially affect the overall efficiency on the cycle ergometer during growth.

Treadmill

It is very difficult to estimate the horizontal work performed while running on a treadmill and to calculate a mechanical efficiency ratio. In order to find the most efficient runners, O$_2$–velocity curves are usually compared. However, this does not produce a single value, such as the mechanical efficiency ratio.

It is tempting to use the slope of the $\dot{V}O_2$–velocity curve; but due to different intercepts, it is possible that the $\dot{V}O_2$ requirement at any particular velocity is different even with identical slopes. The individual with the smaller slope generally appears to be less economical (Kearney & Van Handel, 1989).

Many researchers are using a ratio equivalent for mechanical efficiency and have labeled it *running economy*. It is basically the cost of running 1 km and is expressed in ml · kg^{-1} · km^{-1}. Running economy is obtained by dividing the (ml · kg^{-1} · min^{-1}) by the velocity (km · min^{-1}). Typical values are around 180 to 220 ml · kg^{-1} · min^{-1}. As with any ratio, the mathematical requirements are that the $\dot{V}O_2$–velocity curve must pass through or close to the origin and that the relationship be linear. These requirements are not usually achieved, particularly for the intercept, and it is not valid to compare such ratios if they have been computed at different speeds or at $\dot{V}O_2$max. Therefore, Costill, Thomason, and Roberts (1973) and Sjodin and Svedenhag (1985) measure running economy at one speed (16.1 km · h^{-1} and 15 km · h^{-1}, respectively). This protocol is correct, but potentially misleading; the resulting ratio differs at different velocities because of mathematical bias, even though mechanical efficiency remains the same. On the other hand, children cannot sustain high speeds, such as 15 km · h^{-1}, that are typical of adult competitive speeds in endurance events, and children's running economy must be calculated at lower speeds. There is, therefore, a problem in comparing the running economy values of children and adults: Lowering the speed to one that is feasible at any age results in a speed that is not appropriate for adult athletes.

Thus, running economy as a mechanical efficiency indicator is of limited value during growth. Therefore, mechanical efficiency of children should be assessed using $\dot{V}O_2$–velocity curves, even though no single value summarizes the status. Furthermore, it may be better to do so using power ratio units (ml · $kg^{-0.75}$ · min^{-1}), rather than $\dot{V}O_2$ per body mass units (ml · kg^{-1} · min^{-1}).

Sjodin and Svedenhag (1985) have expressed $\dot{V}O_2$ cost at 15 km · h^{-1} as a %$\dot{V}O_2$max and used it as an indicator of running economy. However, improving $\dot{V}O_2$max alone (the denominator of the ratio) will also improve running economy or lower the percent values even though the energy cost has not decreased (i.e., same running economy). Therefore, expressing running economy as a %$\dot{V}O_2$max is misleading. It measures both the $\dot{V}O_2$max and running economy and may not be an accurate reflection of running economy as the expression suggests. It is suggested to plot $\dot{V}O_2$–intensity curves in order to assess running efficiency during growth.

EXPRESSING AEROBIC FITNESS THROUGH AEROBIC ENDURANCE

Two approaches are used to measure aerobic endurance: measuring endurance time and measuring anaerobic threshold.

Endurance Time

The time an individual can maintain any exercise intensity depends on the three components of aerobic fitness. In order to control for $\dot{V}O_2$max and mechanical efficiency, the exercise intensity has to be expressed as a %$\dot{V}O_2$max.

In adults, using % maximal aerobic speed (MAS) is also acceptable because the %$\dot{V}O_2$max–%MAS regression is very close to the identity line (i.e., 35% MAS $\approx$ 35% $\dot{V}O_2$max). In running, however, the endurance time, using ml · kg^{-1} · min^{-1} units as a function of %MAS, decreases much faster in children versus adults, and the curves are similar when endurance time is plotted against %$\dot{V}O_2$max (Figure 5.12).

From a practical point of view and because running is often used in training activities, it is important to understand that training duration at any speed and %MAS will be shorter in younger individuals because their lower running economy is associated with a $\dot{V}O_2$max (in ml · kg^{-1} · min^{-1}) and true endurance (endurance time at any %$\dot{V}O_2$max) that stay constant with age. The aerobic reserve concept has similar implications, but fails to consider endurance time as a contributing factor.

Anaerobic Threshold

As was the case for the endurance time, anaerobic threshold should be expressed in %$\dot{V}O_2$max in order to control for $\dot{V}O_2$max and mechanical efficiency. As a matter of fact, the rightward shift of the lactate–speed curve that occurs with training is also observed at maximal values. The higher the $\dot{V}O_2$max and the mechanical efficiency, the higher the speed at which the lactate inflexion point occurs. Thus, expressing any lactate inflexion point (or any ventilatory parameters) in km · h^{-1}

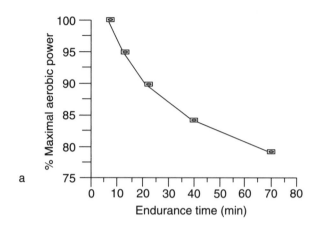

a

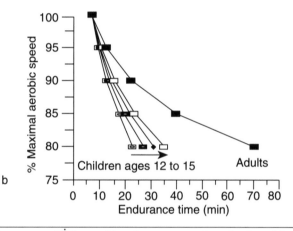

b

Figure 5.12 Percentage of V̇O₂max (a) and percentage of maximal aerobic speed (b) that could be maintained as a function of the exercise duration for adults and children.

(running) or Watt (cycling) depends on the three components of aerobic fitness (i.e., not only on endurance). Consequently, anaerobic threshold in km · h⁻¹ is better correlated with performance than V̇O₂max alone (Sjodin & Svedenhag, 1985). This is misleading because the anaerobic threshold concept is supposed to represent aerobic endurance only. Consequently, anaerobic threshold must be expressed as %V̇O₂max in order to strictly measure aerobic endurance. Correlations with performance are then reduced considerably and are no better than V̇O₂max (Ouvrier-Buffet, 1994; Sjodin & Svedenhag, 1985) as it is commonly thought.

For similar reasons, it follows that expressing anaerobic threshold as a %MAS measures both endurance and economy and expressing it in ml · kg⁻¹ · min⁻¹ measures both endurance and V̇O₂max. It must be realized that manipulating the units of measurement often changes the attribute being measured even though the expression used (i.e., anaerobic threshold) stays the same.

There is also a problem in determining the anaerobic threshold at the same 4 mmol · L^{-1} for children and adults. In children (contrary to adults), the average lactate concentration at the inflexion point of the lactate–intensity curve is much lower than 4 mmol · L^{-1} (Williams & Armstrong, 1991a). Also, 4 mmol · L^{-1} does not mean the same thing for children having maximal lactate values between 4.9 and 14.1 mmol · L^{-1} (Cumming, Hastman, Cort, & McCullough, 1980). Longitudinal data obtained in children between 11 and 15 years confirm these values (Paterson, Cunningham, & Bumstead, 1986).

$\dot{V}O_2$max MAXIMAL TESTING

$\dot{V}O_2$max laboratory test are traditionally divided into maximal and submaximal tests. Each approach is based on different principles; we will talk about maximal tests first. We will discuss the issues of ergometers, the principles of direct and indirect tests, the stage duration and intensity, the criteria for maximal tests, the validity and reliability of maximal tests, and the $\dot{V}O_2$max protocols.

Ergometers

Each ergometer, whether it is the stationary cycle or the treadmill, has its own advantage (Table 5.1). The prevalent testing conditions or the type of subject may also influence the choice of ergometer. A major issue, however, is the fact that $\dot{V}O_2$max treadmill values are 7% to 19% greater than cycle values and that these systematic differences not only vary from study to study but also from individual to individual, making it impossible to estimate the difference. Furthermore, it means that specific norms are required for each ergometer.

Also the cycle ergometer often has to be modified for body size during growth; the lowest resistance as well as resistance increments must be smaller for children. Typically, the Monark friction cycle ergometer has a resistance span of 0 kp to 3 kp with 0.1 kp scale increments; the corresponding values for adults are 0 kp to 7 kp for the resistance span and 0.5 kp scale increments. Most commercial cycle ergometers do not allow the seat to go low enough for children. In addition, the length of the pedal shaft and the distance between the seat and the handlebars is not appropriate for children. According to Klimt and Voight (1971) and Bar-Or (1983), a 13-cm crank length is recommended for 6-year-old children and a 15-cm one is recommended for children 8 to 10 years of age and a cadence of 50 rpm to 60 rpm is considered optimal between 6 to 10 years of age.

Direct and Indirect Determinations

Laboratory tests can be direct or indirect. With the most common method, the open circuit, the $\dot{V}O_2$ can be directly determined by the analysis of collected expired air

Table 5.1   Ergometer Advantages

Cycle ergometer	Treadmill
Easier to measure blood pressure or cardiac output	Less local fatigue, particularly with children
Easier to calculate power output and mechanical efficiency	More natural movement
Inexpensive and portable	Larger muscle mass and larger $\dot{V}O_2$max and heart rate values
Safer and less expensive	Needs no attention to keep the appropriate pace (no metronome), particularly good with children (mental age and attention); thus no need to count revolutions at each stage
Needs less coordination than running on a belt	No need to modify ergometer according to body size
Less interindividual variation in mechanical efficiency (indirect estimation of $\dot{V}O_2$)	
No systematic variation in mechanical efficiency with age (adult metabolic costs are valid for children)	
Easy to calibrate	
No electricity for most models	

Note. Adapted from Anderson et al., 1971; Bar-Or, 1993; Docherty & Gaul, 1990; Rowland, 1993; and Vaccaro and Makon, 1987.

($\dot{V}E$ and O_2 and CO_2 fractions), or the $\dot{V}O_2$ can be indirectly estimated assuming a common mechanical efficiency using an average steady-state O_2 cost for the final stage of a multistage test. Additional assumptions for indirect $\dot{V}O_2$ measurement are that stage duration is long enough or intensity increment per stage is small enough to ensure steady-state conditions and that there is no plateau phenomenon, which is more or less the case in a continuous multistage test (i.e., no rest between stages), particularly with children (Armstrong et al., 1991; Freedson & Goodman, 1993; Massicotte et al., 1985; Vaccaro & Mahon, 1987).

With direct determination, steady-state conditions are not necessary to attain $\dot{V}O_2$max values. This was clearly demonstrated in a classic paper by Åstrand and Saltin (1961) in which $\dot{V}O_2$max was attained with almost any supramaximal single load that exhausted the subject in 1.5 to 5 min. But submaximal $\dot{V}O_2$ values in steady-state conditions are also useful for studying physiological adaptation to a standardized load and in establishing the mechanical efficiency of the subjects.

Finally, with continuous protocols the plateau phenomenon is rare. The observed value is called peak $\dot{V}O_2$ unless a rest is given after the continuous protocol and is followed by an additional supramaximal load without any $\dot{V}O_2$ increment; in the latter case the observed value may be called $\dot{V}O_2$max.

Stage Duration and Intensity Incrementation

If acceleration is too fast or the test discontinuous, the final stage will be supramaximal and indirect $\dot{V}O_2$max will be overestimated. With adults, it is common to use 2- or 3-min stages with no more than 1 MET (i.e., 3.5 ml $\cdot$ kg^{-1} $\cdot$ min^{-1}) increments per stage. In such conditions, $\dot{V}O_2$ at any exercise intensity and $\dot{V}O_2$max are similar to the ones observed in a discontinuous protocol with 5- to 6-min stages (Maksud, & Coutts, 1971; McArdle, Katch, & Pechar, 1973).

With children, the O_2 kinetic is faster (Godfrey, 1974), which means that conditions set up for adults are theoretically valid except that younger children might find it too physiologically and psychologically difficult to sustain these stage increments and durations. This explains why some laboratories reduce the stage of the Bruce protocol from 3 min to 2 min (Rowland, 1993). However, it might be hazardous to extrapolate conditions according to age during growth due to the current state of knowledge. For instance, according to Godfrey it takes only 1 min to reach steady state in children; Bar-Or (1983) suggests a value closer to 2 min. In fact, the time to reach steady state also depends on the magnitude of the intensity of increments as well as the age of the child. In order to be conservative, 2-min stages are suggested. The overall duration of the test should be between 6 min and 12 min (Bar-Or, 1993; Rowland).

As reported by Rowland (1993), maximal power on the cycle ergometer is 3.5 W $\cdot$ kg^{-1} for boys and 3.0 W $\cdot$ kg^{-1} for girls during growth. With an average of 10 min per test, it could be calculated that work increments of 0.35, 0.70, and 1.05 W $\cdot$ kg^{-1} for boys and 0.30, 0.60, and 0.90 W $\cdot$ kg^{-1} for girls should be used with stages of 1-, 2- and 3-min durations, respectively. With such an approach, however, based on the "best" children, the $\dot{V}O_2$ requirement would increase by approximately 8 ml O_2 $\cdot$ kg^{-1} $\cdot$ min^{-1} (or 2 METs) per 2-min stage, which is quite challenging. Along with Mocellin, Lindemann, Rutenfranz, and Sbresny (1971) and Bar-Or (1993), it is suggested that the increments be reduced by half with 0.35 and 0.30 W $\cdot$ kg^{-1} per 2-min stage for boys and girls, respectively.

On the treadmill, adults are subject to the same intensity (speed, grade, or both) increments per stage because the $\dot{V}O_2$ in ml $\cdot$ kg^{-1} $\cdot$ min^{-1} is relatively stable. Children are systematically less economical than adults, mainly because of the higher intercept rather than a different regression slope. Therefore, similar increments (e.g., 1 km $\cdot$ h^{-1} at 0% grade) are valid for adults and children, but initial and final intensity will be much lower for children.

According to Rowland (1993), 2.5% grade increments at 5.6 km $\cdot$ h^{-1} (3.5 mph) induce a 4- to 5-ml $\cdot$ kg^{-1} $\cdot$ min^{-1} change in $\dot{V}O_2$. The most commonly used protocol in pediatric testing (50% of 30 laboratories), the Bruce test, uses large $\dot{V}O_2$ increments in children (i.e., 6 to 7 ml $\cdot$ kg^{-1} $\cdot$ min^{-1} between stages 1 and 2, and 11 to 12 ml $\cdot$ kg^{-1} $\cdot$ min^{-1} between stages 2 and 3 (Cumming, Everatt, & Hastman, 1978, reported by Rowland).

Criteria for Maximal Tests

The occurrence of a plateau phenomenon as $\dot{V}O_2$ increases as a function of exercise intensity is an exception to usual results, particularly with children (Armstrong et al., 1991; Cunninghan et al., 1977; Freedson & Goodman, 1993; Massicotte et al., 1985; Rivera-Brown, Rivera, & Frontera, 1992; Rowland & Cunningham, 1992; Vaccaro & Mahon, 1987). Whether or not a plateau occurs, other criteria must be used to ensure that a maximal effort has been performed. Attainment of age-predicted maximum heart rate (PMHR) is often used as one of the criteria. Although there is a large variability in PMHR for any specific age, it is still regarded as a valid criterion (Freedson & Goodman, 1993). Heart rate often plateaus before $\dot{V}O_2$max or peak $\dot{V}O_2$ is attained in both children (Sundberg & Elovainio, 1982) and adults (Davies, 1968). The maximum heart rate in young trained subjects may be even lower (Davies, 1968). It is, therefore, doubtful that $\dot{V}O_2$max could be reached without attaining PMHR. Because maximal heart rate is relatively constant during growth (Rowland, 1993), and cycle-ergometer MHR is slightly lower than treadmill MHR (Léger, Gutierrez, Choinière, Ricart, & Massicotte, 1990; Mocelin et al., 1971), values of 200 bpm and 195 bpm for the treadmill and cycle ergometer, respectively, are recommended as acceptable criteria (Rowland, 1993).

Perhaps the best criterion of maximal effort is the respiratory equivalent ratio (RER) of $VCO_2/\dot{V}O_2$, maximal RER values being slightly higher for the cycle ergometer (RER = 1.11) compared to the treadmill (RER = 1.04), due to local fatigue and a greater anaerobic contribution (Rowland, 1993). Thus, in both children and adults, RER values above 1 indicate maximal effort.

If blood lactate values are available, a criterion of 9 mmol $\cdot$ L^{-1} is recommended for children (Docherty & Gaul, 1990), knowing that adults usually reach values 3 to 5 mmol $\cdot$ L^{-1} higher. Cumming et al. (1980) recommended a lower value of 6 mmol $\cdot$ L^{-1}. For ethical reasons, however, it is suggested that blood sampling should not be part of routine testing of children. In any event, in view of the large variability in blood lactate levels after maximal exercise (Cumming et al.), Armstrong and Welsman (1994) question the validity of the lactate criterion. Furthermore, sampling time and lactate assay influence the lactate value, and Cumming's value of 6 mmol $\cdot$ L^{-1} obtained on plasma assay corresponds to a 4 mmol $\cdot$ L^{-1} on whole blood (Armstrong & Welsman).

Besides these physiological parameters, signs of extreme exhaustion or fatigue may also indicate that $\dot{V}O_2$max has been reached. Even when a plateau is seen, extreme exhaustion is rare. Its presence obviously indicates that supramaximal loads have been reached and confirms maximal efforts, but its absence does not suggest $\dot{V}O_2$max was not attained.

Validity and Reliability of Maximal Tests

The direct measurement of $\dot{V}O_2$max is the gold standard against which other indirect tests are validated. It is recognized as valid as long as spirometer and O_2 and CO_2 analysers are properly calibrated and as long as a plateau phenomenon is observed or other equivalent criteria are met. The latter is not always so obvious, however, because the plateau is rare in children during a continuous multistage test and because many operators are totally unaware of how their automated metabolic system works.

Since $\dot{V}O_2max$ criteria ($\dot{V}O_2$ plateau, maximal heart rate, high lactate values) are highly questionable, peak $\dot{V}O_2$ tests are the norm. Thus, their validity and their reliability are very similar to performance field tests. Large differences are observed between the AAHPERD standards and the FITNESSGRAM standards for the same test (1.6 km) on the same U.S. population (Safrit, 1990), raising the problem of choosing proper standards and questioning the validity of these tests. A similar situation was observed when the same 20-m multistage shuttle-run was administered to large random samples of the same population 10 years apart (Léger, Massicotte, Gauthier, Tremblay, Cazorla, & Prat, 1992). Of course, it is tempting to say that individual testing in a laboratory environment should reduce these variability problems, but this is not certain. In one study with children, heart rate and lactate values were higher during group field testing than during individual laboratory testing, possibly indicating higher motivation in a group environment (Van Praagh, Bedu, Falgairette, Fellmann, & Coudert, 1988).

Reliability of $\dot{V}O_2max$ tests is more difficult with children than it is with adults due to children's shorter attention spans and poor motivation, particularly in those younger than 8 years (Armstrong & Welsman, 1994). However, test–retest reliability of $\dot{V}O_2max$ or $\dot{V}O_2$ peak in children was reported similar to that of adults (Vaccaro & Mahon, 1987). Acceptable reliability was also found in 3- to 4-year-old children (Shuleva et al., 1990).

Correlation coefficients for the reliability of maximal field tests for children show some variability from study to study: 0.61 to 0.94 with a central tendency around 0.85 (Safrit, 1990). These values are similar to or higher than those observed for direct $\dot{V}O_2max$ tests: 0.42 to 0.95 with a tendency around 0.76 (Safrit, 1990). In fact, the reliability of direct $\dot{V}O_2max$ tests differs whether the plateau criterion is observed (0.74 vs. 0.27) (Cunningham, MacFarlane, Van Waterschoot, Paterson, Lefcoe, & Sangal, 1977). Correlations are, however, affected by the number of subjects and the range of $\dot{V}O_2max$ values, which may explain the lowest reported values. Restricting observations to maximal multistage field tests suggest better correlation than the ones reported above (Léger et al., 1988).

Indirect maximal multistage laboratory tests, such as the Bruce test or the Balke test, have been used extensively with adults. In children, indirect multistage treadmill tests were found valid ($r = 0.84$ to 0.88) (Cumming, Everatt, & Hastman, 1978; Montoye, Ayen, & Washburn, 1986). Maximal multistage cycle tests are also valid in children ($r \sim 0.9$) (Golden, Clarke, & Mahoney, 1991; Hansen, Froberg, Nielsen, & Huldebrant, 1989).

$\dot{V}O_2max$ Protocols

Numerous protocols for $\dot{V}O_2max$ determination in children have been described in the literature (Bar-Or, 1993; Docherty & Gaul, 1990; Freedson & Goodman, 1993;

Rowland, 1993). As expected, the first protocols used with children were originally developed for adults (e.g., like the Bruce and the Balke protocols). In fact, a survey indicated that 50% of pediatric laboratories use the Bruce protocol or modifications of the protocol (Rowland, 1993). These protocols, particularly the Bruce protocol, make it possible to compare data from children and adults while exercising a control for the protocol. In addition, due to its wide use, norms (ages 4-14), and reliability, data have been published for the Bruce protocol (Cumming et al., 1978). However, the Bruce protocol was not designed for children, and almost everyone agrees that its intensity increments between stages are too large and unequal (Rowland, 1993). The Balke protocol is too long and involves too high a grade for fit children (Rowland, 1993). The original walking version (5.5 km h^{-1}) resulted in lower values than the running (7.9 km h^{-1}) version (Paterson, Cunningham, & Donner, 1981).

Although some logical rules may be applied, no single protocol and ergometer will be appropriate for all subjects, trained and untrained, obese and normal, young and old, during growth. That is why Rowland (1993) and Bar-Or (1993) suggest a series of protocols according to weight or height for the bicycle ergometer and the treadmill, respectively. On the cycle ergometer each stage is two minutes in duration. For children ≤119.9 cm, the initial load is 12.5W with subsequent increments of 25W; children 120-139.9 cm start at 12.5W with increments of 25W; children 140-159.9 cm and females ≥160 cm start at 25W with 25W increments. Boys ≥160 cm have an initial 25W load but progress in increments of 50W (Bar-Or, 1993). The continuous protocol for an all-out treadmill test has an initial slope of 10% for all body statures, except for males ≥150 cm, who start at an initial slope of 12.5%, with 2.5% slope increments every 2 min. Treadmill speed is set according to stature: For children ≤109.9 cm, the treadmill speed is set at 4 km · h^{-1}; for children 110-129.9 cm, the treadmill speed is set at 5 km · h^{-1}, and for children ≥130 cm, the treadmill speed is set at 6 km · h^{-1} (Bar-Or, 1993).

$\dot{V}O_2$max SUBMAXIMAL TESTING

The choice of a submaximal test to estimate $\dot{V}O_2$max in children was investigated by Mocellin et al., (1971). Various methods originally developed for adults (e.g. Åstrand and Ryhming, 1954; Margaria, Aghemo, & Rovelli, 1965) yielded the same levels of reliability and validity (test–retest r > 0.90; and r > 0.75 compared to direct $\dot{V}O_2$max) in 13- to 14-year-old trained boys. As is the case for adults (Davies, 1968), random errors associated with these tests are quite large. Moreover, there are systematic errors when formulas developed for adults are used with children (Cumming & Langford, 1985; Godfrey, 1974; Hermansen & Oseid, 1971; Mocelin et al., 1971).

It is not surprising that the reliability of $\dot{V}O_2$max prediction is high because most predictors, such as age, height, and weight, do not change at all in a test–retest design. Only the HR response, the exercise intensity, or both may have changed, but these parameters are often outweighed by the other factors. The choice of proper predictors is critical and although age is often a significant $\dot{V}O_2$max predictor in a multiple regression model, along with submaximal data, it is suggested that age should be eliminated from regression equations in order to predict realistic $\dot{V}O_2$max values on an individual basis. It would be the opposite if the interest were in the $\dot{V}O_2$max value of a group of subjects. $\dot{V}O_2$max is a fitness index and predictors should only be chosen if they reflect a training response. It is inappropriate for the results of a trained individual to be affected by the average pattern of $\dot{V}O_2$ decrease in sedentary persons with similar age or weight. Of course, the correlation between predicted and measured $\dot{V}O_2$max may be less if age is deleted, but that lower correlation better reflects the true state of individual results by eliminating individual systematic errors (e.g., underestimation of a trained person of the same age). Furthermore, age is a complex predictor. It affects both the energy cost of running (in ml $O_2 \cdot kg^{-1} \cdot min^{-1}$) and the maximal heart rate, as well as the average $\dot{V}O_2$max value. These age effects are not all linear, parallel, and similarly important. Considering them all together may introduce some bias in the $\dot{V}O_2$max prediction. For instance, it is true that $\dot{V}O_2$max (ml $\cdot$ kg^{-1} $\cdot$ min^{-1}) decreases almost linearly with age, but only after puberty or after growth. Before that, $\dot{V}O_2$max values are quite stable (Figure 5.3). Thus, entering age in a linear model to predict $\dot{V}O_2$max of children and adults is mathematically wrong. The same rationale applies to the energy cost of submaximal running that decreases until the end of growth, but stays stable thereafter (Figure 5.5).

Keeping these considerations in mind, Léger, Ricart, and Massicotte (1990) and Ricart-Aguirre, Léger, and Massicotte (1990) designed new equations to predict $\dot{V}O_2$max from submaximal treadmill and cycle ergometer exercise, excluding age as a direct predictor. The obtained equations were not superior to previous ones, but eliminate the systematic errors of these equations.

When submaximal $\dot{V}O_2$ is measured directly with heart rate (Bonen, Heyward, Cureton, Boileau, & Massey, 1979), $\dot{V}O_2$max prediction is quite acceptable ($r = 0.95$ and a coefficient of variation of 9.3%); but that procedure is not readily accessible, and most submaximal tests do not rely on the direct measurement of submaximal $\dot{V}O_2$.

Åstrand and Ryhming Test

The Åstrand and Ryhming nomogram is probably the most common procedure used to predict $\dot{V}O_2$max from heart rate and submaximal power on the cycle ergometer. The procedure, originally designed for adults, yields large underestimation for children (12-25%) (Buono, Roby, Micale, & Sallis, 1989; Buono, Roby, Micale, Sallis, & Shephard, 1991; Hermansen & Oseid, 1971; Woynarowska, 1980). Correction equations have been proposed (Buono et al., 1989; Woynarowska), but their external validity or generalization are questionable in view of their different degrees of underestimation. The specific and limited age span of the subjects of these studies may be linked to that problem.

Correlations between predicted $\dot{V}O_2$max and measured $\dot{V}O_2$max vary substantially both within the same study ($r = 0.82$ for girls and $r = 0.52$ for boys) (Woynarowska,

1980) and among studies ($r = 0.52$-0.89). In an earlier study, the Buono, Roby, Micale, and Sallis (1989) group reported a validity correlation of 0.89; but Buono, Roby, Micale, Sallis, and Shephard (1991) later reported a coefficient of 0.49. Corresponding values for the reliability were 0.95 and 0.77, respectively. In 1991, they also reported that these validity and reliability indexes were much lower than those observed for the 1.6-km run (validity of 0.73 and reliability of 0.95) with the same subjects (paired design).

Results from procedures using submaximal treadmill or step-test data were not any better (Binkhorst, Saris, Noordeloos, van't Hof, & de Haan, 1985; Bonen et al., 1979; Buono et al., 1991; Jetté, Ashtar, & Sharratt, 1984; Montoye et al., 1986).

Physical Working Capacity

The Physical Working Capacity, or PWC_{170}, is the maximal steady-state power attained for a heart rate of 170 b $\cdot$ min^{-1} on a cycle ergometer. Because there is no extrapolation to an age-estimated maximal heart rate to predict a maximal aerobic-power value, there is no error associated with this process. Also, because the gross result itself is being used as an aerobic index, there is no error associated with the use of any population-specific equations in predicting $\dot{V}O_2$max. On the other hand, one must be aware that 170 b $\cdot$ min^{-1} does not represent the same %HRmax at all ages during growth. For example, 170 b $\cdot$ min^{-1} for 8- and 18-year-old children is approximately 83% and 86%HRmax, respectively, on average. On a relative basis the 170 beat $\cdot$ min^{-1} criterion is higher for older individuals and may exaggerate the PWC_{170} increase with age. Within the small age span during growth, this error is small and is compensated for with age-adjusted norms (Howell & Macnab, 1968). As for other submaximal tests, however, the major problem is the assumption that children of any age are at the same %HRmax; the reality indicates a considerable interindividual variability (Léger et al., 1990). Finally, even though PWC_{170} does not predict $\dot{V}O_2$max, its correlation with $\dot{V}O_2$max is as good as any other submaximal test that predicts $\dot{V}O_2$max (Mocellin et al., 1971).

A few decades ago, the PWC_{170} was popular, and numerous sets of norms were published (Howell & Macnab, 1968). Although methodological differences make it risky to compare norms, obvious differences were observed between American, Canadian, and Swedish children (Howell & Macnab, 1968), the heavier weight of American children partly explaining their superior PWC_{170} scores. Finally, because these norms were obtained a few decades ago and because MacDougall et al. (1983) have since reported secular improvement in the $\dot{V}O_2$max of Canadians over that period, caution is recommended in using these older PWC norms.

ASSESSING MECHANICAL EFFICIENCY

Mechanical efficiency, or energy cost of exercise, could be assessed using the same protocols used for $\dot{V}O_2$max. The key issue is to ensure that a steady state or a plateau is reached at each stage, which is also one of the conditions for indirect estimation of $\dot{V}O_2$max. To calculate mechanical efficiency, the mechanical-power output has to be measured in addition to the direct energy cost ($\dot{V}O_2$) required to perform that power output. That may be easy on the cycle, but it is much more complicated on the treadmill. The energy cost as a function of speed is usually measured as an index of running efficiency.

On the cycle ergometer, the energy cost is very similar among children and adults of both genders, and interindividual variation is relatively small (< 5%). Thus, there is no need for age and gender norms. On the treadmill, however, the variations are larger, and there are systematic differences according to age (Figure 5.5). These differences may be due to the inappropriate use of ml $\cdot$ kg^{-1} $\cdot$ min^{-1} $\cdot$ units. Still, it is the most common unit and is subject to a systematic age effect (Figure 5.5).

ENDURANCE TESTS

Four different approaches will be covered: the endurance time at maximal load, the lactate threshold, the ventilatory threshold, and the heart rate threshold.

Endurance Time at $\dot{V}O_2$max

A simple way to measure endurance is to measure the time that can be maintained at $\dot{V}O_2$max (Volkov et al., 1975) or at the last stage of an indirect, continuous, multistage test known to ensure $\dot{V}O_2$-steady-state at the end of each stage (Berthoin, 1994). In fact, there is no need to conduct these tests in a laboratory. At $\dot{V}O_2$max or at maximal aerobic speed, the endurance time of children is relatively stable during growth ($\overline{X} \pm SD = 311.5 \pm 104$ s in 108 boys and girls 12-17 years) and is similar to adult values (Berthoin, 1994). Adult female athletes often have higher endurance times than adult male athletes (Péronnet et al., 1987), but girls 12-14 years tend to have lower endurance times than boys (Berthoin, 1994).

The endurance time at 100% $\dot{V}O_2$max depends on motivation, particularly with children. Testing 18 groups, Berthoin (1994) found that endurance time at maximal aerobic speed is less reliable (central tendency of or around 0.40-0.65) than the maximal aerobic speed measured with a field multistage test on the same groups of subjects (r = 0.75-0.95). The reliability of the endurance test is better with trained adults (0.86) (Billat, Renoux, Pinoteau, Petit, & Koralsztein, 1994), but again in adults as in children, this value is lower than reliability for the results of the multistage test.

Lactate Threshold

The anaerobic threshold (AT) implies a sudden increase in blood lactate at a threshold intensity. It is often difficult to clearly identify the threshold point on a lactate-intensity curve made from a few discrete points, and the threshold point usually occurs at around 4 mmol · L^{-1}. Therefore, the anaerobic threshold is commonly defined as the intensity corresponding to a lactate value of 4 mmol · L^{-1} (Williams & Armstrong, 1991a).

However, 4 mmol · L^{-1}, although valid for adults, is much closer to peak $\dot{V}O_2$ in children (11-16 years) (Washington, 1993; Williams & Armstrong, 1991a) and a value of 2.5 mmol · L^{-1} has been suggested (Williams & Armstrong, 1991a).

Although fixed lactate concentrations of 2.5 or 4.0 mmol · L^{-1} increase the objectivity of the anaerobic threshold determination, such a criterion does not respect the individuality of the inflexion point that occurs at different lactate values. This is particularly true for children because the peak percent $\dot{V}O_2$ corresponding to 2.5 mmol · L^{-1} decreases from about 90% to 80% from 12 to 15 years (Williams & Armstrong, 1991a), suggesting lower lactate values at the inflexion point for younger children. In fact, the maximal lactate-steady-state occurs at around 2.2 mmol · L^{-1} in 13- to 14-year-old subjects (Williams & Armstrong, 1991b). Thus, using 2.5 mmol · L^{-1} for all ages during growth makes it difficult to compare AT values obtained at 4 mmol · L^{-1} for adults and may be misleading because the differences observed at different times of growth may be due to a bias introduced by the adoption of a common fixed lactate value of 2.5 mmol · L^{-1}.

If lactate is being used to assess AT in children, finding a method that permits identification of individual threshold points on the lactate-intensity curve is recommended. Even better is establishing the maximal lactate-steady-state as described by Williams & Armstrong (1991b). Protocols that could be used are the same as the ones used for $\dot{V}O_2max$. This is not easy, however, because it is difficult to obtain many data points due to the limited number of stages available (Armstrong & Welsman, 1994). Blood samples must be taken from children earlier in stage recovery because of their shorter muscle-to-blood diffusion time (~ 2.5 min) as compared to adults (~ 5 min) (Armstrong & Welsman, 1994). Finally, it is ethically difficult to justify blood sampling in routine evaluation of children, particularly in view of the trauma and the numerous problems associated with the determination of a threshold point on the lactate curve. Furthermore, and as reviewed by Armstrong and Welsman (1994), no clear age and gender trends appear in the lactate threshold values. It is very difficult to adopt or suggest a set of normative data for the lactate threshold. Higher %$\dot{V}O_2max$ values at the 4 mmol · L^{-1} threshold were reported for children as compared to adults, but the result is an artifact due to the fixed lactate criterion of 4 mmol · L^{-1} that is much higher than the average inflexion in children (Williams & Armstrong, 1991a). It is also difficult to assess sexual differences because of the paucity of lactate-threshold data for girls (Armstrong & Welsman).

Ventilatory Threshold

The use of noninvasive ventilatory threshold is very common, but as pointed out by Armstrong & Welsman (1994), the lack of conceptual and factual agreement between ventilatory and lactate threshold do not support its use. For a particular set of conditions, however, the ventilatory threshold, defined as the point at which the

$VE/\dot{V}O_2$ ratio suddenly increases without a change in the VE/VCO_2 ratio (Wasserman & McIlroy, 1964), is related to endurance performance and can be used for training application (Washington, 1993). However, the large variability of ventilatory threshold values obtained by different reviewers on the same set of data (Yeh, Gardner, Adams, Yanowitz, & Ro, 1983) questions the usefulness of this approach.

The only known study with interobserver reliability data in children (Paterson, McLellan, Stella, & Cunningham, 1987) reveals a high coefficient ($r = 0.93$). More studies, particularly with children, are needed to address this issue. Except for one longitudinal study (Paterson et al., 1987) where it was shown that the ventilatory threshold increased from 56% to 62% $\dot{V}O_2$max between 11- and 15-year-old trained boys, there is insufficient data to present normative values according to age and gender. It is, however, worthwhile to note that the above values (56-62% $\dot{V}O_2$max) are lower than the values observed for trained adults.

Conconi's Heart Rate Threshold

Another popular noninvasive method to assess the anaerobic threshold is the identification of a deflexion point (AT_{HR}), or departure from linearity of the heart rate as it increases in response to exercise intensity in a multistage test (Conconi, Ferrari, Ziglio, Droghetti & Codeca, 1982). Compared to the lactate threshold (AT_{LA}), these authors found identical AT values as measured by LA and HR "deflexion points" ($r = 0.99$). Although the method was designed as a field test with stages of constant length (200 m), the method is often used in the laboratory with constant-duration stages. In the field situation, the stage duration decreases as the speed increases, making it possible to perform a few extra stages and facilitating the appearance of an HR plateau.

In any event, in a field protocol similar to the Conconi's protocol, Tokmakidis and Léger (1988) were unable to identify a proper HR deflexion point in 45% of the cases. Furthermore, their data could not support the original validity study ($AT_{HR} > AT_{LA}$, $p < 0.05$, and $r = 0.50$ only). These discrepancies were attributed to a particular definition of the lactate threshold associated with a mathematical bias in the original study. For instance, the lactate threshold was defined as the intersection point between the two linear curves drawn on three points below and three points above the previously determined HR threshold. It is not surprising that the intersection point falls between point 3 and point 4, very close to the HR deflection point and that both were highly correlated.

The Conconi method is still popular. Gaisl and Hofmann (1990) support its validity for children, but the facts presented in their paper do not support this contention. They contend that AT_{HR} and AT_{LA} coincide, but they used the 4 mmol $\cdot L^{-1}$ criterion to determine AT_{LA} that is too high (Williams and Armstrong, 1991a). In other words, AT_{HR} is higher than true AT_{LA}, as was the case with adults (Tokmakidis & Léger, 1988). In addition, only 64 of 72 eleven-year-old boys reached the 4 mmol $\cdot L^{-1}$ criterion, indicating that the HR threshold is very close to $\dot{V}O_2$max.

Of course, as with $\dot{V}O_2$max, the HR breakpoint is also correlated with performance. Furthermore, in a close analysis of their original work, Gaisl and Weisspeiner (1989) raised some doubts about their 0.98 correlation between AT_{HR} and AT_{LA}. Computation from the data points on their graph indicates a correlation of 0.52, much lower than the reported 0.8. It is interesting to see that Gaisl has co-signed a paper (Steyer, Steyer, Pfeiffer, Kenner, & Gaisl, 1982) where heart rate linearity is questioned and where heart rate increases exponentially rather than logarithmically toward the end of a maximal test. Obviously, such a heart rate pattern negates the existence of Conconi's heart rate breakpoint.

Two other studies (Baraldi, Zanconato, Santuz, and Zachello, 1989; Mahon & Vacaro, 1991) also yielded lower correlations ($r = 0.76$ and 0.80) between the ventilatory threshold and the heart rate threshold, meaning that heart rate is not a valid threshold measure for many children. Although simple and potentially useful, the heart rate threshold method is theoretically and experimentally confusing and is not recommended. In our opinion, It seems better to assess endurance by measuring the time that can be maintained at 100% $\dot{V}O_2$max or 100% maximal aerobic speed.

MULTICOMPONENT TESTING

The unit used to express the results of a test may have a profound influence on the measured variable. For instance, expressing anaerobic threshold in km $\cdot$ h^{-1} instead of %$\dot{V}O_2$max includes all the three components of aerobic fitness, instead of just endurance. An indirect multistage test can predict $\dot{V}O_2$max, assuming constant mechanical efficiency for all. In fact, it essentially measures both $\dot{V}O_2$max and efficiency together. A 12-min test or a time trial (1.6 km or 3000 m) also measures the three aerobic components together.

CONCLUSION

Aerobic fitness has been an important area of research. Paradoxically, the number of unsolved questions seems to increase as the research goes on. The most appropriate method to express $\dot{V}O_2$ and $\dot{V}O_2$max has not been resolved, and there is controversy between the proponents of the ml $\cdot$ kg^{-1} $\cdot$ min^{-1} units and the proponents of power-function units. In addition, the concept of anaerobic threshold is questioned by many researchers, from both a conceptual and methodological point of view. It is difficult to identify standard procedures and normative data for children. Individual research-ers need to consider the various issues and select the tests and units of expression that best reflect the purpose of their investigations. Selected methodologies and protocols need to be described comprehensively.

REFERENCES

American College of Sports Medicine (1986). *Guidelines for graded exercise testing and exercise prescription.* Philadelphia: Lea & Febiger.

Andersen, K.L., Seliger, V., Rutenfranz, J., & Mocellin, R. (1974). Physical performance capacity of children in Norway. *European Journal of Applied Physiology*, **33**, 177-195.

Andersen, K.L., Shephard, R.J., Denolin, H., Varnouskas, E., & Masironi, R. (1971). *Les épreuves d'effort: Principes fondamentaux*. Genève: O.M.S.

Armstrong, N., & Welsman, J.R. (1994). Assessment and interpretation of aerobic fitness in children and adolescents. In J.O. Holloszy (Ed.), *Exercise and Sport Sciences Reviews* (Vol. 22, pp. 435-476). Baltimore: Williams & Wilkins.

Armstrong, N., Williams, J., Balding, J., & Kirby, B. (1991). The peak oxygen uptake of British children with reference to age, sex and sexual maturity. *European Journal of Applied Physiology*, **62**, 369-375.

Åstrand, P.O. (1952). *Experimental studies of physical working capacity in relation to sex and age*. Copenhagen: Munksgaard.

Åstrand, P.O,. & Rodahl, K. (1970). *Textbook of work physiology*. New York: McGraw-Hill.

Åstrand, P.O, & Ryhming, I. (1954). A nomogram for calculation of aerobic capacity from pulse rate during submaximal work. *Journal of Applied Physiology*, **7**, 218-221.

Åstrand, P.O., & Saltin, B. (1961). Oxygen uptake during the first minutes of heavy muscular exercise. *Journal of Applied Physiology*, **16**, 971-976.

Baraldi, E., Zanconato, S., Santuz, P.A., & Zachello, F. (1989). A comparison of two noninvasive methods in the determination of the anaerobic threshold in children. *International Journal of Sports Medicine*, **10**, 132-134.

Bar-Or, O. (1983). *Pediatric sports medicine for the practitioner*. New York: Springer-Verlag.

Bar-Or, O. (1993). Importance of differences between children and adults for exercise testing and exercise prescription. In J.S. Skinner (Ed.), *Exercise testing and exercise prescription for special cases* (pp. 57-74). Philadelphia: Lea & Febiger.

Bergh, V., Kanstrup, I.L., & Ekblom, B. (1976). Maximal oxygen uptake during exercise with various combinations of arm and leg work. *Journal of Applied Physiology*, **41**, 191-196.

Bergh, V., Sjodin, B., Forsberg, A., & Svedenhag, J. (1991). The relationship between body mass and oxygen uptake during running in humans. *Medicine and Sciences in Sports and Exercise*, **23**, 205-211.

Berthoin, S. (1994). *Évaluation des aptitudes aérobies à l'école: leur évolutions avec l'âge, le sexe et l'entraînement*. Unpublished doctoral dissertation, Université de Lille II.

Billat, V., Renoux, J.C., Pinoteau, J., Petit, B., & Koralsztein, J.P. (1994). Validation d'une épreuve maximale de temps limite à VMA (vitesse maximale aérobie) et à $\dot{V}O_2$max. *Science & Sports*, **9**(3), 135-143.

Binkhorst, R.A., Saris, W.H.M., Noordeloos, A.M., van't Hof, M.A., & de Haan, A.F.J. (1985). Maximal oxygen consumption of children (6 to 18 years) predicted from maximal and submaximal values in treadmill and bicycle tests. In J. Rutenfranz, R. Mocellin, & I. Klimt (Eds.), *Children and Exercise XII* (pp. 227-232). Champaign, IL: Human Kinetics.

Bolen, T.A., Roitman, J.L., & Leguizamon, E.E. (1981). The metabolic cost of zero load bicycle ergometry in cardiac patients. *Medicine and Science in Sports and Exercise*, **13**, 124, abstract.

Bonen, A., Heyward, V.H., Cureton, K.J., Boileau, R.A., & Massey, B.H. (1979). Prediction of maximal oxygen uptake in boys, ages 7-15 years. *Medicine and Science in Sports*, **11**, 24-29.

Bosco, C., Montanari, G., Ribacchi, R., Giovendi, P., Latteri, F., Iachelli, G. et al. (1987). Relationship between the efficiency of muscular work during jumping and the energetics of running. *European Journal of Applied Physiology*, **56**, 138-143.

Brooks, G.A. (1985). Anaerobic threshold: Review of the concept and direction of future research. *Medicine and Science in Sports and Exercise*, **17**, 22-31.

Buono, M.J., Roby, J.J., Micale, F.G., & Sallis, J.F. (1989). Predicting maximal oxygen uptake in children: Modification of the Astrand-Ryhming test. *Pediatric Exercise Science*, **1**, 278-283.

Buono, M.J., Roby, J.J., Micale, F.G., Sallis, J.F., & Shephard, W.E. (1991). Validity and reliability of predicting maximum oxygen uptake via field tests in children and adolescents. *Pediatric Exercise Science*, **3**, 250-255.

Buskirk, E., & Longstreet Taylor, H. (1957). Maximal oxygen intake and its relation to body composition, with special reference to chronic physical activity and obesity. *Journal of Applied Physiology*, **2**, 72-78.

Conconi, F., Ferrari, M., Ziglio, P.G., Droghetti, P., & Codeca, L. (1982). Determination of the anaerobic threshold by a noninvasive field tests in runners. *Journal of Applied Physiology*, **52**, 869-873.

Consolazio, C.F., Johnson, R.E., & Pecora, L.J. (1963). *Physiological measurements of metabolic functions in man*. New York: McGraw-Hill.

Cooke, C.B., McDonagh, M.J.N., Nevill, A.M., & Davies, C.T.M. (1991). Effects of load on oxygen intake in trained boys and men during treadmill running. *Journal of Applied Physiology*, **71**, 1237-1244.

Cooper, D.M. (1989). Development of the oxygen transport system in normal children. In O. Bar-Or (Ed.), *Advances in pediatric sport sciences-Biological issues* (Vol. 3, pp. 67-99). Champaign, IL: Human Kinetics.

Costill, D.L., Thomason, H. & Roberts, E. (1973). Fractional utilisation of the aerobic capacity during distance running. *Medicine and Science in Sports*, **5**, 248-252.

Cumming, G.R., Everatt, D., & Hastman, L. (1978). Bruce treadmill test in children: normal values in a clinic population. *American Journal of Cardiology*, **41**, 69-75.

Cumming, G.R., Hastman, L., McCort, J., & McCullough, S. (1980). High serum lactates do occur in children after maximal work. *International Journal of Sports Medicine*, **1**, 66-69.

Cumming, G.R., & Langford, S. (1985). Comparison of nine exercise tests used in pediatric cardiology. In R.A. Binkhorst, H.C. Kemper & W.H. Saris (Eds.), *Children and exercise XI* (pp. 58-67). Champaign, IL: Human Kinetics.

Cunningham, D.A., MacFarlane Van Waterschoot, B., Paterson, D.H., Lefcoe, M., & Sangal, S.P. (1977). Reliability and reproducibility of maximal oxygen uptake measurement in children. *Medicine and Science in Sports and Exercise*, **9**, 104-108.

Cureton, K.J., Sparling, P.B., Evans, B.W., Johnson, S.M., Kong, U.D., & Purvis, J.W. (1978). Effect of experimental alterations in exercise weight on aerobic-capacity and distance running performance. *Medicine and Science in Sports*, **10**, 194-199.

Daniels, J., & Daniels, N. (1992). Running economy of elite male and elite female runners. *Medicine and Science in Sports and Exercise*, **24**, 483-489.

Daniels, J., Oldridge, N., Nagle, F., & White, B. (1978). Differences and changes in $\dot{V}O_2$ among young runners 10-18 years of age. *Medicine and Science in Sports*, **10**, 200-203.

Davies, C.T.M. (1968). Limitations of the prediction of maximum oxygen intake from cardiac frequency measurements. *Journal of Applied Physiology*, **24**, 700-706.

Docherty, D., & Gaul, C.A. (1990). *Critical analysis of available "laboratory" tests used in evaluating the fitness of children and youth*. Report submitted to Fitness Canada (Ottawa).

Ebbeling, C.J., Hamill, J., Freedson, P.S. & Rowland, T.W. (1992). An examination of efficiency during walking in children and adults. *Pediatric Exercise Science*, **4**, 36-49.

Falgairette, G. (1989). Evolution de la puissance maximal aérobie de l'enfance à l'âge adulte: influence de l'activité physique et sportive. *Revue des sciences et techniques en activités physiques et sportives*, **10**, 43-58.

Freedson, P.S., & Goodman, T.L. (1993). Measurement of oxygen consumption. In T.W. Rowland (Ed.), *Pediatric laboratory exercise testing* (pp. 91-113). Champaign, IL: Human Kinetics.

Gaisl, G., & Hofman, P. (1990). Heart rate determination of anaerobic threshold in children. *Pediatric Exercise Science*, **2**, 29-36.

Gaisl, G., & Wiesspeiner, G. (1989). Comparison of the heart rates at the anaerobic threshold determined invasively and noninvasively in eleven year old children. In S. Oseid and K.H. Carlsen (Eds.), *Children and exercise XIII* (pp. 135-143). Champaign, IL: Human Kinetics.

Godfrey, S. (1974). *Exercise testing in children*. Philadelphia: Saunders.

Golden, J.C., Clarke, W.R., & Mahoney, L.T. (1991). New protocol for submaximal and peak exercise values for children and adolescents: The Muscative study. *Pediatric Exercise Science*, **3**, 129-140.

Hagberg, J.M., Giese, M.C., Spitznagle, E., & Mullin, J.P. (1981). Effect of pedalling rate on submaximal exercise responses of competitive cyclists. *Journal of Applied Physiology*, **51**, 447-451.

Hansen, H.S., Froberg, K., Nielsen, J.R., & Hyldebrant, N. (1989). A new approach to assessing maximal aerobic power in children: The Odense school child study. *European Journal of Applied Physiology*, **58**, 618-624.

Hermansen, L., & Oseid. S. (1971). Direct and indirect estimation of maximal oxygen uptake in prepubertal boys. *Acta Paediatrica Scandinavica*, (Suppl. 217), 18-23.

Hollmann, W. (1985). Historical remarks on the development of the aerobic-anaerobic threshold up to 1966. *International Journal of Sports Medicine*, **6**, 109-116.

Howell, M.L., & Macnab, R.B.J. (1968). *The physical work capacity of Canadian children age 7 to 17*. Ottawa, ON: Canadian Association for Health, Physical Education and Recreation.

Hughson, R.L., Weisiger, K.H., Swanson, G.D. (1987). Blood lactate concentration increases as a continuous function in progressive exercise. *Journal of Applied Physiology*, **62**, 1975-1981.

Jetté, M., Ashtar, N.J., & Sharatt, M.T. (1984). Development of a cardiorespiratory step test of fitness for children 7-14 years of age. *Canadian Journal of Public Health*, **75**, 212-217.

Jones, A. (1991). Peak aerobic power in intensively trained young athletes related to puberty (Abstract). *Journal of Sport Sciences*, **9**, 418-419.

Katch, V.L. (1973). Use of the oxygen/body weight ratio in correlational analyses: Spurious correlations and statistical considerations. *Medicine and Science in Sports*, **5**, 253-257.

Kearney, J.T., & VanHandel, P.J. (1989). Economy: A physiologic perspective. In W.A. Grana, J.A. Lombardo, B.J. Sharkey, & J.A. Stone (Eds.), *Advances in sports medicine and fitness* (Vol. 2, pp. 57-87). Chicago: Year Book Medical.

Kemper, H.C.G. (1986). Longitudinal studies on the development of health and fitness and the interaction with physical activity of teenagers. *Pediatry*, **13**, 52-59.

Klimt, F., & Voight, E.D. (1971). Investigations on the standardization of ergometry in children. *Acta Pediatrica Scandinavica*, (suppl. 217), 35-36.

Krahenbuhl, G.S., Pangrazi, R.P., Stone, W.J., Morgan, D.W., & Williamss, T. (1989). Fractional utilization of maximal aerobic capacity in children 6 to 8 years of age. *Pediatric Exercise Science*, **1**, 271-277.

Krahenbuhl, G.S., Skinner, J.S., & Kohrt, W.M. (1985). Developmental aspects of maximal aerobic power in children. In R.J. Terjung (Ed.), *Exercise and sports science reviews* (Vol. 13, pp. 503-538). New York: Macmillan.

Krahenbuhl, G.S., & Williams, T.J. (1992). Running economy: changes with age during childhood and adolescence. *Medicine and Science in Sports and Exercise*, **24**, 462-466.

Léger, L., Cloutier, J., & Massicotte, D. (1986). Energy cost of running, cycling and stepping during growth. In T. Reilly, J. Watkins, & J. Borms (Eds.), *Kinanthropometry III* (pp. 138-145). London: E & FN Spon.

Léger, L., Gutierrez, A., Choinière, D., Ricart, R.-M., & Massicotte, D. (1990). %HR max-%$\dot{V}O_2$max relation according to age (6-50), sex and ergometer. (Abstract). International Congress on Youth, Leisure and Physical Activity and Kinanthropometry IV, Brussels.

Léger, L., Lambert, J., Goulet, A., Rowan, C., & Dinelle, Y. (1984). Capacité aérobie des Québécois de 6 à 17 ans - Test navette de 20 mètres avec paliers de 1 minute. *Canadian Journal of Applied Sport Science*, **9**, 64-69.

Léger, L., Massicotte, D., Gauthier, R., Tremblay, C., Cazorla, G., & Prat, J.A. (1992). Problems in establishing Canadian norms for the 20 m shuttle run test of aerobic fitness. In J. Coudert & E. Van Praagh (Eds.), *Children and exercise XVI* (pp. 119-121). Paris: Masson.

Léger, L., Mercier, D., Gadoury, C., & Lambert, J. (1988). The multistage 20 metre shuttle run test for aerobic fitness. *Journal of Sport Sciences*, **6**, 93-101.

Léger, L., Ricart, R.-M., & Massicotte, D. (1990). Regression models to predict $\dot{V}O_2$max from submaximal treadmill exercise in 6 to 50 years old males and females. In G. Beunen, J. Ghesquiere, T. Reybrouck, & A.L. Claessens (Eds.), *Children and exercise, Band 4* (pp. 104-110). Stuttgard: Verlag.

Lohman, T.G. (1989). Assessment of body composition in children. *Pediatric Exercise Science*, **1**, 19-30.

MacDougall, J.D., Roche, P.D., Bar-Or, O., & Moroz, J.R. (1983). Maximal aerobic capacity of Canadian schoolchildren: Prediction based on age-related cost of running. *International Journal of Sports Medicine*, **4**, 194-198.

Mahon, A.D., & Vaccaro, P. (1991). Can the point of deflection from linearity of heart rate determine ventilatory threshold in children? *Pediatric Exercise Science*, **3**, 256-262.

Maksud, M.G., & Coutts, K.D. (1971). Comparison of a continuous and discontinuous graded treadmill test for maximal oxygen uptake. *Medicine and Science in Sports*, **3**, 63-65.

Margaria, R., Aghemo, P., & Rovelli, E. (1965). Indirect determination of maximal oxygen consumption in man. *Journal of Applied Physiology*, **20**, 1070-1073.

Massicotte, D., Gauthier, R., & Markon, P. (1985). Prediction of $\dot{V}O_2$max from the running performance in children aged 10-17 years. *Journal of Sports Medicine*, **25**, 10-17.

McArdle, W.D., Katch, F.I., & Pechard, G.S. (1973). Comparison of continuous and discontinuous treadmill and bicycle tests for $\dot{V}O_2$max. *Medicine and Science in Sports*, **5**, 156-160.

Mirwald, R.L., & Bailey, D.A. (1986). *Maximal aerobic power - A longitudinal analysis*. London, ON: Sports Dynamics.

Mocelin, R., Lindemann, H., Rutenfranz, J., & Sbresny, W. (1971). Determination of W_{170} and maximal oxygen uptake in children by different methods, *Acta Peadiatrica Scandinavica*, (Suppl.) **217**, 13-17.

Montoye, H.J., Ayen, T., & Washburn, R.A. (1986). The estimation of $\dot{V}O_2$max from maximal and sub-maximal measurements in males, age 10-39. *Research Quarterly for Exercise and Sport*, **57**, 250-253.

Noakes, T.D. (1988). Implications of exercise testing for prediction of athletic performance: A contemporary perspective. *Medicine and Sciences in Sports and Exercise*, **20**, 319-330.

Ouvrier-Buffet, P. (1994). *Modifications physiologiques chez le coureur de demi-fond au cours d'une saison d'entraînement.* Unpublished doctoral dissertation, Université Blaise Pascal-Clermont-Ferrand II.

Paterson, D.H., Cunningham, D.A., & Bumstead, L.A. (1986). Recovery O_2 and blood lactic acid: Longitudinal analysis in boys aged 11-15 years. *European Journal of Applied Physiology*, **55**, 93-99.

Paterson, D.H., Cunningham, D.A., & Donner, A. (1981). The effect of different treadmill speeds on the variability of $\dot{V}O_2$max in children. *European Journal of Applied Physiology*, **47**, 113-122.

Paterson, D.H., McLellan, T.M., Stella, R.S., & Cunningham, D.A. (1987). Longitudinal study of ventilation threshold and maximal O_2 uptake in athletic boys. *Journal of Applied Physiology*, **62**, 2051-2057.

Péronnet, F., Thibault, G., Rhodes, E.C., & McKenzie, D.C. (1987). Correlation between ventilatory threshold and endurance capability in marathon runners. *Medicine and Sciences in Sports and Exercise*, **19**, 610-615.

Quinney H.A., Watkinson, E.J., Massicotte, D., Conger, P.R., & Gauthier, R. (1982). The height, weight and height/weight ratio of Canadian children in 1979. *Canadian Association for Health and Physical Education Journal*, **49**, 17-19.

Ricart-Aguirre, R.M., Léger, L., & Massicotte, D. (1990). Problèmes théoriques et pratiques de la prédiction de la $\dot{V}O_2$max. *Science & Sports*, **5**, 143-153.

Rivera-Brown, A.M., Rivera, M.A., & Frontera, W.R. (1992). Applicability of criteria for $\dot{V}O_2$max in active adolescents. *Pediatric Exercise Science*, **4**, 331-339.

Rowland, T.W. (1989). Oxygen uptake and endurance fitness in children: A developmental perspective. *Pediatric Exercise Science*, **1**, 313-328.

Rowland, T.W. (1992). On body size and running economy. *Pediatric Exercice Science*, **4**, 1-4.

Rowland, T.W. (1993). Aerobic exercise testing protocols. In T.W. Rowland (Ed.), *Pediatric laboratory exercise testing* (pp. 19-41). Champaign, IL: Human Kinetics.

Rowland, T.W., Auchinachie, J.A., Keenan, T.J., & Green, G.M. (1987). Physiological responses to treadmill running in adult and prepubertal males. *International Journal of Sports Medicine*, **8**, 292-297.

Rowland, T.W., & Cunningham, L. (1992). Oxygen uptake plateau during maximal treadmill exercise in children. *Chest*, **101**, 485-489.

Rowland, T.W., Staab, J.S., Unnithan, V.B., Rambusch, J.M., & Siconolfi, S.F. (1990). Mechanical efficiency during cycling in prepubertal and adult males. *International Journal of Sports Medicine*, **11**, 452-455.

Rutenfranz, J., Andersen, K.L., Seliger, V., Klimmer, F., Berndt, I., & Ruppel, M. (1981). Maximal aerobic power and body composition during the puberty growth period: Similarities and differences between children in two European countries. *European Journal of Pediatry*, **136**, 123-133.

Rutenfranz, J., Macek, M., Lange Andersen, K., Bell, R.D., Vavra, J., Radvansky, Klimmer, F., & Kylian, H. (1990). The relationship between changing body height and growth related changes in maximal aerobic power. *European Journal of Applied Physiology*, **60**, 282-287.

Ryschon, T., Kemp, M., Shappart, L., & Johnson, S. (1991). Gross metabolic efficiency of light and heavy children during stepping [abstract]. *Pediatric Exercise Science*, **4**, 180.

Safrit, M.J. (1990). The validity and reliability of fitness tests for children: A review. *Pediatric Exercise Science*, **2**, 9-28.

Shuleva, K.M., Hunter, G.R., Hester, D.J., and Dunawaw, D.L. (1990). Exercise oxygen uptake in 3- through 6-year-old children. *Pediatric Exercise Science*, **2**, 130-139.

Siri, W.E. (1961). Body composition from fluid spaces and density: Analysis of methods. In J. Brozek & A. Henschel (Eds.), *Techniques for measuring body composition* (pp. 223-224). Washington, DC: National Academy of Sciences National Research Council.

Sjodin, B., & Svedenhag, J. (1985). Applied physiology of marathon running. *Sports Medicine*, **2**, 83-99.

Steyer, G.E., Steyer, A., Pfeiffer, K.P., Kenner, T., & Gaisl, G. (1982). Determination of heart rate index and estimation of physical working capacity from that in children. In N. Bachl, L. Prokop, and R. Suckert (Eds.), *Current topics in sports medicine* (pp. 224-231). Vienna: Urban & Schavarzenberg.

Sundberg, S., & Elovainio, R. (1982). Cardiorespiratory function in competitive endurance runners aged 12-16 years compared with ordinary boys. *Acta Pediatrica Scandinavica*, **71**, 987-992.

Tanner, J.M. (1949). Fallacy of per-weight and per-surface area standards and their relation to spurious correlation. *Journal of Applied Physiology*, **2**, 1-15.

Tokmakidis, S.P. (1989). *Anaerobic threshold in perspective: physiological, methodological and practical implications of the concept*. Unpublished doctoral dissertation, Université de Montréal.

Tokmakidis, S.P., & Léger, L. (1988). External validity of the Conconi's heart rate anaerobic threshold as compared to the lactate threshold. In C.D. Dotson and J.H. Humphrey (Eds.), *Exercise physiology - Current selected research* (Vol. 3, pp. 43-58). New York: AMS Press.

Thomas, S.G., Weller, I.M.R., & Cox, M.H. (1993). Sources of variation in oxygen consumption during a stepping task. *Medicine and Science in Sports and Exercise*, **25**, 139-144.

Unnithan, V.B., & Eston, R.G. (1990). Stride frequency and submaximal treadmill running economy in adults and children. *Pediatric Exercise Science*, **2**, 149-155.

Vaccaro, P., & Mahon, A. (1987). Cardiorespiratory responses to endurance training in children. *Sports Medicine*, **4**, 352-363.

Vanden Eynde, B., Vienne, D., Vuylsteke-Wauters, M., & Van Gerven, D. (1988). Aerobic power and pubertal peak height velocity in Belgian boys. *European Journal of Applied Physiology*, **57**, 430-434.

Van Praagh, E., Bedu, M., Falgairette, G., Fellmann, N., & Coudert, J. (1988). Comparaison entre VO_2max direct et indirect chez l'enfant de 7 et 12 ans. Validation d'une épreuve de terrain. *Science et Sports*, **3**, 327-332.

Volkov, N.I., Shirkovets, E.A., & Borilkevich, V.E. (1975). Assessment of aerobic and anaerobic capacity of athletes in treadmill running tests. *European Journal of Applied Physiology*, **34**, 121-130.

Washington, R.L. (1993). Anaerobic threshold. In T.W. Rowland (Ed.), *Pediatric laboratory exercise testing* (pp. 115-140). Champaign, IL: Human Kinetics.

Wasserman, K., & McIlroy, M.B. (1964). Detecting the threshold of the anaerobic metabolism in cardiac patient during exercise. *The American Journal of Cardiology*, **14**, 844-852.

Welsman, J., Armstrong, N., Winter, E., & Kirby, B.J. (1993, September). The influence of various scaling techniques on the interpretation of developmental changes in peak VO_2 [Abstract]. European Group for Pediatric Work Physiology and North American Society of Pediatric Exercise Medicine, September, 1993, Hamilton, ON.

Williams, J.R., & Armstrong, N. (1991a). The influence of age and sexual maturation on children's blood lactate responses to exercise. *Pediatric Exercise Science*, **3**, 111-120.

Williams, J.R., & Armstrong, N. (1991b). Relationship of maximal lactate steady state to performance at fixed blood lactate reference values in children. *Pediatric Exercise Science*, **3**, 333-341.

Williams, K.R., Cavanagh, P.R. & Ziff, J.L. (1987). Biomechanical studies of elite female distance runners. *International Journal of Sports Medicine*, **8** (Suppl.), 107-118.

Winter, E.M. (1991). Cycle ergometry and maximal intensity exercise. *Sports Medicine*, **11**, 351-357.

Winter, E.M. (1992). Scaling: Partitioning out difference in size. *Pediatric Exercise Science*, **4**, 296-301.

Woynarowska, B. (1980). The validity of indirect estimations of maximal oxygen uptake in children 11-12 years of age. *European Journal of Applied Physiology*, **43**, 19-23.

Yeh, M.P., Gardner, R.M., Adams, T.D., Yanowitz, F.G., & Ro, C. (1983). Anaerobic threshold: Problems of determination and validation. *Journal of Applied Physiology*, **55**, 1178-1186.

6

Catherine A. Gaul

Muscular Strength and Endurance

Strength is commonly described as the maximal tension a muscle, or muscle group, can exert against a resistance. Muscular strength is necessary for efficient movement to occur and provides stability within joints, thereby reducing the risk of musculoskeletal injuries. Muscular strength enables individuals to perform everyday activities without undue fatigue (Haskell, Montoye, & Orenstein, 1985). Muscular strength encourages children to participate in physical pursuits at an early age and may be an important factor in the development of healthy lifelong activity habits (Sallis et al., 1992).

The development of muscular strength enables muscles to endure long periods of submaximal force production, thereby effectively delaying the onset of muscular fatigue. This has important implications for children involved in prolonged activities and sport. Reducing fatigue also reduces the risk of injury.

The primary objectives of this chapter are to describe and explain the most commonly used laboratory tests of muscular strength in healthy children up to the age of 18 years. This chapter also includes a brief section describing the development of strength in children and considers the influence that growth and maturation have on the development of muscular strength. The muscle groups discussed were determined by the availability of data from pediatric studies. More detailed discussions of age and sex-associated changes in strength during childhood can be found in a number of recent reviews (Blimkie, 1989; Beunen & Malina, 1988). In addition

Sale (1989) reviews the role of exercise training on the development of muscular strength in children.

DEFINING TERMS RELATED TO MUSCULAR STRENGTH AND ENDURANCE

The Système Internationale d'Unités (International System of Units [SI]) expresses test results for muscular strength and endurance. *Strength* is defined as the maximal force or torque developed by a muscle, or muscle group, during one maximal voluntary action of unlimited duration at a specified velocity of movement.

Muscular endurance is described as the ability of a muscle, or muscle group, to generate force repeatedly or for an extended period of time. Muscular endurance can be determined by measuring time to fatigue. Units used to describe muscular endurance include the number of repetitions to failure at a specific resistance or the number of repetitions at 50% of peak torque.

Work is the amount of torque or force produced. It has no time reference.

Power is defined as the time it takes to perform a specified amount of mechanical work. Power is also expressed as the product of force or torque and velocity.

Muscle Actions

The three types of muscle action are concentric, eccentric, and isometric. Detailed descriptions of the physiological and mechanical characteristics of the various human skeletal muscle actions have been reviewed elsewhere (Blimkie, 1989; Knuttgen & Komi, 1992; Komi, 1984; Osternig, 1986).

Concentric muscle action refers to the tension, or force, generated as muscle length decreases. It is a dynamic action in which the whole muscle length is reduced, resulting in movement. Often the term *isotonic* is used to describe this type of muscle action, as it refers to constant tension produced as the muscle shortens. Weight-lifting exercises are often considered isotonic; the weight of the implement (e.g., barbell) remains constant through the range in which it is moved. However, the application of this term to describe a muscle action has been criticized because the velocity and the actual force (or torque) applied to resistance do not normally remain constant as a limb is moved through a range of motion (Knuttgen & Komi, 1992; Sale, 1991) but varies according to the length of the muscle and the angle of the joint in use. The amount of concentric force a muscle can generate varies inversely with the velocity of movement. This has implications for training techniques and for velocities used in the evaluation of muscular strength. The identification of the force–velocity relationship in children has been limited to concentric actions of the shoulder, elbow, and knee flexors and extensors (Brodie, Burnie, Eston, & Royce, 1986; Burnie & Brodie, 1986; Nemoto, Kanehisa, & Miyashita, 1989; Ramsay et al., 1990).

Eccentric muscle action involves the generation of tension while the muscle is forcibly lengthened. It occurs when external resistance exceeds muscle force, causing the muscle to lengthen while developing tension. This type of muscle activity is common when resisting the force of gravity during movements such as landing following a jump, lowering a barbell, or running. Eccentric force typically exceeds the concentric strength capability of a muscle by 20% to 50%. However, it also results in greater post-exercise muscle soreness. The force–velocity relationship observed in eccentric muscle action is quite different than that of concentric muscle actions. Eccentric actions result in greater force with increasing movement velocities up to a point beyond which force remains constant. The relationship between eccentric force development and movement velocity has been established in adult populations, but has yet to be described in children.

Isometric muscle action involves a constant muscle length during the production of tension. In the past, the assessment of grip strength was the primary means of measuring isometric strength in children. The increasing availability of isokinetic dynamometers with movement velocities that can be set at $0° \cdot \text{sec}^{-1}$ has provided a more reliable and accurate laboratory isometric testing technique for both adults and children. Both methods involve isometric force generation, but caution must be made when comparing data from the different methods.

Involuntary Evoked Contractions

Recently, electrical stimulation of skeletal muscle has been used to assess strength characteristics, contractile properties of skeletal muscle, and motor unit activation in children (Blimkie, Ebbesen, MacDougall, Bar-Or, & Sale, 1989; Chapman, Grindrod, & Jones, 1984; Davies, 1985; Ramsay et al., 1990). Electrical stimulation techniques used to evoke involuntary contractions provide a means of evaluating muscular activity independent of volition and are not influenced by the skill or motivation of the subject.

The evoked twitch contraction measures the intrinsic force-producing ability of muscle. This technique involves the stimulation of a motor nerve by a single percutaneous supramaximal electrical stimulation that produces a single isometric contraction lasting a few hundred milliseconds (msec). Twitch force or torque is recorded at progressively higher voltages until supramaximal stimulation is achieved and a plateau is obtained in the force–voltage relationship. Twitch force, time to peak twitch torque, and time to half-relaxation can be determined. However, it is important to note that a single twitch typically does not induce maximal activation of a muscle. Caution must be used when employing these techniques on pediatric populations. Ramsay et al. (1990) reported that the measurement of evoked contractile properties of knee extensors in children was difficult due to discomfort.

Evoked tetanic contraction involves repetitive percutaneous electrical stimulation of a muscle, resulting in a fused isometric contraction usually lasting from 1 to 3 sec. Maximal tetanic stimulation at the optimal frequency for the generation of force is the best measure of maximal evoked-contraction strength (and, therefore, maximal

Table 6.1 Isometric-Evoked Contractile Characteristics and Methods Used in Children

Author	Sex	Age (yrs)	N	Muscle group	Joint angle (°)	Tetanic tension (N)	Peak twitch tension (TT)	Time to TT (msec)	1/2 relax time (msec)	Fatigue index (%)	MUA (%)	Method
Davies, 1985	M	9	10	Triceps surae	85	569*	70 N	117	90			*Max twitch torque* using 50µs pulses of increasing voltage (10, 20, 50 Hz) to supramax stimulation.
		11	14			765	85 N	123	96			*Tetanic tension* using 50 Hz with 6s stimulus train.
		14	12			1054	97 N	117	87			*Electrically evoked fatigue* measured by intermittent stim of muscle for 2 min at 20 Hz.
	F	9	11			554*	71 N	118	97			
		11	12			706	90 N	128	97			
		14	14			1005	126 N	123	95			
Belanger & McComas, 1989	M	6-13	10	Dorsiflexors Plantarflexors	10° PF• 20° DF•		DF 0.4 N·m PF 8.7 N·m	59.5 115.6	67.6 106.5	39.7 36.8	94.0	*Max twitch torque* using 50 - 100µsec pulses of increasing voltage to supramax stimulation.
	M	15-18	8				DF 1.1 N·m PF 17.6 N·m	72.5 111.3	73.8 99.4	40.1 30.3	99.4	*MUA* from interpolated twitch technique using supramax stim during Max voluntary contraction (MVC). *Fatigue index* measured as % decrease in torque using max contraction for 60s.

Reference	Sex	Age	N	Muscle	Stim	TF			MUA	Description
Blimkie, Ebbesen et al., 1989	M	9-13	11n 13o	Elbow flexors	80		59.3	61.0		Max twitch torque using 50µs pulses of increasing voltage to supramaximal stimulation.
					90		64.5	61.0		
							60.7	68.4		
					120		62.3	71.1		
							59.0	77.5		
							61.8	86.9		
					150		55.3	81.6		
							60.1	90.6		
Blimkie, Ramsay et al., 1989	M	9-11	27	Elbow flexors	80	1.66 N·m	69.3	66.2		Max twitch torque using 100µs pulses of increasing voltage to supramax stimulation.
					100	1.91 N·m	67.6	79.8	89.3	MUA via interpolated twitch using single supramax stim during MVC.
					120	1.84 N·m	65.1	88.0		
					150	1.61 N·m	65.9	88.4		
Ramsay et al., 1990	M	9-11	13	Elbow flexors	80					Max twitch torque using 50µs pulses of increasing voltage to supramax stim.
					100				89	MUA via interpolated twitch using single supramax stim during MVC (at 100° elbow flexion and 90° knee ext only)
					120					
					150					
				Knee extensors	90				78	

Note. Twitch force (TF) represents maximal isometric force (or torque) produced during a single evoked contraction.

Contraction time measured as the time taken from initial deflection in force production to peak twitch force.

Half relax time reflects the time from peak twitch force to a 50% decrease in force.

MUA is the motor unit activation represented as a percentage of total available motor units.

*measure taken at 20 Hz.

•DF = dorsiflexion or dorsiflexors, PF = plantarflexion or plantarflexors.

activation). However, as tetanic stimulation can be a painful technique, it is rarely used in the study of children (Blimkie, 1989; Ramsay et al., 1990; Sale, 1989).

The interpolated-twitch technique is used to measure interpolated twitch torque and to assess the percentage of motor unit activation (%MUA) during an isometric muscle action. This method involves an initial measurement of evoked twitch torque (TT) that is then considered to be 100% activation. Peak torque during a maximal voluntary contraction (MVC) is measured next, followed by a second MVC when an electrical stimulation (similar to the evoked twitch) is superimposed to test for differences between maximum volitional contraction and maximum electrical stimulation of the muscle.

% motor unit activation is calculated as:
$$\% \text{ MUA} = [TT - (ITT)]/TT \times 100$$
where ITT = difference between MVC and the electrically stimulated MVC.

Neural adaptations due to growth, maturation, and training can be identified and distinguished from muscular adaptations by using these methods.

Evoked twitch contraction and interpolated-twitch methods have been used to assess motor unit activation in pediatric populations (Belanger & McComas, 1989; Blimkie, Ebbesen, MacDougall, Bar-Or, & Sale, 1989; Blimkie, Ramsay et al., 1989; Davies, 1985; McComas, Sica, & Petito, 1973; Ramsay et al., 1990). Table 6.1 reviews studies utilizing these techniques in children (see pages 228-229).

DEVELOPMENT OF MUSCULAR STRENGTH IN CHILDREN

The development of muscular strength in children is related to age, gender, maturity status, previous levels of physical activity, and body size (Alexander & Molnar, 1973; Blimkie, Ramsay et al., 1989; Molnar & Alexander, 1973, 1974). This section provides a brief overview of the development of specific variables related to muscular strength in children. Many reviews regarding the development of these strength-related components are referred to within each of the following sections.

Muscle Fiber Type

The development and differentiation of skeletal-muscle fiber type have been extensively reviewed (Baldwin, 1984; Colling-Saltin, 1980; Malina, 1986). Information regarding muscle fiber type in childhood and adolescence is limited by ethical considerations involving the use of invasive techniques to obtain muscle samples. However, based on the information available, there seems to be a high proportion of Type I (slow oxidative) and undifferentiated Type IIc fibers and a lower percent distribution of the fast, Type II fibers during early and mid-childhood than in adulthood (Bell, MacDougall, Billeter, & Howald, 1980; Colling-Saltin, 1980; Du-Plessis et al., 1985). The relative proportions of Type IIa and IIb fibers remain equivocal for this population, with some studies demonstrating a greater proportion of IIa than IIb during childhood (Colling-Saltin, 1980) while others have reported the opposite (Bell et al., 1980). Very little is known about sex-associated variations in skeletal-muscle fiber proportions in children. There is no evidence of a difference in Type I, Type IIa or Type IIb fiber distributions between male and female children.

Metabolic Properties

There are no longitudinal data regarding the metabolic changes that occur in human skeletal muscle during growth and development. The invasiveness of the currently used methods to determine intramuscular characteristics (e.g., muscle biopsy) makes their application to pediatric studies inappropriate. The very few cross-sectional studies of muscle metabolic properties in children have reported muscle adenosine triphosphate (ATP) and creatine phosphate (CP) concentrations at 1 year of age to be approximately 60% of adult levels. By 12 to 14 years they are similar to mature levels. Table 6.2 describes the changes in muscle metabolic characteristics that occur between 1 year of age and adulthood. The rate at which these changes occur is unknown. Unlike ATP and CP, muscle glycogen levels appear to be similar to adult levels by the time a child (male) reaches 15 or 16 years of age (Eriksson & Saltin, 1974). The activity level of the glycolytic rate-limiting enzyme phosphofructokinase (PFK) has been described as being well below adult values in 11-year-old males (Eriksson, Gollnick, & Saltin, 1974). PFK activity levels appear to be influenced by maturity, reaching adult levels in some children by 13 to 15 years (Haralambie, 1982). The activity of succinate dehydrogenase (SDH), an oxidative enzyme, has been reported to be similar to adult values in circumpubertal children (Berg, Kim, & Keul, 1986; Eriksson, Gollnick, & Saltin, 1973, 1974; Haralambie, 1982). The timing of maturity of these enzyme activities has yet to be determined. Until noninvasive methods of determining intracellular content and activities are developed, the roles of growth and physical activity on the metabolic properties and composition of skeletal muscle in children will remain unclear.

Muscle Mass

There is a considerable increase in muscle mass during growth and development that is associated with changes in muscular strength. Post-natal growth in skeletal muscle is due to hypertrophy of fibers. Growth in human skeletal muscle occurs through an increase in the number of sarcomeres and the number of myofibrils, both of which increase muscular strength (Mersch & Stoboy, 1989).

The hypertrophy of skeletal muscle fibers in children increases linearly with age from birth to adolescence (Malina, 1986). The timing and rate of the intracellular changes have not yet been identified. Therefore, it is not possible to determine if chemical maturity of skeletal muscle occurs concurrently with the increase in muscle growth. Malina and Bouchard (1991) suggest that the rate of myofibrillar protein synthesis in children may be influenced by functional activity of skeletal muscle.

Table 6.2   Metabolic Properties of Skeletal Muscle in Children

Variable	Prepubertal level*	Compared to adult values
ATP concentration	3-5 (mmol · kg muscle)	Similar to adults
CP concentration	12-22 (mmol · kg muscle)	Similar to adults
Muscle glycogen	50-60 (nmol · kg^{-1})	Increases with age, similar to adult levels by 16 yrs
PFK activity	8-10 (μmol · g^{-1} · min^{-1})	Below adult levels
SDH activity	5-6 (μmol · g^{-1} · min^{-1})	Similar to, or slightly higher than, adult levels

*values reflect wet weight of muscle

Data from Eriksson et al., 1973, 1974; Haralambie, 1982; Berg et al., 1986.

Gender and Maturity

In a study of 5- to 17-year-old children, Malina (1969) estimated that absolute muscle mass increases 350% and 500% in females and males, respectively. While the males in this study demonstrated an increase in muscle mass from 42% to 53.6% of body weight, the proportion of muscle mass in the females of the same age increased from 40.2% to 42.5%. Significant differences between the sexes are also found for absolute and relative amounts of muscle (kg muscle mass per kg body weight) at all ages above 7 years. The sex- and maturity-associated changes in skeletal muscle strength may, at least in part, be attributed to these differences in the patterns of muscle development.

The variation in the rate of maturation on growth makes it difficult to compare children of a similar age. Maturity status influences both growth status as well as physical performance, especially during midadolescence (Malina, 1989). A typical chronological age group yields considerable variation in levels of biological maturity. Details regarding the influence of maturity status on performance are found in chapter 3.

As discussed previously, males reach puberty approximately 2 years after females. Therefore, muscle breadth may be greater in females than males prior to males reaching puberty. For example, there is a small increase in the gain in calf muscle breadth for females during puberty that results in females having larger calf muscles than same-age males (Figure 6.1). An increase in muscle gain in males occurs approximately 2 years later in males and is of a greater magnitude than that observed in females.

Considering the relationship that exists between muscular strength and muscle size, females may at times be stronger than males. Nevertheless, the greater magnitude of the growth spurt in skeletal muscle when males reach puberty is associated

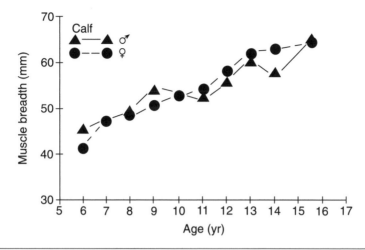

Figure 6.1 Relationship between age and calf muscle breadth in males and females measured from antero–posterior radiographs.
Reprinted from Blimkie (1989).

with the larger increases in muscular strength gains for males compared to females. In fact, studies of females show a strength plateau soon after the attainment of puberty (Blimkie, 1989; Shephard, 1982). It must be recognized that the developmental level of the child will also affect test results. Therefore, when assessing the strength of children, the tester should avoid considering only the chronological age of each subject, especially when comparisons among children are to be made.

Male children exhibit a rapid increase of strength at approximately 13 years of age, corresponding to the increase observed in muscle mass and to the attainment of sexual maturity (Asmussen, 1973). The increase in secretion of testosterone at puberty has been associated with increases in skeletal muscle mass. In a 1-year training study with 11- and 12-year-old males, Mero, Jaakkola, and Komi (1990) reported a significant positive correlation between level of testosterone and strength. Based on the finding that testosterone levels increase significantly in the trained children but not in controls, the authors concluded that training-induced increases in anabolic activity will enhance trainability, at least in the early stages of puberty. However, prior to puberty when levels of testosterone are low, the percentage of muscle mass increases to the same extent as it does between puberty and maturity (Mersch & Stoboy, 1989). Therefore, factors other than testosterone are obviously also involved in muscle hypertrophy during childhood. In addition, strength gains have been reported in prepubescent children following strength training programs, indicating that the responsiveness of muscle to training is not soley dependent upon levels of testosterone.

The gender- and maturity-related influences on both muscle cross-sectional area and force production in children has been reviewed by Blimkie (1989). Muscle strength, measured either by maximal voluntary contractions or electrically evoked contractions, has been positively correlated with muscle size determined anthropo-metrically (Davies, 1985; Davies, White, & Young, 1983), ultrasonically (Ikai & Fukunaga, 1968 as cited in Blimkie, 1989), and through computerized axial tomogra-phy (Ramsay et al., 1990). The relationship between muscle size and strength remains consistent across various muscle groups (Blimkie, 1989). In addition to these relationships, Blimkie (1989) supports the suggestion that factors other than muscle size may be important in the sexual differentiation of strength in children, as well as the maturity-related variation in strength seen during this period of growth. There are still many questions regarding the gender- and maturity-related influences on the development of muscular strength. In particular, the strength characteristics of young females has yet to be thoroughly detailed. Additionally, more longitudinal studies are needed to identify the maturity-related changes in muscular strength that occur in children.

Strength Training

Puberty has been considered a maturational threshold after which great gains in strength can be made through training. The development of strength in children through resistance-strength training prior to puberty has been controversial because of the potential for injury and the lack of significant performance gains (AAP, 1983; NSCA, 1985). A number of recent studies report significant changes in muscular strength for prepubertal boys with no evidence of musculoskeletal injury (Blimkie, Ramsay et al., 1989; Jacobson & Kulling, 1989; Ramsay et al., 1990; Rians et al., 1987; Sewall & Micheli, 1986; Weltman et al., 1986, 1988). Typically, any improvement in maximal voluntary strength has been attributed to neural adaptations rather than to the hypertrophy of skeletal muscle (Blimkie, 1989).

Few studies have examined the influence of resistance training on muscle hypertro-phy in prepubescent children, and none have included females within the subject population. A number of pediatric strength-training studies reporting significant increases in muscle strength have been unable to demonstrate concomitant gains in muscle girth, cross-sectional area, or both, measured anthropometrically (Blimkie, Ramsay et al., 1989; Weltman et al., 1986). Similar findings have been reported following strength-training studies where a cross-sectional area of limb muscle in male children was measured using soft-tissue X-rays (Vrijens, 1978) or computerized axial tomography (Ramsay et al., 1990). Using nuclear magnetic resonance tomogra-phy, Mersch and Stoboy (1989) were able to demonstrate significant increases in isometric leg extension concomitant with hypertrophy of the quadriceps femoris muscle in twin boys following 10 weeks of isometric training.

CRITERIA FOR SELECTING A METHOD
OF STRENGTH TESTING

The selection of a particular strength testing method depends on the reason for testing (such as descriptive information, training evaluation, rehabilitation), the subject population, the available equipment, the cost of equipment, the level of specificity, and the accuracy required by the tester.

While support for the concept of training and testing specificity can be found in the adult exercise physiology literature (Hakkinen, Komi, & Kauhanen, 1986), it seems to be equally applicable to any pediatric population. The level of specificity of the test mode has implications for the interpretation of the data. Levels of specificity of strength testing have been discussed in detail by Sale (1991) and are outlined in Table 6.3.

In some situations the efficacy of the optimal testing method may be constrained due to limited funding or the lack of the most appropriate equipment. It is not always feasible to modify equipment to fulfill all of the levels of specificity described in Table 6.3. Where it is not possible to employ the most appropriate methods, it is still possible to collect useful data provided that, at the very least, the assessment is of the specific muscle group in question. The greater the specificity of strength tests, the more accurate the evaluation of program effectiveness.

In a laboratory setting muscular strength and endurance are typically measured by one of three different methods. In *isotonic* (concentric and eccentric) strength testing, the maximal muscle action occurs within a small part of the total range of motion. This is related to the length-tension relationship exhibited by skeletal muscle.

Table 6.3   Levels of Specificity of Strength Testing

Level	Description
Muscle group	Tests should involve the specific prime movers for the movement of interest and/or involved in the training or rehabilitation movement employed.
Joint angle	During strength testing, limb joint angle should be similar to what occurs within the activity, training or rehabilitation movements. This is particularly important in isometric actions. In eccentric or concentric actions, test range of motion should simulate the movement closely.
Type of contraction	Tests should involve the same muscle action (isometric, concentric, eccentric) as the activity, training or rehabilitation movements.
Speed of contraction	Velocity of test movement should be similar to that of the activity movement pattern.
Movement pattern	Strength testing protocols should simulate the activity movement pattern as closely as possible, including body position (i.e., standing, sitting, supine) and number of joints involved (i.e., single- vs. multijoint movements). Most dynamometers are not arranged for multijoint movement testing, but often can be modified to do so.

During *isometric* testing, force development occurs at a preset joint angle against an immovable resistance. Finally, in strength assessments employing *isokinetic* testing, it is possible to measure maximal torque production through a complete range of motion while speed of movement is maintained. Isokinetic testing is the procedure most widely used for the evaluation of strength and muscular endurance in the laboratory setting. A popular aspect of isokinetic dynamometers is their ability to assess torque, work, and power achieved by muscle actions performed at a variety of velocities. However, compared to the other two methods, isokinetic strength testing equipment is expensive and time consuming.

ISOKINETIC TESTING

Isokinetic refers to constant-velocity muscle actions that may be either concentric or eccentric in nature. Isokinetic muscle action does not often occur during normal movement and sport activities. The measurement of isokinetic muscle action is only possible through the use of special dynamometers developed to provide resistance by precisely matching the force applied against the resistance and prohibiting acceleration beyond the preset velocity. The result is the development of maximal tension through a full range of motion with a constant movement speed.

Criticism of the term isokinetic stems from the fact that during high velocity contractions, the true isokinetic phase is only a very small percentage of the total movement (Sale, 1991). Initial muscle action will often involve an acceleration period, followed by a rapid dynamometer-induced deceleration to the preset velocity. As a result, the velocity of the muscle action will not be constant throughout the measurement. In addition, the term *isokinetic* may refer to either a constant angular velocity of the limb or to a constant linear velocity of muscle action.

Isokinetic strength-testing devices are frequently employed to obtain quantitative information regarding the contraction capabilities of skeletal muscle (Burdett & Van Swearingen, 1987). Many different isokinetic dynamometers are commercially available (Cybex, Kin Com, Biodex); however, most isokinetic research performed with children has been limited to either the Cybex II (Lumex Inc., Ronkonkoma, NY) or Kin Com (Chattanooga Group, Inc., Hixson, TN) dynamometers. To date, there have been no reported comparisons between these two isokinetic testing devices for either adults or children.

The distinguishing features of isokinetic testing methods are a predetermined constant limb velocity and an accommodating resistance (Burnie & Brodie, 1986). This provides for the quantitative study of many factors related to muscle function. In isokinetic testing, the force exerted against the lever arm is used to reflect the tension generated by the muscle applying the torque. That is, the product of the force recorded by the dynamometer and the length of the lever arm is considered to be equal to the product of the force generated by the muscle and the distance between the joint (axis of rotation) and the insertion point of the muscle. In consideration of the fact that the task involves angular motion, strength is expressed as torque (in Newton meters), displacement is measured in radians (rad), and velocity in rad · sec^{-1}. Some of the early studies of strength used the units of foot pound or kilogram meter in the reporting of peak torque data. These data should be converted to the torque SI unit of Newton meter ($N \cdot m$):

$$1 \text{ ft} \cdot \text{lb} = 1.355818 \, N \cdot m$$
$$1 \text{ kg} \cdot \text{m} = 9.80665 \, N \cdot m$$

Variables Measured in Isokinetic Testing

The most frequently used isokinetic measurement has been peak torque (PT), referring to the single highest torque output produced by muscle action as the limb moves through a range of motion (Burnie & Brodie, 1986; Kannus, 1992). Peak torque has been found to be an accurate and reproducible measure of strength in adults and children (Burdett & Van Swearingen, 1987; Mohtadi, Kiefer, Tedford, & Watters, 1990; Molnar, Alexander, & Gutfeld, 1979) and has become a reference point for the measurement of muscular strength in all isokinetic measurements (Kannus, 1992; Sale, 1991).

The interfacing of microprocessors with isokinetic dynamometers allows for rapid and reliable quantification of many specific muscle function parameters in addition to PT. These include total work, peak power, average power, and peak torque acceleration energy (Kannus, 1992). Figure 6.2 demonstrates how these measurements are determined during a concentric muscle action on an isokinetic dynamometer.

Peak torque acceleration energy (TAE) is considered indicative of motor unit recruitment rate and muscular explosiveness; it provides an estimate regarding the rate of torque production. Torque acceleration energy (measured in joules) is used to measure the amount of work performed during the first 125 msec of a single torque production and can be used to determine the time for tension to develop in a muscle or group of muscles. Time to peak torque has also been used to indicate the rate of motor-unit recruitment. However, this technique has been criticized for not reflecting muscular quickness, but simply measuring the relationship of test velocity and starting position to optimal joint position (Brodie et al., 1986). Torque acceleration energy values for children have been reported in only two published studies (Brodie et al., 1986; Burnie & Brodie, 1986).

Isokinetic dynamometers are not without their limitations. The use and interpretation of isokinetically derived torque and force have been criticized for the mechanical imperfections that exist within certain dynamometers (Taylor, Cotter, Stanley, & Marshall, 1991). During concentric actions at high velocities, the momentum of the accelerating limb is absorbed by the servomotor that decelerates the limb. The resulting impact artifact (due to a velocity overshoot) is reflected by an accentuated peak torque (Sapega, Nicholas, Sokolow, & Saraniti, 1982; Winter, Wells, & Orr, 1981). This phenomenon is less common in the testing of young children due to their smaller limb mass and torque values.

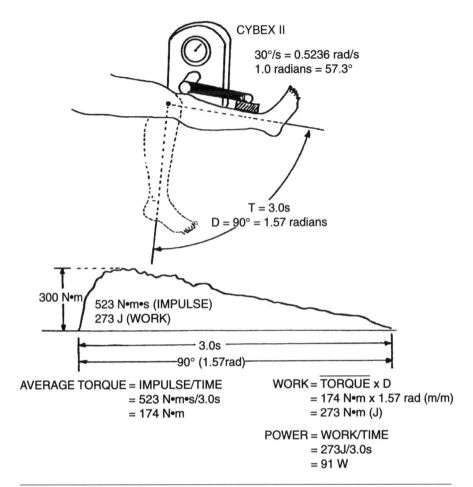

Figure 6.2   Mechanical properties measured on an isokinetic dynamometer. The recording demonstrates the Cybex II print out following leg extension at 0.52 rads · sec⁻¹ through a movement range of 90°. Peak torque was 300 $N · m$ during the muscle action, which lasted 3 seconds.
Adapted from Sale (1991).

The influence of gravity on the measurement of torque must also be taken into consideration in isokinetic testing. In the example of knee flexion and extension, gravity will provide assistance to the leg flexors and opposition to the extensors. The magnitude of the gravitational torque depends on the position of the limb relative to a horizontal plane. At extension and flexion, gravitational torque has been shown to be approximately 5% and 15% of total peak torque and zero when the knee angle is 90° (Sale, 1991). The proportional influence of gravity depends on velocity of movement as well as the strength of the muscle action. During testing with high velocities (and therefore producing smaller peak torque), gravity will play a larger role in measured peak torque. Similar results occur when peak muscle actions are weak. This may have important implications for isokinetic testing of children when absolute peak torque values are small, especially in the upper limb.

Methods for correcting for the effects of gravity have been described elsewhere (Winter et al., 1981). Most commercially available dynamometers provide directions for correction of this problem. These procedures include measurement of limb mass and assessment of torque when limb and lever arm are positioned at the angle of greatest gravitational influence. This information can then be computerized and used during subsequent calculations.

Preparing for Isokinetic Testing

Isokinetic dynamometers provide for the velocity of movement to be preset, typically between 0 and 6.97 rads · sec^{-1} (400° · sec^{-1}). However, pediatric research has been limited to velocities ranging from 0 to 4.18 rads · sec^{-1} (240° · sec^{-1}). There is no commonly recommended velocity for isokinetic testing of children. The fact that pediatric studies have employed various movement velocities, often without providing any explanation for the choice, limits the ability to compare results across studies. Future research should include the identification of optimal isokinetic test velocities for pediatric populations.

Difficulty exists in the comparison of isokinetic torque results obtained from different laboratories. Testing procedures must include standardization of velocities, limb position, and range of movement. Often, these components of testing are not reported clearly, making comparisons with other studies difficult. In addition, the use of isokinetic equipment necessitates repeated and accurate calibration procedures, which are not always reported and may not even be performed.

The choice of velocity for isokinetic testing depends on the goals of the test, the specificity of sport movement velocity (in testing of athletes), and the skill level of the subject. Movement velocities employed for the evaluation of strength range from 0 (isometric) to 1.56 rads · sec^{-1} (90° · sec^{-1}). Velocities greater than 3.15 rads · sec^{-1} (180° · sec^{-1}) are often difficult for young children to perform without adequate familiarization and practice. Often, in order to quantify a strength profile for a group of subjects, a series of 2-5 different velocities is used. The order of administration can be random, although it is recommended that slower velocities be performed first in order to ensure that the child understands the movement pattern and to reduce the risk of injury. It is important to perform velocities in the same sequence when there are repeated evaluations of a child over time.

The number of trials needed for stable isokinetic measurements has been extensively studied with adults (Osternig, 1986). However, the optimal number of muscle-action repeats required with children has yet to be determined. While this is an important protocol variable, it is not always reported in the literature. For the evaluation of muscular strength of children, a minimum of two and a maximum of six actions are recommended to ensure that maximal values are obtained without causing undue fatigue. This number will be partially determined by the velocity employed. A low velocity will not necessitate as many muscle actions as a faster

Table 6.4   Isokinetic Measurement Protocols for the Evaluation of Muscular Strength in Pediatric Populations

Author	Age (yrs)	Sex	N	Muscle group and measurement	Number of reps	Velocity rads · sec⁻¹	Action type	Limb tested	Reliability
CYBEX II									
*Alexander & Molnar, 1973	7-15	M F	36 34	Elbow and knee flexors and extensors Peak torque	NR	5 cycles · min⁻¹ (0.52)	Concentric	R and L	Test–retest (*n* = 3). Chi² = sig.
Brodie et al., 1986	11.72 (±.40)	M	24	Shoulder flexors & extensors Peak torque, TAE, RM Ratio	6	0.52, 1.04, 1.56, 2.09, 2.62, 3.15	Concentric	NR	NR
Burnie & Brodie, 1986	11.4 (±0.59)	M	18	Knee flexors and extensors Peak torque, TAE, RM Ratio	15	1.05, 4.2	Concentric	Dom and NDom	NR
Docherty et al., 1987	12.6 (±0.75)	M	30	Knee flexors and extensors Peak Torque	NR	0.52, 3.15	Concentric	NR	NR
				Arm abduction and adduction Peak torque	NR	0.52, 3.15	Concentric	NR	NR

Reference	Age	Sex	n	Measure		Velocity	Contraction	Side	Reliability
Docherty & Gaul, 1991	10.8 (±0.5)	M	23	Knee flexors and extensors	4	0.52, 3.15	Concentric	R and L	NR
	11.1 (±0.4)	F	29	Peak torque					
Gilliam et al., 1979	7-13	M	28	Knee flexors and extensors	3	0.52	Concentric	R and L	NR
		F	28	Peak torque	5	2.09	Concentric	R and L	
				Elbow flexors and extensors	3	0.52	Concentric	R and L	NR
				Peak torque	5	2.09	Concentric	R and L	
*Molnar & Alexander, 1974	7	M	6	Shoulder and hip flexion, extension and abduction; elbow and knee flexion and extension Peak torque	NR	5 cycles · min⁻¹ (0.52)	Concentric	R and L	Test–retest (n = 50), reported high consistency, no stats provided.
		F	7						
	8	M	67						
		F	64						
	9	M	62						
		F	61						
	10	M	64						
		F	56						
	11	M	35						
		F	30						
	12	M	18						
		F	15						
	13-15	M	5						
		F	10						

(continued)

Table 6.4 *(continued)*

Author	Age (yrs)	Sex	N	Muscle group and measurement	Number of reps	Velocity rads · sec^{-1}	Action type	Limb tested	Reliability
*Molnar et al., 1979	7-15	M F	NR	Shoulder and hip flex, ext, abduc; elbow and knee flexion, extension Peak torque	NR	5 cycles · min^{-1} (0.52)	Concentric	R and L	5.3-5.8% intratest variability ($n = 100$) 8.7-10% intertest variability-same tester ($n = 70$) 7.9-9.8% intertest variability-different testers ($n = 80$)
Nemoto et al., 1989	10-18	M F	132 71	Knee extensors Peak torque Endurance	3 3 50	0 0.52, 3.15, 5.2 3.15	Isometric Concentric Concentric	NR	NR
Pfeiffer & Francis, 1986	prepub. pubesc.	M M	14 10	Knee flexors and extensors Peak torque Elbow flexors and extensors Peak torque	3	0.52, 2.09	Concentric	R and L	NR
Ramsay et al., 1990	9-11 yrs	M	13	Elbow flexors Knee extensors Peak torque	3 3	0 0.52, 1.05, 2.09, 3.14	Isometric Concentric	R and L R	NR

Study	Age	Sex	n	Measure	Velocities	Value	Action	Limb	Comments
Tabin et al., 1985	Prepub	M	15	Knee flexors and extensors Peak torque	4-8	1.04	Concentric	NR	NR
	Postpub	F	15						
		M	15	Ankle dorsi and plantar flexors Peak torque	4-8	0.52	Concentric	NR	NR
		F	15						
Kin Com									
Mohtadi et al., 1990	10-12	M	12	Knee extension Peak torque	3	1.02	Concentric Eccentric	Dom and Ndom	Test–retest $n = 5$, no sig diff found; compared Dom vs Ndom limb to reflect reproducibility.
Rians et al., 1987**	6-11	M	32	Elbow and knee flexion and extension					Correlations between Dom and Ndom limb used to reflect reliability
Weltman et al., 1986**				Mean torque Mean work Shoulder flexion and extension	5	0.52	Concentric	Dom and Ndom	Knee flex and ext; $r = 0.73\text{-}0.91$
Weltman et al., 1988**				Mean torque Mean work	10	1.56	Concentric	Dom and Ndom	Elbow flex and ext; $r = 0.72\text{-}0.79$ Shoulder extension $r = .87$ Shoulder flexion $r = 0.39\text{-}0.62$

NR = not reported; R = right limb; L = left limb; Dom = dominant limb; Ndom = nondominant limb
*indicates testing performed on early Cybex model, not Cybex II.
**reported the use of same subjects and protocols.

velocity, where performance may improve over the first few trials. Of course, this will be influenced by the subject's familiarity with the velocity being used. A subject well versed in the test protocol will require fewer repeats than a subject with little experience. It is also important to note that the development of fatigue will occur earlier with low-movement velocities.

Because most isokinetic dynamometers are designed for the adult population, modification of equipment is necessary when they are used in testing children. For example, extra postural support is typically required to allow the child to sit comfortably and correctly for evaluation of leg strength. This modification should allow for the knee joint to be positioned appropriately relative to the lever arm. Care must be taken to ensure that the extra support used behind the subject does not result in children arching their backs in order to keep their shoulders on the seat back. Torso-length pads, placed behind the seated subject, provide the most effective means of modifying the seat for children. Stabilizing straps may also require modification to ensure that upper body movements are restricted comfortably. The normal position of these straps can be at head height for some children, a position that will not provide adequate or appropriate stabilization during test procedures. It may be preferable to have a tester hold a young child gently against the seat. This tester contact with the subject may help the child to remain focused on the task and may also reduce anxiety. When testing involves the arm (elbow or shoulder), standing support should be used. Weltman et al. (1988) reported that standing support was necessary to raise some of their young male subjects (6-11 years) to an appropriate height for testing of elbow flexion and extension on the Kin Com. This support stabilized and isolated the muscles being tested by effectively preventing synergistic muscle action.

Concentric Isokinetic Testing

Most isokinetic testing of children has involved concentric muscle action utilizing Cybex II or Kin Com isokinetic dynamometers (Table 6.4; see pages 240-243). Once the limb to be tested is fixed securely to the dynamometer lever arm, the subject is directed to accelerate the limb as quickly as possible and apply maximum force against the lever arm at the preset velocity. The speed of the movement accelerates unopposed by the servomechanism of the dynamometer from zero to the preset velocity. As the limb attempts to accelerate the lever movement beyond the preset velocity, the servomotor resists and the torque applied against the lever arm is recorded.

The assessment of concentric strength in adults, and especially athletes, often involves the testing of reciprocal muscle groups. In this method of testing, for example, maximal quadriceps action is followed immediately by maximal hamstring activity, with no recovery time or delay preceding hamstring activity. The movement pattern used in this type of muscle testing requires that the subject have adequate motor control, not only to perform repeated muscle actions of reciprocal muscles, but also to successfully generate tension at the appropriate speed. Many exercise testing laboratories now employ a modified movement pattern that involves the evaluation of one muscle (or group) at a time. For example, quadriceps muscle action is followed by passive return to a knee-flexion position so that the muscle action can be repeated. Similar patterns of muscle action can be applied to strength testing of elbow and shoulder flexors and extensors in children.

Using the Cybex II, Docherty and Gaul (1991) found that when testing nonathletic children (9-11 years), the actions of flexion and extension of the leg had to be separated by a time delay in order to elicit maximal torque values. Many of the subjects were unable to quickly reverse the action of leg extension to leg flexion. The short pause between the two muscle actions appeared to facilitate the neuromuscular demands of the testing protocol.

Children (and adults) typically demonstrate greater peak torque with limb extensors than with the limb flexors (Table 6.5). Peak torque has been reported to be higher in knee extensors than knee flexors (Burnie & Brodie, 1986; Docherty & Gaul, 1991; Gilliam et al., 1979; Molnar & Alexander, 1973; Sunnegardh, Bratteby, Nordesjo, & Nordgren, 1988; Tabin, Gregg, & Bonci, 1985; Weltman et al., 1986, 1988). A few studies have considered the relationship between extensors and flexors of the shoulder and elbow joints; however, the findings remain equivocal. Weltman et al. (1986, 1988) reported significant differences between shoulder flexors and extensors of 8- to 11-year-old males measured using a Kin Com dynamometer. The flexion-to-extension ratios for the dominant limb were 67% and 65% (0.52 rads · sec^{-1} and 1.56 rads · sec^{-1}, respectively). However, the reliability of the shoulder flexor data was questioned. Brodie et al. (1986) reported no difference in the PT generated by the shoulder flexors and extensors of their preadolescent males using

Table 6.5   Reported Hamstring:Quadriceps Strength Ratio in Children at Various Velocities Using Cybex II Isokinetic Dynamometry (Percent)

Velocity	Subjects	Ratio	Reference
0.52 rad · sec^{-1}	M (10-11 yrs)	75%	Docherty and Gaul (1991)
	F (10-11 yrs)	69%	
	M F (7-13 yrs)	60%	Gilliam et al. (1979)
1.04 rads · sec^{-1}	M F preadolescents	65%	Tabin et al. (1985)
	M F postpubescents	60%	
	M (11 yrs)	64%	Burnie & Brodie (1986)
1.56 rads · sec^{-1}	M (8 yrs)	53%	Sunnegardh et al. (1988)
	F (8 yrs)	47%	
	M (13 yrs)	53%	
	F (13 yrs)	46%	
2.08 rads · sec^{-1}	M (11 yrs)	79%	Burnie & Brodie (1986)
3.12 rads · sec^{-1}	M (10-11 yrs)	87%	Docherty & Gaul (1991)
	F (10-11 yrs)	82%	

the Cybex II. In adults, shoulder extensors are much more developed than flexors (Davies et al., 1980).

Brodie et al. (1986) reported that torque acceleration energy (TAE) of the leg and forearm extensors is significantly greater than in respective flexors (Brodie et al., 1986; Burnie & Brodie, 1986). While the finding of higher PT or TAE in leg extensors compared to flexors remains consistent, the magnitude of the flexor–extensor ratio (flexor value reported as a percentage of extensor result) depends on the test velocity.

The literature is inconclusive regarding the relationship between peak torque values for dominant and nondominant limbs. In comparing contralateral limb results, some researchers have demonstrated no difference (Burnie and Brodie, 1986; Mohtadi et al., 1990; Sunnegardh et al., 1988; Weltman et al., 1988), others report higher peak torque values in the dominant limb (Molnar & Alexander 1973; Sunnegard et al., 1988), and others find lower peak torque values in the dominant limb (Weltman et al.). The use of different muscle groups, various movement velocities, and children of different maturity levels combine to make the findings of these studies equivocal. Torque acceleration energy has been reported to be similar for dominant and nondominant limbs of 11-year-old males (Burnie & Brodie, 1986). The generalizability of this finding to various age groups and to female subjects has yet to be determined.

Available data suggest that there is less pronounced asymmetry of muscle strength in children than in adults (Sunnegardh et al., 1988). Based on the finding of no statistical difference between dominant and nondominant limbs, Mohtadi et al. (1990) suggested their results support the use of a contralateral limb as the control for comparison purposes. However, until there is further evaluation of this relationship the use of contralateral limbs in children for this purpose must be done with caution. It has been hypothesized that as children become more selective and experienced in their physical pursuits, strength differences may develop in relation to their natural limb dominance (Burnie & Brodie, 1986).

The reproducibility and validity of isokinetic concentric testing of adults has been tested against isometric, isotonic, and other strength-testing methods. Knapik, Wright, Mawdsley, and Braun (1983) found that tests of isokinetic (Cybex II), isometric, and isotonic strength in knee and elbow extension and flexion of adults measured similar phenomenon, termed *maximal voluntary strength*. They concluded that only one strength-testing method was needed to predict a large portion of the strength derived from several methods of measurement at the same joint angle. However, the strength of the relationships between methods decreased as velocities and joint angles became more widely separated. Similar studies with children have not been conducted.

Dunn and Mayhew (1988) compared isometric, isotonic, and isokinetic strength-measurement techniques to determine muscle imbalance ratios at the knee in male collegiate athletes. Their findings showed that strength-measurement methods may be used interchangeably to determine bilateral strength ratios (dominant vs. nondominant limb). However, the higher hamstring-to-quadriceps ratios observed with isokinetic measurement led to the conclusion that methods should not be used interchangeably when assessing knee agonist-to-antagonist ratios. No similar comparison of strength-testing methods has been performed on children. The relationship between isometric, isotonic, and isokinetic strength-measurement techniques in children should be evaluated to determine if such methods can be used interchangeably to assess muscular strength.

There has been only limited research on the reliability and applicability of isokinetic-strength testing of children. In their comprehensive study of strength testing in 7- to 15-year-olds, Molnar et al. (1979) examined Cybex test reliability of maximal torque generated during shoulder and hip flexion and abduction, as well as knee and elbow flexion and extension. The results of this study demonstrated a small variability among test occasions and between different examiners (mean score deviations of 5.3-5.8% and 7.9-9.8%, respectively) and indicated the consistency of the technical component of measurement procedures used by individual testers. Mean score deviations ranging from 8.7% to 10% were reported when test-retests were conducted using two different testers. The intertester deviations were not found to be statistically significant, and the authors interpreted the results as being within reasonable limits. They concluded that, when performed by trained and experienced testers, Cybex II isokinetic-strength testing of children can be accurate and reproducible. The description of the statistical procedures used in this study was vague, as was the identification of subjects. Another limitation to this research is that the velocity of movement was not clearly stated, but was maintained throughout all testing. The applicability of these findings to other movement velocities has not been determined.

More recently, Sunnegardh et al. (1988) reported a small variability between different trials of isokinetic (Cybex II) strength measurements. Their research involved a variety of muscle groups and testing velocities with 8- and 13-year-old boys and girls. However, the reliability data were not provided, nor were they evaluated statistically.

Very few studies have attempted to evaluate the reliability of Kin Com isokinetic strength testing of children. Weltman et al. (1988) estimated reliability of the Kin Com by comparing dominant and nondominant maximal torque values in young male subjects (6-11 years). Peak torque generated by flexors and extensors of the knee, shoulder, and elbow joints was evaluated at 0.52 rads $\cdot$ sec^{-1} and 1.56 rads $\cdot$ sec^{-1} through a full range of motion. It was observed that for all motions except shoulder flexion, the peak torque was reproducible between dominant and nondominant limbs ($r = 0.65 - 0.94$). Correlations were slightly higher for the extensors of each limb than the flexors. The results of shoulder flexion between contralateral limbs were not as reproducible as results at the elbow and knee. These researchers had difficulty isolating the anterior deltoid and suspected that the subjects required additional assistance with other synergistic muscles (long head of biceps brachii, trunk flexors) in order to complete the full range of motion required in shoulder flexion. They concluded that measures of shoulder flexion may not be reliable in prepubertal boys.

It should be noted that the efficacy of using correlation coefficients between dominant and nondominant limbs as a means of determining reliability is questionable. Considerable differences between the mean values of the dominant and nondominant values were observed by Weltman et al. (1988), but not statistically evaluated. While it is current clinical practice to use the contralateral limb as a control for comparison purposes, the validity of such a statistical technique must be studied further, especially in children. Additional research is required to determine the reliablity of Kin Com data from pediatric populations.

Isokinetic Eccentric Testing

Not all isokinetic equipment can be used to evaluate eccentric muscle action. Kin Com and Biodex systems have the ability to measure both concentric and eccentric strength and power, unlike Cybex machines that are limited to concentric testing. During eccentric actions the subject is instructed to resist the lever arm as it automatically moves to the end of a preset range of motion. In resisting this movement, the subject must generate tension eccentrically. Adult-testing procedures typically involve a dual-phase protocol: The subject begins with a concentric muscle action through the full range of motion, followed immediately by an eccentric action resisting the lever arm as it returns to its initial position.

Only one study is presently available in which eccentric muscle actions have been evaluated in children (Mohtadi et al., 1990). This study of eccentric knee extension and flexion was limited to 12 males (10-12 years) and only one movement velocity (1.04 rad · sec^{-1}). Eccentric strength of the knee extensors was reported to be greater than concentric strength (84-88% of eccentric), which is similar to that observed in the adult population (Highenboten, Jackson, & Meske, 1988).

In our laboratory, attempts have been made to evaluate eccentric strength of male and female children ranging in age from 10 to 17 years. The task of producing maximal eccentric tension is difficult, particularly for children, as it requires much concentration, understanding, and motor control to resist the lever arm appropriately. Children appear to have more difficulty understanding the movement control necessary in eccentric actions than do adults. Special attention must be given to the explanations and directions given to children when utilizing this type of movement. In addition, compared to concentric testing, children require more familiarization trials when learning to generate torque eccentrically at various movement velocities (unpublished observations). It is recommended that eccentric and concentric tests be performed individually in order for the child to produce appropriate movement patterns. With sufficient time and patience, it is possible to teach children the control necessary to perform isokinetic eccentric contractions effectively.

Because rehabilitation from injury is often based on eccentric muscle loading, eccentric testing may be a useful method of quantifying strength in children. Therefore, it is important to encourage more isokinetic eccentric testing of pediatric populations. The efficacy of eccentric testing of children remains speculative, pending additional research in the area. There are no current data to indicate the most appropriate eccentric test velocity for the measurement of strength in children. In addition, the application of eccentric testing to muscle groups other than knee extensors in children has not yet been reported. Future research dealing with the reliability and validity of eccentric testing in children must include both males and females; clear identification of velocity of motion, movement pattern, and joint angles; and should be extended to included various muscle groups.

ISOTONIC TESTING

The use of free weights (or stacked weights) to evaluate muscular strength is not a true laboratory protocol. However, in consideration of the specificity principle regarding training and testing, the measurement of repetition maximum (RM) using free or stacked weights can be used to evaluate the response to resistance training programs, provided strict adherence to technique is employed. Blimkie, Ramsay et al. (1989) used one repetition maximum (1 RM) bench-press and arm-curl protocols with stacked weights (Global Gym apparatus) to evaluate the effects of 10 weeks of heavy resistance training on prepubertal males. In a later study from the same laboratory, Ramsay et al. (1990) used 1 RM performance (Global Gym) for double leg presses and bench presses to evaluate strength. In both studies, testing was preceded by a warm-up consisting of three to seven submaximal repetitions. Resistance was gradually increased so that 1 RM was obtained within six to eight trials. It has been recommended that prepubescent children not be subjected to the risks inherent in the use of 1 RM loads (Freedson, Ward, & Rippe, 1990; NSCA, 1985). Other repetition-maximum protocols (e.g., 6-15 RM) have been used to assess muscular strength (Duda, 1986; Sailors & Berg, 1987; Watkins & Docherty, 1986).

The determination of resistance setting for a particular repetition maximum requires time, consistency of protocol, and motivation of the subjects. Watkins and Docherty (1986) determined that, for untrained 10- to 12-year-old children, resistances of 45% and 40% of body weight corresponded to 10 RM for bench press in boys and girls, respectively. Ten RM loads present minimal risk of injury provided there are proper instruction and supervision. The determination of similar relationships for other movements, while not yet available, will provide valuable information for those interested in using free weights safely with their pediatric groups.

It is important to differentiate between the resistances lifted when using free weights (e.g., barbells) compared to stacked weights. The technical and physical demands in the performance of the same joint actions are typically quite different and will be reflected in the test results. Test procedures, including body alignment and technique, must be strictly enforced to ensure accurate, reliable results, as well as to reduce the potential for injury. Any modification to the lifting technique will influence the test results. When using free or stacked weights to evaluate strength in children, tasks involving a stable base should be employed (e.g., bench press). Complex exercises including those that place stress on the lower back and knee joints should be avoided. Tests should be terminated if the maintenance of technique becomes difficult for the child.

ISOMETRIC TESTING

Isometric tests involve the application of force against some form of immovable measuring device that records the force (N) or torque ($N \cdot m$) developed. Isometric testing can be performed using an isokinetic dynamometer with the velocity set at zero (0 rad $\cdot$ sec^{-1}). Isometric dynamometers are commercially available; however, custom-made units permit specific muscle groups or movement patterns to be tested by isolating strength at a fixed angle for each joint.

Prior to the development of isokinetic devices, the cable tensiometer and grip strength dynamometer were commonly employed to determine muscular strength. As with other types of strength-testing methods, the force or torque generated by a specific muscle group during isometric testing depends on joint angle and body position (Clarke, 1966). It is essential that joint angle be standardized, measured, and recorded along with strength values during an isometric test. Strength varies through a range of joint angles, and strength curves can be developed to determine the influence of joint position on isometric strength. Most strength curves have been produced from adult studies. Similar curves for younger populations have not yet been as clearly defined. Partial isometric strength curves for young (9-13 year) male subjects have been developed for elbow flexion (Blimkie, Ebbesen et al., 1989; Blimkie, Ramsay et al., 1989; Ramsay et al., 1990) (Figure 6.3) and knee extension (Ramsay et al.), using a custom-made dynamometer (Figure 6.4). If only one joint angle is used during isometric testing, it is common practice to choose a joint angle that is close to the peak of the strength curve for the specific joint.

Optimal joint angle for isometric testing depends on the limb being tested and the reason for the testing. Often more than one angle is used in order to construct an isometric profile and evaluate the length-tension (torque) relationships of a specific muscle or group of muscles. This relationship also demonstrates the influence that tendon angle of pull has on the development of force in skeletal muscle.

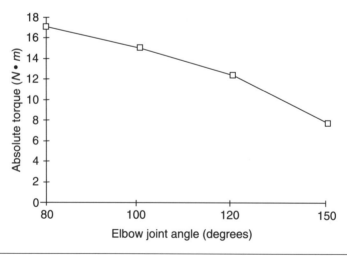

Figure 6.3 Maximal voluntary isometric torque for elbow flexors at various joint angles in males, 9-11 yrs of age. 180 = full extension. Data from Blimkie, Ramsay et al., 1989).

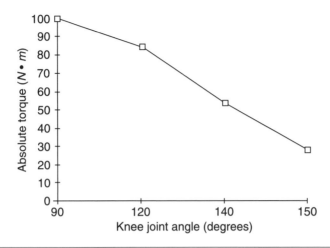

Figure 6.4   Maximal voluntary isometric torque for knee extensors at various joint angles in males, 9-11 yrs of age. 180° = full extension. Data adapted from Ramsay et al. (1990).

Using isokinetic equipment, Ramsay et al. (1990) recorded voluntary isometric torque at four joint angles when testing knee extensors (90°, 120°, 140°, and 160°) and elbow flexors (80°, 100°, 120°, and 150°), where 180° was full extension in both actions. This study provides some evidence of an inverse relationship between peak torque and angle of pull (or muscle length) in children.

Appropriate time should be allotted for the subject to produce peak force or torque during isometric testing. Duration of isometric test protocols are often not reported in the literature; however, they typically range from 2 sec to 5 sec (Andersen & Henckel, 1987). Isometric testing usually includes a minimum of two trials at any joint angle being tested. There is no general agreement on which test result to use. The best of trials (Andersen & Henckel, 1987; Siegel, Camaione, & Manfredi, 1989), the average of two trials (Blimkie, Ebbesen et al., 1989; Blimkie, Ramsay et al., 1989; Ramsay et al., 1990), and the average of the two best attempts when there are more than two trials (Bowie & Cumming, 1972) have all been used as measures of strength. If children are given adequate time and trials to learn the skill necessary to properly complete the test protocol, there should be very little difference between the scores of multiple trials.

Comparison with results from one test session to another, as well as from other laboratories, will be influenced by the method of determining maximal isometric strength. Subjects should be familiarized with the protocol to be used, as performance can be influenced by the way in which instructions are provided (Kroemer & Howard, 1970). Isometric strength scores will also depend on factors such as cooperation and motivation of subjects (Bohannon, 1986). Care must be taken to ensure that children are prepared and motivated to perform to the best of their abilities. Test conditions should be carefully standardized to ensure validity and reliability of the technique.

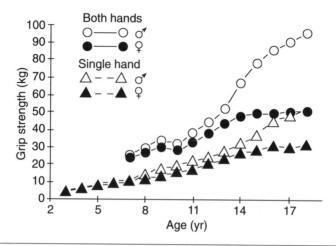

Figure 6.5 Cross-sectional data demonstrating the influence of age on grip strength for male and female children.
Reprinted from Blimkie (1989).

Special mention must be made of the grip strength test, one of the most common methods of measuring isometric strength in children. The grip dynamometer is a portable, noninvasive device that provides a reliable method of evaluating hand grip quickly and easily (Gabbard & Patterson, 1980). In this method, a lever arm is difficult to define, therefore hand grip strength scores are typically reported in kilograms or newtons (kg · 9.80665 m · sec^{-2}). Figure 6.5 demonstrates the age- and gender-related differences in grip strength. Scores differ between males and females as early as 3 years of age, with males having higher scores (both single hand and combined right and left hands) than females (Blimkie, 1989).

As with other isometric tests, scores for grip dynamometry will be influenced by the position of the hand and arm, the experience of the subject in performing the task, and motivational level (Blimkie, 1989; Dawson, Croce, Quinn, & Vroman, 1992). Body position related to grip strength testing is not commonly reported in the literature; however, this information is necessary for appropriate comparisons between studies. For example, in some studies subjects remain standing during the test (Gabbard & Patterson, 1980); in other studies subjects are tested from the sitting position with 90° flexion of the elbow (Sunnegardh et al., 1988).

Grip-strength scores will also be affected by hand dominance. Asymmetry of hand-grip strength has been reported to be greater in left-handed children than in right-handed children (Sunnegardh et al., 1988). Left-handed children tend to have greater differences between their left- and right-hand grip strength scores than do right-handed children. Measurement is usually taken for both the right and left hands and often values are combined for a double-hand performance score (Blimkie, 1989).

TESTING MUSCULAR ENDURANCE

Muscular endurance is the ability to use a muscle (or muscle group) to generate force repeatedly or to sustain force production for an extended period of time. The endurance of skeletal muscle is related to the anaerobic characteristics of the muscle being tested (Bar-Or, 1993). Very few laboratory muscle endurance tests are performed in children due to the lack of available valid, reliable, and standardized tests. The most common method of evaluating muscular endurance in children is the 30-second Wingate Anaerobic Test (WAnT), discussed by Bar-Or in chapter 4.

Isokinetic dynamometers can also be used to measure muscular endurance. The procedure involves repetitive muscle actions, usually of reciprocal muscle groups, through a full range of motion. There are a number of protocols used to produce a quantitative evaluation of muscular endurance. Certain methods involve having the subject continue until either the torque production decreases by 50% of maximum or until the subject can no longer continue. Another method involves preselecting the number of muscle actions to be performed and comparing the torque produced at the end of the test to that produced in earlier actions. A fatigue index can be derived by measuring the decline in the torque produced from peak torque to the lowest score recorded.

Limited information from isokinetic muscular endurance testing of children is presently available. Nemoto et al.(1989), using a Cybex II dynamometer, tested fatigability in knee extensors in junior speed skaters (10-18 years). The protocol consisted of 50 consecutive maximal voluntary-muscle actions at a movement velocity of 1.04 rads $\cdot$ sec^{-1}. A fatigue index was determined by comparing the average PT values calculated from the initial and final 5 contractions. Compared to the younger subjects, older skaters demonstrated larger declines in PT (fatigue index). This study suggests that training-induced improvements to muscular endurance are related to maturation.

Bowie and Cumming (1972) studied hand-grip endurance times, using a sustained hand grip of 40% maximal grip strength in boys and girls (13-17 years). Considerable motivation, concentration, and perseverance was required by the subjects due to the discomfort experienced during the test. It was suggested that the longer grip times performed by the girls (234 sec) compared to the boys (185 secs) was due to the lower maximum strength of the girls, as well as the fact that girls seemed more willing to tolerate the discomfort. Test-retest reliability was moderate ($r = 0.60$); however, the coefficient of variation was high (27%). It was concluded that day-to-day variability of grip time makes this measurement unsuitable for most studies.

Much more research is required in the measurement and evaluation of muscular endurance of children. Normative data for various muscle groups and movement velocities are required. In addition, the relationship between age and muscular endurance suggested by Nemoto et al. (1989) should be investigated further.

CONCLUSION

Strength is an important component of fitness. It is the basis of power, muscular endurance, and speed of movement. The development of strength in children is influenced by maturity status, gender, and activity level. Much of the information available regarding methods of evaluating strength in children comes from studies of young males: Very little data have been reported for females.

There are a variety of methods of evaluating muscular strength in children. The most common laboratory methods include isokinetic and isometric techniques. The selection of a specific technique will depend on the level of specificity and accuracy required by the tester, as well as the availability of equipment. Isometric testing with a grip dynamometer, cable tensiometer, or isokinetic dynamometer can evaluate strength at specific joint angles. While reliable and simple to perform, isometric-strength testing is essentially limited to the measurement of isolated strength at a fixed joint angle. Optimal angles for individual muscle groups in children have not been identified.

Most research utilizing isokinetic techniques has been limited to knee and elbow flexors and extensors and has almost exclusively involved concentric muscle actions. Optimal movement speeds have not been identified; consequently, studies have employed various contraction velocities and ranges of motion. The variety of isokinetic protocols makes it difficult to compare results among studies. It is important to recommend protocols for isokinetic testing in children of all ages. Until such time, caution must be taken when attempting to compare results across studies.

REFERENCES

Alexander, J., & Molnar, G.E. (1973). Muscular strength in children: Preliminary report on objective standards. *Archives of Physical Medicine and Rehabilitation*, **54**, 424-427.

American Academy of Pediatrics (AAP). (1983). Weight training and weight lifting: Information for the pediatrician. *Physician and Sportsmedicine*, **11**(3), 157-161.

Andersen, L.B., & Henckel, P. (1987). Maximal voluntary isometric strength in Danish adolescents 16-19 years of age. *European Journal of Applied Physiology*, **56**, 83-89.

Asmussen, E. (1973). Growth in muscular strength and power. In G.L. Rarick (Ed.), *Physical acitvity human growth and development* (pp. 60-77). London: Academic Press.

Baldwin, K.M. (1984). Muscle development: Neonatal to adult. *Exercise and Sport Science Reviews*, **12**, 1-19.

Bar-Or, O. (1993). Noncardiopulmonary pediatric exercise tests. In T.W. Rowland, (Ed.), *Pediatric laboratory exercise testing: Clinical guidelines* (pp. 165-185). Champaign, IL: Human Kinetics.

Belanger, A.Y., & McComas, A.J. (1989). Contractile properties of human skeletal muscle in childhood and adolescence. *European Journal of Applied Physiology*, **58**, 563-567.

Bell, R.D., MacDougall, J.D., Billeter, R., & Howald, H. (1980). Muscle fiber types and morphometric analysis of skeletal muscle in 6-year-old children. *Medicine and Science in Sports and Exercise*, **12**, 28-31.

Berg, A., Kim, S.S., Keul, J. (1986). Skeletal muscle enzyme activities in healthy young subjects. *International Journal of Sports Medicine*, **7**, 236-239.

Beunen, G. & Malina, R.M. (1988). Growth and physical performance relative to the timing of the adolescent spurt. *Exercise and Sport Sciences Reviews*, **16**, 503-540.

Blimkie, C.J.R. (1989) Age- and sex- associated variation in strength during childhood: Anthropometric, morphologic, neurologic, biomechanical, endocinologic, genetic and physical activity correlates. In C.V. Gisolfi & D.R. Lamb (Eds.), *Perspectives in exercise science and sports medicine: Youth, exercise and sport*, (Vol. II, pp. 99-163). Indianapolis: Benchmark Press, Inc.

Blimkie, C.J.R., Ebbesen, B., MacDougall, D., Bar-Or, O., & Sale, D. (1989). Voluntary and electrically evoked strength characteristics of obese and nonobese preadolescent boys. *Human Biology*, **61**, 515-532.

Blimkie, C.J.R., Ramsay, J., Sale, D.G., MacDougall, J.D., Smith, K., & Garner, S. (1989). Effects of 10 weeks of resistance training on strength development in prepubertal boys. In S. Oseid & K.H. Carlson, (Eds.), *Children and exercise XIII*, International Series on Sport Sciences (pp. 183-197). Champaign, IL: Human Kinetics.

Bohannon, R.W. (1986). Test-retest reliability of hand-held dynamometry during a single session of strength assessment. *Physical Therapy*, **66**, 206-209.

Bowie, W., & Cumming, G.R. (1972). Sustained handgrip in boys and girls: Variation and correlation with performance and motivation to train. *Research Quarterly*, **43**(2), 131-141.

Brodie, D.A., Burnie, J., Eston, R.G., & Royce, J.A. (1986). Isokinetic strength and flexibility characteristics in preadolescent boys. In J. Rutenfranz, R. Mocellin, & F. Klimt (Eds.), *Children and exercise XII*, International Series on Sport Sciences (Vol. 17, pp. 309-319). Champaign, IL: Human Kinetics.

Burdett, R.G., & Van Swearingen, J. (1987). Reliability of isokinetic muscle endurance tests. *Journal of Orthopedic and Sports Physical Therapy*, **8**, 484-488.

Burnie, J. & Brodie, D.A. (1986). Isokinetic measurement in preadolescent males. *International Journal of Sports Medicine*, **7**(4), 205-209.

Chapman, S.S.J., Grindrod, S.R., & Jones, D.A. (1984). Cross-sectional area and force producion of the quadriceps muscle. *Journal of Physiology*, **353**, 53P.

Clarke, H.H. (1966). *Muscular strength and endurance.* Englewood Cliffs, NJ: Prentice Hall.

Colling-Saltin, A.S. (1980). Skeletal muscle development in the human fetus and during childhood. In K. Berg & B.O. Eriksson (Eds.), *Children and exercise IX* (pp. 193-207). Baltimore: University Park Press.

Davies, C.T.M. (1985). Strength and mechanical properties of muscle in children and young adults. *Scandinavian Journal of Sports Science*, **7**, 11-15.

Davies, C.T.M., White, M.J. & Young, K. (1983). Muscle function in children. *European Journal of Applied Physiology*, **52**, 111-114.

Davies, G.J., Halbach, J.W., Carpenter, M.A., Scheid, D.T., Reinbold, T.R., Brandt, J.A., Tesch, J.C., Kirkendall, D.T., & Wilson, P.K. (1980). A descriptive muscular power analysis of the United States cross country ski team. *Medicine and Science in Sports and Exercise*, **12**, 141-147.

Dawson, C., Croce, R., Quinn, T., & Vroman, N. (1992). Reliability of the Nicholas Manual Muscle Tester on upper body strength in children ages 8-10. *Pediatric Exercise Science*, **4**, 340-350.

Docherty, D., and Gaul, C.A. (1991). Relationship of body size, physique, and composition to physical performance in young boys and girls. *International Journal of Sport Medicine*, **12**(6), 525-532.

Docherty, D., Wenger, H.A., Collis, M.L., & Quinney, H.A. (1987). The effects of variable speed resistance training on strength development in prepubertal boys. *Journal of Human Movement Studies*, **13**, 377-382.

Duda, M. (1986). Prepubescent strength training gains support. *Physician and Sports Medicine*, **14**(2), 157-161.

Dunn, K. & Mayhew, J.L. (1988). Comparison of three methods of assessing strength imbalances at the knee. *Journal of Orthopaedic and Sports Physical Therapy*, **10**(4), 134-137.

DuPlessis, M.P., Smit, P.J., DuPlessis, L.A.S., Geyer, H.J., Mathews, G., & Louw, H.N.J. (1985). The composition of muscle fibers in a group of adolescents. In R.A. Binkhorst, H.C.G. Kemper, & W.H.M. Saris (Eds.), *Children and exercise XI* (pp. 323-328). Champaign, IL: Human Kinetics.

Eriksson, B.O., Gollnick, P.D., & Saltin, B. (1973). Muscle metabolism and enzyme activities after training in boys 11-13 years old. *Acta Physiologica Scandinavica*, **87**, 485-497.

Eriksson, B.O., Gollnick, P.D., & Saltin, B. (1974). The effect of physical training on muscle enzyme activities and fiber composition in 11-year-old boys. *Acta Paediatrica Belgica*, **28** (Suppl.), 245-252.

Eriksson, O. & Saltin, B. (1974). Muscle metabolism during exercise in boys aged 11 to 16 years compared to adults. *Acta Paediatrica Belgica*, **28** (Suppl.), 257-265.

Freedson, P.S., Ward, A., & Rippe, J.M. (1990). Resistance training for youth. In W.A. Grana, J.A. Lombardo, & B.J. Sharkey (Eds.), *Advances in sports medicine and fitness* (Vol. 3, pp. 57-63). Chicago: Year Book Medical.

Gabbard, C.P. & Patterson, P.E. (1980). Relationship and comparison of selected anthropometric measures to muscular endurance and strength in children aged 3-5 years. *Annals of Human Biology*, **7**(6), 583-587.

Gilliam, R.B., Villanacci, J.F., Freedson, P.S., & Sady, S.P. (1979). Isokinetic torque in boys and girls ages 7-13: Effect of age, height and weight. *Research Quarterly*, **50**(4), 599-609.

Hakkinen, K., Komi, P.V., & Kauhanen, H. (1986). Electromyographic and force production characteristics of leg extensor muscles of elite weight lifters during isometric, concentric and various stretch-shortening cycle exercises. *International Journal of Sports Medicine*, **7**(3), 144-151.

Haralambie, G. (1982). Enzyme activities in skeletal muscle of 13-15 years old adolescents. *Bulletin of European Physiopathology and Respiration*, **18**, 65-74.

Haskell, W.L., Montoye, H.J. & Orenstein, D. (1985). Physical activity and exercise to achieve health-related physical fitness components. *Public Health Reports*, **100**, 202-212.

Highenboten, C.L., Jackson, A.W., & Meske, N.B. (1988). Concentric and eccentric torque comparison for knee extension and flexion in young adult males and females using the kinetic communicator. *American Journal of Sports Medicine*, **16**(3), 234-239.

Jacobson, B.J., & Kulling, F.A. (1989). Effect of resistance weight training in prepubescents. *Journal of Orthopaedic and Sports Physical Therapy*, **11**(3), 96-99.

Kannus, P. (1992). Normality, variability and predictability of work, power and torque acceleration energy with respect to peak torque in isokinetic muscle testing. *International Journal of Sports Medicine*, **13**(3), 249-256.

Knapick, J.J., Wright, J.E., Mawdsley, R.H., & Braun, J.M. (1983). Isokinetic, isometric and isotonic strength relationships. *Archives of Physical Medicine and Rehabilitation*, **64**, 77-80.

Knuttgen, H.G., & Komi, P.V. (1992). Basic definitions for exercise. In P.V. Komi (Ed.), *Strength and power in sports* (pp. 3-6). London: Blackwell Scientific Publications.

Komi, P.V. (1984). Physiological and biomechanical correlates of muscle function: Effects of muscle structure and stretch-shortening cycle on force and speed. *Exercise and Sport Sciences Reviews*, **12**, 81-121.

Kroemer, K.H. & Howard, J. (1970). Towards standardization of muscle strength testing. *Medicine and Science in Sports*, **2**(4), 224-230.

Malina, R.M. (1969). Quantification of fat, muscle and bone in man. *Clinical Orthopaedics*, **65**, 9-38.

Malina, R.M. (1986). Growth of muscle tissue and muscle mass. In F. Faulkner & J. M. Tanner (Eds.), *Human growth. A comprehensive treatise: Postnatal growth neurobiology* (Vol. 2, pp. 77-99). New York: Plenum Press.

Malina, R.M. (1989). Growth and Maturation: Normal Variation and Effect of Training. In C.V.Gisolfi, & D.R.Lamb, (Eds.), *Perspectives in exercise science and sports medicine: Volume II, Youth, exercise and sport* (pp. 223-272). Indianapolis: Benchmark Press.

Malina, R.M., & Bouchard, C. (1991). *Growth, maturation, and physical activity*. Champaign, IL: Human Kinetics.

McComas, A.J., Sica, R.E.P., & Petito, P. (1973). Muscle strength in boys of different ages. *Journal of Neurology, Neurosurgery, and Psychiatry*, **36**, 171-173.

Mero, A., Jaakkola, L., & Komi, P.V. (1990). Serum hormones and physical performance capacity in young boy athletes during a 1-year training period. *European Journal of Applied Physiology*, **60**(1), 32-37.

Mersch, F. & Stoboy, H. (1989). Strength training and muscle hypertrophy in children. In S. Oseid, & K.H. Carlsen, (Eds.), *Children and exercise XIII* (pp. 165-182). Champaign, IL: Human Kinetics.

Mohtadi, N.G.H., Kiefer, G.N., Tedford, K., & Watters, S. (1990). Concentric and eccentric quadriceps torque in pre-adolescent males. *Canadian Journal of Sports Science*, **15**(4), 240-243.

Molnar, G.E., & Alexander, J. (1973). Quantitative muscle testing in children: A pilot study. *Archives of Physical Medicine and Rehabilitation*, **54**, 224-228.

Molnar, G.E., & Alexander, J. (1974). Development of quantitative standards for muscle strength in children. *Archives of Physical Medicine and Rehabilitation*, **55**, 490-493.

Molnar, G.E., Alexander, J., & Gutfeld, H. (1979). Reliability of quantitative strength measurements in children. *Archives of Physical Medicine and Rehabilitation*, **60**, 218-221.

National Strength and Conditioning Association (NSCA) (1985). Position paper on prepubescent strength training. *National Strength and Conditioning Association Journal*, **7**(4), 27-31.

Nemoto, I., Kanehisa, H., & Miyashita, M. (1989). The effect of training on isokinetic peak torque in knee extensors of junior speed skaters. In S. Oseid and K.H. Carlson, (Eds.), *Children and exercise XIII*, International Series on Sport Sciences (pp. 199-210). Champaign, IL: Human Kinetics.

Osternig, L.R. (1986). Isokinetic dynamometry: Implications for muscle testing and rehabilitation. In K.B. Pandolf (Ed.), *Exercise and sport sciences reviews*, (Vol. 14, pp. 45-80). New York: Macmillan.

Pfeiffer, R.D., & Francis, R.S. (1986). Effects of strength training on muscle development in prepubescent, pubescent, and postpubescent males. *Physician and Sportsmedicine*, **14**(9), 134-143.

Ramsay, J.A., Blimkie, C.J.R., Smith, K., Garner, S., MacDougall, J.D., & Sale, D.G. (1990). Strength training effects in prepubescent boys. *Medicine and Science in Sports and Exercise*, **22**(5), 605-614.

Rians, C.B., Weltman, A., Cahill, B.R., Janney, C.A., Tippett,S.R.,& Katch, F.I. (1987). Strength training for prepubescent males: Is it safe? *American Journal of Sports Medicine*, **15**(5), 483-489.

Sailors, M., & Berg, K. (1987). Comparison of responses to weight training in pubescent boys and men. *Journal of Sports Medicine*, **27**, 30-37.

Sale, D.G. (1989). Strength training in children. In C.V. Gisolfi & D.R. Lamb (Eds.), *Perspectives in exercise science and sports medicine: Youth, exercise and sport* (Vol. II, pp. 165-222). Indianapolis: Benchmark Press.

Sale, D.G. (1991). Testing strength and power. In J.D. MacDougall, H.A. Wenger, & H.J. Green, (Eds.), *Physiological testing of the high-performance athlete*, (2nd ed., pp. 21-106). Champaign, IL: Human Kinetics.

Sallis, J., Simons-Morton, B.G., Stone, E.J., Corbin,C.B., Epstin, L.H., Faucette, N., Iannotti, R.J., Killen, J.D., Klesges, R.C., Pettray, C.K., Rowland, T.W. & Taylor, W.C., (1992). Determinants of physical activity and interventions in youth. *Medicine and Science in Sport and Exercise*, **24**(6), S248-S257.

Sapega, A.A., Nicholas, J.A., Sokolow, D., & Saraniti, A. (1982). The nature of torque overshoot in Cybex isokinetic dynamometry. *Medicine and Science in Sports and Exercise*, **14**(5), 386-375.

Sewall, L., & Micheli, L.J. (1986). Strength training for children. *Journal of Pediatric Orthopedics*, **6**, 143-146.

Shephard, R.J. (1982). *Physical activity and growth*. Chicago: Year Book Medical.

Siegel, J.A., Camaione, D.N., & Manfredi, T.G. (1989). The effects of upper body resistance training on prepubescent children. *Pediatric Exercise Science*, **1**(2), 145-154.

Sunnegardh, J., Bratteby, L.-E., Nordesjo, L.-O., & Nordgren, B. (1988). Isometrics and isokinetic muscle strength, anthropometry and physical activity in 8 and 13 years old Swedish children. *European Journal of Applied Physiology*, **58**, 291-297.

Tabin, G.C., Gregg, J.R., & Bonci, T. (1985). Predictive leg strength in immediately prepubescent and postpubescent athletes. *American Journal of Sports Medicine*, **13**(6), 387-389.

Taylor, N.A.S., Cotter, J.D., Stanley, S.N., & Marshall, R.N. (1991). Functional torque-velocity and power-velocity characteristics of elite athletes. *European Journal of Applied Physiology*, **62**, 116-121.

Vrijens, J. (1978) Muscle strength development in the pre- and post-pubescent age. In J.Borms & M. Hebbelinck (Eds.), *Pediatric work physiology, medicine and sport* (Vol. 11, pp. 152-158). New York: Karger.

Watkins, J. & Docherty, D. (1986). Training loads for the development of uppper limb muscular strength and endurance in pre-adolescents. In J.A. MacGregor & J.A. Moncur (Eds.), *Sport and medicine* (pp. 61-65). Proceeding of the VIII Commonwealth and international conference on Sport, Physical Education, Dance, Recreation and Health. London: F&N Spon.

Weltman, A., Janney, C., Rians, C.B., Strand, K., Berg, B., Tippitt, S., Wise, J., Cahill, B.R., & Katch, F.I. (1986). The effects of hydraulic resistance strength training in pre-pubertal males. *Medicine and Science in Sports and Exercise*, **18**(6), 629-638.

Weltman, A., Tippett, S., Janney, C., Strand, K., Rians, C., Cahill,, B.R., & Katch, F.I. (1988). Measurement of isokinetic strength in prepubertal males. *Journal of Orthopaedic and Sports Physical Therapy*, **9**(10), 345-351.

Winter, D.A., Wells, R.P., & Orr, G.W. (1981). Errors in the use of isokinetic dynamometers. *European Journal of Applied Physiology*, **46**, 397-408.

III

PHYSICAL FITNESS
FIELD TESTING

The use of laboratory tests to measure physiological performance is not always possible. A large number of field tests and batteries of field tests have been used to assess the fitness levels of children. Many of these fitness tests reflect physiological responses to exercise and have been used to assess the status of children and the effectiveness of programs. Recently, there has been considerable concern expressed about the validity of specific test items, the ways in which the data have been used, and the effectiveness of testing as a means of encouraging a physically active lifestyle. Part III of the text discusses the use of field tests and test batteries in the assessment of fitness for children and youth.

Chapter 7, by Patty Freedson and Edward Melanson, examines the measurement of physical activity. Many studies attempt to quantify the frequency, mode, volume, and intensity of physical activity in short-term (single 30-60 min bouts) and long-term (several hours to days) events. The shift towards encouraging the inclusion of physical activity or active living as part of lifestyle requires a valid and reliable assessment technique, and is a major challenge to researchers and a continuing area of investigation. This chapter discusses the use of various measurement techniques including pencil-and-paper evaluations, direct observation, self-reporting, mechanical and electronic monitoring, and physiological measures. Studies that monitor developmental changes or the effect of intervention programs on lifestyle will need to include physical activity as a dependent measure.

Chapter 8 provides an historical perspective on field tests, including the evolution of health-related fitness and criterion-referenced standards of performance. The discussion reflects the current concerns that have been expressed, the potential problems in using such tests to reflect children's fitness, and especially their commitment to a physically active lifestyle.

Specific test items are evaluated in regard to their validity, reliability, and inclusion in health-related fitness test batteries. Also included in the chapter is a description of fitness test batteries that are used in different countries, including the United States, Canada, Australia, New Zealand, and the standardized test of Europe (EUROFIT). Test batteries are evaluated in relation to their "face validity" and the current trends towards health-related fitness and development of a physically active lifestyle. Chapter 8 concludes with recommendations regarding the use of fitness tests and test batteries, especially in school programs.

7

Patty S. Freedson
Edward L. Melanson, Jr.

Measuring
Physical Activity

The relationship of physical activity, coronary heart disease, and other chronic degenerative diseases among adults is well-known. Origins of cardiovascular disease (CVD) have been shown to occur in childhood, with CVD risk factors appearing in early childhood. Thus, in recent years researchers have begun to examine selected behaviors in children that are associated with or protect against future development of disease. Although it has been reported that physical activity behavior patterns develop during childhood (Berenson, 1986), there is limited information on whether or not this behavior carries over into adulthood.

To provide a framework for measurement of physical activity, it is necessary to define common terminology. *Physical activity* is defined by Casperson (1989, p. 423) as "any bodily movement produced by the skeletal muscles that results in energy expenditure." Physical activity is a behavior, and it must be assessed in a real life field setting, in contrast to the other measures described in this text. For example, measurement of physical fitness is accomplished by testing a specific characteristic or set of characteristics using standardized testing protocols. The definition of *physical fitness* is "a set of attributes that people possess or achieve" (Casperson, 1989, p. 424).

Casperson (1989) considers exercise to be a subcategory of physical activity. It is "physical activity that is planned, structured, and results in the improvement or maintenance of one or more facets of physical fitness" (p. 425).

In measuring physical activity behavior, several different units of measurement are used. Caloric expenditure per unit time; metabolic equivalents (METS), minutes spent in moderate, hard, very hard or total activity; frequency of aerobic activity; ordinal rating compared to gender and age peers; and ordinal activity classifications are the more commonly used outcome units for pencil and paper evaluations. Caloric expenditure per unit time, activity counts, and heart rate indexes are the outcome units for motion sensors and physiologic measures.

CHARACTERISTICS OF PHYSICAL ACTIVITY IN CHILDREN AND YOUTH

Testing of fitness characteristics in a pediatric population presents special problems and concerns with regard to developmental characteristics as outlined elsewhere in this volume. In measuring physical activity, these issues are generally not a concern because activity behavior is a measurement where a specific test is not administered. In order to measure a habit or practice in the natural environment, the assessment scheme is obtained by ascertaining the behavior in a normal setting. The primary concern with the measure of activity is that the instrument used can capture activity habits of the child. For example, it has been shown that children under 10 years cannot recall activities accurately and are unable to quantify the timeframe of activity (Baranowski, 1988); therefore, a self-reported activity recall method would be inappropriate. In other types of query procedures, age appropriate lists of activities must be included. It may also be inappropriate to compare activity levels between very young children (less than 6 years) and adolescents, using motion sensors where motor characteristics may prevent the younger child from being classified as equally active as the older child.

Assessment of any behavior is complex and difficult to quantify accurately. Depending on the hypothesis being tested, the measurement of physical activity may address the frequency, duration, and intensity of activity, the type of activity (e.g., walking, cycling, team sport participation), the caloric expenditure of the activity, or some other index that characterizes activity level. A number of different methods have been used to assess activity in children, and there is no standard, accepted technique that can be universally applied. This chapter will review some of the commonly used assessment procedures as well as present some new electronic methods that are promising for more precise evaluation of the physical activity of children.

PENCIL-AND-PAPER EVALUATIONS

A validation instrument for assessing children's level of physical activity is direct observation with a trained observer recording the activity of a child over preselected time intervals, for example, over the course of an hour or several hours in a free play situation. A less time-intensive and more indirect pencil-and-paper method for estimating physical activity is the self-report method. For children under the age of 10, self-report actually refers to parent, teacher or both reporting on the child's activity behavior.

Direct Observation

McKenzie (1991) presented a summary of several different direct observation methods that have been used to assess children's physical activity (see Table 7.1). Direct observation instruments have been used for measuring children under the age of 13 years. This technique for assessing physical activity is the most labor-intensive and costly because of the time required to train observers, the length of the observation period, and the tedious data-coding phase. The environment used for testing must be conducive for observer or video-tape presence, and adequate observation time must be available to allow the children to habituate so that they will behave as they would in a more natural setting. Direct observation is a technique that can validate other less time-consuming pencil-and-paper- and activity-monitoring methods that will be described in subsequent sections.

If energy expenditure is estimated by direct observation, calorie estimates of the observed activities are estimated from published tables. However, the literature-based values are probably inappropriate for use in children and can lead to substantial errors in estimating actual energy expenditure (Sallis, Buono, & Freedson, 1991).

Another concern is the time frame for monitoring and recording activity. Recording activity at set intervals may exclude short bursts of activity; this situation may be a problem when evaluating young children whose activity patterns are constantly changing. Observational systems may be most appropriate in studies where the observation period is short, a precise measure of activity is required, and when alternative methods may be too inaccurate. For example, observation may be preferred because recall error is extremely high in young children and parent or teacher evaluation of the child's activity is too subjective.

Self-Report Measures

The most widely used assessment technique is the self-report measure of physical activity. Ease of administration, convenience, the ability to characterize activity historically, and low cost are the primary advantages of this method. Self-reports are typically used in large sample studies where the use of more precise activity monitoring is not feasible. Numerous instruments have been used, and researchers typically design the self-report that is appropriate for the objectives of the study (Sallis, 1991). The timeframe and amount of detail collected with regard to type, intensity, frequency, and duration of activity varies considerably among the different instruments (Sallis, 1991). It is recommended that the investigator carefully consider the objectives of the study and the hypotheses being tested to determine the appropriate type of self-report (Sallis, 1991). In addition, the age of the children being

Table 7.1 Characteristics of Selected Instruments Designed for Observing Children's Physical Activity

Citation	Name	Location	Observation strategy	Activity categories	Validation summary	Data summary	Associated variables	Training time	Test site
Hovell et al., (1978)	MAL (movement of the arms and legs)	Diverse	Momentary time-sampling; 5-second intervals	3 (no activity, moderate; vigorous), each for upper and lower body	None	% intervals/ time; mean activity score	None	Low	Recess
Epstein et al., (1984)	APEE (activity patterns and energy expenditure)	Free play	Momentary time-sampling; 15-second intervals	5 (sitting/ lying quietly; standing quietly; sitting/ lying while active; standing while active; very active/ moving)	Heart rates	Mean activity score; kcal/ kg/min	None	Low	Free play in gym

Measuring Physical Activity 265

O'Hara et al., (1989)	CPAF (children's physical activity form)	Physical education classes	Partial-time sampling; 1-minute intervals	4 (stationary, no movement; stationary, limb movement; slow trunk movement; rapid trunk movement)	Heart rates	Activity points; kcals	None	Moderate	Physical education classes
McKenzie et al., (1992)	SOFIT (system for observing fitness instruction time)	Physical education classes	Momentary time-sampling; 10-second obs/rec intervals	5 (lying; sitting; standing; walking; very active)	Heart rates	% intervals/time	Lesson context; teacher behavior	Low	Physical education classes
Klesges et al., (1984)	FATS (Fargo activity time-sampling survey)	Home	Partial interval recording; 10-second obs/rec intervals	8 (sleeping; lying down; sitting; crawling; climbing; standing; walking; running; each with 3 intensity levels-minimal; moderate; extreme)	None; correlated with LSI readings	% intervals	Location; persons percent; interactors; interactions; child response	High	Home

(continued)

Table 7.1 *(continued)*

Citation	Name	Location	Observation strategy	Activity categories	Validation summary	Data summary	Associated variables	Training time	Test site
Puhl et al., (1990)	CARS (children's activity rating scale)	Diverse	Partial time-sampling; 1-minute intervals	4 (stationary, no movement; stationary, movement; translocation easy; translocation moderate)	Heart rates; VO_2	% intervals; kcal/kg/min	Location; others present; television; eats; interactors; prompts; consequences	High	Diverse
McKenzie et al., (1991)	BEACHES (behaviors of eating and physical activity for children's health evaluation system)	Diverse	Momentary time-sampling; 1-minute intervals	5 (lying; sitting; standing; walking; very active)	Heart rates	% intervals/time; kcal/kg/min	Location; TV; interactors; eating; prompts; consequences; child response	High	Diverse
Klesges et al., (1990)	SCANCATS (studies of children's activity and nutrition children's activity time-sampling survey)	Diverse	Momentary time-sampling; 10-second obs/rec intervals	4 (stationary; minimal activity; slow movement; rapid movement)	None	% intervals/time	Location, persons present; interactors; prompts	High	Home

Reprinted from McKenzie (1991).

tested must be considered as it has been shown that children under the age of 10 cannot adequately recall their activity (Baranowski, 1988).

Table 7.2 is a summary of the characteristics of a number of different self-report measures of physical activity presented by Sallis (1991). The table is organized according to type of self-report measure: (a) interview-administered recall, where an interviewer conducts a structured question-and-answer session one-on-one with the child; (b) self-administered recall, where children report on their own activities; (c) diary, where the child lists activities throughout a specified time period (day, week); and (d) proxy report, where the parent or teacher or both record the child's activity.

Reliability coefficients ranged from $r = .47$ (5th graders) to $r = .96$ (11th graders). Nineteen of the 23 instruments were validated with either a direct criterion (observation or objective activity monitor) or an indirect criterion ($\dot{V}O_2$max, lipoprotein measure, % fat). Validity coefficients for studies that used a direct criterion measure were generally less than $r = .60$. This cannot be interpreted to mean that the self-report measures were not capturing activity. It may be that the criterion measures were not assessing dimensions of activity similar to the ones in the self-report measure.

Self-report measures will continue to be the most widely used method of assessing physical activity in epidemiological studies. It is likely that no standardized format will be accepted because each investigation requires specific information about physical activity that is consistent with the objectives of the study. This table details the characteristics of each instrument and should be used to identify the appropriate self-report. If other self-report measures are designed, it is essential that adequate reliability and validity studies be conducted prior to use in experimental investigations.

MECHANICAL AND ELECTRONIC MONITORING

Recent advances in electronic circuit technology have led to the development of a number of devices that can be worn on the trunk or extremities to directly monitor movement and store the data for subsequent analysis. Freedson (1991) summarized studies that have investigated the validity and reliability of a variety of motion sensors that are used to assess physical activity in children (see Table 7.3).

Actometer

Direct assessment of motion is not a new concept and was used as early as 1959 to quantify movement intensity using a device called an actometer. The actometer, worn on the wrist or ankle, is similar in design to a self-winding wristwatch; movement of a limb causes a rotor inside to move and measure acceleration and deceleration. Saris and Binkhorst (1977a) verified that the device could differentiate movement of different intensities.

Table 7.2   Characteristics of Self-Report Physical Activity Measures for Children and Adolescents

Citation	Instrument characteristics					Study characteristics		
	Instrument name	Dimensions: mode/freq./ inten./ duration	Weekday/ weekend	Time period	Summary variables	Items	Burden respondent/ staff	Time req'd	Subject characteristics
Interviewer-administered measures								
Linder et al., (1983)	usual activity interview	yes/no/yes/no	no	usual	none	6: TV, sports, jogging, cycling	med/high	5-10 min	11-17-year-old white males
Verschuur et al., (1985a, b)	3 month activity survey	yes/yes/yes/ yes/	no	3 months	time in activities; MET score; kcals	19 types of activities	high/high	10-15 min	13-14 years old
Wallace et al., (1985)	7 day physical activity recall	no/no/yes/yes	yes	7 days	kcals	min or kcal in mod, hard, very hard, or total activity	high/high	10-20 min	11-13-year-old white males
Sallis et al., (1988)	7 day physical activity recall	no/no/yes/yes	yes	7 days	kcals	min or kcal in mod, hard, very hard, or total activity	high/high	10-20 min	Anglo and Mexican Americans; mean age = 12 years

Sallis et al., (1990)	1 day physical activity recall	no/no/yes/yes yes	1 day	kcals	min or kcals in mod, hard, very hard, or total activity	med/high	5-10 min	8-13 years old
Sallis et al., (1991)	7 day physical activity recall	no/no/yes/yes yes	7 days	kcals	min or kcals in mod, hard, very hard, or total activity	high/high	10-20 min	5th, 8th, 11th graders; 50% female; 69% white
Self-administered measures								
Sallis et al., (1991)	Godin-Shephard activity survey	no/yes/yes/ partial no	usual	total weekly exercise (freq × METS)	freq per week in light, moderate, strenuous	low/low	2-5 min	5th, 8th, 11th graders; 50% female; white
Sallis et al., (1991)	Activity rating	no/no/no/no no	usual	rating compared to same age and sex peers	1 rating	low/low	1 min	5th, 8th, 11th graders; 50% female; white
Murphy et al., (1990)	Activity poster	no/no/yes/no no	usual	classification	choose 1 of 3 posters showing sedentary, moderate, or vigorous activities	low/low	1 min	10-18-year-old boys and girls
Diary measures								
Seliger et al., (1974)	Activity record-interview	no/yes/yes/ yes yes	1 day	min in 7 intensity categories	7 intensity codes	high/high	1 day	12-year-old boys

(continued)

Table 7.2 (*continued*)

	Instrument characteristics						Study characteristics		
Citation	Instrument name	Dimensions: mode/freq./inten./duration	Weekday/weekend	Time period	Summary variables	Items	Burden respondent/staff	Time req'd	Subject characteristics
Bouchard et al. (1983)	Activity record	no/yes/yes/yes	yes	daily	kilo calories	1 of 9 intensities coded each 15 min	high/med		mean age 15 (SD = 3); boys and girls
Proxy report measures									
Halverson and Waldrop (1973)	Activity and play rating	no/no/no/no	no	usual	factors of participation and hyperactivity	27 ratings	med/low	5-10 min	middle class white 2.5-year-olds
Thorland & Gilliam (1981)	5-day activity diary	no/no/yes/yes	yes	5 days	time at 6 intensity levels	6 intensity levels	high/high	white males, aged 8-10 years	55
Murphy et al. (1988)	Activity classification	no/no/no/no	no	usual	activity class	sedentary, slightly active, active	low/low	1 min	black and white; 6-18 years
Klesges et al. (1990)	energy balance questionnaire	no/no/no/no	no	usual	ratings compared to peers	3 ratings: structured, leisure, aerobic	low/low	1 min	3-6 year old white children
Noland et al. (1990)	parent rating of activity	no/no/no/no	no	usual	mean of ratings	9 ratings	low/low	2 min	white and black; 3-5 years
Noland et al. (1990)	Teacher rating of activity	no/no/no/no	no	usual	mean of rating	5 ratings	low/low	2 min	white and black; 3-5 years

Reprinted from Sallis (1991).

Table 7.3 Validity and Reliability of Motion Sensors and Heart Rate to Assess Activity in Children

Study	N	Ages (years)	Criterion measure	Tested measure	Reliability	Validity
Saris et al., (1977a& b)	11	4-6	direct observation and teacher questionnaire	pedometer actometer	NR	$r = .93*$ $r = .97*$
Fenster et al., (1989)	5 males 13 females	6-8	peak VO_2	LSI	NR	$r = .59*$
LaPorte et al., (1982)	22 males	12-14	three-day food intake Taylor Leisure Time Activity Survey	LSI	NR	$r = .30$
Klesges et al., (1985)	18 males 12 females	1.7-5.7	LSI Caltrac	direct observation	NR	$r = .16$ $r = .40*$ (LSI) $r = .35*$ (Caltrac)
O'Hara et al., (1989)	18 males 18 females	8-10	heart rate	direct observation	NR	$r = .64*$
Freedson and Evenson, (1991)	13 males 17 females	5-9	NR	Caltrac	$r = .38*$ (D1 vs D2) $r = .79*$ (D2 vs D3) $r = .42*$ (D1 vs D3)	NR

(continued)

Table 7.3 *(continued)*

Study	N	Ages (years)	Criterion measure	Tested measure	Reliability	Validity
Klesges and Klesges, (1987)	17 males 13 females	2-4	direct observation	Caltrac	r v .90 inter-observer correlation (direct observation)	r = .57 – .95* (hourly) r = .54* (whole day)
Mukeshi et al., (1990)	11 males 9 females	2.4-3.3	direct observation	Caltrac	NR	r = .62*
Sallis et al., (1990)	20 males 15 females	8-13	heart rate recall of previous 10 hours	Caltrac Caltrac heart rate	r = .10 (heart rate) r = .30 (Caltrac) r = .06 (recall)	r = .49* r = .49* (day 1 Caltrac) r = .39* (day 2 Caltrac) r = .54* (day 1 heart rate) r = .42* (day 2 heart rate)

*Statistically significant correlation
NR = not reported
Reprinted from Freedson (1991).

Pedometer

A pedometer is another example of a mechanical device; it monitors distance covered by measuring acceleration using a lever arm, spring, and gear assembly. Limitations of this type of monitor include errors in step rate and distance covered that primarily result from individual variability in stride length as well as impact force variation. Nevertheless, Saris and Binkhorst (1977b) reported a validity coefficient of $r = .93$ between pedometer readings and observed activity among 4- to 6-year-old children. This result was surprising given the potential sources of error.

Large Scale Integrated Sensor

The Large Scale Integrated Sensor (LSI) (GMM Electronics, Inc., 1200 Riverview Dr, Verona, PA, 15147) was originally designed to monitor hyperactive children. It is a small (51 gm, 3.8 cm x 4.5 cm x 2.2 cm) plexiglass unit that can be worn on the arm, leg, or hip. A movement that is greater than a 3° displacement is recorded as a count by a mercury column activating a switch and counter. A limitation of this device is that it is designed to function purely as a movement counter and does not differentiate the intensity of motion. The correlation of LSI activity versus direct observation was reported to be higher in adults ($r = .60$) than in children ($r = .17-.33$) (Klesges, Klesges, Swenson, & Pheley, 1985).

Caltrac

Most recent research that has employed a motion sensor to access activity in children has used the Caltrac accelerometer (Hemokinetics, Inc., 2923 Osmundsen Rd., Madison, WI, 53711). It is relatively inexpensive ($65/unit) and easy to use. It weighs 400 gm and is 14 cm × 8 cm × 4 cm in size and is worn on the nondominant hip. The Caltrac measures vertical acceleration that causes a ceramic transducer to twist, resulting in an intensity dependent voltage output. The assumption underlying the validity of the device is that body or limb accelerations closely reflect energy cost of the movement. The Caltrac sums and integrates the absolute value of the acceleration versus time curve and derives a numerical count that is displayed. Unlike other motion sensors, the Caltrac is designed to provide activity counts that reflect the intensity and quantity of movement. A limitation of the Caltrac is that it is calibrated to a single activity (walking) and may not accurately reflect the intensity and quantity of other types of activity.

When used for children under the age of 12, the device should be secured on the hip in a fanny pack or some other type of pouch to discourage children from tampering with the device. The output appears on a liquid crystal display, and several buttons on the front panel are used to program the device. The Caltrac can be programmed to provide the output either in caloric expenditure units or in activity counts. For caloric expenditure, the subject's height, weight, age, and gender must be entered. It is recommended that for children, the device is programmed with constants (height = 36, weight = 25, age = 99, and gender = 0) to assess activity counts because the caloric expenditure output was originally designed for use in adults. Validation and reliability studies generally have shown that the device is an excellent tool for assessing activity behavior in children (see Table 7.3).

Wrist Activity Monitor

A relatively new product that was originally designed to measure G-forces in fighter jets shows promise as a tool for measuring physical activity in children. The Wrist Activity Monitor (WAM) (Computer Science and Applications, Inc., 2 Clifford Dr., Shalimar, FL, 32579) is a small electronic motion sensor that estimates motion based on the deflection of deformation of a single-axis internal piezoelectric plate. The data are stored in the WAM memory and are downloaded into a computer for analysis. The WAM can be worn on any limb or secured to the hip or belt, similar to the recommended placement of the Caltrac. The WAM unit contains an internal real-time clock that allows data to be analyzed over time intervals as short as 1 sec. This feature is attractive for monitoring constantly changing physical activity patterns of children (Klesges & Klesges, 1987).

Figure 7.1 illustrates the WAM output from a 12-year-old who participated in a number of different activities. The summed magnitude mode of data collection was used; each activity count represents a movement and intensity of movement each time the signal crosses above the set baseline reference. This output is converted to a numerical value and is accumulated over the specified time-sampling period. At the end of the time-sampling period, the value is stored in memory and the accumulator is reset to zero.

Mini-Logger

The Mini-Logger (Mini-Mitter Company, Inc., PO Box 3386, Sunriver, OR, 97707) has three channels for data collection. Channel 1 monitors body or environmental temperature. Channels 2 and 3 are activity channels that use a multidirectional mercury switch system to assess motion. Sensors are placed on the arm or ankle or both, which send motion signals to the device. The data can be sampled from once every 8 sec up to once every 34 min. Figure 7.2 illustrates the computerized output from the Mini-Logger for a 12-year-old boy.

Tritrac-R3D

A new version of the Caltrac, the Tritrac-R3D, (Hemokinetics, Madison, WI) monitors motion horizontally, vertically, and diagonally and internally records motion for intervals ranging from one time per min to one time per 15 min for up to a 20-day period. The output is in integrated acceleration that can be converted to caloric expenditure using proprietary software. Figure 7.3 presents a sample of data downloaded from the Tritrac to a computer.

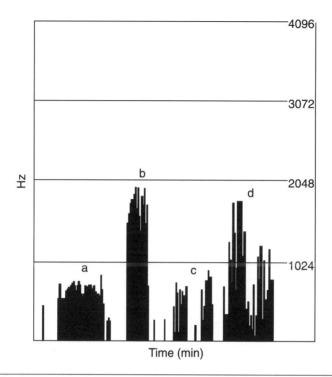

Figure 7.1   Sample ankle WAM output from a 12-year-old boy using the summed magnitude mode: (a) walking, (b) running, (c) cycling, (d) soccer.

PHYSIOLOGIC MEASURES

Physiologic responses to exercise, such as an increase in heart rate and an increase in oxygen consumption, have also been used as markers to assess physical activity. The gold standard for assessing energy expenditure in a field setting is doubly-labeled water. Continuous heart rate monitoring has also been used to quantify both the quantity and quality of movement (low- vs. high-intensity).

Doubly-Labeled Water

This method assesses the rate of carbon dioxide production based on the differences in the disappearance rates of ^2H_2O and $H_2^{18}O$. Following the stable isotope dosing, urine is collected and analyzed for up to 14 days. Total energy expenditure (TEE) is calculated from standard respiratory gas exchange equations. A detailed description of the technique is presented by Coward (1988). The major limitation of this procedure is the cost, which is approximately $350 to $450 per dose. In addition, it is not possible to determine the proportion of energy expenditure associated with activity. Nevertheless, the procedure is highly accurate for assessing total daily

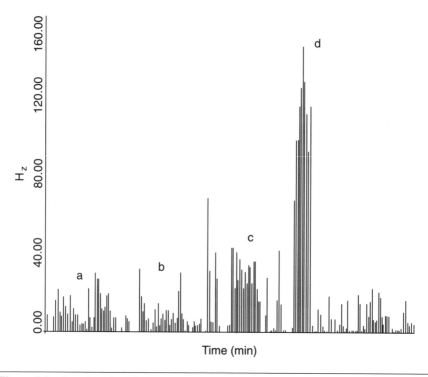

Figure 7.2   Sample wrist Mini-Logger output from a 12-year-old boy: (a) walking, (b) running, (c) cycling, (d) soccer.

energy expenditure. It is generally used to assess energy expenditure over a 1- to 2-week period. It has been suggested that maximal precision is obtained when monitoring is done over a 6-to 7-day period for children and 14 days in adults.

Average daily rates of TEE have been determined for children using the doubly-labeled water technique (Davies, 1992). Total daily energy expenditure is expressed as a multiple of either resting or basal metabolic rate (TEE/BMR) and is called the physical activity level (PAL). The range of PAL scores for children ages 3 to 10 years is 1.44 (3- to 4-year-old girls) to 1.95 (Mean age = 9.3-year-old boys). These values are similar to those reported by Livingstone et al. (1992) in Figure 7.4.

Heart Rate

Relatively inexpensive heart rate monitors with full-day storage capacity for minute-by-minute heart rate have made heart rate techniques more feasible for assessing daily activity. This method has an advantage over both questionnaires and doubly labeled water in that it is possible to trace activity patterns within the monitoring period.

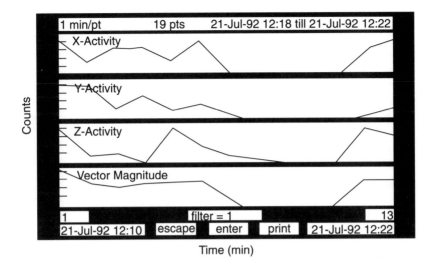

Figure 7.3   Output from the Tritrac-R3D for the horizontal, vertical, and diagonal plane from a 12-year-old boy. The vector magnitude represents the summation of movement in the three planes.

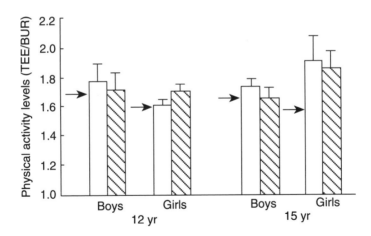

Figure 7.4   Comparison of the World Health Organization estimates of energy intake requirements (shown by arrows) with energy expenditure as measured by heart rate monitoring (open bars) and doubly-labeled water (cross bars). Data are presented as PAL units (total energy expenditure [TEE] basal metabolic rate [BMR]).
Reprinted from Livingstone et al. (1992).

The use of heart rate to quantify physical activity is based on the linear relationship between heart rate and energy expenditure. Factors such as active muscle group, anxiety, ambient temperature, type of muscle contraction, and training influence the relationship between heart rate and energy expenditure and potentially affect the accuracy of the translation of heart rate into energy expenditure units. Thus, it is not uncommon to use the number of minutes that heart rate is above a certain level as the activity score. Sallis, Buono, Roby, Carlson, and Nelson (1990) calculated the difference between resting and exercise heart rate as the activity score to account for individual differences in baseline heart rate.

Livingstone et al. (1992) reported that heart rate converted to energy expenditure, using individually determined heart rate/$\dot{V}O_2$ regression equations, compared quite favorably to doubly-labeled water estimates of energy expenditure among 7- to 15-year-old children when the group responses were compared. However evaluation of individual responses revealed differences among methods ranging from −16.9% to +18.8%.

Figure 7.5 illustrates the estimates of energy expenditure from doubly-labeled water and heart rate for 7- to 15-year-old boys and girls. This study also reported that over the course of a day, younger and older boys spend 91 and 52 min in moderate-to-vigorous physical activity, whereas girls spend only 39 and 15 min in this intensity level.

NORMS AND RECOMMENDATIONS

The 1988 Campbell Survey on Well-Being in Canada reported physical activity data among children and youth ranging in age from 10 to 19 years (Russell, Hyndford, & Beaulieu, 1992). Figures 7.6 and 7.7 present these data. Children were classified as active if daily caloric energy expenditure was greater than or equal to 3 kcal · kg^{-1} · day^{-1}. The activity assessment used in this survey was a questionnaire, and no validity data are available. Seventy-two % of males, 10 to 14 years old, and 69% of males, 15 to 19 years old, were classified as active. Forty-nine % of females, 10 to 14 years old, and 39% of females, 15 to 19 years old, were considered active. A trend towards lower activity that appears to continue into the second decade of life is evident (Stephens & Craig, 1990).

A recent report from the Centers for Disease Control (1992) reported vigorous physical activity levels among high school students. This information was obtained from the national school-based Youth Risk Behavior Survey (YRBS) in 1990. Over 11,000 students in grades 9 to 12 were asked the number of days over the previous 2 weeks in which they had participated in "at least 20 minutes of hard exercise that made you breathe heavily and made your heart beat fast." *Vigorously active* was defined having participated in this type of activity at least 3 days per week. Thirty-seven % of the high school students were classified as being physically active (24.8% of females, 49.6% of males). Vigorous-activity rates declined for girls as they got older (30.6% for 9th grade vs. 17.3% and 23.4% for 11th- and 12th-grade girls).

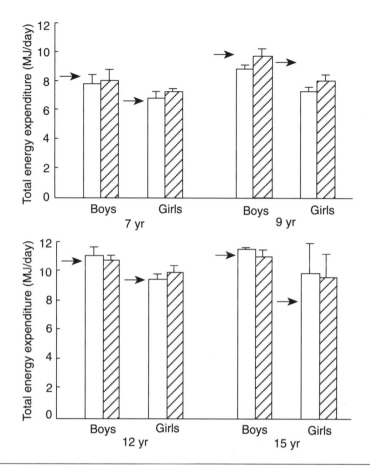

Figure 7.5   Comparison of World Health Organization estimates of energy intake requirements (shown by arrows) and absolute energy expenditure as measured by heart rate monitoring (open bars) and doubly-labeled water (crossed bars).
Reprinted from Livingstone et al. (1992).

Norms for physical activity for younger children are not available, particularly below the age of 10. The major difficulty in establishing norms for activity is that it is extremely difficult to measure behavior precisely. Activity behavior is particularly difficult to measure in younger children because of their inconsistent daily and seasonal patterns of physical activity. In addition, there is no standard accepted method for assessing activity behavior.

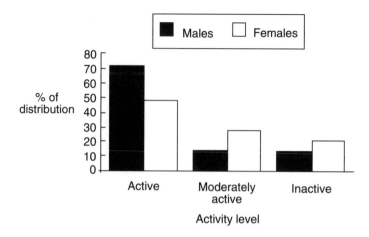

Figure 7.6   Physical activity levels of 10-14 year olds.
Reprinted from Russell, Hyndford, and Beaulieu (1992).

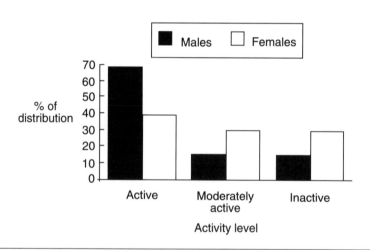

Figure 7.7   Physical activity levels of 15-19 year olds.
Reprinted from Russell, Hyndford, and Beaulieu (1992).

CONCLUSION

Heart rate and motion-sensor monitoring seem appropriate for relatively small samples (< 100 subjects) where this type of evaluation is feasible and practical. Heart rate monitoring may be particularly attractive, as it is possible to examine specific time segments within a measurement period when heart rate remains elevated. The new Tritrac triaxial motion sensor also has the capacity to store information, so it is now possible to look at elevated activity periods over the course of a day. It may be desirable to monitor physical activity with both heart rate and this new type of motion sensor so that elevated heart rates can be functionally linked to increased activity rather than other influencing factors.

Limited information is available regarding the consistency and stability of heart rate measures. A recent study reported by Durant et al. (1993) investigated this question among 5- to 7-year-old children. Within-day and between-day reliabilities were $r = .92$ and $r = .81$, respectively, for the proportion of heart rates that were 25% above rest (PAHR-25). This heart rate based physical activity index should be considered in future studies because it minimizes age and fitness effects on heart rate during physical activity and it has been shown to be a reliable measure.

Doubly labeled water, motion sensors, heart rate, and direct observation can be used to validate a proposed standardized self-report method, and appropriate modifications to the instrument can be made to insure that physical activity behavior is being accurately characterized. In addition, the instrument needs to be sensitive to historical patterns of activity in the child so that developmental patterns of activity behavior can be examined.

REFERENCES

Baranowski, T. (1988). Validity and reliability of self report measures of physical activity: An information-processing perspective. *Research Quarterly for Exercise and Sport, 59,* 314-327.

Berenson, G.S. (Ed.) (1986). *Causation of cardiovascular risk factors in children.* New York: Raven Press.

Bouchard, C., Tremblay, A., Leblanc, C., Lortie, G., Sauard, R., & Theriault, G. (1983). A method to assess energy expenditure in children and adults. *American Journal of Clinical Nutrition, 37,* 461-467.

Casperson, C.J. (1989). Physical activity epidemiology: Concepts, methods, and applications to exercise science. *Exercise and Sport Science Reviews, 17,* 423-473.

Centers for Disease Control (1992). Vigorous physical activity among high-school students— United States, 1990. *Morbidity and Mortality Weekly Report, 41,* 33-35.

Coward, W.A. (1988). The doubly-labelled-water ($^2H_2{}^{18}O$) method: Principles and practice. *Proceedings of Nutrition Society, 47,* 209-218.

Davies, P.S.W. (1992). Developments in the assessment of physical activity. In N.G. Norgan (Ed.), *Physical activity and health* (pp. 45-56). Cambridge: Cambridge University Press.

Durant, R.H., Baranowski, T., Davis, H., Rhodes, T., Thompson, W.O., Greaves, K.A., & Puhl, J. (1993). Reliability and variability of indicators of heart-rate monitoring in children. *Medicine and Science in Sports and Exercise*, **25**, 389-395.

Epstein, L., McGowan, C., & Woodall, K. (1984). A behavioral observation system for free play activity in young overweight female children. *Research Quarterly for Exercise and Sport*, **55**, 180-183.

Fenster, J.R., Freedson, P.S., Washburn, R.A., & Ellison, R. (1989) The relationship between peak oxygen uptake and physical activity in 6- to 8-year old children. *Pediatric Exercise Science*, **1**, 127-136.

Freedson, P.S. (1991). Electronic motion sensors and heart-rate as measures of physical activity in children. *Journal of School Health*, **61**, 220-223.

Freedson, P.S. & Evenson, S.K. (1991). Familial aggregation in physical activity. *Research Quarterly for Exercise and Sport*, **62**, 384-389.

Halverson, C.F., & Waldrop, M.F. (1973). The relations of mechanically recorded activity level to varieties of preschool play behavior. *Child Development*, **44**, 678-681.

Hovell, M., Bursick, J., Sharkey, R., & McClure, J. (1978). An evaluation of elementary students' voluntary physical activity during recess. *Research Quarterly for Exercise and Sport*, **49**, 460-470.

Klesges, L.M. & Klesges, R.C. (1987). The assessment of children's physical activity. A comparison of methods. *Medicine and Science in Sports and Exercise*, **19**, 511-517.

Klesges, R., Coates, T., Meldenhauer-Klesges, L., Holzer, B., Gustavson, J., & Barnes, J. (1984). The FATS: An observational system for assessing physical activity in children and associated parent behavior. *Behavioral Assessment*, **6**, 333-345.

Klesges, R., Haddock, C.K., & Eck, L.H. (1990). A multimethod approach to the measurement of childhood physical activity and its relationship to blood pressure and body weight. *Journal of Pediatrics*, **116**, 888-893.

Klesges, R.C., Klesges, L.M., Swenson, A.M., & Pheley, A.M. (1985). A validation of two motion sensors in the prediction of child and adult physical activity levels. *American Journal of Epidemiology*, **122**, 400-410.

Laporte, R.E., et al. (1982). The epidemiology of physical activity in children, college students, middle-aged men, menopausal females, and monkeys. *Journal of Chronic Diseases*, **35**, 787-795.

Linder, C.W., DuRant, R.H., & Mahoney, O.M. (1983). The effect of physical conditioning on serum lipids and lipoproteins in white male adolescents. *Medicine and Science in Sports and Exercise*, **15**, 232-236.

Livingstone, M.B.E., Coward, W.A., Prentice, A.M., Davies, P.S.W., Strain, J.J., McKenna, P.G., Mahoney, C.A., White, J.A., Steward, C.M., & Kerr, M.J. (1992). Daily energy expenditure in free-living children: Comparison of heart-rate monitoring with the doubly labelled water ($^{2}H_2{}^{18}O$) method. *American Journal of Clinical Nutrition*, **56**, 343-352.

McKenzie, T.L. (1991). Observational measures of children's physical activity. *Journal of School Health*, **61**, 224-227.

McKenzie, T., Sallis, J., & Nader, P. (1992). SOFIT: System for observing fitness instruction time. *Journal of Teaching Physical Education*, **11**(2), 195-205.

Mukeshi, M., Gutin, B., Anderson, W., Zybert, P., & Basch, C. (1990). Validation of Caltrac movement sensor using direct observation in young children. *Pediatric Exercise Science*, **2**, 249-254.

Murphy, J.K., Alpert, B.S., Christman, J.V., & Willey, E.S.L. (1988). Physical fitness in children: A survey method based on parental report. *American Journal of Public Health*, **78**, 708-710.

Murphy, J.K., Alpert, B.S., Dupaul, L.M., Wiley, E.S., Walker, S.S., & Nanney, G.C. (1990). The validity of children's self-reports of physical activity: A preliminary study. *Journal of Human Hypertension*, **4**, 130-132.

Noland, M., Danner, F., Dewalt, K., McFadden, M., & Kotchen, J.M. (1990). The measurement of physical activity in young children. *Research Quarterly for Exercise and Sport*, **61**, 146-153.

O'Hara, N.M., Baranowski, T., Simons-Morton, B.G., Wilson, B.S., & Parcel, G.S. (1989). Validity of the observation of children's physical activity. *Research Quarterly for Exercise and Sport*, **60**, 42-47.

Puhl, J., Greaves, K., Hoyt, M., & Baranowski, T. (1990). Children's activity rating scale (CARS): Description and evaluation. *Research Quarterly for Exercise and Sport*, **61**, 26-36.

Russell, S.J., Hyndford, C., & Beaulieu, A. (1992). *Active living for Canadian children and youth: A statistical profile*. Ottawa: Canadian Fitness and Lifestyle Research Institute.

Sallis, J.F. (1991). Self-report measures of children's physical activity. *Journal of School Health*, **61**, 215-219.

Sallis, J.F., Buono, M.J., & Freedson, P.S. (1991). Bias in estimating caloric expenditure from physical activity in children: Implications for epidemiological studies. *Sports Medicine*, **11**, 203-209.

Sallis, J.F., Buono, M.J., Roby, J.J., Carlson, D., & Nelson, J.A. (1990). The Caltrac accelerometer as a physical activity monitor for school-age children. *Medicine and Science in Sports and Exercise*, **22**, 698-703.

Sallis, J.F. Patterson, T.L., Buono, M.J., & Nader, P.R. (1988). Relation of cardiovascular fitness and physical activity to cardiovascular disease risk factors in children and adults. *American Journal of Epidemiology*, **127**, 933-941.

Saris, W.H.M. & Binkhorst, R.A. (1977a). The use of a pedometer and actometer in studying daily physical activity in man. Part I: Reliability of the pedometer and actometer. *European Journal of Applied Physiology*, **37**, 219-228.

Saris, W.H.M. & Binkhorst, R.A. (1977b). The use of a pedometer and actometer in studying daily physical activity in man. Part II: Validity of the pedometer and actometer measuring the daily physical activity. *European Journal of Applied Physiology*, **37**, 229-235.

Seliger, V., Trefny, Z., Bartunkova, S., & Pauer, M. (1974). The habitual activity and physical fitness of 12-year-old boys. *Acta Paediatrica Belgica*, **28**, 54-59.

Stephens, T. & Craig, C.L. (1990). *The well-being of Canadians: Highlights of the 1988 Campbell's survey*. Ottawa: Canadian Fitness and Lifestyle Research Institute.

Thorland, W.G., & Gilliam, T.B. (1981). Comparison of serum lipids between habitually high and low active pre-adolescent males. *Medicine and Science in Sports and Exercise*, **13**, 316-321.

Verschuur, R., & Kemper, H.C.G. (1985a). Habitual physical activity. *Medicine and Science in Sports and Exercise*, **20**, 56-65.

Verschuur, R., & Kemper, H.C.G. (1985b). The pattern of daily physical activity. *Medicine and Science in Sports and Exercise*, **20**, 169-186.

Wallace, J.P., McKenzie, T.L., & Nader, P.R. (1985). Observed vs. recalled exercise behavior: A validation of a seven-day exercise recall for boys 11 to 13 years old. *Research Quarterly for Exercise and Sport*, **56**, 161-165.

8

David Docherty

Field Tests and Test Batteries

Fitness testing of children has enjoyed considerable popularity in many countries for the past 30 to 40 years. Such widespread interest has resulted in a proliferation of fitness tests and test batteries purporting to measure the physical status of children and youth. Initially the focus of most tests was on motor fitness, and tests were designed to measure the efficiency of muscle function. More recently attention has shifted to tests that are considered to be indicators of health and wellness. Many of the original tests have been retained and included in test batteries that purport to measure health-related fitness components. Usually the tests are used with the intent to motivate children to achieve higher levels of fitness and to include optimal levels of physical activity in their present and future lifestyles.

It is apparent from evaluating these tests and test batteries, measuring either motor fitness or health-related fitness, that the basic tenets of test construction (including validity, reliability, and objectivity), are seldom reported or addressed. In addition, many of the tests that have been developed in recent years appear to be very similar in content and perpetuate some of the problems inherent in earlier tests. Understandably, there has been increasing criticism of physical fitness tests and identification of many issues and concerns that need to be addressed (Franks, Morrow, & Plowman, 1988; Safrit, 1990; Seefeldt & Vogel, 1989).

There has also been concern about the way in which fitness tests have been used in educational settings (Corbin, Whitehead, & Lovejoy, 1988; Fox & Biddle, 1986, 1988). Such criticism has been extended to the use of normative-referenced standards in which an individual's fitness performance is compared to his or her peers. Often normative-referenced standards are linked to reward systems. This approach is considered by many educators to be counterproductive to the development of a fitness-oriented lifestyle. Consequently, more recent test batteries have used criterion-referenced standards (Cooper Institute for Aerobics Research, 1987; American Alliance, 1988; Manitoba Education, 1989). Unfortunately, there is a lack of empirical support in establishing the criterion-referenced standards and considerable arbitrariness in identifying "acceptable" levels of performance (Safrit, 1990).

Considerable thought has been given to the development of tests and test batteries to assess the fitness of children (Safrit, 1990). There are many reasons to measure and evaluate the fitness of children and a growing scientific body of knowledge to suggest its importance to future health and wellness. Safrit suggests there is a role for norm-referenced standards and the need to recognize excellence in fitness. In fact the case can be argued for inclusion of both normative- and criterion-referenced standards in the publication of test manuals. However, individuals who administer these tests and test batteries need to be aware of the strengths and weaknesses of the test items and batteries and the purpose of the testing. They should also be aware of the rationale for either criterion- or normative-referenced standards and the basis upon which the standards have been determined.

FITNESS ASSESSMENT OF CHILDREN: AN HISTORICAL PERSPECTIVE

Interest in fitness testing in the United States was stimulated in the 1950s with the development of the Kraus-Weber Minimal Fitness Test and the subsequent use of the test to compare U.S. and European children (Kraus & Hirschland, 1953, 1954). Despite the limitations of the test, it did stimulate government and educational institutions to develop programs and tests to enhance the fitness status of U.S. children. A project entitled "The Development of Criteria of Physical Proficiency" was funded by the Office of Naval Research and resulted in the publication of a more comprehensive and valid measurement of fitness (Fleishman, 1964). The Youth Fitness Test (American Association, 1957) was developed by AAHPER and gained greater visibility in 1966 when the President's Council on Physical Fitness and Sport (PCPFS) adopted it as the basis for the Presidential Physical Fitness Award (Franks et al., 1988). The Presidential Fitness Award Program was designed to motivate boys and girls to develop and maintain a high level of fitness, promote testing programs in schools, stimulate health and physical education programs, and provide information on the fitness status of children (Corbin et al., 1988).

In 1975 AAHPER started a process to revise the original Youth Fitness Test and distinguish between health-related fitness and physical performance related to athletic ability (Franks et al., 1988). The revision resulted in the establishment of the Health-Related Physical Fitness Test (American Alliance, 1980) and a modified Youth Fitness Test. The PCPFS recognized only the AAHPERD Youth Fitness Test and required students to perform at the 85th percentile or better on all seven items. AAHPER introduced two additional awards for students attaining either the 50th percentile (the achievement award) or the 80th percentile (the gold seal award), neither of which was sponsored by PCPFS (Corbin et al., 1988). In 1985 PCPFS developed its own fitness test battery, keeping only five of the original seven AAHPER Youth Fitness Test items, and retained the 85th percentile as the performance standard for the Presidential Award.

A task force was established with representatives from PCPFS and AAHPERD to develop one AAHPERD test. Discussions on the definition of physical fitness, selection of test items, evaluation, and allocation of awards were divisive and resulted in many task force members resigning (Corbin et al., 1988; Franks et al., 1988). The members who resigned from the task force helped develop the Fitnessgram (Cooper Institute for Aerobics Research, 1987) under the auspices of the Cooper Institute for Aerobics Research and the sponsorship of Campbell Soup Company (Corbin et al., 1988). AAHPERD subsequently developed the Physical Best program (American Alliance, 1988), which was intended to replace all previous fitness programs developed by AAHPERD. Both the Fitnessgram and Physical Best programs include award systems that are based primarily on regular involvement in exercise, though special awards are available for attaining minimum criterion performance standards.

Fitness testing has been extensively used in Canadian schools since the publication of the *CAHPER Fitness-Performance Test Manual* in 1966. The Centennial Athletic Awards were introduced one year later and were based on the percentile norms of the CAHPER Fitness-Performance Test (Dahlgren, 1983). In 1979 the initial test was revised to include a more valid measure of aerobic fitness, update the norms, and convert distances to metric terms. The new *CAHPER Fitness Performance II Test Manual* was published in 1980. The Canada Fitness Award Program (CFA) was developed from the Centennial Athletic Awards by Fitness and Amateur Sport in 1970. In 1980 several changes were made to the CFA, including the adoption of a performance standard on the endurance run as a prerequisite to any award. Further changes were made to the CFA program in 1984: in particular, a revision of the standards; replacement of the flexed-arm hang by a push-ups test; and partial sit-ups in place of speed sit-ups.

The Manitoba Physical Fitness Performance Test Manual and Fitness Objectives, published in 1980, evolved from the Manitoba Schools Physical Fitness Survey conducted from 1976 to 1977. The Manitoba test preceded the CAHPER II test with inclusion of a more valid measure of aerobic fitness, as well as tests to estimate adiposity and flexibility. *Manitoba Schools Fitness 1989* has been published with a particular focus on developing fitness and establishing criterion-referenced standards of fitness for the various test items.

In 1979 a physical education assessment was conducted in British Columbia to determine the status of students and programs in physical education. Part of the assessment included evaluation of physical fitness, utilizing a variety of tests to measure cardiovascular endurance, static and dynamic muscular endurance, static and explosive strength, and flexibility (British Columbia Assessment, 1979). Tests were also included to assess knowledge of nutrition, body structure and function, and development of fitness.

The Canadian Standardized Test of Fitness (CSTF) was first published in 1977 as a simple test of fitness, including a cardiovascular performance test. It has been revised several times, most recently in 1986 through Fitness and Amateur Sport. The CSTF was the basis of the Canadian Fitness Survey (CFS) conducted in 1981 with a random sample of Canadians, 7 to 69 years of age. However, although the CSTF includes norms and data for younger children, it is currently recommended only for individuals 15 years and older.

In 1968 CAHPER published the Physical Working Capacity Test (PWC_{170}) that was a modification of a test developed by Sjostrand and Wahlund. The modification included adaptations of the Monark Cycle Ergometer for use with children and the establishment of norms for Canadian children 7 to 17 years of age. The norms were updated in 1983.

The Canadian Home Fitness Test (CHFT) was developed in 1976 for Health and Welfare Canada as a self-administered motivational test. Fitness Canada has adopted the CHFT as its measure of cardiovascular, or aerobic, fitness in the CSTF and renamed it the Canadian Aerobic Fitness Test (CAFT). When conducted in a controlled setting, the CAFT can be used to predict maximal oxygen consumption ($\dot{V}O_2$ max). Although initially developed for individuals 15 to 69 years old, the test has been extended to the junior high school age range of 11 to 14 years (Bailey & Mirwald, 1978).

HEALTH-RELATED FITNESS VERSUS MOTOR-FITNESS PERFORMANCE TESTS

It is important to distinguish between tests that measure various aspects of health and tests that measure components of motor performance. There is some degree of commonality between health-related fitness (HRF) and motor performance, but there are important differences that need to be recognized by teachers and students. Health-related fitness tests should measure factors that are concerned with the health and wellness of the individual. Measures of cardiorespiratory fitness and body composition (especially adiposity) are generally regarded as critical risk factors related to optimal health. Some authors include strength, muscular endurance, flexibility, and posture as components of health-related fitness (Fox & Biddle, 1986). Motor-fitness performance tests include measures of explosive power, agility, coordination, and speed. Some tests may involve items requiring a specific motor-skill level, such as the softball throw.

Motor-fitness performance tests can be used to predict individuals with good athletic ability who may excel in a variety of sports. However, they do not relate to health and wellness. Educators need to clearly distinguish between those tests that are related to health and those tests related to general motor performance. The ability to score well on motor-fitness performance tests often depends upon genetics and physical maturation. It has little to do with a lifestyle committed to improving or maintaining health. If the objectives of a physical education program include enhancing children's health and instilling a lifetime commitment to physical activity, measurement of health-related fitness seems to be of more concern than motor-fitness performance.

AAHPERD developed a test battery in 1984 designed to assess factors related to health rather than the original AAHPER Youth Fitness Test (1976) that contained tests requiring motor ability and skill. The new Health-Related Physical Fitness Test (HRPFT) (American Alliance, 1980) is accompanied by school- and college-age-related norms, including norms recently developed for 6- to 9-year-old boys and girls (Ross, Pate, Delpy, Gold, & Suilor, 1987). Unfortunately, the HRPFT has not been widely adopted in schools, nor is it well understood (Safrit & Wood, 1986).

Currently, there is no National Canadian Test (battery) for school-aged children that focuses solely on health-related fitness. The *Manitoba Schools Fitness 1989* does provide a test and suggestions to measure and develop "positive attitudes and lifestyle habits that are conducive to healthy living." The manual also provides "criterion-referenced measurement" in an attempt to inform students of their performance in regard to desired standards. At present some caution needs to be applied in the utilization of this approach since the desired standards do not consider biological (physical) age, and the desired standards that are recommended have not been empirically established. In addition, one could question the relationship of measures that include force generation, local muscular endurance, and flexibility to health and control of coronary heart disease (CHD) risk factors.

It has already been stated that performance on many motor fitness tests is attributable to genetics and physical maturation. Fox and Biddle (1986) suggest that scores on tests of health-related fitness also have a significant genetic component. Physical maturation also plays an important part in performance on these tests. It is well-known that children of the same chronological age will have widely disparate biological ages, often up to 6 years (Clark, 1973). To judge children's test performance according to chronologically-based norms is obviously inappropriate and can be disheartening to the late-maturing boy and early-maturing girl. In addition fitness tests are "still plagued by severe limitations which cause validity, reliability, and interpretation problems in educational settings" (Fox & Biddle, 1986). It also seems inappropriate to pursue the presentation of "Fitness Awards" based on biological inheritance rather than a commitment to an active lifestyle. The administration of health-related fitness tests or motor-fitness performance tests needs careful consideration if it is intended to promote fitness and positive attitudes towards health in children (Corbin et al., 1988). This does not imply that there is no educational value in the use of fitness tests. Fitness can be effectively developed through the use of health-related tests but educators need to be judicious in their application and constructive in their prescription (Fox & Biddle, 1988).

The trend towards health-related fitness tests associated with an award system based on commitment to exercise behavior rather than fitness status appears to be commendable. However, there is no empirical data to validate the effectiveness of the different programs in promoting health, fitness, positive attitudes towards physical activity, and adoption of an active lifestyle into adulthood (Corbin et al., 1988).

NORM- VERSUS CRITERION-REFERENCED STANDARDS

Recently there has been considerable discussion about the relative merits and problems associated with norm-referenced measurement compared to criterion-referenced measurement (Ross et al., 1987; Manitoba Education, 1989). Most tests have some form of *normative scale*, or standards by which individuals can compare their performances to their peers'. Norms are frequently expressed as percentiles or standard scores (e.g., *T* score, Hull scores). When performance is converted to a normative standard, it is referred to as norm-referenced measurement. Many physical educators believe that such peer comparison is useful for discriminating within and among ability groups (Safrit, 1990). However, peer comparison is inappropriate for interpretation of performance on health-related fitness tests and, in many situations, motor-fitness performance tests. As Fox and Biddle (1986, 1988) have indicated, results on such tests largely depend on physical maturity and genetic endowment rather than a commitment to regular physical exercise. In fact, the use of norms and comparisons among students may prove counterproductive to the promotion and development of health and wellness (Docherty & Bell, 1990). Students may perceive the standards beyond their capabilities or competence and, consequently, withdraw from exercise (Corbin et al., 1988).

Criterion-referenced measurement attempts to set specific standards or levels that all students are expected to meet. In the context of health-related fitness tests, the standards are supposedly related to performance levels commensurate with optimal health. However, many of the criterion standards are established arbitrarily, often using specific percentile cut-off points. Many of the criterion standards do not take into account the developmental age of the student. It is also questionable whether or not all the items included in many health-related fitness tests are really associated with health and wellness. Unfortunately, there is little empirical information to help in setting standards or identifying those fitness components critical for optimal health. Until more information is available, the dilemma cannot be resolved, and test developers must rely on intuition and construct validity.

In using fitness tests it should be clear to the students which items are related to health and which items are related to motor performance. Motor-fitness performance tests can be used to identify children with athletic ability, but should be used with discretion and recognition of individual differences. Care must be taken not to discourage students, especially those who are late-maturers.

Based upon current trends and opinions, most testing in schools should involve health-related fitness tests. The use of normative standards should be discouraged. Instead, test results should be used to provide information to students to indicate their current status and desirable future actions (Fox & Biddle, 1988). Personal goals should be established to achieve criterion-referenced standards for health, realizing the limitations previously discussed. Students should be retested to determine if the goals are being met; the retests should give the students a sense of "fitness competence." Tests can also be used as a vehicle to impart knowledge about various aspects of fitness and particular methods of enhancing performance. It seems inappropriate, and possibly counterproductive to health, to reward students solely on the basis of performance in fitness tests. However, fitness-awards programs need to be carefully evaluated to determine if they do recognize a commitment to physical activity and promote positive attitudes to health and wellness.

EVALUATING FITNESS TESTS

In order for a test or test battery to be considered *good*, it "should measure what it is supposed to measure (*validity*), with consistency (*reliability*), using an accurate scoring system (*objectivity*)" (Safrit, 1986, p. 118). These concepts need to be discussed as they relate to the development or selection of fitness tests and test batteries.

Validity

There are several ways in which tests can be determined to be valid. *Logical validity*, or *face validity*, is defined as the extent to which a test measures the components or parameters of the attribute being measured. If flexibility is regarded as the range of motion around a joint and a tester measures the range of motion, the test would have logical validity. In measuring any fitness attribute, it is important that motor skill does not significantly influence performance; otherwise, the validity of the test is severely compromised.

Criterion-related validity involves comparing one test with an established or valid test (i.e., the criterion or gold standard). There are two types of criterion-related validity: *concurrent validity* and *predictive validity*. Both types of validity require statistical analysis, usually some form of correlation coefficient. Concurrent validity is used when the test is a substitute for a more elaborate or costly test. Predictive validity, as it relates to fitness testing, is essentially an extension of concurrent validity; the criterion performance is predicted from performance on the substitute test.

Concurrent validity and predictive validity are used extensively in the measurement of aerobic power, or cardiovascular fitness. The criterion measure is generally regarded as maximal oxygen consumption ($\dot{V}O_2max$). If the correlation coefficient is sufficiently high ($> \pm 0.80$), the substitute test(s) are considered valid. However, the test should only be considered valid when it is used to measure a population similar (in sex, age, activity level, etc.) to the one on which the initial validity was established.

Predictive validity is also used to describe the current status (as opposed to future status or behavior) of an individual and involves estimating performance on a complex criterion test by obtaining a score on a simple predictor test (Safrit, 1986). In order to be accurate in such prediction, there should be a high relationship between the two tests (> ±0.80). A regression equation permits the prediction of the score on the criterion test to be made from performance on the substitute test. For example, $\dot{V}O_2$max can be predicted in ml · kg^{-1} · min^{-1} from a submaximal stepping test (Canadian Standardized Test of Fitness, 1986) or a distance run.

Construct validity is defined as the degree to which a test or test battery measures an attribute or ability that cannot be directly measured. In the present context the attributes of health-related fitness, motor-fitness performance, and motor ability are not readily measured by a single test. Although the attribute, or *construct*, cannot be measured precisely, indicators of the *construct behaviour* are often measurable. The begging question is how to establish validity when no criterion test is available? (Safrit, 1986).

The two areas of measurement addressed in this report are health-related fitness and motor-fitness performance. Most educators agree that motor skill should not significantly effect the test results. However, there is considerable debate regarding test items on a health-related fitness test battery, and even for a motor-fitness performance test battery.

Logical validity is often employed in determining which aspects of fitness are to be included in a health-related fitness test battery. Unfortunately, there is little empirical support for inclusion of specific attributes, especially the standard of performance required for optimal fitness and health. Flexibility is often incorporated in health-related fitness test batteries, but there is little or no support related to its contribution to health or physical performance (Hubley, 1991). The significance of local muscular endurance (arms and abdomen) to health and wellness may also be questioned. Most educators would agree that cardiovascular fitness and body composition (particularly adiposity) are considered CHD-risk factors but there is little empirical data to indicate the levels needed for optimal health or decreased risk of CHD. There is more agreement in the tests indicative of motor-fitness performance. Motor-fitness-performance test batteries usually measure attributes of strength, power, local muscular endurance, and agility. However, recommended standards of performance, and even test selection, are usually established arbitrarily or based on normative scales.

One technique for establishing construct validity is referred to as *the group differences method* (Safrit, 1986). This method compares the performances of two groups on the tests or test battery. One group should be regarded as highly fit or healthy based on a number of criteria, such as lifestyle, whereas the other group should be less fit or sedentary. If the tests or test battery have a level of construct validity, the physically active, or "healthy," group should obviously score better than the sedentary group.

In deciding whether or not to use a test, the user should be satisfied that the test has established validity. The type of validity should be clearly indicated in the test description, including correlation coefficients and the criterion tests (if criterion-related validity has been used). Few, if any, test batteries report validity or even give a rationale for including specific test items.

Reliability

Reliability refers to the consistency of an individual performing a test. Within the context of a norm-referenced test, reliability also implies the ability of a test to detect reliable differences among individuals. In other words, an individual doing a test on two occasions under the same conditions and close proximity in time should obtain similar results. On repeat testing, two individuals should also score the same distance apart (i.e., the same percentile score). Reliability related to criterion-referenced tests refers to the consistency of classification. Most of the tests in the context of this report are norm-referenced, and the reader is directed to Safrit (1986) for a more complete explanation of reliability as it relates to criterion-referenced tests.

For most tests measuring attributes of health-related fitness or motor-fitness performance, reliability should be established on a test-retest basis. Traditionally, an *interclass correlation coefficient* $(r_{xx}{}^1)$ is computed (often Pearson product-moment) from the two sets of scores on the same variable. However, this technique is insensitive to systematic increases or decreases in an individual's score and is a bivariate statistical technique. In other words, a high correlation coefficient occurs if everyone scores higher on Trial 1 than on Trial 2, even though the performances were not consistent.

The *intraclass correlation coefficient* $(R_{xx}{}^1)$ is estimated by calculating an analysis of variance and is regarded as a univariate statistic. The correlation coefficient $(R_{xx}{}^1)$ is still interpreted in a similar way to the interclass coefficient $(r_{xx}{}^1)$, but takes into account the actual change, or variance, in performance. Consequently, it is regarded as the more appropriate method for describing test reliability.

Reliability can also be expressed in relation to the individual's score using the standard error of measurement (SE_m). The standard error of measurement is calculated from the standard deviation (s) and the intraclass correlation coefficient. It is expressed in the units of the actual measurement. The smaller the SE_m, the more stable or reliable is the test. If the SE_m is approximately half of the standard deviation, the subject stability is regarded as low, whereas an SE_m approximately one quarter of the standard deviation is considered reasonably stable or reliable. The standard error of measurement, therefore, reflects the degree a test score can be expected to vary due to measurement error.

In relation to fitness testing it is important to consider the reliability of the specific test items, especially when the instructor is interested in monitoring change due to programming. Instructors must also use extreme care when testing to ensure that the measurement is precise and accurately reflects performance. Test conditions should be standardized, taking into consideration the time of day, test environment, internal and external motivation, number of test trials, and the individual's familiarity with the test. Reliability is also population specific and should be established for groups based on age, gender, and level of experience. When interpreting reliability coefficients it is also important to consider the effect of practice on performance (i.e., the number of trials or tests required to produce stable or reliable performance) and the level of experience of the test administrator. Frequently test reliability is reported without inclusion of this information.

Objectivity

Objectivity refers to the degree of accuracy in scoring a test. It is frequently described as the degree of agreement between the scores assigned to each individual by two or more testers (Baumgartner & Jackson, 1987). The clearer the test description and scoring technique, the greater should be the objectivity. Tests that rely on considerable subjectivity in assigning scores generally have poor objectivity.

The degree of objectivity in a test is calculated by using an intraclass correlation coefficient rather than the interclass correlation coefficient that is often reported. The intraclass correlation coefficient takes into account differences in the mean and standard deviation (variance) between the two sets of scores from the different testers. If one tester consistently scores individuals higher than another tester, the interclass correlation coefficient is high but the objectivity of the test is low.

In fitness testing, especially when the same tests are used from year to year, it is important the tests are administered in a standardized method by different testers. Scores on "simple tests" such as push-ups and sit-ups can vary between testers if they impose different criteria on the way in which the test is performed.

FITNESS COMPONENTS MEASURED IN FIELD TESTS

Several components or attributes of fitness have already been discussed but not clearly defined. Prior to critically analyzing tests designed to assess these attributes, it is useful to define them according to generally accepted definitions.

Strength

Strength refers to the maximum force or torque a muscle or muscle group can generate in one contraction (Sale, 1991). It is not included in many field tests of fitness because it typically requires expensive equipment and is time consuming. One repetition-maximum (1RM), or the maximum weight a student can lift, is a measurement of strength that can be employed in a school setting. However, such a test should be confined to older students who have considerable experience in weight training.

Power

In most testing and training contexts, *power* relates to explosive strength, or the ability of a muscle group to contract both forcefully and quickly (Sale, 1991). Typically the contraction propels the body (vertically or horizontally) or a heavy object (e.g., a medicine ball).

Muscular Endurance

Muscular endurance refers to the ability of specific muscle groups to do repeated contractions, usually to fatigue or failure as in push-ups. Some tests may employ static contractions for as long as possible (the flexed-arm hang) or require the maximum number of repetitions within a set time (one minute speed sit-ups).

There is a relationship between strength and endurance as long as the energy demands of the physical task do not change. For example, if Student A has a maximum bench press of 100 kg compared to Student B who can press 60 kg, Student A will be able to complete more repetitions if the barbell is 50 kg. Student A is lifting only 50% of maximum strength, whereas Student B is lifting nearly 80% of maximum strength. Consequently, some tests are considered to measure strength even when they involve a maximum number of repetitions. It is probably more appropriate to refer to such tests as measures of local muscular endurance to distinguish them from strict measures of strength.

Flexibility

The range of motion about a specific joint is referred to as *flexibility* (Hubley, 1991). Typically, most practical (or field) tests measure only a part of the range of motion. For example, the sit-and-reach really measures forward flexion of the trunk rather than the range of motion from full flexion to full extension. Such tests also measure linear rather than angular displacement of the limb.

Body Composition

Body composition refers to the proportion of the different types of tissues that contribute to body weight (Ross & Marfell-Jones, 1991). The tissues are usually identified as skeletal mass, muscle mass, fat mass, and residual mass (which includes major organs and intestines). However, in fitness testing it is most common to assess only the fat mass, or adipose tissue. Body composition has almost become synonymous with measuring body fat. Body fat has received unique attention because it is most related to health problems and regarded as a potential health-risk factor.

Cardiorespiratory Fitness

Cardiorespiratory fitness is dependent upon efficient lungs, heart, and blood vessels; oxygen carrying capacity of the blood; and oxygen utilization by the working muscles (Thoden, 1991). The ability to continue prolonged heavy work depends on an efficient cardiorespiratory system. Since the total system includes the lungs (respiration) and the oxidating capability of blood and muscle, cardiovascular fitness is also referred to as *cardiorespiratory fitness* and *aerobic fitness* (*aerobic* means with oxygen).

Other Attributes

Other attributes, such as balance and agility, are frequently included in motor-fitness-performance tests. *Balance* refers to the ability to maintain equilibrium when the body is either stationary (static balance) or moving (dynamic balance). *Agility* is usually described as the ability to change direction or body position.

EVALUATION OF SPECIFIC TEST ITEMS

The different fitness components have been measured in a variety of ways. Analysis of Tables 8.1 to 8.8 shows the way in which the components have been measured and the psychometric considerations associated with each test item. Many of the tests fail to meet the basic psychometric requirements related to validity and reliability.

Sit-Ups

Sit-ups have frequently been used as a measure of abdominal strength, endurance, or both. There is considerable variation in the way sit-ups are performed and scored (Table 8.1). Early tests involved straight-legged sit-ups with feet unsupported (American Association, 1957), whereas later tests incorporated bent-legged sit-ups with the feet supported (American Alliance, 1976). When the legs are straight or the feet supported, the hip flexors (especially iliopsoas) are considered to be primarily activated, rather than the abdominal muscles. If the tests are designed to measure abdominal strength or endurance, they are obviously testing an inappropriate muscle group. Strengthening, or measuring, the hip flexors is regarded by many health specialists to produce or exacerbate low back pain and postural deviations (especially lordosis). The evidence to support these contentions and concerns is somewhat limited. Jetté, Sidney, & Cicutti (1984) conducted a critical analysis of sit-ups, including those frequently used for testing. They completed an extensive literature review with special reference to studies that had used electromyographical (EMG) analyses to identify the muscles primarily activated under different sit-up protocols.

Jetté et al. (1984) concluded that there was a lack of evidence to clearly indicate the best procedure for "safely assessing (or improving) abdominal muscular endurance." Even clinical studies examining the detrimental effects of different sit-ups on the lumbar and cervical regions of the spine were limited and inconclusive. However, based on their review, Jetté et al. proposed that the most suitable procedure for evaluating abdominal muscular endurance was the partial curl-up. In the partial curl-up the subject begins in a supine position, knees bent at an angle of 140°, feet together, heels in contact with the ground, arms extended along the thighs, and fingers pointing toward the knees.

This is followed by flexion of the neck and a slow curling-up of the upper spine until the tips of the fingers touch the patella. At this point, the trunk should be raised at an angle of no greater than 30° to the floor. During the sit-up, the heels must remain in contact with the floor.

Using the procedures for the partial curl-up, Dickinson, Bannister, Allen, and Chapman (1984) conducted an independent study to evaluate the validity, reliability, objectivity, and safety of the test. Based on EMG data and radiographic analyses,

Table 8.1 Test Evaluation Criteria for Sit-Ups

Test description	Test battery	Validity (pop)	Reliability (pop)	Objectivity (pop)	References
Hands behind head; legs straight; 1-min speed	AAHPER (YFT)		.57 to .68 (150 grade 10 boys)		Klesius, 1968
Hands across chest; knees bent; feet braced; 1-min speed	AAHPER		.77 to .93 (545 boys) / .62 to .89 *(girls 11-14 yrs) / .68 to .94 (not reported)		Safrit & Wood, 1987 / Miller, 1988
2-min speed / Hands behind head; knees bent; feet unbraced		Face	.69 to .75 (high school boys) / .94 (not reported)	.98 (not reported)	Clarke & Clarke, 1987 / Johnson & Nelson, 1986
Hands behind head; knees bent; feet braced; 1-min speed	CAHPER (1966)		.86 (80 boys, 13-14 yrs)		Crawford, 1970
Legs straight; 2-min speed			.89 to .98 (152 boys, 10-17 yrs) (with practice 1 wk prior to test)		McGraw & McClenney, 1965
Partial curl-up; feet unbraced	CFA (1984)	Critical analysis EMG	.88 (43 school children)	.99 (43 school children)	Dickinson et al., 1984 / Jetté et al., 1984

*Intraclass correlation coefficient

they concluded that the partial curl-up is a valid and safe test for measuring abdominal muscular endurance. Using 43 school children, the same authors established a reliability coefficient of 0.88 and an objectivity coefficient of 0.99. Normative data (percentiles) were established from subsequent testing of 740 boys and 665 girls, aged 6 to 17 years, in Quebec, Ontario, and Manitoba (Massicotte, 1984).

A test of abdominal muscular endurance is considered preferable to testing hip flexors because the former is regarded as important in controlling excessive curvature of the lumbar spine. In contrast, because the psoas major and minor originate on the transverse processes of the lumbar vertebrae, they are considered to place stress on this area. It is possible that the curvature will be accentuated by inappropriate strengthening and conditioning of the iliopsoas muscle group. For some sports groups it may be appropriate to evaluate both the abdominal muscles and the hip flexors. However, if the test is to be used, particularly in a school environment, it should be a test of abdominal muscular endurance.

Pull-Ups

Pull-ups are usually incorporated into a fitness test battery as a measure of "arm and shoulder strength" (American Alliance, 1976). From previous discussion it was suggested that strength refers to a single maximal contraction. Once the student can do more than one pull-up the test is no longer a measure of strength but muscular endurance. This is particularly the case when the number of repetitions exceeds 10. Usually the overhand grip is advocated, which actually reduces the effectiveness of the biceps brachii in performing flexion of the arm and forearm. In the overhand grasp it is probable that the latissimus dorsi contributes most to the pull-up action. An undergrasp would primarily activate the biceps; the origin and insertion of the muscle are aligned, allowing for more direct generation of force.

The pull-up test has been extensively criticized as a test since many students are unable to successfully complete even one pull-up. Pate, Ross, Baumgartner, and Sparks (1987) reported that 30% of boys age 10 to 11 years and 60% of girls age 10 to 18 years scored zero on the pull-ups test (undergrasp) when administered as part of the National Children and Youth Fitness Test I. Ten percent of boys 9 to 17 years were also unable to perform one pull-up. Children who are unable to perform one pull-up have strength and endurance in the arms, but the test is obviously unable to measure it. The test has, therefore, been regarded as invalid since it eliminates a large proportion of people it is supposed to test. It may also be regarded as invalid if the objective of the test is to measure strength.

Validity of the test is also challenged in that students must lift (raise) their own body weight. To use pull-ups as a measure of absolute strength or endurance is invalid since body weight is inversely related to the number of pull-ups performed (Baumgartner & Jackson, 1987; Berger & Medlin, 1969). Children with large body mass would be considerably disadvantaged and may be unable to score above zero in the test. Woods, Pate, and Burgess (1992) found that laboratory measures of upper body muscular strength and endurance (1RM, sum 1RM, and endurance tests of 50% 1RM) failed to account for significant fractions of variance in performance in four of five field tests (pull-ups, New York modified pull-ups, flexed-arm hang, and push-ups). Only the Vermont modified pull-up (VMPU) attained a significant standardized regression coefficient (.40, p < .05). The results indicated that body fat significantly hindered performance in the field tests, even when controlled for body weight. Percent body fat explained from 9% to 35% of the variance in each of the five field-test measures of upper body muscular strength and endurance.

When the pull-ups tests have been successfully performed, reliability coefficients of .82 to .89 have been reported with boys 9 to 17 years as subjects (Klesius, 1968) (see Table 8.2). However, McGraw and McClenney (1965) found that performance consistently improved in boys 10 to 17 years over four trials even though the correlation coefficients from test to test were quite high (.89 to .98). There is, therefore, a significant practice effect on the performance of the pull-ups test.

A modified pull-up test was developed by Baumgartner and Wood (1978, 1984) and is included in the health-related fitness test battery. It is performed on an inclined board with a moveable scooter. Validity is enhanced because all students score above zero, and reliability has been estimated as high as .89 (Baumgartner & Wood, 1984). However, Erbaugh (1990) found an intraclass correlation coefficient of .52 and a total variance of 15% for trials and 41% for error for 26 boys and girls age 8.3 years (SD = 1.0).

The Vermont modified pull-up test was developed by Pate et al. (1987) and has been incorporated into the National Children and Youth Fitness Survey II (NCYFS II). The major features of the test are:

- The child is positioned on his or her back with the shoulders directly below a bar that is set at a height 1" or 2" beyond the child's reach.
- An elastic band is suspended across the uprights parallel to and about 7" to 8" below the bar.
- In the start (down) position, the child's buttocks are off the floor, the arms and legs are straight, and only the heels are in contact with the floor.
- An overhand grip (palm away from body) is used and thumbs are placed around the bar.
- A pull-up is completed when the chin is hooked over the elastic band. The movement should be accomplished using only the arms and the body must be kept straight.
- The child executes as many pull-ups as possible, keeping the hips and knees extended through each attempt.

The only reported estimate of validity has been provided by Woods et al. (1992), in which the VMPU obtained a .40 standardized regression coefficient with sum 1-RM (the composite score for bench press, forearm curl, and "lat" pull-down 1RM). However, such a regression coefficient only accounts for 16% mutual variance, reflecting a significant but weak relationship. In addition, the VMPU failed to account for any of the variance in the endurance score (the composite score for the tests using 50% of 1RM referred to as *sum end*). Coefficients for reliability and intertestor objectivity have not been reported.

Table 8.2   Test Evaluation Criteria for Pull-Ups and Flexed-Arm Hang (Arm/Forearm Flexions Endurance)

Test description	Test battery	Validity (pop)	Reliability (pop)	Objectivity (pop)	References
Overgrasp pull-ups	AAHPER (1976)	Face	.87 (not reported)	.99	Johnson & Nelson, 1986
		Face	.90* (not reported)		Miller, 1988
			.89 to .98 (152 boys 10-17 yrs) (incl. non sig t ratios)*		McGraw & McClenney, 1965
			.83 to .97 (high school boys)		Clarke & Clarke, 1987
			.82 to .96 (150 boys grade 10)		Klesius, 1968
Modified pull-ups	HRFT**	Face	.52*		Clarke & Clarke, 1987
			.89 to .91 (all ages)		Erbaugh, 1990
					Baumgartner & Woods, 1978, 1984
Modified pull-ups (VMPU)	NCYFS II		not reported		Pate et al., 1987
Flexed arm hang (undergrasp)	AAHPER	.40 (standard-ized regression with sum 1 RM, 56 girls and 38 boys 9-11 yrs)	.90 (not reported)		Woods et al., 1992
					Miller, 1988
	CAHPER (1966)		.75 (80 boys 13-14 yrs)	.99 (not reported)	Johnson & Nelson, 1986
			.90 (not reported)	.99	Crawford, 1970

*Intraclass correlation coefficient

**Health-related fitness test (HRFT)

The flexed-arm hang has been used to estimate local muscular endurance. Although it seems to have adequate reliability, the validity of the test can be challenged on the basis that body weight (especially body fat) is again a critical factor in performance (Woods et al., 1992). Most children can score within the test protocols because it is measured on the basis of how long the child is able to hold the criterion position on the chinning bar. However, it is essentially an isometric contraction that may restrict blood flow and impair the attribute that is being measured (i.e., local muscular endurance).

Push-Ups and Dips

Push-ups are frequently incorporated in test batteries as a means of assessing muscular endurance of the arms, in particular the extensors of the arms and forearms. Validity of the test is not reported in relation to any criterion test. There are some children who are unable to score one push-up, especially girls, which further challenges the validity of the test because many children will be excluded. The reliability coefficients are generally moderate-to-high but there is a potential practice effect in repeated trials (McGraw & McClenney, 1965). Some authors (Clarke & Clarke, 1987; Johnson & Nelson, 1986) report high objectivity coefficients (.93 = .99) but fail to provide details regarding the specific populations on which they were established. Push-ups as a test needs to be carefully administered from test to test and between testers; performance can be markedly affected by differences in protocol. Some researchers have used a metronome to set the cadence, permitting a clearer observation of adherence to the test protocol. However, this approach has not been empirically validated.

Modified push-ups, in which the knees are on the ground, are often utilized, especially for girls. Reliability coefficients of .83 to .97 have been suggested by Clarke and Clarke (1987) but population specifics are not provided. A validity coefficient of .78 with Rogers Short Index is reported by Johnson and Nelson (1986) based on an unpublished study (see Table 8.3).

Dips, using some form of parallel bars, also measure muscular endurance, especially of the forearm extensors (triceps). Validity coefficients are generally not reported. Johnson and Nelson (1986) report respective coefficients of .90 and .99 for reliability and objectivity but again do not provide details on their sources of information.

Standing Broad Jump and Vertical Jump (Leg Power)

Standing broad jump (SBJ) and vertical jump (VJ) are used to test muscular power, or explosive strength, of the extensor muscles of the thigh, leg, and foot. Validity has been reported as .61 with a "pure" test of power (Johnson & Nelson, 1986) and .79 with vertical jump as the criterion measure (Larson, 1974). However, as with pull-ups, body weight is a critical factor in performance when power is assessed as height or distance jumped. If power is to be measured as an absolute rather than a relative measure, body weight must be considered in determining performance.

Table 8.3   Test Evaluation Criteria for Push-Ups and Dips (Arm/Forearm Extensor Endurance)

Test description	Test battery	Validity (pop)	Reliability (pop)	Objectivity (pop)	References
Full push-ups (knees & hips off-ground)		Face	.69 to .97 (152 boys 10-17 yrs) *t* values sig different from test 1 to test 4		McGraw & McClenney, 1965
			.83 to .97 (not reported)	.93 (not reported)	Clarke & Clarke, 1987
				.99 (not reported)	Johnson & Nelson, 1986
Modified push-ups (knees on ground)		.78 (with Rogers Short Index)	.83 to .97 (not reported)		Clarke & Clarke, 1987
Dips (parallel bars)			.90 (not reported)	.99 (not reported)	Johnson & Nelson, 1986

Reliability coefficients are generally high (.93–.99) but based on a limited sample of Grade 10 boys (Klesius, 1968). An objectivity coefficient of .96 is supplied by Johnson and Nelson but without providing the source information and population specifics (see Table 8.4).

Vertical jump is often used in lieu of SBJ as a measure of muscular power. Larson (1974) reports a coefficient of .79 between SBJ and VJ, assuming either SBJ or VJ has established validity and can be used as a criterion measure for the other. However, no studies have examined the specific issue of validity for either test. Miller (1988) reports a correlation of .78 between VJ and performance in four power events in track and field, but does not elaborate on the specific events or population. It is possible to convert performance (height jumped) to power output in watts using the Lewis nomogram (Fox & Mathews, 1981). Converting height jumped into watts does take into account differences in body mass and enhances test validity. Procedures in test administration should be carefully followed.

Since height jumped is usually calculated as the difference between standing-reach height and the jump-and-reach height, it is important to ensure the subjects are in the full standing-reach position. In addition, during the jump-and-reach phase of the test there is considerable opportunity for intersubject variability in the way subjects mark their absolute jump-and-reach height. Variations in the administration of these parts of the test can lead to considerable error measurement among subjects. Reliability coefficients of .91 to .93, reported in several texts (Johnson & Nelson, 1986; Miller, 1988), suggest good intrasubject consistency. However, the texts fail to provide information related to the test-retest conditions or the specific populations.

Sit and Reach (Flexibility)

The sit-and-reach test is generally considered as a measure of low back and hamstring flexibility. It is frequently included in test batteries of health-related fitness due to the hypothesized relationship between low back pain and low back and hamstring flexibility (American Alliance, 1980). Jackson and Baker (1986) tested 100 young females ($\bar{X}$ age = 14.1 yr, SD = .83) to determine the relationship of sit and reach to criterion measures of low back and hamstring flexibility. They found a moderate relationship (r = .64) between the sit and reach and hamstring flexibility. Low relationships were found between sit and reach and total back flexibility (r = .07), upper back flexibility (r = −.16) and lower back flexibility (r = .28). They concluded that the sit and reach is not a valid assessment of back flexibility, including lower back flexibility, and is limited as a measure of hamstring flexibility (see Table 8.5).

The sit and reach test can also be challenged in regard to the relationship of limb length and stature to flexibility. Although relationships have been found to be low, various combinations of limb and trunk lengths can significantly affect test performance (Broer & Galles, 1958). This is an important consideration in testing children because the relationship between trunk and limb lengths changes during growth, and results on flexibility tests (especially using linear displacement) will be influenced by growth and development. Valid assessment is further compromised by the possible discrepancy in growth between bone and muscle length. The potential

Table 8.4　Test Evaluation Criteria for Standing Broad Jump and Vertical Jump (Leg Power)

Test description	Test battery	Validity (pop)	Reliability (pop)	Objectivity (pop)	References
Standing broad jump best of 3 trials	AAHPER (1976)	.61 (cp to "pure" power)	.96 (not reported)	.96 (not reported)	Johnson & Nelson, 1986
		Face	.83 to .99 (not reported) .93 to .99 (150 boys grade 10) .88		Miller, 1987 Klesius, 1968 Larson, 1974
		.79 (with vertical jump)			
	CAHPER (1966)		.83 (80 boys 13-14 yrs)		Crawford, 1970
Vertical jump		.78 (using 4 power events in track and field)	.93 (not reported)	.90 (not reported)	Miller, 1988
		.79 (with standing broad jump)	.93 (not reported) .84 (not reported) .91 (not reported)	.93 (not reported)	Johnson & Nelson, 1986 Larson, 1974 Clarke & Clarke, 1987

Table 8.5 Test Evaluation Criteria for Sit and Reach (Flexibility)

Test description	Test battery	Validity (pop)	Reliability (pop)	Objectivity (pop)	References
Sit and reach (using specially constructed box)	AAHPERD, HRFT (1980)	.64 (hamstrings) .07 (total back) −.16 (upper back) .28 (lower back)	.90* (100 girls 13-15 yrs)		Jackson & Baker, 1986
	AAHPERD, HRFT (1980)	Face	.90 .89 to .97* (545 boys) .80 to .85 (girls 11-14 yrs)		Clarke & Clarke, 1987 Safrit & Wood, 1987
		.80-.90 (not reported)	.70 (not reported)		Miller, 1988
	AAHPERD, HRFT (1980)	Face	.84 to .98 (not reported)		Johnson & Nelson, 1986

*Intraclass correlation coefficient

lag in muscle length was suggested as a possible explanation for the inverse relationship between flexibility and measures of morphological linearity found by Docherty and Bell (1985). It should also be remembered that flexibility is joint specific and inclusion of one test in a fitness test battery cannot be regarded as reflecting the subject's general flexibility (Harris, 1969; Hupprich & Sigerseth, 1950). Based on the concerns related to test validity, practitioners should use the sit-and-reach test with caution, especially if measuring flexibility of the lower back is the objective of the assessment (Jackson & Baker, 1986).

Shuttle Run and 50-m Dash (Agility and Speed)

The shuttle run and 50-yd (later changed to 50-m) dash have been included in the Youth Fitness Test (American Alliance, 1976) and the CAHPER Fitness-Performance Test (1966, 1980). The shuttle run is considered to measure agility, but leg power is also a significant factor in performance (Docherty and Collis, 1976). Although regarded as a measure of agility, there is little empirical evidence to support this contention. Van Mechelen, Hlobil, & Kemper (1986) found moderate correlations between the shuttle run and $\dot{V}O_2max$ (.68 = .69). Such a relationship suggests there is only 46% mutual variance and could be used to rationalize inclusion of both measures in a test battery. However, it does not validate the shuttle run as a measure of agility. Reliability coefficients have been reported between .46 to .94 (Marmis, Montoye, Cunningham, & Kozar, 1969; Klesius, 1968). However, Marmis et al. recommend at least two, and preferably three, practice trials (see Table 8.6).

The 50-m dash is included in most test batteries as a measure of running speed. Generally face validity is accepted for this test (Johnson & Nelson, 1986). No attempts were found to establish other forms of validity, such as criterion-related or construct validity. Reliability coefficients of .66 to .94 have been found for this test, but the test has been confined to boys. There was no reported practice effect for this test.

Skinfolds (Body Fat)

Body composition refers to the different tissues that compose the body mass, usually identified as muscle, fat, bone, and residual masses. However, the estimation of body fat has almost become synonymous with the concept of body composition. Estimation of body fat is included in most test batteries that purport to assess health-related fitness.

There appears to be considerable evidence to link obesity with increased morbidity and mortality (Going, 1988). Although most diseases become symptomatic in adulthood, there is evidence that the risk factors, including those associated with obesity, are present in children. Following a comprehensive review of studies, Going (1988, p. 33) concluded that ''With the overwhelming evidence of an association between obesity and an increased health risk and..., the assessment of body composition [sic, body fat] as part of youth fitness tests is clearly important.'' It is important to monitor body fat on a continuing basis throughout childhood and into adolescence.

Table 8.6 Test Evaluation Criteria for the Shuttle Run and 50-m Dash (Agility and Speed)

Test description	Test battery	Validity (pop)	Reliability (pop)	Objectivity (pop)	References
Shuttle run - 30 ft 4 times (best of 2 trials)	AAHPERD, YFT (1976)	Face	.68 to .75 (not reported) .68 to .94 (150 boys grade 10) .4 to .82 (2060 boys and girls 9-8 yrs)*		Miller, 1987 Safrit, 1986 Klesius, 1968 Marmis et al., 1969
		.68 to .69 $\dot{V}O_2$max, (82 boys and girls 12-14 yrs)			Van Mechelen et al., 1986
Shuttle run - 30 ft 2 times (best of 2 trials)	CAHPER, 1966		.71 (80 boys 13-14 yrs)		Crawford, 1970
50-yd dash	AAHPERD, YFT (1976)		.83 to .95 (not reported)		Safrit, 1986
	CAHPER (1966)	Face	.68 (80 boys 13-14 yrs) .66 to .94 (2060 boys 9-18 yrs) .83 to .94 (150 boys grade 10)		Johnson & Nelson, 1986 Crawford, 1970 Marmis et al., 1969 Klesius, 1968

*2 practice trials (3 recommended)

Table 8.7   Test Evaluation Criteria for Skinfolds (Body Fat)

Test description	Test battery	Validity (pop)	Reliability (pop)	Objectivity (pop)	References
Triceps and subscapular	AAHPERD, HRFT (1980)	Face	.94 to .98* (545 boys) .89 to .97 (girls 11-14 years)		Safrit & Wood, 1987
Triceps and subscapular	AAHPERD, HRFT (1980)	.78 to .85 (boys) .81 to .82 (girls 8-17 years) Concurrent % body fat for both sites .73 to .86 (hydrostatic weighing) .80 to .90 (hydrostatic weighing)			AAHPERD Technical Manual HRFT, 1984 Lohman et al., 1986 (reported by Going, 1988) Verducci, 1980
Triceps and calf	Physical Best	.78 to .85 (pre- and postpubertal boys) .83 to .88 (pre- and postpubertal girls) .76 to .83 (boys and girls 6-16 years) (hydrostatic weighing)			Slaughter et al., 1988 Harsha et al., 1978

Sum of skinfolds (triceps, subscapular, biceps, suprailiac)	Manitoba (1977, 1989)	R = .91 to .96 (boys and girls 11-13 years) (sum of skinfolds)	Nelson & Nelson, 1986
		.87 to .91 (boys 13.03 years) (hydrostatic weighing)	Mukherje & Roche, 1984
		Content validity	Manitoba Education, 1977 Manitoba Education, 1989
O scale			Ross & Ward, 1984

*Intraclass correlation coefficient

The commonly regarded criterion for estimating percent body fat is based on hydrostatic weighing, in which total body density is determined. Using a two-component model, a fat mass and fat-free mass are estimated, assuming the densities of both components are known and constant. Such an assumption has been questioned through the cadaver studies of Martin (1984). However, hydrostatic weighing continues to be regarded by many authors as the best technique for determining percent body fat. Since hydrostatic weighing is impractical for large numbers, alternate measurement techniques must be used. Skinfold thickness is an inexpensive and practical means of estimating total body fat. Several authors have reported moderate to high correlations (.70–.91) between skinfolds (triceps and subscapular) and percent body fat (Boileau et al., 1984; Lohman, 1986, Slaughter et al., 1984). However, it is important to note that adult equations for predicting percent body fat are inappropriate for children. Children have a lower bone mineral content and higher water content than adults, which leads to an overestimation of children's percent body fat if adult equations are used, especially with prepubertal populations (Lohman, 1986). Slaughter et al. (1988) have developed newer equations that take into account the differences in density of the fat-free mass. Lohman (1987) has provided charts that classify body fat from very low to very high based on skinfolds (triceps and subscapular) and percent body fat (Figure 8.1). The charts are useful in identifying children at risk and also negate the necessity to convert skinfold thickness to an estimate of percent body fat (see Table 8.7, pp. 308-309).

The Physical Best test battery (American Alliance, 1989) has replaced the subscapular skinfold site with a medial calf skinfold to eliminate any problems that might be associated with subscapular measurement in large groups and mixed sexes. The triceps and calf skinfolds are considered good predictors of percent body fat (Murkhejee and Roche, 1984; Nelson & Nelson, 1986; Slaughter et al., 1988). Lohman (1987) also provides a classification chart based on the sum of the triceps and medial calf skinfolds (Figure 8.1). However, in adults, fat distribution, especially trunk fat, is considered to be related to health risk (Bray & Bouchard, 1988; Canadian Standardized Fitness Test, 1986). Omission of the subscapular skinfold may detract from the construct validity of skinfolds as a relevant measure in a health-related fitness test. Content validity may also be threatened by exclusion of a trunk skinfold measurement (Going, 1988). Safrit and Wood (1987) and Shaw (1986) have reported good test reliability for the triceps and subscapular skinfold measurements (.89 = .98), including intraclass correlation coefficients. Going (1988) also suggests that the objectivity of skinfold measurements is good when standardized measurement procedures are followed, although no empirical support for such a statement is provided.

The Manitoba Test Battery (Manitoba Education, 1977) uses the sum of four skinfolds (biceps, triceps, subscapular, and suprailiac) to reflect body fat. However, little empirical support, especially related to children, is provided to justify the selection of these sites.

The O-scale (Ross & Ward, 1984) was developed as a means of assessing body composition and avoiding the problems associated with the prediction of body fat

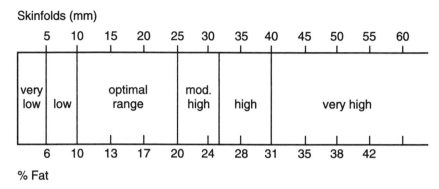

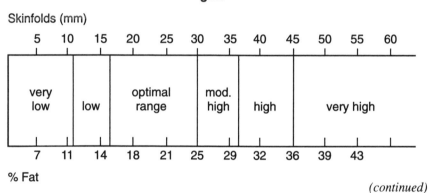

Figure 8.1 Risk associated with skinfold measurements.
Reprinted from Lohman (1987).

from hydrostatic weighing. It is based on a measure of adiposity (calculated from the sum of six skinfolds corrected for height) and proportional weight (pWT)

$$pWT = Wt \times \left(\frac{170 \cdot 18}{Ht}\right)^3.$$

The two scores are expressed as stanines (0-9) and interpreted in relation to each other. For example, a high score on proportional weight (> 7.0) implies the individual is heavy relative to height. A low score on adiposity (< 3.5) indicates that the mass is nonfat.

Distance Runs (Cardiorespiratory or Aerobic Fitness)

Cardiorespiratory fitness can be considered to have construct validity when used as part of a health-related fitness test battery. Several authors suggest that training of

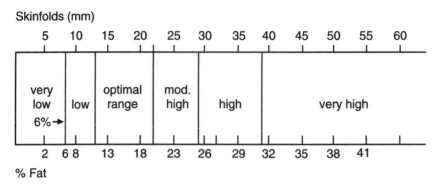

**Triceps plus subscapular skinfolds
boys**

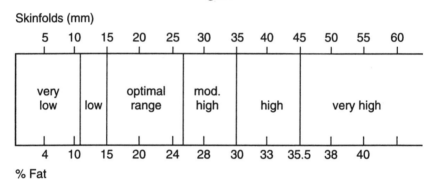

**Triceps plus subscapular skinfolds
girls**

Figure 8.1 *(continued)*

the cardiorespiratory, or aerobic, system is important to reduce the risk of coronary heart disease (Wood, Williams, & Haskell, 1984). It is also proposed that coronary heart disease has pediatric origins (Vaccaro & Mahon, 1989). It would, therefore, seem appropriate to include a measure of cardiorespiratory fitness in a test battery used to assess health status and provide exercise counseling.

Measurement of maximal oxygen consumption ($\dot{V}O_2$max) is generally regarded as the most precise and valid method of assessing cardiorespiratory (or aerobic) fitness (Åstrand & Rodahl, 1977; Cooper, 1968). However, the equipment costs and expertise required to measure $\dot{V}O_2$max are not feasible for testing large populations in a school environment. A variety of distance runs are used to reflect the cardiorespiratory fitness of children (see Table 8.8). Safrit, Hooper, Ehlert, Costa, and Patterson (1988) examined the validity generalization of the various studies that used distance runs and maximal oxygen uptake ($\dot{V}O_2$max) on a treadmill. The intent of this approach was to determine the generalizability of the validity of distance runs as measures of cardiorespiratory fitness. From analysis of five studies for girls and eight studies for boys Safrit et al. concluded that validity of distance runs might be generalizable for boys and girls. However, the authors suggest the results should be interpreted with caution owing to small sample sizes and the shortness (less than 1K) of the distance runs.

The mean "true validity" coefficients were .71 and .78 for girls and boys, respectively (Safrit et al., 1988). Table 8.8 shows the test evaluation criteria for distance runs. Validity correlation coefficients generally range from .70 to .82 among the various distance runs and $\dot{V}O_2$max, with the notable exceptions of .22 and .26 for the 1.2K and 1.6K runs for 8-year-old girls (Krahenbuhl, Pangrazi, Burkett, Schneider, & Peterson, 1977). There is a general trend for the correlation coefficients to increase with distance from .22 to .76, with the 1600m distance proving to be the best predictor of $\dot{V}O_2$max for both boys and girls (Krahenbuhl, Pangrazi, Burkett, Peterson, Burkett & Schneider, 1978).

It may be concluded that distance runs are useful tests of cardiorespiratory fitness for young children. However, there is considerable variance that is unaccounted for, and further studies need to be conducted to determine the optimal distance and practice conditions that most accurately reflect this important aspect of fitness.

The multistage 20-m shuttle run test has been proposed as a valid and reliable method for evaluating functional maximal aerobic power (Léger & Galboury, 1989; Léger & Lambert, 1982; Léger, Mercier, Lambert, & Garboury, 1984). The test involves running back and forth as long as possible in a 20-m course. Speed starts at 7.5 km·hr^{-1} and is increased every minute by .5 km·hr^{-1} until the student is unable to maintain the pace or voluntarily withdraws from the test. A validity coefficient of .70 with $\dot{V}O_2$max has been reported for 188 boys and girls, 8 to 19 years of age (Mercier, Léger, & Lambert, 1983) and a reliability coefficient of .89 (Léger & Godbois, 1983). The test has these possible advantages over distance runs: It can be administered indoors, is less dependent on pacing, and is of relatively short duration. However, the validity coefficient of .70 still only accounts for approximately 50% of the variance.

Anderson (1992) determined the validity of using the 1600m distance run and the multistage shuttle run as predictors of aerobic [capacity] in active boys, 10 to 12 years of age. Both field tests were related to $\dot{V}O_2$ max (−.83 and .72, respectively, for the distance run and shuttle run) but the predicted $\dot{V}O_2$max values from the shuttle run differed significantly from the measured values. Anderson suggested that running efficiency and the utilization of anaerobic energy sources may account for the differences in performance between the field and laboratory measures of aerobic [capacity]. It should be noted that in the shuttle run test a "person trained in running the shuttle run serves as a visual pacing cue by running with the children," but such a strategy was not employed for the 1600m distance run. The effect of pacing on performance in both field tests should be further investigated.

GENERAL CRITIQUE AND CONCERNS

The components of fitness have been discussed and evaluated for their validity, reliability, and objectivity. There are several concerns resulting from the analysis

Table 8.8 Test Evaluation Criteria for Distance Runs (Cardiovascular/Aerobic Fitness)

Test description	Test battery	Validity (pop)	Reliability (pop)	Objectivity (pop)	References
6 min	AAHPERD HRFT (1980)	.71 to .82 ($\dot{V}O_2$max, 22 boys and 25 girls 9-11 yrs)			Jackson & Coleman, 1976
		.71 to .82 ($\dot{V}O_2$max, 38 boys and girls 8 yrs)			Krahenbuhl et al., 1977
9 min	EUROFIT (1988)	.70 (with 1000m)	.87 (not reported)		Van Mechelin et al., 1988
			.61 to .90* (545 boys and girls 11-14 yrs)		Safrit & Wood, 1987
12 min	AAHPERD HRFT (1980)	.90 ($\dot{V}O_2$max, 9 boys 14 yrs)	.94 (150 boys grade 9)		Doolittle & Bigbee, 1968
		.75 ($\dot{V}O_2$max, 15 boys and girls 11 yrs)			Gutin et al., 1976
		.71 to .82 ($\dot{V}O_2$max, 22 boys and girls 9-11 yrs)			Jackson & Coleman, 1976
		.65 ($\dot{V}O_2$max, 17 boys 11-14 yrs)	.92		Maksud & Coutts, 1971
			.94 (not reported)		Miller, 1988 and Johnson & Nelson, 1986

Test	Test/Norm	Value	Reference
1200 yds (1097 m)		.81 (V̇O₂max, 15 boys and girls 11 yrs)	Gutin et al., 1976
		.64 (V̇O₂max, 20 boys 8 yrs)	Krahenbuhl et al., 1977
		.22 (V̇O₂max, 18 boys 8 yrs)	Krahenbuhl et al., 1977
1800 yds (1646 m)		.76 (V̇O₂max, 15 boys and girls 10 yrs)	Gutin et al., 1977
1 mile (1609 m)		.66 (V̇O₂max, 140 boys and 56 girls 10 yrs)	Cureton et al., 1977
		.71 (V̇O₂max, 20 boys 8 yrs)	Krahenbuhl et al., 1977
		.26 (V̇O₂max, 18 girls 8 yrs)	Krahenbuhl et al., 1977
500 meters	Manitoba (1977)	.80-.90 (161 girls 12-19 yrs)	Beunen et al., 1977
	CAHPER (1980)	.22-.50 (V̇O₂max, 49 boys and 34 girls grades 1-3)	Krahenbuhl et al., 1978
1000 meters		.77-.89 (174 boys 12-19 yrs)	Beunen et al., 1977

(continued)

Table 8.8 (*continued*)

Test description	Test battery	Validity (pop)	Reliability (pop)	Objectivity (pop)	References
1200 meters	Manitoba (1977)	.23 to .47 ($\dot{V}O_2$max, 49 boys and 34 girls grades 1-3)			Krahenbuhl et al., 1978
	Manitoba (1989)	.60 to .76 ($\dot{V}O_2$max, 49 boys and 34 girls grades 1-3)			
1600 meters	CAHPER (1980)		.82-.92 (120 boys and girls grades 1-3)		Krahenbuhl et al., 1978
Shuttle run (20 meters, multistage, 1 min)		.70 ($\dot{V}O_2$max, 108 boys and girls 8-19 yrs) .71 ($\dot{V}O_2$max, 13 boys 10-12 yrs)	.89 (139 boys and girls 6-16 years)		Leger & Godbois, 1982 (unpublished data) Mercier et al., 1983 Anderson, 1992
Shuttle run (20 meters, multistage, 2 min)	EUROFIT (1988)	.97 (not reported)	.84 (not reported)		Van Gerven et al., 1982

*2 practice trials (3 recommended)

that should be addressed prior to consideration of test batteries that have been developed to assess the fitness of children and youth.

Validity

Validity can be determined by the use of several techniques. For many of the fitness-performance test items, face or logical validity appears to be the most prevalent method. Although it appears obvious that some tests are measures of what they purport to measure (e.g., 50-yard dash as a measure of speed), the relationship is less clear in many of the test items. Seldom is criterion-related validity used for fitness-performance tests, in part a problem of identifying appropriate criterion measures. It should also be remembered that validity may not be generalizable across age and gender. A test that is found to have good criterion-related validity for a specific age and gender population may not retain its validity when used with a different age and gender population. Validity, therefore, should be obtained for a test with consideration of the age and gender groups with whom it is likely to be used. However, other forms of determining validity could be used, but frequently are omitted. Tests are usually incorporated into test batteries to either predict future performance (as in motor-performance test batteries) or assess current status of fitness (as in health-related test batteries).

In most test batteries that assess motor performance there is little attempt to determine the effectiveness of predicting future behavior or distinguish among groups of different athletic capabilities. For example, how effective is performance on push-ups or standing broad jump in predicting future athletic success? What do they really tell the instructor about the fitness of the individual? There are some basic questions that need to be resolved before more tests and test batteries are designed to assess fitness performance. It should be possible to utilize construct validity techniques in selecting specific test items and developing test batteries.

There is also the additional problem of overlap among test items in test batteries as reflected by intercorrelation coefficients. Docherty and Collis (1976) found the CAHPER Fitness Performance Test (1966, 1980) to be dominated by tests that were dependent upon explosive leg strength (power). Test batteries must be evaluated to ensure that the tests within them are independent and do not contain unnecessary duplication. Such an analysis is seldom reported.

The problem of validity of specific test items has been more extensively addressed in health-related fitness tests, especially in the areas of body composition (body fat) and cardiorespiratory fitness. There is considerable support for inclusion of body fat and cardiorespiratory assessment in health-related fitness test batteries because both components are considered to be coronary heart disease risk factors. Therefore, they can be regarded as having construct validity in relation to health. In addition, the field tests used to evaluate body fat and cardiorespiratory fitness have been validated against concurrent criterion measures. It would be desirable to have a higher relationship between the field tests of cardiorespiratory fitness and the criterion ($\dot{V}O_2max$), but the relationship is generally regarded as acceptable. There is also some debate about the legitimacy of hydrostatic weighing as the criterion measure for body composition. However, sum of skinfolds is an acceptable method of assessing body fat and negates the need for converting to estimations of percent body fat.

Flexibility is often justified as a component of health-related fitness based on the possible relationship of hamstring and lower back flexibility to low back pain, although this assumption has been questioned by Dr. Alf Nachemson, a leader in the field of low back pain (Nachemson, 1991). The sit-and-reach test currently used to assess this aspect of fitness lacks criterion-related validity. In addition, the sit-and-reach test cannot be rationalized as a general assessment of flexibility. Neither does it appear to be related to performance or the reduction of injury (Hubley, 1991).

Reliability

Reliability of tests has received considerably more attention than the validity of tests as evidenced in Tables 8.1-8.8. This is particularly true for tests related to motor-fitness performance that generally appear to have good reliability based on test–retest conditions. However, it should be noted that most studies use interclass correlation coefficients that are not sensitive to actual shifts in performance and do not reflect the effects of practice or number of trials on performance. Analysis of the populations on which the reliability coefficients were determined, as shown in Tables 8.1-8.3, indicates a limited sampling of age and gender. Reliability for fitness tests could be gender and age specific. Future studies examining the reliability of tests should use intraclass correlation coefficients (or similar statistics sensitive to performance changes, the effects of practice, the effects of the number of trials) and ensure there is comprehensive population sampling in relation to sex and age. Most textbooks on measurement and evaluation in physical education fail to report details with reference to the determination of validity and reliability.

Objectivity

Objectivity refers to the ability of two different test administrators to produce the same results on an individual. Good test objectivity is closely related to the clarity of the test protocol and the precision of scoring. It also depends on the test administrator's rigor in ensuring standardized procedures are closely followed. Many of the motor-fitness performance and health-related fitness tests are deceptively simple to administer. However, results will be markedly affected by the way in which procedures are followed. Speed tests requiring maximum repetitions in specific time periods can be difficult to control. For example, maximum speed sit-ups often result in excessive arm action, raising of hips to facilitate trunk flexion, and the use of momentum from the mat to help the sit-up action. Other tests such as push-ups, pull-ups, and vertical jumps also require careful enforcement of test protocols if the measurement is to remain consistent between different testers. Skinfold measurement is also a deceptively simple test, but requires accurate location of the specific sites and considerable experience in applying the correct amount of pressure in the "pinch" phase and placement of the calipers.

Few, if any, tests provide objectivity coefficients, assuming the tests can be effectively administered without training or experience. Test objectivity is a critical consideration in test selection and application because the tests are often administered by individuals with considerably different levels of testing knowledge and experience. Development of tests and test batteries must consider the potential users of the test and the level of skill required for correct administration of the test.

Based on the current review there are few, if any, tests that have proven validity, reliability, and objectivity. Before selecting specific tests, there should be a comprehensive evaluation to ensure all criteria are satisfactorily met. Where criteria are lacking or omitted, comprehensive studies need to be conducted, including representative population sampling.

FITNESS TEST BATTERIES

Numerous test batteries have been developed to assess fitness of children and youth (see Tables 8.9-8.11 on pp. 322-327). The test batteries are usually purported to motivate participants to engage in a physically active lifestyle to increase their fitness and health. In addition, some batteries have been developed to provide normative data regarding fitness performance. Such information can be used to compare different populations within and between countries and to monitor secular trends related to fitness. The historical perspective on the evolution of fitness test batteries reflects the trend of changing from a motor-fitness performance concentration to one that focuses on health-related fitness. Some test batteries (such as Eurofit) have attempted to serve both purposes. Addresses for obtaining the various fitness test batteries can be found in Appendix 8.1.

Tables 8.9 to 8.11 show the various components that are generally included in the test batteries used to measure the fitness of children and youth. There is some disagreement regarding the components to include in a health-related fitness battery. Most researchers agree on the inclusion of some form of assessment for cardiorespiratory fitness and body composition (especially body fat). The other components are important in motor-fitness performance and may be included in health-related fitness. Those batteries with a health-related fitness focus are identified with an asterisk (*). Also indicated in the tables is whether the test items in the battery are norm or criterion referenced.

As previously noted, norm-referenced tests need to be interpreted with caution if they are used to promote fitness or an active lifestyle. When tests are used for personal goal setting or to monitor secular trends, it is not necessary to convert the raw scores to normative scales or values. If scores are converted to normative values, the developmental level of the child must be considered. Some of the test batteries have provided criterion-referenced standards but often fail to provide a rationale for the specific levels of acceptability. The Physical Best (AAHPERD, 1988) and Fit Youth Today (American Health and Fitness Foundation, 1986) are exceptions and attempt to rationalize the standards. However, the standards are generally based on levels of fitness "thought to be associated with minimal health risk" (AAHPERD, 1988). The FYT provides a criterion standard for the "steady state jog" test based on a duration and intensity that is considered to produce the minimum energy expenditure needed to develop and maintain aerobic fitness. Unfortunately, this does not really establish a fitness level compatible with health or decreasing CHD risk factors. Obviously there needs to be continued research to try to identify standards that are associated with optimal health or potential CHD risk factors. Until such standards are established, the current practices must suffice but the users must be aware of the inherent limitations.

Several of the health-related fitness tests have incorporated recognition systems for a commitment to exercise behavior as well as fitness achievement. Because any level of fitness is transient, it is educationally more desirable to motivate children to adopt "healthy" exercise habits than to acclaim current fitness. The Physical Best program includes several awards: "Physical Activity" for a commitment to physical activity outside of the physical education program; "Fitness Goals" for the achievement of cognitive, affective, and/or psychomotor goals; and "Health Fitness" for reaching criterion-referenced standards. The Fitnessgram (Cooper Institute for Aerobics Research, 1987) also includes similar awards: the "Get Fit" award for committing to a 6-week program of fitness activities; the "I'm Fit" award for achieving specific fitness levels on five test items; and the "Fit for Life" award that recognizes children or adults who have shown commendable exercise behavior. The recently developed Canadian Active Living Challenge (Fitness Canada, 1993) also rewards a commitment to active living or exercise behavior. It has been developed to replace the Canadian Fitness Award (1984) program that was based solely on fitness performance or status. Reward systems that recognize a personal commitment to activity attempt to reinforce exercise behavior on the assumption that this will have greater long term effects into adulthood. Unfortunately, the effectiveness of such programs has not been empirically determined but they are worthy in their intent.

Most of the test items included in the fitness test batteries have been reviewed in the previous discussion on "Evaluation of Specific Test Items." The reader should be able to evaluate the content validity of the specific test batteries based on the comprehensiveness of the test items. The ecological validity (i.e., appropriateness of the test battery to assess or predict health) must be judged by the individual reader and related to the purpose(s) of testing. Similarly, the validity of motor-fitness performance tests must be judged in regard to the type of information they provide and the purpose(s) of testing. The assumption that motor-fitness performance is related to sport performance or provides a foundation for skill development has not been empirically established.

CONCLUSION

The current assessments of health-related fitness and the inclusion of criterion-referenced standards are obviously not without problems. A major criticism is that the developers of test batteries have largely failed to attend to the basics of good test construction. As Seefeldt and Vogel (1989) conclude, the construct of physical fitness needs to be operationally defined, the specific components identified, valid tests developed to measure the components, and criterion standards established that are empirically defensible.

There is some evidence to suggest that tests can be effective in promoting and enhancing the fitness of children and youth. Pate (1989) makes a good case for the continuation for physical fitness testing provided certain conditions are met. The conditions he outlines are summarized below.

1. Fitness tests must be integrated into the curriculum and used as a pedagogical tool.
2. Testing should be only one component of a comprehensive fitness education program.
3. Fitness testing should emphasize health-related fitness.
4. Fitness tests must be administered in a caring, sensitive, and positive manner.
5. Results of fitness tests must be interpreted for students and parents in a meaningful way.
6. If reward systems are used, they must be motivating for all students.

Criterion-referenced standards are currently, at best, based on arbitrary criteria rather than empirically determined relationships to health or health-risk factors. These relationships must be clearly established. Until this happens authors of fitness programs must more clearly acknowledge the limited basis on which the criterion-standards have been established.

It is encouraging that there has been a shift from normative-referenced criteria to criterion-referenced standards and reward systems that recognize exercise behavior. Most of the recognition systems described in this chapter are designed to reward the development and attainment of appropriate fitness behaviors, individual improvement based on goal setting and achievement, and the achievement of standards considered compatible with health. This approach is certainly more appropriate to the encouragement of a physically active lifestyle than are systems that simply reward achievement, especially achievement based on normative standards of performance.

Table 8.9   Fitness Test Batteries Most Common in United States

Test battery	Anthropometric measurements	Body composition	Cardiorespiratory	Flexibility	Speed	Agility and balance	Muscular endurance	Strength	Power (explosive strength)
AAHPERD Youth Fitness Test (norm-referenced)			options: 600-yd run 1600-m or 9-min run; 2400-m or 12-min run (13-17 yrs)		50-yd run	Shuttle run	pull-ups (boys); flexed-arm hang (girls); 1-min sit-ups (feet braced)		standing long jump
*AAHPERD Health-related fitness test (norm-referenced)		Sum of skin-folds (tri-ceps & subscapular)	1600-m or 9-min run; 2400-m or 12-min run	Sit and reach			1-min sit-ups (feet braced)		
*AAHPERD Physical Best (criterion-referenced)		Sum of skin-folds (tri-ceps & calf) options: Sum of tri-ceps & subscapular; Body mass index	1600-m run options: 800-m run (younger) 2400-m run (older)	Sit and reach			pull-ups; 1-min sit-ups (feet braced)		

Fitnessgram (norm-referenced)	Sum of skinfolds (triceps and calf); Body mass index (option)	1600-m run	Sit and reach	Shuttle run (optional)	pull-ups; flexed-arm hang (optional); 1-min sit-ups (feet braced)
Fit Youth Today (criterion-on-referenced)	Sum of skinfolds (triceps and calf)	20-min steady-state jog	Sit and reach		2-min sit-ups (feet braced)
Get Fit (norm-referenced)		1600-m run	V-sit and reach; Sit and reach (optional)	Shuttle	pull-ups; 1-min sit-ups (feet braced)

*Health-related fitness test

Table 8.10 Fitness Test Batteries Most Common in Canada

Test battery	Anthropometric measurements	Body composition	Cardiorespiratory	Flexibility	Speed	Agility and balance	Muscular endurance	Strength	Power (explosive strength)
Canada Fitness Award (norm-referenced)			800-m run (6-9 yrs); 1600-m run; (10-12 yrs); 2400-m run (13-17 yrs)		50-m run	Shuttle run	Partial curl-ups		Standing long jump
CAHPER Fitness Performance Test II (norm-referenced)	Height Weight		800-m run (6-9 yrs); 1600-m run (10-12 yrs) 2400-m run (13-17 yrs)		50-m run	Shuttle run	1-min speed sit-ups (feet braced); Flexed-arm hang		Standing long jump
MANITOBA Fitness Performance (norm-referenced)	Height Weight	Sum of skinfolds (biceps, triceps, subscapular, and suprailiac; Percent body fat (13-18 yrs)		Sit and reach		Shuttle run	1-min speed sit-ups (feet braced); Flexed-arm hang		

*MANITOBA Schools Fitness 1989 (Criterion referenced)	(Optional) Height Weight	(Optional) Sum of skinfolds (triceps, biceps, suprailiac, (two-site and four-site methods)	1600-m run	Sit and reach	Push-ups and modified push-ups; 1-min sit-ups (feet braced)	
*Canadian Standardized Test of Fitness (norm-referenced); Skinfolds are criterion-referenced	Height Weight Girths (chest, waist, hip, and thigh)	Sum of five skinfolds (triceps, biceps, suprailiac, subscapular, medial calf); Body mass index; Sum of two trunk skinfolds; Waist–hip rates	Canadian Aerobic Fitness Test (CAFT)	Sit and reach (feet braced)	Push-ups; Modified push-ups; 1-min sit-ups	Grip strength

*Health-related fitness test

Table 8.11   Fitness Test Batteries from Australia, New Zealand, and Europe

Country, test battery	Anthropometric measurements	Body composition	Cardiorespiratory	Flexibility	Speed	Agility and balance	Muscular endurance	Strength	Power (explosive strength)
*Australia Field tests (Health and Fitness Survey, 1985)	Height; Weight; Girths (arm, waist, hip)		1.6-km run	Sit and reach	50-m run		Sit-ups (partial curl-ups); Push-ups (on chair)		Standing long jump
**New Zealand Test of Health-related fitness, 1989 (norm-referenced)	Height; Weight	Sum of skinfolds (triceps and subscapular)	9-min run (6,8 yrs); 12-min run (10,12,14 yrs) Optional CAFT	Sit and reach			Otago curl-ups		

Europe								
Eurofit	Height; Weight	Sum of skin-folds (biceps, triceps, subscapular, suprailiac, and medial calf)	PWC$_{170}$; Endurance shuttle run	Sit and reach	10 × 5-m shuttle; Plate tapping	Flamingo balance	Sit-ups (feet braced)	Hand grip	Standing broad jump

(no norm-reference)

*This test battery also has a series of laboratory tests.
**Health-related fitness test

Appendix 8.1

Sources of Fitness Test Batteries

Test	Address
AAHPER Youth Fitness Test Manual (1976)	AAHPERD 1900 Association Drive Reston, Virginia 22091 U.S.A.
AAHPERD Health-Related Fitness Test (1980)	AAHPERD 1900 Association Drive Reston, Virginia 22091 U.S.A.
AAHPERD Physical Best (1988)	AAHPERD 1900 Association Drive Reston, Virginia 22091 U.S.A.
Fitnessgram (Cooper Institute for Aerobics Research, 1987)	FITNESSGRAM Cooper Institute for Aerobics Research 12330 Preston Road Dallas, Texas 75230 U.S.A.
"Get Fit" (1987)	President's Council on Physical Fitness and Sports 450 - 5th Street N.W. Suit 7103 Washington, D.C. 20001 U.S.A.
Canada Fitness Awards (1984)	Fitness and Amateur Sport 365 Laurier Avenue West Ottawa, Ontario K1A 0X6 Canada
CAHPER Fitness Performance Test II (1980)	CAHPER 1600 James Naismith Drive Gloucester, Ontario K1B 5N4 Canada
Manitoba Fitness Performance (1977)	Physical Education Consultant 409-1181 Portage Avenue

	Winnipeg, Manitoba R3G 0T3 Canada
Manitoba Schools Fitness (1989)	Physical Education Consultant 409-1181 Portage Avenue Winnipeg, Manitoba R3G 0T3 Canada
Canadian Standardized Test of Fitness (CSTF) (1986)	Canadian Society for Exercise Physiology 1600 James Naismith Drive Suite 311 Gloucester, Ontario K1B 5N4 Canada
Australian Health Fitness Survey (ACHPER, 1985)	Australian Council for Health, Physical Recreation Inc. 128 Glen Osmond Road Parkside South Australia Australia 5063
New Zealand Fitness Test Handbook (Russell, 1989)	Education Officer, P.E. Curriculum Development Division Department of Education Private Box 1379 Government Buildings Wellington, New Zealand
Eurofit (1988)	EUROFIT (European Test of Physical Fitness) Council of Europe Committee for the Development of Sport Rome: Edigrat Editionale Grafica
Canadian Active Living Challenge	Canadian Active Living Challenge CIRA/CAHPERD 1600 James Naismith Drive Gloucester, Ontario K1B 5N4 Canada
Fit Youth Today (FYT)	American Health and Fitness Foundation 6225 U.S. Highway 290 East Suite 114 Austin, Texas 78723 U.S.A.

REFERENCES

American Alliance for Health, Physical Education, Recreation, and Dance (1988). *Physical Best: The American Alliance physical fitness education and assessment program.* Reston, VA: Author.

American Alliance for Health, Physical Education, Recreation, and Dance (1976). *Youth fitness test manual.* Reston, VA: Author.

American Alliance for Health, Physical Education, Recreation, and Dance (1980). *AAHPERD health-related fitness test.* Reston, VA: Author.

American Association for Health, Physical Education, and Recreation (1957). *Youth fitness test manual.* Washington: NEA Publications.

American Health and Fitness Foundation. (1986). *Fit Youth Today.* Austin, TX: Author.

Anderson, G.S. (1992). The 1600 m run and multistage 20 m shuttle run as predictive tests of aerobic capacity in children. *Pediatric Exercise Science, 4,* 302-311.

Astrand, P. and Rodahl, K. (1977). *Textbook of work physiology.* New York: McGraw-Hill.

Bailey, D.A., & Mirwald, E.L. (1978). A children's test of fitness. *Medicine in Sport, 11,* 56-64.

Baumgartner, T.A., & Jackson, A.S. (1987). *Measurement for evaluation in physical education and exercise science.* Dubuque, IA: Brown.

Baumgartner, T.A., & Wood, S.S. (1978). Modified pull-up test. *Research Quarterly, 49,* 80-84.

Baumgartner, T.A., & Wood, S.S. (1984). Development of shoulder-girth strength-endurance in elementary children. *Research Quarterly of Exercise and Sport, 55,* 169-171.

Berger, R.A., & Medlin, R.L. (1969). Evaluation of Berger's IRM chin test for junior high males. *Research Quarterly, 40,* 460-463.

Beunen, G., Van Gerven, D., & Vanden Eynde, B. (1977). Reliability of three cardiorespiratory field tests. In H. Lavalle and R.J. Shephard (Eds.), *Frontiers of Activity and Child Health* (pp. 75-81). Quebec: Editions du Pelican.

Boileau, R.A., Lohman, T.G., Slaughter, M.H., Ball, T.E., Going, S.B., & Hendrix, M.K. (1984). Hydration of the fat-free body in children during maturation. *Human Biology, 56,* 651-666.

Bray, G.A., & Bouchard, C. (1988). Role of fat distribution during growth and its relationship to health. *American Journal of Clinical Nutrition, 47,* 551-552.

British Columbia Assessment of Physical Education 1979 (1979). Learning Assessment Branch, Ministry of Education, Province of British Columbia.

Broer, M.R., & Galles, N.R. (1958). Importance of relationship between various body measurements in performance of the toe-touch test. *Research Quarterly, 29,* 253-263.

CAHPER Fitness Performance II: Test Manual (1980). Canadian Association for Health, Physical Education and Recreation.

CAHPER Fitness Performance Test (1966). Canadian Association of Health, Physical Education and Recreation.

Canadian Association of Health, Physical Education and Recreation. (1968). *The physical work capacity of canadian children: 7-17 years* Ottawa, ON: Author.

Canada Fitness Award Manual (1984). Fitness Canada, Government of Canada Fitness and Amateur Sport.

Canadian Standardized Test of Fitness: Operations Manual (1986). Third Edition. Fitness and Amateur Sport, Government of Canada.

Clarke, H.H. (1973). Individual differences, their nature, extent, and significance. *Physical Fitness Research Digest,* Series 3 (4).

Clarke, H.H., & Clarke, D.H. (1987). *Application of measurement to physical education* (6th ed.). Englewood Cliffs, NJ: Prentice Hall.

Cooper Institute for Aerobics Research. (1987). *Fitnessgram.* Dallas: Author.

Cooper, K.H. (1968). A means of assessing maximal oxygen intake. *Journal of the American Medical Association, 203,* 125-138.

Corbin, C.B., Whitehead, J.R., & Lovejoy, P.Y. (1988). Youth physical fitness awards. *Quest, 40,* 200-218.

Crawford, G.L. (1970). *A reliability study of the CAHPER fitness-performance test.* Thesis, University of Victoria, Victoria, BC.

Dahlgren, W.J. (1983). CAHPER Fitness Performance, Test, Canada Fitness Award, and PWC$_{170}$: What's the difference? *CAHPER Journal, 49,* 23.

Dickinson, J., Bannister, E., Allen, M., & Chapman, A.E. (1984). Reliability, validity, objectivity, and safety of a proposed partial curl-up test. Final report. Ottawa, ON: Fitness and Amateur Sport.

Docherty, D., & Bell, F.I. (1990). Fitness testing: Counter-productive to health. *CAHPER Journal, 56,* 4-8.

Docherty, D., & Bell, R.D. (1985). The relationship between flexibility and linearity measures in boys and girls 6-15 years of age. *Journal of Human Movement Studies, 11,* 279-288.

Docherty, D., & Collis, M.L. (1976). The CAHPER Fitness Performance Test Revisited. *CAHPER Journal, 42*(6), 35-42.

Doolittle, T.L., & Bigbee, R. (1968). The twelve minute run-walk: A test of cardiorespiratory fitness of adolescent boys. *Research Quarterly, 39,* 491-495.

Erbaugh, S.J. (1990). Reliability of physical fitness tests administered to young children. *Perceptual and Motor Skills, 71,* 1123-1128.

European Test of Physical Fitness (EUROFIT). (1988). Council of Europe, Committee for the Development of Sport. Rome: Edigrat Editionale Grafica.

Fitness Canada (1993). *Canadian Active Living Challenge.* Ottawa; Author.

Fleishman, E.A. (1964). *The structure and measurement of physical fitness.* Englewood Cliffs, NJ: Prentice Hall.

Fox, E.L., & Mathews, D.K. (1981). *The physiological basis of physical education and athletics.* Toronto, ON: Saunders College.

Fox, K.R., & Biddle, S.J. (1986). Health related fitness testing in schools: Introduction and problems of interpretation. *Bulletin of Physical Education, 22*(3), 54-64.

Fox, K.R., & Biddle, S.J. (1988). The use of fitness tests: Educational and psychological considerations. *JOPERD, 59*(2), 47-53.

Franks, B.D., Morrow, J.R., Jr., & Plowman, S.A. (1988). Youth fitness testing: Validation, planning, and politics. *Quest, 40,* 187-199.

Going, S. (1988). Physical best—Body composition in the assessment of youth fitness. *JOPERD, 59*(7), 32-36.

Gutin, B., Fogle, R.K., & Stewart, K. (1976). Relationship among submaximal heart rate, aerobic power, and running performance in children. *Research Quarterly, 47,* 536-540.

Harris, M.L. (1969). A factor analytic study of flexibility. *Research Quarterly, 40*(1), 62-70.

Harsha, D.W., Frerichs, R.R., & Berenson, G.S. (1978). Densitometry and anthropometry of black and white children. *Human Biology, 50,* 251-280.

Hubley, C. (1991). Testing flexibility. In MacDougall, J.D., Wenger, H.A., & Green, M.J. (Eds.), *Physiological testing of the high performance athlete* (2nd ed., pp. 309-360). Champaign, IL: Human Kinetics.

Hupperich, F.L., & Sigerseth, P.O. (1950). The specificity of flexibility in girls. *Research Quarterly, 21*(1), 25-33.

Jackson, A.S., & Coleman, A.E. (1976). Validation of distance run tests for elementary school children. *Research Quarterly*, **47**(1), 87-94.

Jackson, A.W., & Baker, A.A. (1986). The relationship of the sit and reach test to criterion measures of hamstring and back flexibility. *Research Quarterly*, **57**(3), 183-186.

Jetté, M., Sidney, K., & Cicutti, N. (1984). A critical analysis of sit-ups: A case for the partial curl-up as a test of abdominal muscular endurance. *CAHPER Journal*, **51**(1), 4-9.

Johnson, B.L., & Nelson, J.K. (1986). *Practical measurements for evaluation in physical education* (4th ed.). Edina, MN: Burgess International.

Klesius, S.G. (1968). Reliability of the AAHPER youth fitness test items and relative efficiency of the performance measures. *Research Quarterly*, **39**(3), 809-811.

Krahenbuhl, G.S., Pangrazi, R.P., Burkett, L.N., Schneider, M.J., & Petersen, G. (1977). Field estimation of $\dot{V}O_2$max in children eight years of age. *Medicine and Science in Sports*, **9**(1), 37-40.

Krahenbuhl, G.S., Pangrazi, R.P., Petersen, G.W., Burkett, L.N., & Schneider, M.J. (1978). Field testing of cardiorespiratory fitness in primary school children. *Medicine and Science in Sports*, **10**(3), 208-213.

Kraus, H., & Hirschland, R.P. (1953). Muscular fitness and health. *Journal of Health, Physical Education and Recreation*, **24**, 17-24.

Kraus, H., & Hirschland, R.P. (1954). Minimum muscular fitness test in school children. *Research Quarterly*, **25**, 177-188.

Larson, L.A. (1974). *Fitness, health and work capacity: International standards for assessment*. International Committee for the Standardization of Physical Fitness Tests. New York: MacMillan.

Legér, L., & Gadboury, C. (1989). Validity of the 20m shuttle run test with 1 min stages to predict $\dot{V}O_2$max in adults. *Canadian Journal of Sport Sciences*, **14**(1), 21-26.

Legér, L., & Lambert, J. (1982). A maximal 20 m shuttle run test to predict $\dot{V}O_2$max. *European Journal of Applied Physiology*, **49**, 1-12.

Léger, L., Mercier, D., Lambert, J., & Gaboury, C. (1984). The multistage 20 meter shuttle run. Unpublished paper.

Lohman, T.G. (1986). Applicability of body composition techniques and constants for children and youths. In K.B. Pandolf (Ed.), *Exercise and Sport Sciences Reviews*, **14**, 325-357.

Lohman, T.G. (1987). The use of skinfold to estimate body fatness on children and youth. *Journal of Physical Education, Research and Dance*, **58**(9), 98-102.

Manitoba Education. (1977). *Manitoba physical fitness test manual and fitness objectives*. Winnipeg, Manitoba: Author.

Manitoba Education. (1989). *Manitoba schools fitness 1989*. Winnipeg, Manitoba: Author.

Maksud, M.G., & Coutts, K.D. (1971). Application of the Cooper twelve minute run-walk test to young males. *Research Quarterly*, **42**, 54-59.

Marmis, C., Montoye, H., Cunningham, D., & Kozar, A. (1969). Reliability of the multi-trial items of the AAHPER youth fitness test. *Research Quarterly*, **40**(1), 240-245.

Martin, A. (1984). *An anatomical basis for assessing human body composition*. Unpublished doctoral dissertation, Simon Fraser University, Burnaby, British Columbia.

Massicotte, D. (1984). Norms (centiles) pour les redressments partiels en position assise et les extensions des bras en position couchee ventrale de jeunesse en forme Canada. Preliminary report, Fitness and Amateur Sport, Ottawa, Canada.

McGraw, L.W., & McClenney, B.N. (1965). Reliability of fitness strength tests. *Research Quarterly*, **36**(3), 289-295.

Mercier, D., Léger, L., & Lambert, J. (1983). Relative efficiency and predicted $\dot{V}O_2$max in children (abstract). *Medicine and Science in Sports and Exercise*, **15**(2), 143.

Miller, D.K. (1988). Measurement by the physical educator: Why and how. Indianapolis, Indiana: Benchmark Press, Inc.

Murkherjee, D., & Roche, A.F. (1984). The estimation of percent body fat, body density, and total body fat by maximum *r* regression equations. *Human Biology, 56*, 79-109.

Nachemson, A. (1991, April). *Exercise and back pain.* Thematic address at the International Congress and Exposition on Sport Medicine and Human Performance, Vancouver, BC.

Nelson, J.K., & Nelson, K.R. (1986). Skinfold profiles of black and white boys and girls ages 11-13. *Human Biology, 58*, 379-390.

Pate, R.R. (1989). The case of large scale physical fitness testing in American youth. *Pediatric Exercise Science, 1*(4), 290-294.

Pate, R.R., Ross, J.G., Baumgartner, T.A., & Sparks, R.E. (1987). The modified pull-up test. *JOPERD, 58*(9), 71-73.

President's Council on Physical Fitness and Sports. (1987). *Get Fit.* Washington, DC: Department of Health and Human Services.

President's Council of Physical Fitness and Sports. (1987). *The Presidential Physical Fitness Award Program.* Washington, DC: Author.

Ready, E. (1986). *Fitness assessment for youth: A resource manual.* Gloucester: Ontario, CAHPER.

Ross, J.G., & Gilbert, G.G. (1985). Summary of findings from national children and youth fitness study. *Journal of Health, Physical Education, Recreation and Dance, 56*, 43-90.

Ross, J.G., Pate, R.R., Delpy, L.A., Gold, R.S., & Suilar, M. (1987). The national children and youth fitness study II: New health-related fitness norms. *JOPERD, 58*(9), 66-70.

Ross, W.D., & Ward, R. (1984). *The O-scale system.* Victoria, B.C.: 3S Fitness Group Ltd.

Ross, W.D., & Marfell-Jones, M.J. (1991). Kinanthropometry. In J.D. MacDougall, H.A. Wenger, & H.J. Green (Eds.). *Physiological testing of the high performance athlete* (2nd ed., pp. 223-308). Champaign, IL: Human Kinetics.

Safrit, M.J. (1990). The validity and reliability of fitness tests for children: A review. *Pediatric Exercise Science, 2*(1), 9-28.

Safrit, M.J. (1986). *Introduction to measurement in physical education and exercise science.* St. Louis: Times Mirror/Mosby College.

Safrit, M.J., Hooper, L.M., Ehlert, S.A., Costa, M.G., & Patterson, P. (1988). The validity generalization of distance run tests. *Canadian Journal of Sport Science, 13*(4), 188-196.

Safrit, M.J., & Wood, T.M. (1986). The health-related physical fitness test: A tri-state survey of users and non-users. *Research Quarterly for Exercise and Sport, 57*(1), 27-32.

Safrit, M.J., & Wood, T.M. (1987). The test battery reliability of the health related physical fitness test. *Research Quarterly for Exercise and Sport, 58*(2), 160-167.

Sale, D.G. (1991). Testing strength and power. In J.D. MacDougall, H.A. Wenger, & H.T. Green (Eds.), *Physiological testing of the high performance athlete* (2nd ed., pp. 21-106). Champaign, IL: Human Kinetics.

Seefeldt, V., & Vogel, P. (1989). Physical fitness testing of children: A 30-year history of misguided efforts? *Pediatric Exercise Science, 1*(4), 295-302.

Shaw, V.W. (1986). The accuracy of two training methods of skinfold assessment. *Research Quarterly for Exercise and Sport, 57*, 85-90.

Slaughter, M.H., Lohman, T.G., Boileau, R.A., Stillman, R.J., Van Loan, M., Horswill, C.A., & Wilmore, J.H. (1988). Influence of maturity on relationship of skinfolds to body density: A cross-sectional study. *Human Biology, 56*(4), 681-689.

Slaughter, M.H., Lohman, T.G., Boileau, R.A., Stillman, R.J., Van Loan, M., Horswill, C.A., & Wilmore, J.H. (1984). Influence of maturation on relationship of skinfold to body density: A cross-sectional study. *Human Biology, 56*, 681-689.

Thoden, J.S. (1991). Testing aerobic power. In J.D. MacDougall, H.A. Wenger, & M.J. Green (Eds), *Physiological testing of the high performance athlete*. Champaign, IL: Human Kinetics.

Vaccaro, P., & Mahon, A.D. (1989). The effects of exercise on coronary heart disease risk factors in children. *Sports Medicine, 8*(3), 139-153.

Van Gerven, D., Beunen, G., Ostyn, M., Ronson, R., Simons, J., Claessons, A., & Vanden Gynde, B. (1980). Reliability of a relation between 2 sub-maximal incremental bicycle ergometer tests in children. *Cardiorespiratory fitness in Canada: A current view of youth and sports*. International Council for Physical Fitness Research XVth Meeting of ICPER (XXIst Symposium of Maglingen), Maglingen, Switzerland.

Van Mechelen, W., Hlobil, H., & Kemper, H.C.G. (1986). Validation of two running tests as estimates of maximal aerobic power in children. *European Journal of Applied Physiology, 55*, 503-506.

Verducci, F.M. (1980). Measurement concepts in physical education. Toronto: C.V. Mosby Co.

Wood, P.D., Williams, P.T., & Haskell, W.L. (1984). Physical activity and high density lipoproteins. In N.E. Miller & G.J. Miller (Eds.), *Clinical and metabolic aspects of high density lipoproteins* (pp. 133-165). New York: Elsevier Science.

Woods, J.A., Pate, R.R., & Burgess, M.L. (1992). Correlates to performance on field tests of muscular strength. *Pediatric Exercise Science, 4*, 302-311.

Index

About the Contributors

David Docherty, PhD, is a professor in and director of the School of Physical Education at the University of Victoria. He has conducted research and written extensively on the fitness of children and youth and their responses to acute and chronic exercise. He was the principal author of the two manuals for the National Fitness Appraisal Certification and Accreditation Program of the Canadian Society for Exercise Physiology, *Critical Analysis of Available Laboratory Tests Used in Evaluating the Fitness of Children and Youth* and *Critical Analysis of Available Field Tests in Evaluating the Fitness of Children and Youth*. These two manuals provided the initial impetus for the development of *Measurement in Pediatric Exercise Science*. Docherty was also on the Advisory Board for the Canadian Active Living Challenge, which replaced the Canada Fitness Awards program.

Oded Bar-Or, PhD, is a professor of pediatrics and director of the Children's Exercise and Nutrition Centre, McMaster University, and Chedoke-McMaster Hospitals in Hamilton, Ontario. He is an expert on several areas related to the responses of children and adults to exercise. Bar-Or's research has been published extensively in such journals as *Journal of Applied Physiology* and *Pediatric Exercise Science* and he has had leadership roles in several organizations, including president of the Canadian Association of Sports Sciences, vice president of the American College of Sports Medicine, and chair of a task force of the American Medical Association on the participation of children in sports. He was the founder and director of the Department of Research and Sports Medicine at the Wingate Institute in Israel until assuming his current position.

Susan M. Crawford, PhD, is a registered dietitian with a doctorate in kinesiology. She is a faculty associate at the Institute for Health Promotion Research at the University of British Columbia and an adjunct professor in the Gerontology Diploma Program at Simon Fraser University. She also teaches in the areas of sport nutrition and health promotion for the School of Human Kinetics and the School of Kinesiology at these respective universities. Her research and writing have included a focus on anthropometry of children and young athletes. In addition to her academic functions, Crawford serves as a consultant to the fitness industry as well as elite amateur and professional athletes.

Robert A. Faulkner, PhD, is a professor of physical education and an associate member in Community Health and Epidemiology at the University of Saskatchewan. His major research interest is pediatric exercise, with a focus on factors affecting bone mineralization in growing children. Faulkner is a co-investigator in an ongoing longitudinal study investigating bone mineral accrual in children and adolescents. He has published extensively in pediatric exercise and physical activity and health.

Patty S. Freedson, PhD, is a professor in the Department of Exercise Science at the University of Massachusetts–Amherst and an adjunct professor in the Department of Medicine at the University of Massachusetts Medical School–Worcester. She has over 75 peer-reviewed publications on a variety of topics, including a number of papers on children's physical activity. She teaches undergraduate and graduate courses in exercise physiology and also offers a course on the biological basis of children and exercise. Freedson's research interests include pediatric exercise physiology, methods of physical activity assessment, and fitness test development and validation. She is a Fellow of the American College of Sports Medicine and of the Research Consortium in the American Alliance of Health, Physical Education, Recreation and Dance.

Catherine A. Gaul, PhD, is an assistant professor in the School of Physical Education at the University of Victoria, where she teaches anatomy, physiology, and growth and maturation. She is actively involved in the study of pediatric exercise physiology. Her primary areas of research include the responsiveness of children to exercise, particularly young females; maturational influences on physical performance; and strength characteristics in children and youth. She is currently chair of the Certified Fitness Appraiser (CFA) Technical Committee for the Canadian Society for Exercise Physiology.

Luc Léger, PhD, has been a full professor at the Université de Montréal since 1973. He earned his PhD from the University of Alberta in 1978. His research focuses include methodological problems of fitness testing (aerobic status and body composition) and performance determinants in sport and work. He has written more than 100 articles and given more than 250 presentations or conferences. Léger is the author of two popular multistage field tests of aerobic fitness, the 400-m track test and the 20-m shuttle run. He is active on many Canadian committees and organizations related to fitness or physical activity sciences. He is the assistant editor of *Science et Sports*, the journal of the Société Française de Médecine du Sport.

Alan D. Martin, PhD, has degrees from the University of Leeds and the University of British Columbia and a doctorate from the School of Kinesiology at Simon Fraser University. Martin has been director of the Sport and Exercise Sciences Research Institute at the University of Manitoba and is an associate professor in the School of Human Kinetics at the University of British Columbia and the president of the International Society for the Advancement of Kinanthropometry, which trains and